Advance Praise for *Fly Solo*

"Whether your dream adventure involves catching waves on Waikiki or scoring bargains in Bangkok, this is the only travel companion you'll need."

—Carrie Sloan, senior editor, *Marie Claire*

"*Fly Solo* is a must for every girl's coffee table. Teresa offers you solid, fun, honest information about the best places to go alone. I love the Top 10 listings of things to do—what a great way to get started on a new adventure. I'm ready to pack my bags!"

—Holly Payne, award-winning, bestselling author of
The Virgin's Knot and *The Sound of Blue*

"Teresa perfectly captures the adventure and excitement of traveling alone with her pithy, practical, and insightful summaries of exotic destinations. As a woman who has traveled solo to six of the seven continents, I highly recommend this guide as an indispensable insider's take on how any girl with gumption can best enjoy exploring the world on her own."

—Cheryl Dahle, author of *No Horizon Is So Far*
and contributing writer at *Fast Company* magazine

p 65 Zagreb
275 wholes San Diego

OCT   2007

FLY SOLO

The 50 Best Places on Earth
for a Girl to Travel Alone

Teresa Rodriguez Williamson

A PERIGEE BOOK

A PERIGEE BOOK
Published by the Penguin Group
Penguin Group (USA) Inc.
375 Hudson Street, New York, New York 10014, USA
Penguin Group (Canada), 90 Eglinton Avenue East, Suite 700, Toronto, Ontario M4P 2Y3, Canada
(a division of Pearson Penguin Canada Inc.)
Penguin Books Ltd., 80 Strand, London WC2R 0RL, England
Penguin Group Ireland, 25 St. Stephen's Green, Dublin 2, Ireland (a division of Penguin Books Ltd.)
Penguin Group (Australia), 250 Camberwell Road, Camberwell, Victoria 3124, Australia
(a division of Pearson Australia Group Pty. Ltd.)
Penguin Books India Pvt. Ltd., 11 Community Centre, Panchsheel Park, New Delhi—110 017, India
Penguin Group (NZ), 67 Apollo Drive, Mairangi Bay, Auckland 1311, New Zealand
(a division of Pearson New Zealand Ltd.)
Penguin Books (South Africa) (Pty.) Ltd., 24 Sturdee Avenue, Rosebank, Johannesburg 2196,
South Africa

Penguin Books Ltd., Registered Offices: 80 Strand, London WC2R 0RL, England

While the author has made every effort to provide accurate telephone numbers and Internet addresses at the time of publication, neither the publisher nor the author assumes any responsibility
for errors, or for changes that occur after publication. Further, the publisher does not have any con-
trol over and does not assume any responsibility for author or third-party websites or their content.

FLY SOLO

First edition: February 2007

Perigee trade paperback ISBN: 978-0-399-53310-5

An application to register this title for cataloging has been submitted to the Library of Congress.

PRINTED IN THE UNITED STATES OF AMERICA

10   9   8   7   6   5   4   3   2

PUBLISHER'S NOTE: Outdoor recreational activities are by their very nature potentially hazardous.
All participants in such activities must assume the responsibility for their own actions and safety. If
you have any health problems or medical conditions, consult with your physician before undertak-
ing any outdoor activities. The information contained in this guide book cannot replace sound judgment and good decision making, which can help reduce risk exposure, nor does the scope of this
book allow for disclosure of all the potential hazards and risks involved in such activities. Learn as
much as possible about the outdoor recreational activities in which you participate, prepare for the
unexpected, and be cautious. The reward will be a safer and more enjoyable experience.

Most Perigee Books are available at special quantity discounts for bulk purchases for sales promo-
tions, premiums, fund-raising, or educational use. Special books, or book excerpts, can also be
created to fit specific needs. For details, write: Special Markets, The Berkley Publishing Group,
375 Hudson Street, New York, New York 10014.

TO

Stephanie Block
Thank you for the words when I am speechless and for your direction when I am lost.

Patti Mangan
Thank you for your steadfast determination and loyalty when I am jet-setting.

Sarah Naimark
Thank you for your passionate trailblazing when I am fastened to my computer.

Heidi Arrizabalaga
Thank you for the champagne and conversations when I want to chill.

Acknowledgments

Jetting off to new places alone is a cinch; it's skillfully writing about where to go and what to do that's the hard part. This book would not be in your hot hands without the help of some remarkable spirits who believed in this project as much as I did. I am so grateful to have an incredibly supportive and handsome husband, Timothy Williamson, who kisses me goodbye and always wishes me good fortune, as I fly off to distant shores solo. The biggest influence on this book is from my director, cheerleader, coach, therapist, and friend—Stephanie Block. She is a rock star, and I adore her for her unending dedication to me and *Tango Diva*. She was able to take my broken thoughts and string them back together like magic. I am forever grateful for her skillful editing and fierce honesty. Stephanie's brilliant writing shimmers in Waikiki, Buenos Aires, Tokyo, Cartagena de Indias, Panama City, Montreal, and Beijing. A million *mercis* to the diligently delightful Sarah Naimark for her positively awesome research, editing, and management of the mêlée of chapters. Her input on Vienna, Dubrovnik, and Moab is beautiful. With her help, I was able to tackle each chapter—one by one.

I am so grateful to Cheri Molnar for her skillful suggestions, support, and kind words just when I needed them. Many thanks to Suzanne Dunning for her research and lovely presence at *Tango Diva*. May the world be filled with more souls like her. Willow Cook's editing skills are stellar, and I thank her for her input. To the global gallivanting girls who shared insights about their travels: Jennifer Crawford for meeting me in Paris to show me the sights and her wonderful tips about Dubai, Krissie Dempsey for her enthusiastic information on Thailand, Anna Alioto's Waikiki expertise, Amy Chen's help on Hong Kong, Meegan Adamson's ideas for Sydney, and Jill Christina Hansen's thoughts on Copenhagen—I thank you all for your precious time to share. I am so grateful for all the fantastic editorial staff at *Tango Diva* who shared their personal experiences with me. Stephanie Kulik, Alyssa Morrissey, Janet Lipkin Bein, Ashly Roof, Alexa Trotta, Ashley Zoellner, Lisa Esquivel, Callie Silver, Ashly Zoellner, Melissa Josue, and Daniel Lasman. I am so thankful for Monica Woelfel's fact-checking skills and patience, as I careened into the writing abyss.

Super-duper special thanks go out to Eli Block, who cared enough about this project to find my fifty chapters that mysteriously went missing on my hard drive. And extra-special thanks to all those in the travel world who believed me when I said I was writing a book and helped me out with resources, information, press passes, and insights. From the fabulous people at Hotel Josef in Prague to the amazing tourist boards in Dublin, Lisbon, Berlin, Budapest, San Diego, and London. I really appreciate your priceless information.

There are a few others who were lucky enough not to be a part of my daily run-on sentences, dangling modifiers, and misplaced pronouns—but they were there from the beginning and will be there forever. I would not be where I am without the love and constant support from Patti Mangan. She met me when I was a young girl returning from five years in Australia, and she has watched me grow, marry, travel, and write a book. Together we built *Tango Diva*. And to my best friend and favorite playmate, Heidi Arrizabalaga. She believed in me, took the idea of *Tango Diva*, created an inspiring brand, and lovingly designed my first book, which ended up transforming into this travel guide.

Finally, to Christel Winkler, my editor at Perigee, for the inspiring phone calls, encouragement, and direction. To Meg Leder for enthusiastically running with this project and managing it through its completion. And most of all, I thank Stephanie Kip Rostan, my agent extraordinaire, mentor, friend, and coach. Without her passion for this project, this book would still be stuck somewhere between my heart and my head.

Contents

Introduction

Before zipping up your suitcase filled with untold pairs of stilettos and Brazilian bikinis, or snorkeling gear and sunscreen, take a moment to reflect on what you want to do (besides flirt!) on your next vacation. Are you setting out to discover why the world went crazy over Dada, or do you plan on getting cozy with jet-setters? Or both?

In *Fly Solo*, I'm going to share with you the 50 best places on earth for a girl to travel alone, so that you can. How did I magically choose these fabulous 50 destinations?

1. **Safety:** These destinations have safe places for women to stay and explore. The general attitudes toward women are positive.
2. **Transportation:** These locations have good public transportation options and easy access to an airport. Trains, buses, and taxis are easy to come by, or everything is in walking distance.
3. **Social Center:** You will find a place where you can go to meet others. Even if you plan on spending your trip completely alone, it's good to have that option.

4. **Variety:** These places have a variety of venues to stay, dine, adventure, and relax. You won't get bored.
5. **Friendliness:** These places like entertaining visitors.
6. **Cost:** I found hotels, resorts, or tours that are realistically affordable for a solo traveler.
7. **Climate:** The weather is something I have researched so you won't be surprised by midday thunderstorms, for example.
8. **Size:** These destinations have plenty to do and see and are manageable in size. A place that is too big or too small can be overwhelming, or boring.
9. **Communication:** These locations are equipped with a way to dial home if you need to. If an emergency arises, you have a way of contacting someone.
10. **Medical and Health:** These destinations have reliable medical and health services.

With the help of my friend and partner in crime Stephanie Block, I have made it my *CAWS célèbre* to help you find your ideal vacation destination.

Over hours of champagne-induced brainstorming, Stephanie and I isolated the key characteristics that define any location: Culture, Activity, Weather, and Social—aka CAWS. Through our brief, yet uncannily intuitive CAWS quiz, you'll understand how important each of the CAWS is to you—and be well on your way to arriving at a destination uniquely suited to your interests and preferences.

With so many places to see—and so little time to see them—this handy-dandy quiz will save you hours of research and investigation that may uncover only what *other people* might enjoy. The CAWS quiz, in contrast, is about *your* trip! It's all about pinpointing what *you* want out of your travels—so when choosing your answers, be truthful, have fun, and follow your instincts.

The Four CAWS

1. **CULTURAL OPPORTUNITIES: Do you look forward to exploring a place's art, history, and traditions?**

2. **ACTIVITY LEVEL: Do you want your trip to be an active adventure or a restful escape?**

3. **WEATHER PREFERENCE: Do you care what the weather will be like?**

4. **SOCIAL INTERACTION: Do you want to meet new people—or spend quality time with yourself?**

Follow These Simple Directions

*T*his fun, insightful quiz will allow you to determine what you want out of your next getaway. So sit back and reflect on what would make your next vacation better than a double-dark-fudge chocolate cake, then answer each question as if you were concocting your dream trip.

Let your heart's desire be your guide!

1. **When you think museum, you think . . .**
   - The best way to avoid those long lines is to buy your tickets ahead of time! (5)
   - Great! If there's a huge storm and you can't do any of the things you wanted to do. (2)
   - You should. You really should. After the latte and before hitting the shops. (3)
   - Which way to the Cubists? (4)
   - Blah. Melatonin is cheaper if you're having trouble sleeping. (1)

2. **Your idea of a night of entertainment is . . .**
   - An opera followed by a symphony followed by a ballet. Oh, if only time would allow it! (5)
   - A play, which is good foreplay to dinner and dancing. (4)
   - Brad Pitt in . . . anything! (2)
   - A pub crawl. (3)
   - A curtain call. As in the ones in your hotel room. As in good night. (1)

3. **In your guidebook, the history section is . . .**
   - Dog-eared and worn to the bone with highlighting. (4)
   - In mint condition. (1)
   - A place you've perused. (3)
   - Committed to memory. (5)
   - Next on your list. (2)

4. **At the crack of dawn you . . .**
   - Have already been jogging. (5)
   - Are asleep and will be until 10:50 a.m., giving you 10 minutes before the hotel kitchen stops serving breakfast. (2)
   - Are groggy and pulling on yoga pants. (4)
   - Were told to catch the area's famous sunrises, so here you are. Just this once. (3)
   - Are stumbling home. (1)

5. **There's a health club in your hotel. You . . .**
   - Love the sauna. (2)
   - Had no idea. (1)
   - Work it into your daily schedule, so you can squeeze into that new outfit you bought. (4)

- Glare at the man on the stair climber. He's hogging it on your only gym day! (3)
- Spend more time here than in your "other" room. (5)

6. You are packing your luggage for your big trip. You make sure to include . . .
- A travel guide and your journal. (2)
- A few pairs of sweats, your Nikes, and your heart rate monitor. (5)
- Your camera, sunscreen, and bathing suit. (3)
- Your running shorts and water bottle. (4)
- Your Gucci heels, your cutest cocktail dress, and a French translation book. (1)

7. London fog is legendary. You . . .
- Barely have time for the British Museum after all that shopping and eel pie. (1)
- Might agree to meet a friend there, but only if Barcelona were part of the bargain. (4)
- Head to St. Tropez. (5)
- Deal with it. After all, most of what's fun in London is indoors, including tweed-wearing Englishmen. (3)
- Enjoy the vividness of what feels like a Sherlock Holmes mystery around every corner. (2)

8. Piña coladas and getting caught in the rain are . . .
- What they are. After all, rain is great for your hair. (1)
- Romantic. The soft fingers of rain caressing your window make poetry of the night. (2)
- Irrelevant! A mere umbrella is all that stands between you and the world. (3)
- Devastating. Before you unpack, you plan to file suit against the Weather Channel. (5)
- Threatening. You brought mostly suede. (4)

9. It's high noon and it's hot! The sand sparkles, the water beckons, and . . .
- You wished someone had engineered a way to air-condition the tropics. (5)
- High school physics helps you angle two umbrellas against the sun over your deck chair. (4)
- Your SPF is 50 so you can romp in the waves without losing ten years off your face. (3)
- So does Antoine, the lifeguard on duty with chiseled pectorals and abs that don't quit. (1)
- Your body glistens with baby oil. Against dark paneling, you'd be totally camouflaged! (2)

10. Happy hour? What would make you devilishly happy is . . .
- The Australian national rugby team, a magnum of champagne, and kissing and telling. (5)

- To have a glass of wine in your hotel's bar with the locals you met while shopping. (4)
- A sidewalk seat in a café overlooking the bustling square where you might connect with someone. (2)
- If that oversized reading chair in the lobby by the fireplace were finally vacant. (1)
- An evening epicurean tour where you'll share a meal with new friends. (3)

11. Want to share your table?
- That's the whole idea: dinner (and hopefully breakfast!) for two . . . (4)
- As if you have a choice with that mad bunch of Brazilians you just befriended! (5)
- Yes, if you count the room service guy and the eight o'clock movie. (2)
- No, thank you, you say confidently. I'll take the prix fixe menu and a carafe of your house red. (1)
- Perhaps. If you meet some jet-setting cuties. (3)

12. If your best friend had to describe you, she would say . . .
- Our friendship is one-on-one, she likes her space. (1)
- Great friend, but she can get shy around strangers. (2)
- We have so much fun going out and meeting up with our friends. (3)
- I can't keep track of her, she's always socializing with others. (5)
- If there were a contest for having the most friends, she would win. (4)

Pack your bags, *Principessa*, you're off to . . .

That wasn't too hard, was it? Good, because here comes the easy math. Simply follow the directions below for each CAWS section, tally your score, and discover the global hot spots with your name on them. Then, turn to the chapter where your destination is outlined in detail—and start packing!

Culture: Add up your points for questions 1, 2, and 3.
10 to 15 points: Well, hello, kitty—looks like you're full of curiosity! For your trip to be absolutely *purr*fect, you'll need to sink your claws into some art, history, and culture. Some of the destinations that you might want to prowl around at include:
- **Thailand:** Parasail over the gentle blue Indian Ocean, venture into the jungle for some coconut ice cream, and savor the slow, peaceful pace of this Asian paradise.
- **Tokyo, Japan:** Enjoy one of the safest countries on the planet, visit Shinto and Zen shrines, geisha-watch, catch a sumo-wrestling match, and be sure to go during cherry blossom season.
- **St. Petersburg, Russia:** Glow in the aura of the white nights, ogle art at the Hermitage, and discover why Catherine the Great was so great.
- **Prague, Czech Republic:** Get lost in medieval castles, shop in the stylish city, and relax the day away while spa-ing in some of Europe's oldest mineral baths.
- **Budapest, Hungary:** See if the Danube is really blue, rummage through Petofi Csarnok flea market for some post-communist deals, and dance the night away in one of the city's many international discos.

- **Vietnam:** Watch farmers and water buffalo cultivating rice paddies, take a sobering look at the Hanoi Hilton, and hunker down in the old Viet Cong tunnels that stretched for more than a hundred miles under enemy territory.

5 to 10 points: It's okay that you don't plan on spending your vacation deciphering hieroglyphics. Here are some places that will be just right for you:
- **Buenos Aires, Argentina:** Learn to Tango, study Spanish, and get closer to the greatest Diva *ever*—Evita Perón.
- **Hong Kong, China:** Order the perfect silk cheomsang, purchase exquisite knock-offs, and have a few fabulous suits made-to-order.
- **Beijing, China:** Hike the Great Wall, and enter the Forbidden City.
- **Vienna, Austria:** Be enchanted by a magical, musical evening with the Vienna Boys Choir, glide through the gilded halls of the Kunsthorische Museum, then head to the Alps for some après-ski sports.
- **Brussels, Belgium:** Dive into this delicious destination by dining on its famous chocolate and to-die-for *pommes frites*. Find out why the Belgians are nothing like the French—and take a ride on the flower carpet.

0 to 5 points: Darling, it's not that you don't appreciate historical monuments and museums. It's just that you're here to make some history of your own! Below are a few gems that incorporate the best of both worlds:
- **Paris, France:** The shopping. The dining. The sightseeing. The Frenchmen! Ooh la la, this place is a must for every solo gal.
- **Rome, Italy:** Stroll through the idyllic cobblestone streets of Rome, take the train to Florence, continue on to Venice, and relish the flavorful zeal of Italy.
- **Bali, Indonesia:** Indulge in a massage on the beach, visit a Hindu temple, and embrace the gentle kindness of the Balinese culture.
- **London, England:** Savor afternoon tea at the Ritz, bathe in Bath, and find that oh-so-perfect pair of boots on Canterbury Lane.

Activity: Add up your points for questions 4, 5, and 6.
10 to 15 points: The only chilling you'll be doing on this trip will involve champagne—to celebrate all that hiking, biking, trekking, surfing, skiing, and sweating you'll be doing. To keep your heart racing, try out:
- **Machu Picchu, Peru:** Hike the sacred Inca Trail, climb massive, high-altitude ruins, and quietly meditate at the top of Huayna Picchu.
- **Moab, Utah:** Find out why they call it slick rock as you river raft with a team of hot guides (prepared to render mouth-to-mouth when needed), and explore secret trails in Utah's mysterious red rocks.
- **Queenstown, New Zealand:** Get wet and wild on a jet boat cruise, let the rapids on the Kawarau River carry you away, and take the ultimate leap at 15,000 feet.
- **Belize:** Canoe through stillwater caves, explore the colorful rain forest while floating down a gentle river, and meet some shy manatees while snorkeling.

- **Bhutan:** Trek the steep mountains of Paro Valley, spin a prayer wheel, and spend the day hiking to sulfurous hot springs in the Kingdom of the Lost Horizon.

5 to 10 points: Still don't know the difference between carbo-loading and cardio? No worries! For you, I'd recommend:
- **Reykjavik, Iceland:** Soak in milky-blue hot geothermal pools, gape at the Northern Lights, get racy on a snowmobile, and party in Reykjavik till the sun comes up—wait a minute, it never sets in summer!
- **Crested Butte, Colorado:** Mountain bike in the spring, go horseback riding in the summer, hike in the fall, and when winter arrives, come play in the snow with the new cool. Aspen is *so* last-millennium.
- **Fairbanks, Alaska:** Track bears, mush along a dogsled, and take a wild ride through the wilderness on an all-terrain vehicle.

0 to 5 points: It's just fine if you don't plan on lifting anything other than your glass (to toast your independence!) on this vacation. Find some peace in these delightful destinations:
- **Ibiza, Spain:** Worship the sun on this heavenly island while chilling in the Mediterranean heat to the super DJ beats at Café del Mar and other clubs.
- **Waikiki, Hawaii:** Learn how to surf at an all-girls surf spa, kayak with the dolphins, snorkel with sea turtles, and salute all those military boys at the surrounding bases.
- **Panama City:** Indulge in investment property fantasies, visit the endangered harpy eagles at the Summit Zoo, and enjoy a night out on Calle Uruguay.
- **Lisbon:** Eat your way through Lisbon, then spend the next day spa-ing.

Weather: Add up your points for questions 7, 8, and 9.
10 to 15 points: For all you fair-weather darlings and snow bunnies, weather is vital for your vacation. Sun or snow, here are my top picks:
- **Playa del Carmen, Mexico:** With a name like Carmen, you know all things—snorkeling, relaxing, and playing—will be wonderful on this sun-kissed Mayan beach in the Caribbean.
- **Port Douglas, Australia:** Say g'day to crazy summer days packed with scuba diving, sky diving, and horseback riding in this rugged, tropical coastal town on the Great Barrier Reef.
- **The Caribbean:** Chant *Om* on Paradise Island, soar through the air on a flying trapeze in Turks and Caïcos, and sail the crystal blue sea of the Caribbean.
- **Turin, Italy:** No need to be an Olympic skier to slide down the slopes in this famous Italian ski town. Unless you want to relive the 2006 Olympics.
- **Whistler, Canada:** With a guaranteed six months of skiing a year, you'll be sure to find powder here. In the summer, view elk and moose and bears—oh my!—wandering the idyllic countryside.

5 to 10 points: These locations are sure to keep you smiling, even when the sun sneaks behind a cloud or two. Spend some time in:

- **Athens, Greece:** Sip champagne from a yacht, take the Greek Islands like a goddess, and stroll through some of the most fantastic ruins in the world.
- **San Diego, California:** Rollerblade along Pacific Beach, join a volleyball game in the sand, rent a convertible, and take a road trip to the desert.
- **St. Moritz, Switzerland:** The perfect après-ski spot for those who love snow but not the slopes.

0 to 5 points: Weather, schmeather! If that's your feeling, you have a whole lot of choices! No reason to list cities with wanton weather, because you're degrees beyond Fahrenheit! Your spirit isn't dampened by Scotland's moors, nor would California's Death Valley at its summertime 100+ degrees raise your eyebrow. And Stockholm's dark winters sure won't keep you from taking that dream vacation. Good for you!

Social: Add your points for questions 10, 11, and 12.

10 to 15 points: In addition to jet-setting, you're about to become a worldwide socialite! You're sure to meet some amazing people in these super-social locations:

- **Rio de Janeiro, Brazil:** Dance your nights away in this passionate city where jungle meets gentry.
- **San Francisco, California:** Leave more than your heart in this glimmering city on the bay. Stay busy with wine tasting, dining, flirting, and sailing.
- **Berlin, Germany:** Move with ease from the wild old West to the funky new East, sip absinthe in cool cafés, and proclaim yourself a Berliner as you hop from one posh bar to the next.
- **Dublin, Ireland:** Do a jig, drink Guinness in a pub, and kiss an Irishman! Oh, the luck of the Irish.
- **Stockholm, Sweden:** Get glamorous in Gamla Stan and make new friends on the pedestrian-friendly Drottninggatan. You'll understand why this is a top vacation destination for Europeans.

5 to 10 points: Even if you don't plan on hooking up with a rugby team, it's always nice to have some company. Here are a few picks for great destinations with great people:

- **South Beach, Miami:** Dress like a supermodel, party like a rock star, smoke a cigar, and drink a mojito in this insanely wonderful place.
- **Sydney, Australia:** Rock on in The Rocks, sport a sarong on Bondi Beach, and find a darling in Darling Harbour—and perhaps join him on his yacht.
- **Amsterdam, The Netherlands:** Paddle through the famous flower market, ride a bike from nightclub to nightclub, and remember to visit Anne Frank.
- **Edinburgh, Scotland:** Visit the home of Loch Ness, Braveheart, and golf, and find out what's really under those kilts.
- **Dubrovnik, Croatia:** Sail along the Peljesac Peninsula, stroll the narrow streets on the Hrvatskas, and ferry down to Hvar, where you'll find jet-setters dancing to the latest Europop hits.

0 to 5 points: If you are your own ultimate traveling companion—as well you should be—then girl, these destinations are solo superb!

- **Montreal, Canada:** Discover the Underground City, go antique shopping in Old Montreal, catch the summer jazz festival, and celebrate your solo-ness in this femme-friendly city.
- **Barcelona, Spain:** Learn how to flamenco dance, try tapas, sip sangria, relive Picasso's blue period, and go crazy for Gaudi architecture.
- **Copenhagen, Denmark:** Get swept away during Fairytale season in Tivoli Garden or just hit the cafés and enjoy the hospitality of the Danes.
- **Dubai:** Go snow skiing in the desert and shop like an Arabian princess.

From learning how to surf to strolling down historic cobblestone streets, you've got the whole world in your hands. Thinking about playing with dolphins or dancing with drag queens? It's all in here! Have fun exploring your chosen destinations, and remember, you can always read this book cover to cover if you can't decide what great adventure you want to experience.

EUROPE

AMSTERDAM, THE NETHERLANDS

Teresa cycling through the canals of Amsterdam.

Why This Place Rocks for Flying Solo

Forget everything you've ever heard about Holland's favorite city and its pot-smoking, Red-Light-District-walking denizens. In Amsterdam, the focus is on beauty, not brothels. This jewel of Northern Europe is decorated with dreamlike canals that drape around the city like silver strands. And on each canal, proud, corniced mansions line the cobblestone streets, capturing the rich history and beauty that is Amsterdam. It's easy to lose yourself in this timelessness and forget you're in the twenty-first century. Of course, you can still legally smoke pot and check out naked chicks if you want—but there's so much more to life, and the Amsterdammers know that. Tulips, Van Gogh, style sages, darling gentlemen, and cheese reign supreme in this canal-filled city. The Netherlands, also known as Holland, is the largest supplier of fresh flowers in the world, and wherever you stroll in Amsterdam, tulips, roses, and gladiolas greet you with their vibrant rays of fragrant joy.

And as for the people who call Amsterdam home? You'll be pleasantly surprised that almost everyone speaks English—and is willing to use it! Between the charming gabled homes in the Canal District and Oud-Zuid, you'll discover (most likely while bicycling) streets lined with high-end fashions, busy cafés, galleries, and museums. I must admit that Amsterdam is one of my favorite destinations in the world. After a week here, it will be one of yours, too. The only way you can have a bad trip here is by having a bad trip, if you know what I mean . . .

Culture: 5

With 60 theaters, 42 museums, and 141 art galleries, you'll need to stay an extra few months to experience all that this historic city has to offer. Some of the great places to catch drama in Dutch include the Concertgebouw and the Stadsschouwburg. For opera and ballet, head to the modern Muziektheater. If the arts melt your butter, then this is the city for you. The famous Rijksmuseum is home to the masterpieces of local artists including Rembrandt, Vermeer, and Frans Hals. The Van Gogh Museum is a must, even for those who don't care much for art. Seeing Van Gogh's colorful expressions up close is overwhelming. Don't be surprised if your eyes tear up looking at his emotionally charged artwork. Really.

Activity: 2

If you're training for a marathon and the only thing you want to get high is your heart rate, then you might want to skip this spot on the map. Amsterdammers are not big on kickboxing or Pilates, but they do ride their last-century bikes all around town. So if daily bygone-cycle rides through enchanting flower-lined streets and over steep canal bridges are enough exercise for you, you'll love this place.

Weather: 2

Let's just say that if you want a nice bronze tan as proof of your globe trekking, then maybe you should head south. Amsterdam is pretty high up there on the latitudinal lines; so, even in the summer, it's wise to bring a nice warm jacket. The best times to visit are in April and May. The weather is fair and the tulips are in full bloom.

Social: 5

Girl, get ready to party like a tabloid heiress. If you're a member of any organization that ends in "Anonymous," then socializing here will be challenging. Amsterdammers love their cocktails and meeting up at bars. You'll soon be familiar with the city's legendary "brown cafés," *the* place for the daily ritual of after-work socializing. By the time you leave one, you'll have a few new Dutch friends—and you'll know what *gezelligheid* means. If you don't make it to Amsterdam, the word loosely means "all things fabulous like friends, coziness, fun, and good times." Think Disneyland for grown-ups.

Flying Foreplay

The great thing about visiting historical, cosmopolitan cities like Amsterdam is that there's not a lot you need to preplan. The national language is Dutch, but for the most part, everyone in Amsterdam speaks English. It's always a good idea to learn a few Dutch words before landing in Schiphol Airport. So, for your convenience, I've included some very important phrases:

Thank you. *Dank u.*
Please. *Tevreden.*
Excuse me. *Excuseer me.*
I'm sorry. *Ik ben droevig.*
Where are all the cute guys? *Waar alle leuke kerels?*
Where can I get some good cheese? *Waar kan ik één of andere goede kaas krijgen?*
Do you have any condoms? *Hebt u om het even welke condoms?*

This destination is truly ready-to-wear. You can show up and enjoy this place without too much planning. Of course, book your hotel before you go and exchange some cash for euros. Great neighborhoods to stay in include the canal district, Oud Zuid, Jordaan, and De Pijp. Stay away from the Red Light District—unless you need to make a few euros to get home.

Read Before You Go

Amsterdam Cops: Collected Stories, by Janwillem van de Wetering
Anne Frank: The Diary of a Young Girl, by Anne Frank
The Green Face, by Gustav Meyrink

Amsterdam Accessories

Leave those Jimmy Choos at home. Everyone gets around on bicycles, and even if you don't plan on pedaling your way around town, you'll be walking across beautifully ornate brick canal bridges with ridiculously steep sidewalks and cobblestone deathtraps. Bring some solid wedge boots or sturdy sandals that you can pedal in, because it's not about being glam in Amsterdam.

Backpack it! If you have the choice of taking your Birkin or backpack, leave the Birkin at home and schlep the backpack (a cute one) to Schiphol Airport. In this city, which is way more casual than

Paris or London, traversing on two tires is way easier with your weight equally distributed across your back.

Stay dry. Even if you plan on visiting during the summer, you might want to bring along a small umbrella, one that you can throw into your really cute backpack.

You are, I am. For easy access to all the hot spots swarmed by tourists, invest in an Iamsterdam Card. This card gives you access to public transportation and a free canal ride (whoo-hoo!). It includes admission to most of the museums in town. You can also receive a 25 percent discount at a host of tourist-centric restaurants (yum!—*not*). Depending on how quickly you can get through the museums, you can purchase a 24-, 48-, or 72-hour card. If you're not big into the touristy scene, I'd recommend getting a 24 or 48 Iamsterdam Card. It's a great way to pay for a bunch of attractions in one fell swoop. Remember that this card *won't* show the local side of Amsterdam. That's why you've got this book.

The Top 10 Extraordinary Experiences

1.   Spend time on the nines: De 9 Straatjes. Between Leidsestraat and Raadhuisstraat, you'll come across a nine-street wonderland of antique shops, vintage boutiques, trendy restaurants, and cozy cafés. Glide in and out of colorful shops and pick out some unique pieces of clothing that you can only find in this darling neighborhood. End your day with a plate of oysters and at least one glass of champagne at Barok. Wolvenstraat 22–24; www.restaurantbarok.nl.

2.   Float away on the world's only floating flower garden. Plan on spending a few hours admiring the colorful blooms on this magical floating market. The Dutch name is Bloemenmarkt. Look for the mysterious, rare black tulip. Monday through Saturday 9:30 a.m. to 5 p.m. (Singel, 1071 AZ).

3.   Discover the Dutch masters. Van Gogh, Rembrandt, and Frans Hals are a terrific triumvirate for the art-loving girl. You can spend more than a day trekking through the Rijksmuseum, Stedelijk Museum, and Van Gogh Museum. These magnificent collections are in the Oud Zuid district, so if you want to take a break from art, it's easy to find a buzzing café or restaurant nearby.

4.   Wander through Waterlooplein. If cheap, funky clothes and smoking paraphernalia are what you plan on taking back for the folks, then head over to the open-air flea market that the locals call Waterlooplein. Once upon a time, this was the central trading center for Amsterdam's Jewish population (think Anne Frank), but the Second World War brought things to a dramatic halt. Over the past few years, this area is again burgeoning, and now you're more likely to find fishnet stockings than gefilte fish.

5. Pedal away on a high-end pub crawl. Get acquainted with the locals on a self-guided bar hop. You're likely to meet a bunch of cute Amsterdammers at your first stop—and party with them all night. But if not, follow this plan: Start at the College Hotel (Roelof Hartstraat 1, www.collegehotel.com), where you'll find a host of local hotties. If you don't connect after drinking one of their crazy concoctions (which include "Amsterdam Swingers"), pedal on to the Mansion (Hobbemastraat 2, www.the-mansion .nl), where they serve a deadly absinthe number. (If you're going to head to the next location, you might want to take a breather and ask for a waterback.) For an over-the-top fifteenth-century nightclub experience, find your way to the Odeon (Singel 460, www.odeonamsterdam.nl). End the night at the refreshing watering hole Rain (Rembrandtplein 44). Hydrate before you go to bed.

6. Take a walk on the wild side. Don't go to the Red Light District alone! The kind gents at Amsterdam Tourist Center offer daily, or should I say nightly, tours of the area. It's a raw look at the oldest profession in the oldest part of Amsterdam. Unless you're up for a crazy night with horny, gross men and/or frisky college boys, stay in a group! The tour starts at the Prostitution Information Center, of course.

7. Pay your respects to an amazing girl. Anne Frank is one of the most inspirational souls ever to walk this planet. And if you don't believe me, take a tour of the annex she called home for 25 months during the Second World War. Get there by 8:45 a.m. because by 9 a.m., when the doors open, there'll be a line around the block. Prinsengracht 267, www.anne frank.org.

8. Day-trip it to the windmills and The Hague. If you're up for a whole day outside the grand center of Amsterdam, why not try an all-day Holland tour? You'll check out the world-famous Aalsmeer flower market, the iconic Za-anes windmills, a cheese factory, a clog factory, and best of all, The Hague and the Peace Palace. This will take up a whole day—and a bit of cash. For current information, visit the Amsterdam Tourist Center.

9. Treat yourself to the theater, ballet, opera, or symphony. Be a princess for the evening and enjoy a night of high society and culture at one of the 16,000 performances offered every year. Bookings can easily be made at the Amsterdam Tourist Office, located at Sationsplein across from Central Station.

10. Get *Gezelligheid*! Before trendy clubs and hotel hot spots, there were *bruine cafés* (brown cafés). These pubs, some of the oldest in Europe, all have the same dark interior and can be found in most every neighborhood in Amsterdam. Chill with the locals—and experience *gezelligheid*.

ATHENS,
GREECE

Melissa sun-worshiping
in Santorini.

Why This Place Rocks for
Flying Solo

-----

*T*he Greek gods knew what they were doing when they chose Athens as their home. What more could a god want? Dancing hues of azure waters stroke Athens's shores, dramatic cliffs crowned with temples deco-rate the skyline, and Greece's gorgeous culture drips with decadence everywhere you turn. Athens is a sensual city, nestled in the rocky shores of the Mediterranean, and it beckons the solo sister to dive into its mythical ruins, dine on its comforting cuisine, and die a thousand times over while watching the sunset.

No other place on earth lives up to its astounding reputation; whitewashed

Cops and Concierges

Just as a concierge dishes out the details, tourist police can also answer questions in English about getting a bus or cab, finding a doctor, and locating addresses and phone numbers for hotels and restaurants. You'll find these folks at all the main tourist spots.

buildings with turquoise domes perch lazily over sparkling seas as dark stray cats scamper along bougainvillea-covered walls. Hunched grandmothers dressed in black carry baskets full of fresh vegetables home from the open markets, and strapping, swarthy Greek youth splash in clear waters. You can watch it all unfold while sipping gritty Greek coffee or crisp white wine. From the Acropolis to Zorba the Greek, this destination dazzles with timeless, iconic images. You've seen pictures of the charming Greek islands that glisten in the Mediterranean, you've watched the torch runner sprint up Mount Olympus, and now it's time to experience all these timeless moments in this exquisite destination. Perhaps you are not a Greek god, but you do hold the title "Global Goddess." So grab your laurel leaves and get ready to frolic in the pious playground of Athens.

Culture: 5

Athens is a mosaic masterpiece of culture and history, and you'll find as many fascinating artifacts snuggled in with modern architecture as you will in all the fine museums. You won't need to, nor should you, make rigid plans when in Athens. A solo traveler can take in as much Greek culture wandering

aimlessly through the Plaka shopping district as she can following a strict itinerary to pack in all the museums. Relax—you're in Greece! And Athens isn't going anywhere!

Activity: 3

The Olympics were invented in this region, but unless you come representing your country for the Games, you won't have the opportunity to do much sporting. If you insist, water sports are available at local beach clubs, and you can find a few hiking trails in the nearby mountains. However, I'm sure you will work up enough of a sweat trekking from the Parthenon to the National Archaeological Museum to leave you happily weary at the end of the day. The only activity you'll want to do is to sip a cool libation under the shade of a white linen umbrella. Plato considered contemplation a serious activity; it should be enough for you, too.

Weather: 3

Don't let the word *Mediterranean* fool you. You might be thinking that Greece boasts year-round warm weather and a delicious cool climate when the sun sets. It can get hot, hot, hot in summer and oh-so-chilly in winter.

Social: 4

If socializing were an Olympic sport, then Athens would boast a fine team of gold medal winners. The social scene starts buzzing at Plaka and Kolonaki Square, where you'll find locals and visitors practicing the fine art of *volta* (strolling). Dinner is a big social event and most meals heat up around 10 p.m. in summer and a bit earlier in winter. Many cafés are tucked in next to each other, so meeting others at the next table is easy. After dinner, the crowds move to nightclubs and discos, and by this time you should have a troop of new friends.

Flying Foreplay

*A*thens is remarkably unique because of its language and culture. For some, it takes time to get used to the weird letters and interesting language. You'll find that most service staff speak English.

Looks like Greek to me! Even though Athens is a thriving international metropolis, you are not going to find much English spoken outside of your hotel. So invest in a good Greek translation book.

Breathe easy. Unfortunately, Athens is pretty polluted, so if you suffer from any lung ailments, make sure to bring your asthma medication. And always carry eye drops to keep your lovely eyes nice and moist.

Read Before You Go

Dinner with Persephone, by Patricia Storace
The Light of Day, by Eric Ambler
A Midsummer Night's Dream, by William Shakespeare

The Toilet

If you use a public toilet (beware, some are not that clean), plan on paying the attendants around .50 euros (that's about $1.00) for the few sheets of toilet paper she'll give you. Bring TP or tissues with you everywhere; many toilets do not have toilet paper available.

Athens Accessories

*A*n all-day public transportation ticket is an excellent value and can be used for any 24-hour period from the validation time. Once it's validated, you can hop on and off without further transactions. There is also a weekly pass available that can be used on all public transport except the train to the airport. Most buses stop running at midnight but there are several lines that go for 24 hours, including the airport buses and the buses from Syntagma to Pireaus.

Appalling apparel. If you plan on visiting the many unbelievable monasteries and religious venues, make sure you cover your arms and legs. You will not be allowed in holy places if you wear low-cut tops or sleeveless shirts. Carry a scarf everywhere you go, so you can cover up in a flash.

Rubber hits the road. Jimmy Choos weren't around during the building of Athens. And those slippery ancient rocks can ruin your trip if you are not wearing sturdy, rubber-soled shoes. Darling, don't run around looking like a tourist either, so invest in some lovely, low-healed espadrilles or Campers and stay away from running shoes.

The Top 10 Extraordinary Experiences

1. **Become a bronze goddess.** Suntan, naturally. Pack your trashiest novel and order the frostiest cocktail—these two private beach clubs are ready to make you feel like a bathing beauty. You'll avoid the lecherous masses that are known to ogle assets on public beaches.

Astir Beach Club Vouliagmeni. This is considered to be one of the best beaches in Athens. You're given a beach chair and sun umbrella once you enter. They have a snack bar and offer shower rooms with lockers. Windsurfing equipment can be rented and water-skiing lessons are offered. Apollonos St., Athens, Greece; tel: (+30) 210-890-2000; alternate reservations: tel: (+30) 210-890-1765/766; www.astir-palace.com/en/astir/membership_club.php.

Karavi Beach Club. This private beach club is the place where European beauties play in the sun. Well worth the one-hour drive from Athens, there are two restaurants, windsurfing rental, water-ski classes, and a beach volleyball court. For more on the beach clubs, visit www.10best.com. 198 Posidonos Ave., Schinias, Greece; tel: (+30) 210-945-5950.

2. Get cultured. All museums should be held to the standard of the National Archaeological Museum in Athens. I dare you not to feel awed and humbled by the sheer breadth in style, time period, and visceral beauty that lies protected inside this museum. This is by far the most important museum in Athens, if not the world, and contains artistic highlights from every period of ancient Greek civilization, from Neolithic to Roman times. Inside you can view the famed golden *Mask of Agamemnon.* 44, Patission St.—106 82 Athens; tel: (+30) 210-821-7717; www.culture.gr.

3. Frolic at the flea market. Monastiraki Flea Market is the place to buy everything from backgammon sets to Byzantine icons. The flea market runs all week, but Sunday is the day that the place is jumping with a sea of vendors and crowds of curious shoppers. This is an all-day event. Get there before 11 a.m. to avoid crowds and spend the day strolling and shopping through hundreds of tiny, unique stalls. Stop for lunch at one of the many cafés,

and end your evening with a shot of ouzo and dinner in Psiri. For more information on how to get there, visit www.athensguide.com/monastiraki.html.

4. He loves me, he loves me yacht. Why not try your hand at sailing and meet a few Greek sailors in the process? No promises that you'll meet a future Onassis, but it's a great way to try! The Athens Institute of Sailing offers courses for beginners and experienced sailors anytime of the year. Weeklong cruise sailing instruction with an English-speaking skipper includes use of yacht, instructor fee, course materials, taxes, permits, and harbor fees. Tel: (+30) 210-931-7018; e-mail: info@azureyachting.com; www.sailingcoursesingreece.com.

5. Get starstruck. Put those Cineplexes at home to shame. Sit under a constellation-filled sky with a perfect view of the floodlit Parthenon and munch popcorn while watching a movie, in English, at Cine Paris, a rooftop garden theater located right in Plaka Square. You can buy kitschy posters of old Greek movies in the lobby. Kidathineon 22, Athens, Greece; tel: (+30) 210-322-2071.

6. Go for the gold! Okay, so you've missed your chance to win an Olympic medal in Athens for this decade, but that doesn't mean you can't bring home the gold. Here are some great places to seek out the finest gold pieces that antiquity and modernity have to offer:

Lalaounis: **Panepistimiou Ave., tel: (+30) 210-361-1371.**
Elena Votsi: **7 Xanthou, tel: (+30) 210-360-0936. She redesigned the Olympic gold medal!**

Magea: 18 Charitos, tel: (+30) 210-724-0697. You can find her work in Barney's, but buying it in Athens is way cooler!

Zolotas: 10 Panepistimiou St., tel: (+30) 210-360-1272. A Greek institution.

7.   Island hop. If you have come this far, then a boat ride over to Mykonos or Santorini is a must. Unlike the whiplash pace of Athens, these islands rest quietly in ancient Greece with restful (repeats "rest") walking streets and endless horizons overlooking the sea. On these islands, you'll find the iconic Greece you've dreamt about—proud, whitewashed buildings, a piercing blue sea, and the best seafood in the world. Unfortunately, ferry schedules are never published and change randomly. For details on getting to Mykonos, visit www.mykonosgreece.com. For Santorini, www.santorini-greece.biz.

8.   Go square dancing. My favorite things to do in Athens involve finding a busy café in one of the many squares and spending the early evening writing in my journal, taking pictures, eating a plate of Greek treats, and people watching. Every neighborhood has a square and they are all very different. Here's a list of the best ones for the solo sister:

Kolonaki square. This is the place to chill and watch the glitterati take to the streets like it was a catwalk.

Kydathinaion square. Located in Plaka neighborhood. Packed with beautiful people sipping coffee.

Thisseion square. The hunting ground for frisky 20- to 30-year-olds, it has a great view of the Acropolis.

Exarhia square. The place you can find people who wear incense as perfume and think body piercing is the perfect accessory.

Plateia Kesariani square. The place to be if you are hungry. The square is lined with fantastic restaurants.

9.   Athens by Night. A fabulous way to meet other travelers is to hop on one of the Athens by Night tours. If you are interested in folk dancing, there is a four-hour evening tour from April to October, which includes the Sound and Light Spectacle and a performance of Dora Stratou folk dances. Another evening tour follows the Sound and Light Spectacle with a dinner show at a Plaka taverna. Other evening tours include a scenic drive through the illuminated boulevards of Athens and the Athens Harbor, followed by a live dance show at a typical Greek taverna. Ask your travel agent or concierge about these tours.

10.   Get down into history. Syntagma Square is not your everyday run-of-the-mill metro stop; it is an unbelievable archeological find. Even if you are not the kind of princess who takes public transportation, you need to check out the amazing antiquities that were found during the excavation for the metro line. They wanted to keep the train line going, but also felt it important to preserve the priceless historical finds. It's worth the price of a one-way ticket just to check out a frenetic public striding past still, priceless antiquities behind Plexiglas. The juxtaposition is startling.

BARCELONA, SPAIN

Marie strolling through Park Güell.

Why This Place Rocks for Flying Solo

I f I won the lottery, I'd pack my soon-to-be-purchased Louis Vuitton luggage with only the bare essentials and move to Barcelona for at least a year. It is a destination that has left a bright, enduring imprint on my heart. Every time I think of Barcelona, I smile. Barcelona is an energetic, vibrant European city that doesn't take herself too seriously. Everyone loves her: the warm Mediterranean kisses her sandy shores, famous artists decorate her streets and parks, and fragrant, spicy foods wrap their delicious scents around her. Barcelona is a dream, and this is the place to watch your dreams unfold in Technicolor glory.

Remember that sparkling sand castle you built as a little girl? Now throw in a pinch of exotic flavors and splash of rainbow hues and you've got the grown-up version of beachside paradise in Barcelona. A tactile city, Barcelona wants you to experience her with all your senses and emotions. Walk down streets lined with Gaudi's gingerbread-like houses, run your hands over the sun-warmed mosaic lizards that guard garden paths, and taste the aromatic Catalan cuisine. In Barcelona, you can smell the Mediterranean sea as it breaks against the shore and eavesdrop on the happy chatter of citizens telling their stories in a choir of diverse languages. Oh, and yes, you can dance the nights away with new friends you'll meet from the four corners of the world.

Culture: 5

Barcelona is a living, breathing museum. Like a surrealist dream come true, just walking the streets will leave you dazed by the historical richness and unsuspecting splendor of the city. You can spend weeks just wandering through endless museums. And for you lovers of art, you'll find several great museums dedicated to renowned local artists such as Picasso, Miro, Gaudi, and Dali (a short train ride to Dali's place). You'll stumble on Spanish and the regional Catalan culture displayed in museums, spilling out of tapas bars, while sitting at open-air cafés and strolling down the main avenue, La Rambla, at all hours of the day and night.

Activity: 3

Barcelona's narrow streets and intricate districts lend themselves to strolling, not jogging, and people will think you robbed someone if you go faster than a healthy clip. A bike can be handy transport through the city, but keep in mind that this *is* a city, and unless you want to hit the gym like a local, you'll probably have to be satisfied with the cardio you get dancing the night away at one of the many nightclubs and flamenco bars.

Weather: 5

If heaven were on earth, Barcelona would be the divine address. The climate is gentle and warm all year, with slight temperature dips in winter that require you to bundle up with a sweater and pants. No matter what time of year, you are bound to find someone sunbathing on the three miles of beaches that line Barcelona.

Social: 5

Take an early-morning stroll and you are likely to see more sleepy-eyed people on their way home from the discos than on the way to work. Clubs and bars get started late and stay open late, conforming to the nocturnal rhythms of the Spanish metropolis. Dinner doesn't start until 9 p.m., the last dish won't be cleared from the table until 11 p.m., and the bartenders don't start really mixing it up until midnight. During the day, the backbone of Barcelona social life is La Rambla, a sweeping boulevard lined with newspaper stands, flower shops, cafés, and street performers. This is the only city in the world where I partied until breakfast; too bad it was the morning of my flight home.

Barcelona is a big, meaty metropolis, so there is not much you won't be able to find. They speak Spanish and Catalan (you might want to get a Catalan phrase book), and it is wise to bring a translation book with key Spanish phrases. Here is a list of some that might come in handy:

I would like a glass of sangria, please. *Quisiera un cristal de sangria, por favor.*
Where are all the hot nightclubs? *¿Dónde están todos los nightclubs poplares?*

Where are you from, handsome? *¿De dónde es usted, hermoso?*
My mother will love you. *Mi madre le amará.*

Be cool. LeCool.com is a weekly e-mail about all the fabulous events and activities that are happening in Barcelona. Just go to their website and sign up before you go. Then you'll have a good idea about some of the places you'll want to hit when you get to town.

Read Before You Go

The Time of the Doves (La Plaza del Diamante), by Merce Rodoreda

Barcelona Accessories

The fashion in Barcelona is a saucy mix of sheer playfulness and European brilliance. If you have a few extra dollars, then invest in at least one new ensemble. You can tell

The Barcelona Barri Gotic area is also known as the Gothic Quarter, and is a fantastic little area to wander through. It is the oldest and largest Gothic area in the world! Keep your eyes out for great architecture and funky shops and cafés, but if you stay out after sunset, the only people there are tourists and pickpockets.

your friends, "Oh this number? I picked it up in Barcelona."

Skinny-dipping. Barcelona has a social, urban beach strip: you'll want to strip off your clothes and bask away. If you are not into skinny-dipping, then you might want to bring a bathing suit. The shops tend to sell items that are season-specific.

Throw on some thongs. You might want to invest in some thong underwear, because the Spanish really don't like *las lineas pantalones* ("panty lines").

The Top 10 Extraordinary Experiences

1. Swing at the bar. La Fira is a nightclub that would be out of business in the United States because of crazy, sometimes dangerous, objects that fill the venue. Some of them being the swings surrounding the bar, where you can swing and sip the night away; the others would be the old metal carnival figures that make up some of the seating by the dance floor. The place is decked out in old fairground equipment from years gone by. Walking into the club's underground locations will send you back to the time when you played in funhouses at carnivals, or when you dated that

really *loco* guy in college. The music is great and most of the guys are gay, so you don't have to worry about getting hit on all night. They don't take credit cards, unfortunately. You can't have everything, darling. La Fira, c/Provenca 171—The Eixample; www.bcn-nightlife.com, look up "La Fira."

2. Muse with Picasso. If you always wondered why Picasso was so blue, then so red, the answers can be found in his museum. It is a remarkable edifice with some of the most iconic images in the world hanging on the walls. Plan on being awestruck, overwhelmed, and amazed. If you didn't like Picasso before your tour, you will love him afterward. Okay, maybe not love him, but you will appreciate his eccentric work and ever more unconventional life.
Picasso Museum; Montcada, 15-23, 08003 Barcelona; www.museu picasso.bcn.es/index.htm.

3. Go gaga over Gaudi. Gaudi was a genius, really. He took his passion for nature, color, and texture and wrapped it into some of the most exhilarating architecture on the planet. A few of his masterpieces do look like they came from out of this world. His creations need to be seen, touched, and experienced on a personal level. And that's pretty easy to do, because the city is chock-full of them. The most famous is the Templo Expiatorio de la Sagrada Familia, which is a monolithic cathedral bursting through the sky. Part of its fascination is that the cathedral has yet to be finished. Other Gaudi gems include several unbelievable apartment buildings in the Eixample neighborhood and the glorious Park Güell, which was declared a universal monument by UNESCO in 1984. Visit www.gaudiclub.com for more information about all of Gaudi's works. Visit www.barcelonaexperience.com or www.euroadventures.net for information on a half-day walking tour.

4. Eat your way through Spain. For a truly mouthwatering tour, join the Culinary Tour on a Friday and eat your way through Barcelona. The crew of the Culinary Tour has done all the fieldwork for you, leaving you to enjoy the best that Catalan food has to offer. The tour includes breakfast at Barcelona's oldest Granja Café, where you can enjoy homemade dairy products; a visit to La Boqueria, the city's most colorful food market, where you'll nosh on some tasty tapas; followed by wine at a bodega. You'll sample some traditional Catalan cheeses at a unique cheese shop, visit an impressive list of delicious food shops, and drop into a local champagne bar for a glass of *cava*. All this is capped off with a hearty

meal at Angel's, where, surrounded by an eclectic mix of antiques and junk, you will be fed and entertained by the eccentric host. All with detailed explanations of your tour, a little recipe book to take home, and juicy anecdotes. The food is to be paid for separately.
Meeting Point: At the corner of La Rambla and Calle Carmen, at the entrance of the church "BETLEM" (Rambla 107).
Booking: e-mail: info@myft.net.

5. Feel the Magic. How long has it been since you've been mesmerized? (Don't answer that if you have already been to La Fira and Park Güell.) Visit the Magic Fountain of Montjuic and you'll be gasping with delight. Created for the Great Universal Exhibition of 1929, the magic fountain is an impressive spectacle of light, color, music, and feats of aqua technology. For all you solo sisters who've gone to Vegas to stare in awe of the Bellagio's shooting water and light show, then prepare to meet the next level of fountain shows. Not convinced? Check it out and I promise you'll feel like a little girl on the Fourth of July.

6. Soar above Barcelona. Well, not really. But you can pretend at the Tibidabo Amusement Park, which is over 1,600 feet above sea level. The park has been around since 1899 and it has such a breathtaking view of Barcelona that at first it does not seem real. The best way to see the sites is in one of the many not-so-kiddy rides. Fly around in the airplane ride, glide through the air on a magic sled, or rise and fall in a colorful Ferris wheel with a gorgeous view of Barcelona beneath. Make sure to take your camera because you will score some spectacular pictures of Barcelona for your desk at work. If you want to join a tour, check out www.barcelonaexperience.com. Pl. del Tibidabo, 3–4.08035 Barcelona; tel: 93-211-79-42.

7.   Get Crazy. For a spectacular secular sensation, spend the evening with a bunch of not-so-holy monks and nuns at Santa Locura. The venue is a themed club where all the waitstaff serves you more than communion and you dance the night away along with your sins. Oh, Santa Locura means Holy Craziness. And this is the place where you can let go of those private schoolgirl rules and party like a reprobate. Santa Locura, Consell de Cent 363; tel: 93-200-14-66.

8.   Dance, baby. I can't think of anything sexier than learning how to flamenco dance in Barcelona. A rose in your hair, a strapping young Spaniard whisking you around the dance floor, and a glass of fruity sangria to quench your thirst. Yum. And thanks to a group of Andalucians who are now living in Barcelona, you, too, can learn how to dance like a Latin lover. Not too sure if he'll stay for drinks with you, but it won't hurt to ask. For two hours you will be taught Sevillanas, which is a popular form of flamenco, with others in a cozy group of beginners. Contact Katrien or Carline. Tel: 34-637-26-5405; e-mail: info@myft.net; www.myft.net/index_fla.html.

9.   Ride, Sally, ride. For the fun-loving solo sister, there's no better way to burn off the chorizo and stuffed mushrooms from the night before, meet other travelers, see the sights, and learn the history of Barcelona than with Fat Tire Bike Tours. You ride around Barcelona with an entertaining native English-speaking expert guide, while pedaling and chatting with others. The guide will share some helpful tips and advice on the do's and don'ts of Barcelona while waxing poetic about the sites you visit. The tour is about 4½ hours long, and you ride through the Barri Gotic, to the Sagrada Familia, the Parc de la Ciutadella, the Olympic Village, the beach, and Port Vell. The ride takes you on bike paths and boardwalks, down Gothic alleyways, and through parks, so just pedal away and enjoy the ride as you learn all about this fascinating city. For more information, visit www.fattire biketoursbarcelona.com.

10.   Beach Blanket Barcelona. Pass el SPF and get ready to enjoy the newly redeveloped and fully outfitted urban beach strips that stretch from the Palau de Mar to the Rambla de Mar and on into the Olympic Port area. There are more than three miles of beaches where you can tan and chill, so put that sangria on ice and join the nearly seven million annual visitors to Barcelona's beautiful beaches. Particularly enjoyable are the beaches of Mar Bella, Sant Sebastià, and Nova Icària. For more details, visit www.bcn.es/turisme.

My favorite beach is in the charming town of Calella on the Costa del Maresme 30 miles from Barcelona. It is a quick hour-long train ride from the city.

The best thing about the town is that it is the strawberry capital of Spain. You can get strawberries on freshly made crepes from street vendors, you can sip fresh strawberry juice, and my favorite is the homemade ice cream filled with fresh strawberries. Calella is a much-loved vacation spot for Europeans and Russians; the beaches are topless and some are nude. Calella Tourist Board, Sant Jaume, 231 08370-CALELLA (Barcelona) Spain; tel: +34 93-769-05-59; e-mail: pt-calella@publintur.es; www.publintur.es/calella.htm.

BERLIN, GERMANY

Teresa loving life under the
Brandenburg Gate.

Why This Place Rocks
for Flying Solo

*B*erlin will stir your soul. It's an
electric city that buzzes with
remnants of a troubled past and
seedlings for a bright future. Because
Berlin has gone through so much drama,
the people try hard to take great care of
its visitors. The city is safe, the public
transportation is great, and the people
are willing to help out. But more than
that, you can't visit without thinking
about war and peace, or questioning your
own beliefs on the subject. Berlin stands
up and says, "Hey, how do you feel about
that?" This was where Einstein was educated and the Nazi movement started. It
was in Berlin where the Soviets put up

If you're not into the bus tour scene, simply take the local Bus 100 or 200. It carries you to all the same historic places but it's less than 3 euros, versus 16–19 euros. You don't get the narrative, but if you do a free walking tour, you can get plenty of information.

the eleven-foot wall that separated East Berlin from West Berlin, and just 28 years later, the residents of both sides tore it down. That was the beginning of the end of Soviet communism throughout Eastern Europe. It's mind-boggling to think that less than two decades ago this was a city split in half, a place where a wall divided a community that in the 1920s was the epicenter of culture and the arts. This is where Marlene Dietrich's career took off, and where the iconic cabaret culture of the roaring twenties began.

As the host of many pivotal moments in the twentieth century, Berlin leaves an indelible mark on all who visit. One minute you're standing in front of the glorious Brandenburg Gate dedicated to the unification of Germany then walk one block to the most moving Memorial to the Murdered Jews of Europe dedicated to the victims of the Holocaust. There, you get lost in a labyrinth of large cement stones and intuitively feel the loneliness of war, being lost and without a home—just like the innocent victims. In mere steps, you've traversed from the gates of unification to the gates of Hell. So, if witnessing history up close is your passion, Berlin is an intellectual delight.

And not only does Berlin possess some of the most infamous places in the world, but you'll fall in love with a city that pulses with innovation, offers some of the best shopping in Europe, and has great nightlife to boot!

Culture: 5

History ain't behind no three inches of Plexiglas in this city. It's right there in front of you, under you, above you, all around you. The city of Berlin is a museum in itself, but if you want more, there's plenty: 175 museums, 3 opera houses, 7 professional symphony orchestras, more than 300 galleries, and countless historical sites. They have a whole island, called Museumsinsel, that's packed with five mind-blowing museums. The Pergamonmuseum is filled with one of the most famous collections of antiquities in Europe. So between history and art collections, you'll be very busy in Berlin.

Activity: 2

If you're looking to Jet Ski, hike, or kayak in Berlin, this place just might disappoint you. Berliners love their bikes, so you can get lots of cardio on a bicycle while dodging speeding Mercedes and BMWs. But remember, although it's a great way to see the city, Berlin is a big place. In fact, Berlin is nine times the size of Paris!

Weather: 3

Unless a vicious cold front blasts through Germany, Berlin's winters are tolerable. Their summers are usually mild, but check before you go if you have heat or cold issues. The public transportation and taxis are reliable, so you won't ever be stuck out in the cold (or heat) for too long anyway.

Social: 4

Germans have this reputation of being, well, German. This stereotype is not true in Berlin. In general, everyone is friendly and many Berliners speak some English. The night scene is *huge*, especially in East Berlin, so if you want to go out, there are plenty of fantastic places safe for solo women. A fantastic way of meeting others to spend some quality time with is through one of the many tours offered.

Flying Foreplay

Good to go. Because Berlin is a true metropolitan city, there's not much you need to plan before you visit. Berlin likes to host some big celebrations, so you should make sure you're not showing up during the World Cup or some other huge event.

Pack light. Germany is part of the European Union, so they use euros. Things are pretty reasonably priced, compared to other big cities in Europe, so you might want to pack less than you would usually and shop for some cool, trendy threads. There are plenty of wonderful boutiques in Berlin, and it is also home to the largest department store in Europe, the KaDaWe.

English magazines. *EXBERLINER* is the monthly Berlin magazine that lists happenings such as clubs, live music, theater, and readings. This magazine also carries great articles on various Berlin-centric topics. You can get this at many shops and hotels.

Setting Your Scene

Depending on your reasons for coming to Berlin—i.e., to shop, eat, socialize, or explore—the neighborhood you stay in matters. As I mentioned, Berlin is huge! So, you can't just stroll from one side of town to the other. Here is a list of a few places and the reasons why you'd like to stay there:

Mitte. This is the fun, trendy (once East Berlin) center of town. It's the home of the Brandenburg Gate, State Museums, libraries, Opera, Humbolt University, the Berlin Cathedral, and the charming Gendarmenmarkt Square. It's also home of the old Jewish area. Brimming with cool galleries and lots of gorgeous shops, Mitte's alleyways are splashed with open-air courtyards filled with boutiques and cafés.

Prenzlauer Berg. This neighborhood is northeast of Mitte and was famous for the punk scene in the eighties. Now these punks are parents. One of the attractions is the nineteenth-century brewery complex that is now the Kulturbrauerei culture center, full of night clubs and restaurants. A good time to visit is on the weekends when the street market Kollwitzplatz is open.

Charlottenburg. This is the hot West side that's packed with great shopping and very close to the main train station,

Zoologischer Garten. It is the home of KaDeWe, the largest department store in Europe, and the famed shopping street Kurfuerstendamm (known to Berliners as Ku'damm). Some of the best design hotels are in this neighborhood. Try the Bleibtreu Hotel at www.bleibteu.com or the Ku'Damm 101 at www.kudamm101.com, both centrally located.

Kreuzberg. Home to the more alternative Berliners, this neighborhood is lined with cafés where you can find locals smoking cigarettes and contemplating some deep philosophical ideologies. It's also where you'll find the last standing remnants of the Wall, Checkpoint Charlie, and the newly opened Jewish Museum.

Berlin Accessories

Berlitz, baby. Get yourself a Berlitz *German for Travelers* guide. It lists all the basic phrases that you need to know, but more importantly, it helps you pronounce the words somewhat correctly. It's easy to slaughter the German language.

Comfy shoes. Berliners are very casual, and they don't get dressed up unless they are going to the opera. So you won't be breaking any style rules here if you bring your comfiest, yet ugliest, pair of shoes. There are not many places in Europe that you can get away with this, so enjoy.

Read Before You Go

The Tin Drum (Die Blechtrommel), by Günter Grass

Shadows of Berlin, by David Bergelson
The Weather in Berlin, by Ward Just

The Top 10 Extraordinary Experiences

1. Tours Gratis. There's a group called New Berlin that offers free tours daily of all the important spots in Berlin. Basically you make a donation at the end of the four-hour tour and it's worth every euro you decide to part with. The catch is that the tour guides want to sell you other tours like the pub crawl tour, the Red Berlin tour, Third Reich Berlin, and a few others. Meet at the Dunkin' Donuts across the street from Zoo Station. New Berlin Free Tours; 12:30 p.m. everyday; www.newberlintours.com.

2. Drink absinthe in a communist bar. The trendy neighborhood of Mitte was one of the first East Berlin districts to welcome capitalism. And with capitalism comes trendy, expensive bars—but Ost-Zone remains true to its East Berlin, underground roots: rough around the edges, with a fabulous cast of local characters, and still serving absinthe—which is completely illegal in most Western countries. Don't drink more than one or two—this is a hallucinogenic—and you need to get back to your hotel safely. Details: It's located at Monbijoupark beneath the S-Bahn tracks that overlook the River Spree and the back of Museum Island. No closing hours on the weekends. Monbijoupark/ S-Bahnbogen 153, Mitte. S-Bahn Hackescher Markt.

3. Shop on the Spree. The phrase *shopping spree* could have well been invented in Berlin, because the river that runs through this style capital is named the Spree. Berlin offers the best German designer labels, leather goods, china, art, and accessories, and if you get bored there, head over to West Berlin, and shop Kurfurstendamm Boulevard or KaDaWe, Europe's biggest department store. On the sixth floor you'll find the best gourmet food ever. You could spend all day up there just eating samples.

4.   Visit Marlene. For you lovers of Marlene Dietrich and cabaret culture, you'll need to check out Marlene Dietrich and Entertainment of the 1920s. It's an extraordinary exhibition of Marlene Dietrich's dresses, suitcases, movie costumes, and personal items, and they are on permanent display at the Film Museum (www.filmmuseum-berlin.de). After your tour, check out a real cabaret show at the famous Wintergarten (www.wintergarten-berlin.de).

5.   Go club hopping. Berlin's nightlife is one of the best in Europe. People are friendly, the variety is fantastic, and there are a ton of different night spot tours you can take. I think this is a great way to see Berlin's nightlife without worries about being alone. You get to meet a great group of other travelers and you get escorted to at least four different bars and clubs with a guide who knows Berlin. www.brewersberlintours.com; www.newberlintours.com.

6.   Concentrate on the past. There are a few things that everyone should do in his or her lifetime, and visiting a former concentration camp is one of them. During this solemn day of seeing what really happened during the Second World War, I hope that we all get a clearer perspective of war and ignorance. The closest camp is the Sachsenhausen Concentration Camp. New Berlin offers tours three times a week, or you can go out there alone. www.newberlintours.com.

7.   Enjoy a winter wonderland. Berlin transforms into a winter wonderland from the last weekend in November until the first weekend in January. Stroll the charming stalls of one of the 50 Christmas markets in Berlin, drink hot mulled wine, and eat crispy sausages while admiring hand-crafted gifts and other delightful German items. After all that shopping, strolling, and eating, catch a beautiful horse-drawn carriage ride past illuminated and beautifully decorated buildings. You can find these markets throughout Berlin.

8.   Take flight. Soar 200 meters above Berlin in a mere 40 seconds. The Berliner Fernsehturm is the highest building in Berlin and was built as a symbol of communism's power. While getting used to the altitude, enjoy a cocktail in the restaurant, which revolves twice an hour. They do serve dinner, but don't expect the best meal of your life. Berliner Fernsehturm, Panoramastr. 1A, D-10178 Berlin; tel: +49 (0) 30242-3333.

9.   Enjoy the opera. Berliners love their opera, so they make sure that everyone can afford a ticket. It's possible to buy tickets at the door for most of their performances. There are three operas in Berlin, and you're bound to find a performance almost every night of the week, all year round. Before the show at Staatsoper Unter den Linden Opera, check out the memorial to the 25,000 books that the Nazis burned, buy a book on Humboldt University's front lawn, and pay your respects to the Unknown Soldier. If you're there during Christmas, go explore the Christmas market next to the opera. All these sites are right next to each other, and you only have to cross the street once to experience them all.

Staatsoper Unter den Linden, Unter den Linden 5, 10117 Berlin-Mitte; tel: 2035-4555; www.staatsoper-berlin.org

Komische Oper Berlin, Behrenstrasse, 55-57 Berlin-Mitte; tel: 4799-7400

Deutsche Oper Berlin, Bismarckstrasse 35, Charlottenburg; tel: 343-841.

10. Get SchauLUST. The three-day SchauLUST-MuseenBERLIN ticket costs a whopping 12 euros and lets you visit more than 70 museums and collections on any three consecutive days. The pass is available at the Berlin Tourismus Marketing GmbH Tourism Info Centers.

Europa-Center, Budapester Strasse

Brandenburger Tor, side entrance to Brandenburg Gate

Tourist Info Café, under the tower at Alexanderplatz

BRUSSELS, BELGIUM

Teresa feasting on mussels
in Brussels.

Why This Place Rocks
for Flying Solo

I f you want to experience European culture in all its glorious flavors, but aren't ready to tackle a huge city like London or Paris, then you'll find the darling city of Brussels *la taille parfaite*—the perfect size. Belgium is nestled between France and the Netherlands and has not one, but three, national languages—French, Flemish, and German. Luckily, most people speak some English. From its enchanting old city center that looks like it drifted out of the pages of a fairytale to its epicurean wonders, you'll be anything but bored in Brussels.

Don't let Brussels's bite size fool you. With over 1,800 restaurants and more museums and historic sites than you can shake a *pomme fritte* at, this itty-bitty city is filled with a ton of surprises. Home of Godiva Chocolates, the Belgian waffle, and the seat of the European Union, Brussels is a small city with big flavor. Once thought of as Paris's and London's redheaded stepchild, Brussels has moved out of the shadows and is showing off her beauty and rich culture with unadulterated pride.

And if you don't fall in love with her majestic architecture, delicious food, and spirited shopping venues, then you'll fall in love with her residents. The Belgians are a fun, ironic group who don't take themselves too seriously—how can they when their claim to fame is a statue of a boy peeing?

Culture: 4
Alice's Wonderland could just as well have been Brussels. The Grand-Place is an outdoor museum and feast for the eyes. And walking in any direction from the center, you might end up in the Comic Strip, or the Art Nouveau district, or perhaps the trendy fashion streets, and if you keep walking, you're sure to discover Mont des Arts, the home of a dozen different museums. Brussels likes to surprise her guests, so during the day, just keep on walking and see what amazing areas you find.

Activity: 2
If you consider eating as a way to burn calories, then give this destination a 5. But if cardio-chocolate tasting is not on your aerobic schedule, you might find the lack of physical stimulation rough. Although, if you really need some physical activity between eating, don't fret because 20 percent of Brussels is lush parks. Just grab your workout shoes and head to one of the many beautiful open spaces that are lined with safe walking paths.

Weather: 3
You'll be so busy dashing from great restaurant to amazing museum that you won't even notice the weather. Brussels is in Northern Europe, where it's known to get chilly. The summers are nice and toasty while the winters are pretty darn cold.

Social: 4
The people are so friendly here that at first you might feel a bit suspicious of everyone's kindness. Well, it's genuine. And they love hanging out and drinking flavored wine together. Many speak English, so it's easy to spark up conversations. If you want to practice your French, this is the place to do it; they are way more patient than the French. If you're not too sure where to go for a nightcap, walk into any of the many cool boutiques at Rue Antoine Dansaert—Place Saint-Géry district and ask the shopkeepers. They will be happy to tell you where they go after work— and they might even invite you for a drink.

Flying Foreplay

Reserve your restaurant. You must have dinner in one of the world-renowned restaurants. And the only way that's going to happen is if you make reservations seconds after you book your airline ticket. Many of the hot spots have a three-month waiting list.

Stay warm. Unless you own a full-length mink stole or can cope with really cold weather, try to avoid Brussels in the winter. I admit it is unbelievably gorgeous then with all the decadent Christmas fairs and twinkling lights, but the temperature likes to dive below zero. It's not fun walking on frozen cobblestones or eating a waffle that gets cold seconds after you order it. The sun sets at 4 p.m. during the winter, too, so you don't get that much time to wander the many side streets and parks.

Be close to old. Brussels is a two-part city. It's a magnificent city of rich heritage and ornate, antiquated buildings with a distinct old town area call the Grand-Place. It is also a city of immense commerce, the capital of the European Union and a thriving community. When you book your hotel, make sure to stay near the Old Center, not the New Center. If you stay in the New Center, you will be staying in the business district. This is great if you plan on doing business. But if you're visiting Brussels to experience all her charm and loveliness, then stay near the Grand-Place. Otherwise, you'll need to take a cab into the energetic, happening part of town.

Brussels Accessories

An appetite and stretch pants. Home of the Belgium waffle, 300 different beers, famous chocolate makers, fried potatoes, mussels, cheese, and 1,800 restaurants—plan on eating your way through this city. And enjoy! No guilt is allowed.

Solid shoes are a must. The streets of Brussels owe their charm to the wonderful cobblestone, but if you're not prepared, you can break your ankle or neck, depending on how you fall. The only place you'll need to wear heels is a top-notch restaurant, and if you go, make sure to take a cab.

The Top 10 Extraordinary Experiences

-- -- -- -- -- -- -- -- -- -- -- -- --

1.   **Buy Brussels.** Visit one of the burgeoning fashion communities in trendy Brussels. You'll find some cutting-edge designers without the pomp and price of other European cities.

The main shopping districts include:

Rue Antione Danseart—Place Saint-Gery district
Saint Jacques district
Galeries Royales, Saint Hubert district
Sablon—Marolles district
Avenue Louise and Boulevard de Waterloo district
Rue du Bailli, Place du Chatelain, Place Brugmann quarter
Rue de Namur—Matonge—Saint Boniface—Flagey quarter
European—Cinquantenaire quarter

2.   **Death by Chocolate.** This is the chocolate capital of the world—and don't let the Swiss or Mr. Hershey tell you different. Try a walking tour where you visit a half-dozen chocolate shops and taste away. Don't miss the Cocoa and Chocolate Museum either. Rue de la tête d'Or 9-11—1000 Brussels; www.mucc.be.

3.   **Hike the Atomio.** At first, it looks like an obnoxious science project gone wrong, but once you get inside and learn the history of this amazing structure, you'll appreciate its symbolism. You can spend

the day in the park and visit other sites like Mini-Europe (no need to go to Paris after seeing this!), the museums of the Far East, and the Planetarium. If you're into jogging off those yummy snacks from the night before, this is the place.

4. Iconic eating. Eat all the things that Brussels is famous for. Have a meal of mussels and *pommes fritte*, drink Belgian beer; finish off with a Belgian waffle slathered in whipped cream and chocolate. Then after all that eating, enjoy some Belgium chocolate made by Godiva, the famous chocolatiers. This meal can be had most anywhere, but my favorite area—albeit touristy—is right off the Grand-Place. You'll find rows of seafood restaurants that are all more adorable than the next.

5. Go backstage. Every Saturday at noon, Mrs. Isabelle Van Honnaker takes a group of opera lovers backstage on guided tours of the opera house. You get to see the costumes, sets, and props in an intimate setting. This is also a great way to meet others. La Monneire house, the opera building, is located in the historic heart of Brussels, near the City Hall and the Grand-Place. Place de la Monnaie—1000 Brussels.

6. Know Art Nouveau. Brussels loves its art nouveau, and you'll understand why after enjoying a guided tour of the famous buildings around town. The Association du Patrimoine Artistique offers tours daily. Rue Charles Hanssens 7; tel: 32 (0)2-512-34-21; http://users.skynet.be/APA. Another tour you'd enjoy is the Brukselbinnenstebuiten (say that ten times fast!) group. This group is on a constant quest for the avant-garde, from the sublime to the ridiculous, and these are the guides who can lead you off the beaten track. For info check out http://brukselbinnenstebuiten.vgc.be.

7. Get happy with hops. Spend a night getting basted in Brussels's breweries. Now this won't be your cheap night out drinking stale beer as in college. This country prides itself on creating the best and most alcoholic beer in the universe. Try these spots:

Belgium Brewer Museum—Maison des Brasseur, Grand—Place 10; www.beerparadise.be

Brasseurs de la Grand-Place, Rue de la Colline 24; www.brasseaurs-brouwers.be

Brussels Gueuze Museum, Cantillon Brewery, Rue Gheude 56; www.cantillon.be

Belle-Vue Brewery, Quai du Hainaut 33; www.breweryvisits.be

The Dark Beer

For you Goth chicks, you can drink beer from a skull-shaped glass at Le Cercueil (The Coffin). Sip beer while listening to funereal music and chilling out on coffins and purple velvet seats. If you dare. Rue des Harengs 10–12; (tel: 02/512-30-77).

Schaerbeek Museum of Beer, Av. Bertrand 31/33; http:/users.skynet.be//museedelabiere

8. Visit the Royals. This is a city fit for a queen, and sure enough, there is a real royal family that calls Brussels home. Well, in summer they head off to their holiday palace in Spain, so you can peek into their pad and check out their China collection. If you're not in Brussels during the summer and can't crash the royal palace, check out these amazing royal digs:

The BELvue Museum, Hotel Bellvue, Place de Palais; www.belvue.be

Royal Crypt at church of Notre-Dame de Laeken, Parvis Notre-Dame

Royal Museum of Central Africa, Leuvensesteenwewg 13; www.africanuseum.be

Royal Greenhouse of Laeken, Avenue du Parc Royal (Domaine royal)

9. Brussels's beaches. During the summer months, alongside Willebroek canal, 500 meters from the Grand-Place, a colorful riverside village pops up. The crazy Belgians ship in sand and turn this urban stretch of land into a beachside paradise. Take a boat trip or go brewery hopping, check out the galleries, visit the open markets at Le Port du Livre or the Midi Market (both on Sundays), or just grab a beach chair and spend the day people watching.

10. Meander through Mont des Arts. This is a lovely district, just a short walk from the Grand-Place, where you can get lost in the many museums, shops, and galleries. Plan on spending the whole day just wandering. Make sure to bring your camera because you'll get some great shots of beautiful Brussels. The museums here include: Royal Museum of Fine Arts, Musical Instruments Museum, BOZAR—Centre for Fine Arts, Former Palace of Brussels and Coudenberg's archaeological site, Royal Library of Belgium, Royal Film Library, BELvue Museum, and ING Center. On Sundays you'll find a market selling books and antiques.

Midnight Museums

To help make the long winter nights easier to endure, the museums in Brussels stay open late on Thursday evenings. Fifty museums participate in this program.

BUDAPEST, HUNGARY

Fee enjoying the rain
in Budapest.

Why This Place Rocks
for Flying Solo

With seven countries kissing Hungary's border and a thousand-year history that reads like a mystery novel/fairy tale, it's no wonder Budapest's entrance onto the world stage was so highly anticipated after the iron curtain drew back. And rightly so—this has to be one of the most dramatic cityscapes in Europe. On one side of the blue Danube is perched the enchanting town of Buda. Here, the impeccable castle and a host of other famous Budapest icons reside. The city of Pest on the river's other side is the home of a flurry of trendy shops, bustling restaurants, and the picturesque City

The Bar

For you young at heart who want to check out the bar scene in Budapest, try Absolute Tours (www.absolutetours.com). They have pub crawls three times a week.

Park. These two equally amazing parts of town are connected by seven bridges; the most famous and striking being the Chain Bridge. At night the bridges and all the buildings on the river are festooned with white lights that twinkle and glisten against the remarkably dark Danube. Walking on the banks of the river, you'll have to stop and catch your breath from the overwhelming splendor of Budapest.

Sprinkled within the granite-lined roads and public squares are scores of delicious, chic restaurants and retailers who've creatively mingled the Old East with the New East. The result is rich, inviting flavors and fashions that leave lasting impressions. Budapest's turbulent past has been transformed into a fascinating, energetic present. This historically rich and remarkably beautiful city is ideal for a solo girl who's ready to explore, uncover, and enjoy one of the most stunning cities in Europe. The size of the city is manageable, and the transportation system is a dream. It's easy to get around, and the city layout is pretty basic, although the language can get a bit tricky at times, and the inhabitants of Budapest are not the friendliest in the world. Once you understand that "it's not you," you can easily navigate your way around.

Culture: 5

Wow! Step back and drink in the splendor of Budapest for a moment, then spend your time wandering the many museums,

historical sites, and parks that fill this city. Even if you're not big into culture and history, you can't help wanting to learn more about Budapest. This destination beckons you to uncover the many secrets that are hidden in its crazy past. Walk the Buda castle's soulful labyrinth, or stroll through one of the over 60 museums that are scattered throughout the city.

Activity: 3

Hungarians love their parks and have plenty of outdoor sports that can keep your heart rate elevated. During the winter (December to March), the City Park Lake is transformed into the largest ice-skating rink in Central Europe. This is the place not only where the locals burn a few calories, but also where they socialize and celebrate. Margaret Island, a small island on the Danube, is a great place to jog or walk.

Weather: 3

Spring and summer are divine in Budapest. Many of the outside terraces and squares morph into wonderlands of socializing, eating, and drinking. You can find plenty of places during the warm months to just sit and watch the locals, read a book, or practice your Hungarian. Winter is another story. It's cold and it gets dark at around 4:30 p.m. Christmas markets pop up, hotels are much less expensive, and the city lights up even more during this time. So, if you don't mind cold weather, you polar bears might really enjoy Budapest this time of year.

Social: 2

Unless you hook up with a group of tourists or go on a tour with English speakers, meeting people here is pretty tough. It's a combination of the language and the residual iron curtain feelings. This should not stop you from visiting; just understand that your nights might be a bit quiet, which will give you more time to journal.

Flying Foreplay

People love to shop in Budapest, so you're sure to find what you need. But be warned that it's very seasonal.

Bath baby. Visiting one of the many historic bath houses is a must, so don't forget your bathing suit. If you're visiting in winter, you won't find any of the stores carrying them. You might want to keep your Brazilian bikini at home and pack your one-piece number. The baths are enjoyed by everyone in Budapest and they feel much like a community center.

Get Hungary. A translation book is a good idea. The *Berlitz Hungarian Phrase Book* has most of the expressions you need to know. Sorry, no section on flirting.

Setting Your Scene

Staying in a hotel on the Danube is a must. If you've come all the way to Budapest, you should get the best view available. Plenty of hotels sit on both sides of the river, but the Pest side is the more social area. The most amazing hotel I've ever stayed at is the Four Seasons Gresham Palace. It's perched at the foot of the iconic Chain Bridge and has views of the river, Palace, Funicular train, and Fisherman's Bastion. Plus they know how to treat you like a princess. Roosevelt Tér 5-6. 1051, Budapest; tel: 36-1-268-6000; www.fourseasons.com/budapest.

Budapest Accessories

Sturdy and sexy. A girl's got to look great while strolling *après* Eastern Bloc. Comfy shoes, especially ones with wedge heels—or no heels—are a requirement. In Buda you will be doing lots of castle and cave exploring; while in Pest you will be busy museum power walking and boutique shopping.

Quell the chill. It gets freaking cold in winter. So, if all you own is a Californian windbreaker, you'd better step up and invest in a coat to keep you cozy.

Love the gloves. Not only will they keep your fingers warm, they act as a nice barrier between you and all the handrails you'll be using to climb on and off trains, trams, and funiculars.

The Top 10 Extraordinary Experiences

1.   Ice it. If you're in Budapest between December and March, then you should try ice skating. The oldest and most popular ice rink is located in Városliget (City Park) on the lake next to Vajdahunyad castle. You might want to do this at the end of your trip, just in case you break something. http://mujegpalya.hu.

2.   Steam it. This place is packed with natural thermal springs, and to take advantage of the healing waters, they've built some of the most beautiful urban spas in the world. Some of the local faves include:

St. Gellert Spa, 1118 Budapest, Kelenhegyi ut 4, www.gelertfurdo.hu

Kiraly Spa, 1027 Budapest, Fo ut 84, www.kiralyfurdo.hu

Rudas Thermal Baths, 1013 Budapest, Dobrentei ter 9, www.rudasfuro.hu

Szechenyi Spa, 1146 Budapest, Allatkerti krt. 11, www.szechenyifurdo.hu

St. Lukacs Spa, 1023 Budapest, www.lukascsfurdo.hu

3.   Get lost. Under the charming streets of Castle Hill lies an intricate maze of tunnels and walkways created by thousands of years of hot water springs rushing through the area. Somewhat less wet now, it has become an amazing maze, called the Labyrinth of Buda Castle. Within the web of passageways are smaller labyrinths with names like: Personal Labyrinth, Labyrinth of Courage, Labyrinth of Love, and Labyrinth of an Other-World. It's really spooky and a great way to test your ability to let go and get lost. H-1014 Budapest, Uri u. 9; tel: 36-1-489-3281; www.labirintus.com.

4.   Take a walk. For an invigorating morning and afternoon, start at the Chain Bridge on the Pest side and cross over it to the Buda side. Take the Funicular train to the top of the Castle district. Stroll the palace garden, walk over to the Mattjias Church, then to the Fisherman's Bastion. Make sure to bring a camera because the views from here are unbelievable. After all that walking, head over to Ruszwurm Cukraszda (Szentharomsag utca 7), just a couple of blocks from the Fisherman's Bastion, for the best pastry or piece of cake in the world.

5.   Fly with the birds. The Budapest Eye is a huge balloon that soars high above the picturesque roofs of Pest. It's a fantastic way to see the Buda side of the city in all its glory. VI. Váci út 1-3, West End City Center Roof Garden; tel: 238-7623.

6.   Visit Margaret. Floating on the Danube between Buda and Pest, Margaret Island is the city's favorite park and for good reason. Hidden behind its lush trees are sports grounds, the capital's largest open-air swimming pool, an outdoor theater, and two spa hotels. The island, which you can get to by small boat, is free from traffic, so you don't have to worry about getting run over by crazy Hungarian drivers.

7.   World Heritage by tram. The Number 2 tram is the perfect way to visit some of the most remarkable locations in Budapest. You can board it in Kossuth Square, in front of the Parliament building. The tram follows the Danube, and from its windows the entire World Heritage section of Budapest can be seen.

8.   Explore antiques. Near Margaret Bridge, you'll find Falk Miksa Street. Here you can spend your money on antiques and fun bric-a-brac. The tiny shops have everything from ancient porcelain, interesting silk carpets, and carved furniture to old violins and faded paintings. Pick up something out of the ordinary, so you can tell all your friends, "Oh, I got that in Budapest." Other fun shopping adventures can be had at: Ecseri flea market: 1194 Budapest, Nagykorosi ut 156, Monday to Saturday, or Budapest Antique Market on the corner of Devai ut and Kassak Lajos ut in Budapest XIII district.

9.   Float on the silky Danube. After sunset is the ideal time to drink in the illuminated views of Buda Castle. The best place to enjoy the scene is on a boat cruise. Some cruises are quick sightseeing tours with narrations that last an hour, and others are full-on dinner cruises. Depending on how much you like water, find one that suits you at www.budapestinfo.hu.

10. Trek out to Statue Park. This is an unreal park of statues from Budapest's era of communism. It's the only one in the world because when the iron curtain dropped in 1989, most of the statues were immediately destroyed. I warn you—it's bleak, unreal, and way out in the middle of nowhere. If you can find a tour group to take you out there, such as Absolute Walking Tours in Budapest, it really is worth the trip. Not only do you get to touch statues of Marx and Lenin, but you can buy some really cool garb as well. They sell CDs of the greatest proletarian dictatorship hits and Soviet Union hip flasks complete with communist rhetoric. Szobopark, Budapest XXII; www.szoborpark.hu or www.absolutetours.com.

COPENHAGEN, DENMARK

Christina exploring the cobblestone streets
of Copenhagen.

Why This Place Rocks
for Flying Solo

Somewhere between those gossamer dreams of a perfect destination and your mercurial habits of jetting around like a firefly, you are bound to find Copenhagen. Just when you think you have experienced all the gorgeously fantastic places on the planet, the capital of Denmark gets on your radar like a glowing spear of energy. At first, it's easy to miss this city that gets overlooked for destinations such as Paris and London. But for the savvy solo sister, this place should be on your Top 10 list. Because once you set foot in this world-class kingdom, you'll be mesmerized by its splendor, kind people, and

You can't translate the Danish word *hygge* directly into English, but the word means "cozy, friendly, fun, and pleasant atmosphere" all in one. The Danes have a very relaxed attitude about life, and this is evident in everything they do.

remarkable culture. You wouldn't be amiss to think this place is a present-day fairytale, because it is! Denmark is the world's oldest kingdom. The reigning monarch, the very modern Queen Margrethe II, who lives in Copenhagen, can trace her ancestry all the way to the Viking era—over 1,000 years ago. Queen Margrethe has a reputation for being one of Europe's most modern and progressive monarchs. She attended five universities, she openly grants television interviews, and she is fond of casual public appearances. She is also a critically acclaimed painter and has worked as a translator in French, Swedish, English, and German. No wonder the Danes love her, and you will love her country.

With royalty come castles, and Denmark has plenty. But this doesn't mean Copenhagen is stuck in the stagnant past. Alongside these antiquated touches you'll see signs of constant renewal, including the sleek new Copenhagen Opera House, the daring modern art museum Ordrupgaard, and the quick underground metro. The canals and cobblestone streets that line this Scandinavian gem are superbly cluttered with chic nightclubs and eclectic restaurants. In the summer the city is buzzing with activity, Copenhagen is one of the top vacation spots for Europeans, and now it can be yours, too.

Culture: 5

This place is first-class when it comes to culture. Just walking the medieval streets of Copenhagen is like spending days in museums; the place pulses with the past. From its humble origins as a fishing village to its heyday as the glittering capital of the Danish Empire, Copenhagen has done a great job mixing old with new. Oh, and you can forget to visit the Republic of Christiania, which was formed by hippy squatters in the 1960s and is considered a "free state" separate from Denmark's governing.

Activity: 3

If biking around all day long isn't enough exercise for you, then hit me with a Danish. Copenhagers are very bike-friendly, and you will find well-marked cycle lanes so you don't end up killing yourself. And if you like to jog, the city has a few jogging tracks you can run around on. Really, you are not coming here to lose ten pounds, so get ready to lounge around in cafés and dance the nights away in trendy hot spots.

Weather: 3

Luckily, Copenhagen is not as high up in latitude as other Scandinavian cities. The weather is categorized two ways—light and dark. What that means is it never really gets very hot, nor does it get totally unbearably cold. Remember, you are still in Scandinavia, and it's not the warmest place on the planet, but it's not the coldest either!

Social: 4

Great Danes might be dogs, but not here. This country is famous for their fabulously friendly folks. You will have plenty of opportunities to meet others—from cozy cafés to rocking nightclubs, be assured you will never be bored or lonely.

Flying Foreplay

This is a cosmopolitan city and you can find everything you might accidentally leave at home. There is plenty to do, so you don't have to worry about booking anything special or making restaurant reservations before you leave home.

Doing Danish. Yes, most Danes speak English. They are very cosmopolitan in the city, and they are not under any fantasy that the rest of the world is going to pick up Danish anytime soon. Everyone learns English in school. But you might want to pick up a Danish phrase book anyway.

Read Before You Go

Hamlet, by William Shakespeare
Hans Christian Andersen's Fairy Tales

Copenhagen Accessories

Bar it. Pack your favorite energy bar. You'll need a quick snack to replenish your energy as you walk around exploring all day, and most food options can be expensive in Copenhagen.

Shoe business. Bring good walking/biking shoes. The Danes are not as fashion-forward as the Parisians, so you don't need to jet around in your

Prada heels. But don't look like a tourist either, so keep your running shoes at home. Think low-key sophisticated style.

Layers. The weather can run the climatological gamut all in the span of one day. Bring a layer to cover up in a spring shower and peel off when the sun pokes out again.

The Top 10 Extraordinary Experiences

1. Check out a "Freetown." What, a place completely separate from the rules and regulations of government in the heart of a modern city? Yup, and it's called Christiania. This ecocentric enclave was founded in 1971 when a group of hippies took over an abandoned military barracks and developed their own set of rules, completely independent of the Danish government. You have to love a place that has a street called Pusher Street, where hash was sold openly until 2004.

The area that Christiania inhabits is around 85 acres and it is totally open to the public. Feel free to stroll around the streets, peek into the homes that are not owned by anyone, or chill at one of the cute cafés. Everywhere you go in Christiania there are paintings and sculptures, and you'll always find live music or something theatrical playing somewhere. They even offer daily walking tours of the tiny town. www.christiania.org.

2. Be cool. CPH:cool is all about the latest hip venues and cool shopping boutiques in Copenhagen. Forget the museums; go hang out with cool locals who know where to see and be seen! For you urban explorers, this sublime tour is for you. In their tours, they show you the trendy shops, secret backyards, cool cafés, and hot spots of the vibrant city. They offer individual walks in the trendiest neighborhoods of Copenhagen. They give you an insider's view of Copenhagen while telling you all about life, culture, and people living here. If you want a true glimpse into the life of the Danes, this is the way to do it. By the time your tour ends, you will know about the best places to go for a meal, some great secret cafes, and a few stylish, cozy bars. www.cphcool.dk.

3. Dine with a Dane. You know a place is amazing when they have a service called Dine with the Danes, and that's exactly what you do. After filling out the application on their website, you will get a confirmation about your dinner plans. They will let you know whom you are having dinner with and all the other important information that you will need. For a few bucks, you get to check out the local hospitality and enjoy a typical Danish dinner with your Danish host. The meal includes two to three courses with drinks followed by coffee, tea, and pastries. How neat is that! Try to book it before you leave home, and ask to dine when you first get into Copenhagen, so you can make new friends. Who knows, you might be so charming that they invite you to another meal! FYI: In order to improve the chances of being suitably matched up, they recommend you complete and return the booking form a minimum of one week before the date of your expected arrival to Denmark. Copenhagen Tourist Information; tel: +45-2685-3961; www.dinewiththedanes.dk.

4. Meet the Mermaid. The small but sturdy statue of Hans Christian Andersen's "Little Mermaid" has become the unofficial symbol of Copenhagen. Think life's easy as a mascot with fins? Think again. She's had a tough life: Her arm was cut off, she's been pushed into the water, had a bra painted on her, been given a red-dye job on her hair, and even been decapitated. But she is so beloved by the population that they bring her back good

as new each time. The police homicide department was even put on the case to solve her decapitation! Celebrate the merlady's birthday every August 23 with her fellow devotees, who bring balloons and flowers to decorate this fairytale survivor.

5. Frivolity at Tivoli. Tivoli is the gold standard when it comes to twinkling city amusement parks. No roaring megacoasters or oversized mice here. Tivoli has been the setting (whether you know it or not) of every lovely fantasy you've had of sharing cotton candy with a Scandinavian stranger, holding hands on the Tilt-a-Whirl, smooching at the top of the Ferris wheel, and making out on a bench under sparkling lights. Founded in 1843, the park's old-time romance lingers among the classy rides, and the fairgrounds are carpeted in tulips. Even if you don't love amusement park rides, strolling through Tivoli at night along boulevards lined with lanterns and low-lying weeping willows adorned in white lights will have you feeling like the star of your own dream come true. And as you get peckish while perusing, Tivoli won't let you down with its impressive list of restaurants and cafés that line the lush walkways. www.tivoligardens.com.

6. Visit Nørrebro and lounge with Hans. Three hundred years ago, Nørrebro was mostly fields and farmland, but today it is a buzzing neighborhood with trendy shopping areas, scores of cafés, and yummy restaurants. Sankt Hans Torv is one of the great places in the area and has several young chic cafés, like Pussy Galores and Café Sebastopol, that are usually packed to the gills during weekends. When strolling the hood, look for the big yellow wall that surrounds Assistens kirkegården. Yes, it's a cemetery, where the famous writer H. C. Andersen and famous philosopher Søren Kirkegaard are buried. It's not just the dead that are lying around here. During the summer you can find people tanning among the graves and tombstones. Bring a good book, sunscreen, and a flower for Hans, and enjoy the warm afternoons.

7. To see or not to see Kronborg? Kronborg was the setting of Shakespeare's *Hamlet*, and you, too, can pace the halls reciting monologues just like the most famous Prince of Denmark. The castle is located on the sea in Elsinore (Helsingør). The castle burned down in 1629 but was rebuilt again in 1638. Kronborg contains the 68-yard-long Knight's Hall—one of the longest halls in Europe—and the famous statue of Holger Danske. He is an important Danish hero who fought for his country. He didn't die in battle, but he came home because he was homesick, fell asleep immediately, and there he stays. Legend says that if Denmark is ever threatened, the stone figure will spring to life and fight for the kingdom again. If you have an iPod, you might want to download *Hamlet* as an audio book and listen while you are there. You can take a half-day tour with City Discover Tours. www.city-discovery.com.

8. Cruising with coffee or champagne. Seeing a city in a double-decker can be fun, but nothing beats sitting back in a cozy boat, drinking hot coffee, and looking out over the sparkling lights of Copenhagen. Flyvefisken Canal Tour offers short cruises that give you a glimpse into the beauty of boating on the charming spire-lined canals. During the winter they offer champagne cruises, too. Sorry, they don't have a website, but your concierge will know where to find them. Tel: 3296-4964.

9. Spa at Skodsborg. Darling, I can't think of anything better than getting pampered at a seaside palace. King Frederik VII purchased Skodsborg in 1857 as a love nest for the Countess Danner and himself. More than 100 years later, in 1992, the palace was renovated into a modern over-the-top hotel spa and rehabilitation center. I don't know if your health insurance will cover a week of physiotherapy here, but it wouldn't hurt to ask! Skodsborg is just 20 minutes from Copenhagen by train on the Øresund Line, so you can go for the day, or spend the night in one of the magnificently appointed rooms. The building and grounds have been restored to their nineteenth-century majesty, while the surrounding seaside landscape is just waiting for you to explore. Combine a history tour with peerless pampering at Skodsborg, and don't forget to bring your journal and trashy novels. www.skodsborg.dk.

10. Cozy up to the bar/restaurant. Forget the fusion of food; that is so last millennium. I am talking about the fusion of restaurants and bars. Imagine having the social scene at the hottest new bars in town fused with the best chefs around? You don't have to sacrifice that perfect "social butterfly" bar side locale just because you want world-class cuisine. In Copenhagen you can have both! One of these is Aura at Nytorv. It's like a stylish, intimate restaurant, but it has one big table where everyone can share food and conversations. www.aok.dk/infosites/10260/3.html.

Viva is a boat restaurant that is thriving. At Viva, the houseboat has outdoor seating on the top deck, along with a cocktail bar and lounge. Mediterranean specialties, fish, and shellfish with a Scandinavian twist are what you see on the menu. www.aok.dk/infosites/11220.

Restaurant Olsen is the largest of these types of restaurants. It has a spectacular location, right across the canal from the Christiansborg Palace. In the summer months, the terrace is buzzing with international jet-setters and Copenhagen's beautiful people. On Thursdays, Fridays, and Saturdays the bar is open until 2 a.m. www.restaurantolsen.com.

Some More Local Favorites

Ida Davidsen. Ida Davidsen is known for her *Smørrebrød*, which is an open sandwich. Her menu card is over six feet long.

Nyhavn. *New Habour* is a lively street in the center of town. In the summer, this is where you want to be. You can sit outside and enjoy a drink and take in all the beautiful men walking past. Or you can journal.

Zeze. It is a small café that is always packed with people. The best time to go there is Friday afternoon/evening. You'll find this place packed with Copenhagers enjoying an après-work drink before heading to the next venue. It is a great place to meet new people. Tourists don't know about this gem (until now).

Bar Rouge. Bar Rouge is a hotel bar in the five-star hotel Skt. Petri. It is one of the hottest places in Copenhagen and it has a very international atmosphere.

Vinbaren. A great place to go during the weekend. It has a cozy atmosphere and great drinks.

DUBLIN, IRELAND

Nicole toasting in
Dublin.

Why This Place Rocks for Flying Solo

------

*M*aybe it is under a four-leaf clover, or in the pocket of a leprechaun, or perhaps in the pot of gold at the end of the rainbow where you can find the magic that makes the Irish so wonderfully friendly and welcoming. Or possibly you can find this special elixir in a freshly poured pint of Guinness stout in a warm pub alive with laughter. No matter where it might be, you are sure to experience plenty of it when visiting the spirited city of Dublin. Know as the Land of Saints and Scholars, Dublin's spectacular castles, mysterious Druid fortresses, and impressive list of famous authors who've called it home

Winter Solstice

Get to Newgrange during Winter Solstice. Newgrange is thought to be a Druid place of worship built about 3200 BCE. That makes it the oldest standing structure in the world—older than Stonehenge and the great pyramids in Egypt! The 60-foot inner passage is dramatically illuminated by the Winter Solstice sunrise. Admission to the chamber of the tomb to witness this feat of nature is by lottery, and application forms are available at the reception desk in the Brú na Bóinne Visitor Centre. For more information visit www.knowth.com/newgrange.htm.

make it one of the most interesting spots on the planet. And it sure does help that the Irish are some of the friendliest folks in the world. Years after your visit, don't be surprised if you silently grin with the memories of the dreamlike sounds of Celtic fiddles and flutes, or if you stop to inhale the smell of fresh air after a rainstorm, and think of your beloved Ireland.

Beyond the mystical ruins, ageless castles, and stone ramparts of Dublin is a country wrapped in sheer beauty. For those who adore nature and the crisp outdoors, you will be forever entertained with an endless list of things to do. And for you urban beauties who prefer to stay city-side, trendy boutiques lining ancient cobblestone streets, pubs, and elegant five-star restaurants will keep you happily shopping, eating, and drinking. Unlike many destinations that cater to a specific crowd, like Monte Carlo to the rich, Patagonia to the adventurous, and South Beach to the wild at heart, Dublin welcomes all.

Culture: 4

From the Book of Kells to James Joyce's *Ulysses*, Dublin, like an academic library,

is crammed with famous literary luminaries and scholars whom you can study and enjoy reading in a dark pub with a beer at hand. And for those who are more interested in art and history, you won't get bored in this city. Most of Dublin's museums and galleries are centrally located and are graciously gratis.

Activity: 4

Gallop across infinite green pastures, play a round of golf on one of Ireland's fine courses, or join a walking tour. Dublin and the surrounding areas are overflowing with activities that will keep you moving at an energetic cadence.

Weather: 1

The only predictable thing about Ireland's weather is its unpredictability. You can plan on winter being wet and summer being less wet. The trick is to view the rain the way the Irish do, as giving you more time to listen to fantastic *trad* (Irish music) at one of the many venues throughout Dublin.

Social: 5

The Irish love good company and great conversations, so plan on meeting

Dubliners who will want to wax poetic about life everywhere you go. *Craic* is what the Irish call good conversation, and it is a national pastime. Expect to be included in a *craic* session the second you meet a Dubliner. The Irish are an ageless group; you can find a young man laughing at a table with a group of women double his age or vice versa. This is one of the great things about Ireland. As my dear Irish friend Moira told me, "Irish don't see age, they see life."

Flying Foreplay

Dublin is a grand city that is well equipped to handle any of your requests; so don't get your knickers in a knot if you forget something.

Weather or not. You may not be able to predict the rain, but you can, to some degree, predict the crowds. Summer is the time when the world heads to Dublin. The temperature is at its peak and so are the room rates. Fall is a great time to travel, especially in September when it's still dry and warm (most of the time!).

Best of the Books

Anything by James Joyce: *Dubliners, Portrait of the Artist as a Young Man, Finnegan's Wake,* or *Ulysses*
The Barrcks, by John McGahern
Gulliver's Travels, by Jonathan Swift

Dublin Accessories

An umbrella, a good book, and a sense of humor.

The Top 10 Extraordinary Experiences

1. Drink from the source. Black magic, Irish medicine, Cloudy heaven, whatever you call it, it's called Guinness here in Dublin. Founded in 1759, Guinness is the world's largest single beer-exporting company, sending out about 300 million pints a year. Visit the brewery and learn about the history and manufacture of the famous stout. And of course, the tour would not be complete without a pint of Guinness. Located a mile west of Christ Church, the Guinness Brewery covers 64 acres on either side of James's Street. Daily 9:30 a.m.–5 p.m. www.guinness-storehouse.com.

2. Observe a raucous Gaelic football match. Do as the Dubliners do and get to the Croke Park stadium early on a Sunday morning, but even then, you'll likely have to bite, pinch, and kick your way to the ticket booth on Fitzgibbon Street. Once inside, the GAA museum will teach you everything you need to know about the game before it begins. From "Hill 16" or "Hogan's Stand," which are some of the best seats, you'll be able to cheer with the locals. After the game, exit on the left side of the street if your team lost and on the right side if they won.

3. Tap your toe to *trad*. One of the most memorable experiences you'll have in Ireland is sitting in a warm, cozy pub with a pint in your hand. Fiddlers and pipers draw impromptu step dancers to the floor and everyone taps along. A spontaneous session occurs when independent musicians gather together at a pub to play jigs, hornpipes, reels, slow airs, and folk songs, sung to mandolin or guitar accompaniments. Normal pub hours in Ireland end at 11:30 p.m. Sunday through Wednesday and 12:30 a.m. Thursday through Saturday. Most pubs, however, will give you an extra half hour after "closing" to kill your drink. Some of my favorites:

The Long Stone. Hand-carved banisters and an enormous carving of a bearded man whose mouth serves as a fireplace sets the tone of the medieval pub. 10 Townsend Street.

The Bleeding Horse. A cozy pub with lots of nooks for kissing those Irish. They have a DJ most nights. 24 Upper Camden Street.

The Palace. This is the only true Irish pub in Temple Bar. Loved by the locals. 21 Fleet Street.

The Celt. Nightly *trad* can be heard at this small, *Olde Irish* favorite. 81 Talbot Street.

The Brazen Head. Dublin's oldest and one of the more spirited pubs, established in 1198. 20 North Bridge Street.

Hot Toddy

Unless you want everyone in the pub to know you are a tourist, don't order an Irish Coffee. It was invented in San Francisco at the Buena Vista. If want something hot, try a Hot Toddy instead.

4. Peek into Ireland of olde in the Book of Kells. Around 800 years after the life of Jesus, the monks in Ireland decided to write out the four Gospels in an ornate book with elaborate scripting and illustrations. Believe it or not, that book has survived over 1,200 years of wars, famines, kings, and queens. You can view this ornate piece of artwork and incredible historic artifact at Trinity College (between Westmoreland and Grafteon Street in the center of Dublin). It is located in the Colonnades, an exhibition area on the ground floor of the Old Library. The Old Library opens at 9:30 a.m. In spring or fall, you might get the library to yourself, especially during midweek. But in summer, getting there early as possible offers your only fighting chance of surviving the organized bands of curious tourists, who quickly pack the place.

5. Too hot to trot. If you have always dreamed of horseback riding with a fine Irishman at your side, then I've got the rides for you. My favorite is the Blind Date Ball Ride.

- Kilarny Ring of Kerry
- Connermara ride, taking you over seven different beaches in Ireland
- Training and riding at Clonshire Equestrian Centre
- Castle trail ride, riding from castle to castle and spending the night in the castles
- Ireland's trail and steeple chase ride
- Ireland's Blind Date Ball Ride, held the week of Valentine's Day
- Haunted castle ride, staying in one castle, visiting a haunted castle, and enjoying a banquet the week of Halloween

Cross Country International; tel: 800-828-8768; www.equestrian vacations.com.

6. See a play at the Abbey Theatre. The Irish love their theater as much as the Brazilians love their soccer, and I know you'll love it all! The Abbey Theatre, which is Ireland's national theater, offers an impressive selection of plays from the Irish repertoire, as well as presenting classics from the European and world theaters. Get lost in some Irish culture after getting lost on the Dublin streets. They have a full bar and offer backstage tours (subject to availability). Opening times: Monday–Saturday: 8 p.m. Saturday matinee: 2:30 p.m. For details contact: +353-1-887-2223; e-mail: info@abbeytheatre.ie; www.abbeytheatre.ie.

Located off O'Connell Street. How to get there:

By bus: Main bus routes to city center
By DART (train): Tara Street and Connolly Stations
By Luas: Red line to Abbey Street

7. Take a stroll down Grafton Street. Possibly the busiest street in Ireland, this pedestrians-only thoroughfare is one of Dublin's best places for strolling and people watching. Everything for the shopaholic is close at hand—from clothes to music to crafts—and malls on streets radiating off Grafton provide sheltered browsing on rainy days. After you've made the day's purchases and checked out the street performers, stop for a cup of tea and a pastry in Bewley's, a multilevel teahouse with comfy places to sit. Late afternoon is perhaps the only time Grafton Street takes a breather. As teatime becomes evening, stores close and the street becomes a major nightlife destination, with drinking spots that reflect Dubliners' tastes for public houses and posh lounges.

8.   The National Gallery. Spend the day strolling the mesmerizing halls of the National Gallery. This is especially fun if the weather is a bit nippy. The gallery houses Ireland's national art collection, as well as an impressive collection of European art spanning from the fourteenth to the twentieth centuries. The highlight of the Irish collection is the room dedicated to the extraordinary works of Jack B. Yeats, brother of the poet W. B. Yeats. Free! Monday–Saturday 9:30–5:30, Thursday 9:30–8:30, Sunday noon–5:30. Merrion Square West, Dublin 2, tel: 353-1661-5133; www.nationalgallery.ie.

9.   Enjoy a literary stroll. For a perfect evening of literary learning, pub crawling, and socializing, join the folks at Dublin's Literary Pub Crawl. It's a tour of the city's famous literary pubs in the company of two actors who introduce the writers and perform scenes from their works. The tour is just over two hours and they feature works from James Joyce, Samuel Beckett, Brendan Behan, Mary Lavin, Oscar Wilde, Eavan Boland, and Paula Meehan. You'll visit about eight pubs on the tour and they always include a stop in Trinity College to talk about Oscar Wilde and other writers. www.dublin-pubcrawl.com Dublin Literary Pub Crawl. "Suffolk Chambers," 1 Suffolk Street, Dublin 2; tel: 353-1-670-5602.

10.   Be Irish for a day. For you bucolic beauties who long for the green grass of Ireland, here's your chance to work on a real farm. You'll learn how to cut turf, speak Gaeilge, play hurling, make a sugan rope, work a sheepdog, milk a cow, play a bodhram, dance a jig. Stay for dinner and enjoy a traditional Irish *ceili.* Causey Farm, Girley, Fordstown, Navan, Co. Meath, Ireland. Tel: +353-0-4694-34135; e-mail: info@causeyexperience.com; www.causeyexperience.com.

DUBROVNIK, CROATIA

Claire discovering Dubrovnik.

Why This Place Rocks for Flying Solo

Just on the other side of the narrow Adriatic Sea, the Croatian coast is Italy without the attitude. While eating fresh seafood in tiny restaurants sprinkled on the shore, you might ask yourself, "Did I just die and go to heaven, or am I really in Croatia?" The coastline has long been a favorite vacation destination for European royalty, and the ancient Romans enjoyed the fine wine produced in this beautiful climate. The sea is amazingly peaceful and transparent, so plan on getting lost in its serene beauty. When not admiring the beauty of the sea, check out the gorgeous people who line the beaches. Bronzed men play water polo and tanned Europeans chill and watch the impromptu matches.

Irish playwright George Bernard Shaw said, "If you want to see heaven on earth, come to Dubrovnik." Europeans have always adored the tiny Eastern European country, with over a thousand picturesque islands to choose from, as a divine destination. Remarkably, Croatia has been able to regain its superstar status after the chilling civil war that devastated the country from 1991 to 1995. War scars healed and infrastructure rebuilt, Dubrovnik accommodated new crowds of tourists, and olive and lemon trees shared their abundant harvests with guests once again. For a truly, old-world experience with a stunningly impressive lineup of historical sites, Dubrovnik is the place to play.

Culture: 3

Croatia has a long but little-known history. I gave it less than a 5 because the museums seem hastily put together and not terribly informative. The best way to take in Croatian culture is to find yourself a good history book to read on the beach, and then appreciate your delicious wine and succulent grilled fish at dinner that night. There are concerts and a new focus on "traditional" folk performances, so you can mix in a little

Croatian folk singing in between beach days.

Activity: 5

There's plenty to do on the Croatian coast, whether it's kayaking, biking, hiking, or scuba diving. The proximity of the ocean provides all kinds of opportunities and a good swim is never far away. With special permission, intrepid divers can view a sunken Roman shipwreck. Bungee jumping is offered just outside Dubrovnik.

Weather: 4

Weather can be temperamental but more often than not relentlessly gorgeous. Clear skies and warm sun are sure things in the summer, and long, warm nights are treasures in themselves. It is typical Mediterranean weather with hot summers and rainy winters.

Social: 4

Dubrovnik is called the "New Riviera," and the sparkling Adriatic gem gives Monaco a run for its money. Great clubs, cheap drinks, and happy, beautiful people: What more can you ask for? The social scene can dip fairly young, and in certain bars, be prepared to elbow teenagers for spaces to sit. There's not a ton of selection in the small towns in Croatia, but the offerings tend to be good. Locals gladly point out their favorite spots; take their advice.

Olive Oil

Don't be afraid to buy olive oil out of refilled soda bottles; this is the traditional way local oil presses store their product. If you trust the seller, you can trust the goods, even if the setup looks pretty sketchy.

Flying Foreplay

Route it. Figure out how you'll get there before you leave home. Dubrovnik Airport is in Cilipi, about ten miles from downtown, so you'll need to organize a shuttle or a bus to take you the rest of the way. Alternatively, ferries operated by Jadrolinija (www.jadrolinija.hr) connect Dubrovnik with Split, Rijeka, and a few cities between.

Speak easy. Try to learn key Croatian words, as English is not as widespread as in Western Europe. If that fails, dust off your Italian, which is spoken especially along the coast.

Hook up your hotel. Find a hotel before you leave, or you'll probably end up staying in someone's home. Finding rooms upon arrival is typical and generally safe in this part of the world, but some-times a woman traveling alone doesn't want to take the risk of entering a stranger's home. If you are with a pal, or feel especially trusting of human goodness, look for signs that advertise rooms for rent; the signs might use the Croatian word for room, *sobe*, or the German word, *zimmer*, the Italian *camere*, or even the French *chambre*.

Interesting Books Set in Croatia

On the Edge of Reason, by Miroslav Krleža
The Sound of Blue, by Holly Payne

Dubrovnik Accessories

Protection. Sunscreen, sunscreen, and more sunscreen. Croatians live their

Topless

Plan on seeing more people wearing designer sunglasses than tops with their bikinis. Modesty is not the key on the beaches. If you have never gone topless, this is the perfect place.

Safety First

Some remote areas in Croatia still contain land mines, so don't just go out and tour empty fields.

lives in the sun, and if you want to really enjoy your time there, take precautions against wicked sunburn. Everyone laughs at the peeling tourists.

Take cover. Invest in a big brimmed hat to keep your face out of the sun. No one likes sunspots, darling.

Waterproof boots. Shoes with tread are a must. The streets of Dubrovnik are alternately very slick or very cobbled: those trendy slip-ons will have you slipping on your rear end in front of all the gorgeous Croatians. But no tennis shoes! I'll pretend I don't know you if you walk down the beautiful main promenade looking like Aunt Millie from Peoria.

Rubber protection. Bring sturdy water shoes to wear while flirting in the water; you don't want to stub your beautifully manicured toenails on the rocky beaches.

Something Swiss. A Swiss Army knife will save your nails and make your beach picnics easier. Grab a hunk of bread, some cheese, and a nectarine, and slice up the perfect seaside lunch. Remember to pack the knife in the luggage you check in, not your carry-on.

The Top 10 Extraordinary Experiences

1. **See and be seen along the Stradun in Dubrovnik.** The main promenade in Dubrovnik, also called the Placa Stradun, has been walked over by thousands of people for thousands of years, shining the ordinary cobblestones into glossy marble. The Croatians are an attractive breed, so don't count on comparative advantage over people reared under communism. Bring your A-game or risk looking like a frumpy American.

2. **Get naked on the beach!** Croatians are very much into and accepting of

Directions

The wanderer is rewarded with many levels of restaurants and charming bars in the stone-paved back alleys of the tiny island town. Don't expect any guidance from street signs—there are none. Locals and fellow travelers are more than willing to give directions to their favorite spots.

naturalism. No, that's not a love of botany, but rather an affinity for baring your booty. Most beaches are clothing optional, and a traveler can find strands that are hopping or seek out more secluded sections, depending on degrees of modesty. Women's bodies are appreciated but not gawked at or drooled over. You'll feel comfortable and in good company, and that Adriatic sun feels so good on those bits that rarely see the light of day.

3.   Walk the walls. Dubrovnik is an ancient town, and has towering city walls to prove it. A thin, stone path atop these walls circle the whole town—walk along its rim for a perfect view below. It's also an important reality check: It's easy to see the brighter spots on roofs repaired after Dubrovnik was attacked in 1991. The town was shelled and many historical treasures were destroyed, including a priceless collection of medieval books in the monastery. Dubrovnik is making its recovery (thanks to travelers like you paying homage—and hotel rates—to the fine town), but it's important to take a step back and see the marks left by war.

4.   Go island hopping. The islands off the coast are delightful, and suited for every kind of traveler. If you are looking to escape crowds, the small nature preserve Lokrum is only a 10-minute ferry ride away from Dubrovnik's port. Mellow gals looking for some rest and relaxation can go to Korcula, where the seafood is delicious and the wine is grown locally. Korculans claim that Marco Polo was born on this island; you can visit his house and decide for yourself. Party divas should head to Hvar, a small island carpeted in lavender and Italians. Hvar, practically dead in the winter, comes back with a bang during the summer, and Euro travelers outnumber locals in the tiny town. The harbor is lovely, and there are clubs and bars for the wilder and milder ones alike. All islands can be reached by reasonably priced ferries.

5.   Catch a sword dance. Like Capoera with swords and marching, the traditional Croatian sword dances (held mostly on Korcula) are exhilarating and fun to watch. Croatian folk tales are reenacted with dancers in traditional costumes performing with breathless athleticism. Any resident can tell you where to see this musical entertainment.

6.   Put faith in your waiter. Pick a restaurant that you think is going to be great, and ask what the waiter recommends. There is almost always an "off-menu" delicacy usually reserved for locals who know what to ask for. You might not be able to pronounce it, but your taste buds will thank you.

7.   Enjoy music with no boundaries. Palace atriums, echoing rectory staircases, stone cathedrals, and nearby islands all serve as unique acoustic venues for Dubrovnik's Summer Music Festival. This 45-day music extravaganza has time to cover a lot of bases, including a broad spectrum of genres, with even theater, film, and dance performances. The whole city takes part in the festival: Children run back and forth carrying set pieces, artists linger after shows to talk shop with locals, and city dignitaries sit alongside the attending celebrities. The big-ticket items are the opening and closing nights, but because of the frequency of events, you are likely to find the artist and venue that are just right. www.dubrovnik-festival.hr.

8.   Taste the Adriatic. As soon as the sun sets, aggressive maître d's line the streets to convince the strolling visitor that their food is positively the best in Dubrovnik. Try not to be swayed by the eager restaurant staff courting you like a celebrity—it's perfectly acceptable to say "No thanks" with a smile and keep walking. So much of dining in Dubrovnik is atmosphere and setting, so spend some time perusing your options. There are tiny alcove restaurants tucked near the city walls as well as huge patios with outdoor seating—perfect for people watching. Once you've picked your venue, settle in for a treat. The local catch of the day on the Croatian coast is divine, especially when paired with the regional wines.

9.   Love your layover. If you take a train to Dubrovnik, odds are you'll have a few hours stopover in Croatia's capital and transportation hub, Zagreb. While tempted to spend these hours reading trashy novels or writing upbeat postcards without ever leaving the train station, you'll miss out on exploring an Eastern European gem. It all starts out as you stumble straight from the train station onto lush, green Kraljia Tomislava Square, followed by rows of stately nineteenth-century houses standing shoulder to baroque shoulder. Tiny winding lanes unfold in front of you, overflowing with jewelry stores, art galleries, and strolling Croatians. Make your way up to Zagreb's highpoint, where you'll find Tolkien's House, a pub dedicated to the fantasy master's work, each room decorated as one of his darkly magical worlds. Snack on boiled corn on the cob bought from old women with shiny carts clanking through the streets as you watch Zagreb fall into darkness. Finish off your stay with a few drinks on Tkalciceva Street—a long strip of open-air restaurants and bars packed with cheerful groups toasting another long day's end. Trust me, it beats crosswords in the train station.

10. Take your breath away. If you can spare a day on your trip, make your way over to Montenegro, the tiny mountainous Balkan country that borders Croatia. You are guaranteed to be awestruck. It requires some effort—this is a separate country and will take a few hours on a ferry or a bus to reach—but a sense of wonder will wash over you as you pull into Montenegro's Bay of Kotor. Enormous black mountains rise straight out of a mirror-surface natural bay and nestle the small, magical island of Sveti Stefan, where Elizabeth Taylor used to summer. This is a secret you'll want to keep from the glitzy tourists you see in Dubrovnik. You can book tours from Dubrovnik to Kotor for under $60. Check Croatian tour guides for more information.

EDINBURGH, SCOTLAND

Jeanette on the Royal
Mile in Edinburgh.

Why This Place Rocks
for Flying Solo

I f you didn't get the memo about how fantastic Edinburgh is for the solo bonnie, then here it is: This place rocks! Once a fortified town wrapped in rolling, green ramparts and home to the British gentry, now

Edinburgh is a bustling city swirling with activities and dripping in iconic Scottish sites. In this fair city, you'll find everything from men in kilts welcoming you at the Balmoral Hotel, to style-centric Europeans lounging at the newest trendy venues. Unlike other major destinations in Europe, where the locals can be less than friendly, here everyone has a smile to share and a story to tell. The men are delightful, yet ornery, and the pubs are always charming and good for a beer or two.

Coming to Edinburgh is not just about seeing the amazing edifices perched about the city, or taking a trip up to meet the Loch Ness Monster; it's a place that offers you plenty of opportunities to chill with the locals. From enchanting bed-and-breakfast homes that line the streets to cozy neighborhood pubs filled with regulars, it is not hard to connect with others here. Come alone and leave with a long list of new friends.

Most locals speak English, as well as the bizarrely charming Gaelic, a Celtic language spoken in Scotland (Gàidhlig) with a range of sounds that can be learned only by hearing them. You'll be well served to pick up a few Gaelic words here and there, and don't be offended if someone calls you a "hen." It's a term of endearment in these parts.

Culture: 4

Edinburgh has a rich and unique cultural heritage, and aye, lass, they are proud of it! They won't let you forget that the town is filled with historic, intellectual, and literary associations. Think Mary Queen of Scots, inventor Alexander Graham Bell, economist Adam Smith, and author Robert Louis Stevenson—they are all part of Edinburgh's influential cultural past.

Activity: 3

There seem to be three main ways of getting your blood pumping in Edinburgh and its environs. You can golf at St. Andrews, where the game was invented. You can stroll through Edinburgh's delightful parks and gardens—for example, the Meadows, the splendid Royal Botanic Gardens, or Calton Hill. Alternatively, you can try your hand (feet?) at climbing the many hills and mountains that surround Edinburgh. Here you can trek up quiet volcanoes and over rocky crags, which rise from the generally flat landscape. If all else fails, you can go on a ghost tour in one of Scotland's castles. That's sure to get your adrenaline surging.

Weather: 1

If all you own are tank tops and shorts, then you might want to think twice about descending on Edinburgh. It's usually cold, no matter what season it is. If you really want to go when it's the warmest, then try September, which will be in the lovely mid-60s F.

Social: 5

Let's do the math: There are over 700 pubs in a city with 450,000 residents. This gives Edinburgh the honor of having the most drinking establishments per capita of any city in the world. Just pace yourselves, girls, or they'll be calling you a *besom* (a difficult woman) for years to come.

Flying Foreplay

*E*dinburgh revels in its many attractions—from the supernatural to the literary. If you are going in high season, you should definitely book before you depart, as numbers are limited. You'll be glad you are one of the select few.

They say that if you shake a family tree hard enough, a Scotsman is liable to fall out. So you might want to check to see if that's true for you. If you are lucky enough to be Scottish, you'll have lots of fun tracking down your long-lost relatives and buying some clan garb. And if you don't want a run-of-the-mill fabric design, ask to get a kilt made with you clan's specific tartan. You will need to find a kilt maker before you depart from home so that they can order the fabric before your arrival. It's easy—just search the Internet for "kilt makers in Edinburgh" and a long list will show up.

Read Before You Go

Black & Blue, by Ian Rankin
The Heart of Midlothian, by Sir Walter Scott
Kidnapped, by Robert Louis Stevenson
Lanark: A Life in Four Books, by Alasdair Gray
The Prime of Miss Jean Brodie, by Muriel Spark
Trainspotting, by Irving Welsh

Edinburgh Accessories

I really don't know how those Scotsmen survive with only a mere kilt covering their bits. This place is cold! Bring clothes that you can layer, because once you step into a warm pub, you'll want to start undressing (and the men will love you forever).

Comfy shoes. Style is not as important as comfort here. You'll be doing lots of walking, and your feet with thank you if you are in shoes that support your feet.

The Top 10 Extraordinary Experiences

1. **Bag a Munro.** Bagging the Munros essentially means hill walking in Scotland. The goal is to stand atop all 284 Scottish Munros, or mountains above 3,000 feet. (Munro is taken from Sir Hugh Munro, the man who first catalogued these peaks.) Scotland is blessed with a lush, dramatic landscape of sweeping hills and fields of heather. If you enjoy walking, then this is the best way to experience Scotland's amazing beauty. For different walking tours, check out www.maketracks.net.

2. **Canoe the River Tay.** Considered to be one of the United Kingdom's Top 20 Adventures, canoeing the River Tay or one of the many lochs is an experience you'll never forget. Depending on your level, you'll spend the day paddling on wild waters or calm, inviting streams. You'll pass old castles, and meadows filled with highland horses and rugged migrating birds. Don't be surprised if you see a seal pop up and follow you as you work your way toward the ocean. Go to www.beyondadventure.co.uk.

3. **Linger with literary greats.** For the *real* bibliophile, satisfy your author adoration at the Writers Museum and Makars Court, dedicated to the lives and works of Scotland's great literary figures as well as contemporary Scottish authors. And for more nightly fun with authors, head to the Beehive Inn, where you can join other literary lovers on a tour of taverns frequented by the likes of Robert Burns, Robert Louis Stevenson, and Sir Walter Scott. You'll hear the dramatic tale of Dr. Jekyll and Mr. Hyde and get lost in the erotic love poetry of Robert Burns. The tours leave nightly at 7:30 p.m. from the Beehive Inn on the Grassmarket. 18 Grassmarket; tel: 0131-226-6665; www.scot-lit-tour.

4. **Meet Nessie.** Find out for yourself if the Loch Ness Monster is fact or fiction. You can rent a car from Edinburgh and try your hand at driving on the wrong side of the road, or you can take a bus tour to Loch Ness. Even if you aren't a big fan of the spooky creature, the drive up to the Loch is stunning. Bring your camera, jacket, hat, and gloves because the temperature tends to drop a bit. For bus tour information, visit www.scotlinetours.co.uk. For information about Loch Ness, visit www.lochnessdiscovery.com.

5. **Get wasted on whiskey, water, and Wallace.** The William Wallace, Scottish Whisky and Water Tour is a quirky way of seeing the stunning countryside of Scotland while tasting whiskey and learning about William Wallace—who looked nothing like Mel Gibson. The first port of call is the picturesque South Queensferry; next you get to gawk at the amazing glassworks at Caithness Glass, a Scottish institution. Then you get to tour the Glenturret Whisky Distillery, which is the oldest malt whiskey distillery in Scotland. The

tour continues its scenic journey along the banks of Loch Tay, making a photo stop at the Falls of Dochart in Killin. The final stop is the Wallace Monument. Here you can learn the details about one of Scotland's greatest heroes. You'll be back by 6 p.m. so you can continue your whiskey drinking in a local pub.

6.   Get Close to Mary. Deep beneath the bustling streets of Edinburgh is hidden The Real Mary King's Close. It was originally narrow streets with houses on either side, stretching up to seven stories high. The houses at the top of the closes were knocked down and part of the lower sections were kept and used as the foundations for the Royal Exchange. The remnants of the closes were left beneath the building, dark and ancient dwellings steeped in mystery. Visit the Close and see an interpretation of life in Edinburgh from the sixteenth to the nineteenth centuries. You will be guided through the underground closes by one of the char-

acters from the past whose life touched Mary King's Close. Your guide will reveal dramatic episodes and extraordinary apparitions from the past, including ghost stories over 300 years old. And for you ghost lovers, they offer weekly ghost tours. www.realmarykingsclose.com.

7.   Swing on the greens. Famous St. Andrews Golf Course is the home of golf and one of the most honored golf courses in the world. It's a mere thirty miles northeast of Edinburgh, so if you love swinging, putting, and slicing, this iconic patch of green is the place to hit a round. Even if you are not a golfer, it's worth a ride out there just to pick up a few golf shirts for the golf fanatics in your life. They will be forever grateful to you. www.standrews.org.uk.

8.   Go hog wild at Hogmanay. If you are crazy enough to be in Edinburgh in the winter, then you deserve to party like a Scotsman on the nights that never seem to end. Hogmanay is the Scottish solution for the holiday blues. The parties start the day after Christmas, then climax on New Year's Eve with a full-blown street party. If you are in town, the best places to witness the chaos are the Royal Mile and Princes Street. And just when you thought it was safe to start detoxing on New Year's Day, you better wait because the celebrations keep going until January sixth.

9. Buy a 24- to 72-hour Edinburgh Pass. If you are really into experiencing all you can while in town, then think about getting yourself an Edinburgh Pass. Whether you're looking for heritage, culture, whiskey, ghosts, or nature, the pass gives you free access to 27 top attractions in Edinburgh and surrounding sites. The pass includes these top attractions: The Cadies & Witchery's Ghost & Gore Tour, Camera Obscura and World of Illusions, The Edinburgh Dungeon, Edinburgh Zoo, Gladstone's Land, Hopetoun House, Secrets of the Royal Mile, National Galleries of Scotland, Scotch Whisky Heritage Centre, Scottish Seabird Centre, The Cadies & Witchery Tours, Murder & Mystery Tour, Dynamic Earth, Edinburgh Literary Pub Tour, Georgian House, Glenkinchie Distillery, Lauriston Castle, The Vaults Tour, and the Scottish Mining Museum. Oh, and it includes unlimited travel on public transportation. Phew, are you tired yet? The pass can be purchased as a one-day, two-day, or three-day pass. You can buy it before you depart at www.edinburgh .org.

10. I dare you to try haggis! Try the nasty-looking national delicacy of Scotland: haggis. What is haggis? It's made up of the heart, liver, and lungs of a sheep mixed with oatmeal, well seasoned and put into bags made from the paunch of the sheep. The haggis is then boiled for 2 to 3 hours and left to get cold. Only you can decide if it tastes as foul as it sounds. Go to the Doric Wine Bar and Bistro at 15 Market St., if you dare. Tel: 131-225-1084.

IBIZA, SPAIN

**Bernessa contemplates
perfection in Ibiza.**

Why This Place Rocks
for Flying Solo

H ikers have Mount Everest, bikers have the Tour-de-France,
and jet-setters have Ibiza. It's
pronounced "Ibitha" in Spain. Called
Eivissa in the local dialect, the British hippies in the 1960s dubbed it the "Island of
Ecstasy." Call it whatever you want because when summer rolls in, this is *the*
spot in the Mediterranean and perhaps
the whole world. You'll trip over wild club
parties every night and fall onto warm
beaches wherever you turn. Once a jet-
setter has successfully climbed the social
ladder of soirees, the last stop on the
gauntlet of global gallivanting is Ibiza.
You can hear from crowded, chic

nightspots around the world, "See you in Ibiza, darling!"

Walk the streets at night and feel like you're in a music video: good tunes, gorgeous bodies, and skimpy costumes float on a dizzy sea of champagne and foam parties. Wear strappy stilettos and a sparkling sexy skirt and you'll fit right in with the International Pilgrims of Party that flock to Ibiza. Be prepared to party like a rock star, dress like a supermodel, and act like a princess—this is a destination that celebrates beauty, culture, and hot bodies.

Culture: 2

Rich in archeological history, you can explore the Museo Arqueologic de Ibiza, the necropolis of the Puig des Molins, or the Ciudad de Ibiza, founded by the Carthaginians 2,500 years ago. Today the town consists of a lively marina district around the harbor and an old town, D'Alt Vila, with narrow cobblestone streets and flat-roofed, whitewashed houses. Cultural elements can be subtle so you might have to seek them out. The real culture of Ibiza lives and breathes in the clubs that speckle the island. Honestly, you don't come to Ibiza if you're studying archeology or history.

Activity: 2

Pretend that you're going to Ibiza for the water sports, and the locals will humor you. There are dive shops and boat rentals, as well as great snorkeling spots and hiking trails. You can play golf, tennis, or squash; go horseback riding; windsurf; sea dive; or fish. But the truth is you'll probably see more people baking off their hangovers and lying supine on the sparkly beaches than lacing up hiking boots.

Weather: 5

If you want to travel to Ibiza, go in July through the end of September. The beginning of August is packed with beautiful men from Italy, Brazil, and Argentina. It's more about when the playboys show up than the weather.

Social: 5

Know what you're signing up for before you walk through the streets in the daylight and see the party shrapnel from the night before: broken beads, empty beer bottles, the smell of stale debauchery. If you love clubbing and partying, this is your paradise. If you're a mellow, knit-by-the-fire kind of girl, you might feel a little out of place on this island of sin. All the clubs are open seven days a week, and they host different themed parties

Predictions

Party like it's the end of the world as we know it! "Ibiza will be Earth's final refuge," predicted Nostradamus. According to the sixteenth-century prophet, when nuclear disaster wipes out most life on Earth, the peculiar wind patterns over Ibiza will ensure that it is the sole remaining life-supporting environment.

with varied DJs and promoters. Never a dull moment.

Flying Foreplay

*I*biza is a tiny Mediterranean island known globally for its summer parties: you do the math. Hotels are expensive and book up fast, and hostels are packed with hung-over teenagers. Plan accordingly.

Consider going off-season. If you avoid the summer, you'll also evade sweltering sun, sweaty crowds, and the high prices of the high season. The weather will be temperate and pleasant in the shoulder seasons. But you might also miss all the gorgeous man-stock from around the world—so it's your call.

Local Newspapers/ Newsletters

*T*wo decent websites are www.ibiza-online.com and www.ibiza-spotlight.com. Both give information on nightlife, restaurants, bars, clubs, accommodations, ecology, politics, and beaches. Both sites publish a weekly newsletter with the latest news from the island.

Read Before You Go

History of Ibiza, by Emily Kaufman
I Remember Ibiza, by Harold Liebow
A Short Life on a Sunny Isle, by Hannah I. Blank
Sober Life, by Sinclair Newton

Ibiza Accessories

Sparkle, darling! This place doesn't fool around when it comes to looking like a million bucks. So, pull out those hot threads you haven't worn since that private jet trip you took to the Grand Caymans.

Immune ammunition. Be safe and pack your favorite over-the-counter remedies—you're likely to be very sleep deprived and vulnerable to getting sick. Also, if you plan to mix with the singles scene, bring protection.

Pack light! When packing, remember that airlines tend to leave heavier luggage behind in Barcelona for a few hours as the small planes can only carry so much. Put your swimsuit in your carry-on—just in case.

Itty-bitty bag. You'll need a little bag to carry your essentials (money, credit card, hotel key, and condoms) when you go out nightclubbing. Make sure it's small and you can connect it to your body. Try a sexy belt-like wallet or light strappy bag; you want to keep your hands free while dancing.

Shoe selections. You'll need flips-flops for the beach, but you might want closed-toe shoes for the clubs; the chances of someone stepping on your freshly manicured tootsies are high.

Water works. The running water in Ibiza is saltwater—you'll need a bottle of fresh water in the bathroom to brush your teeth.

The Top 10 Extraordinary Experiences

1. DJ, spin that wheel! If you've always wanted to be a DJ, but have no idea how to mix like a pro, here's your chance. Point-Blank DJ school trains soon-to-be mix masters in Ibiza. Make sure you book in advance for the three-hour courses held most days from June to October at the Kasbah Sunset Café on San Antonio's sunset strip. You'll learn how to time beats and bars, mix music, along with a few other DJ tricks. Information: tel: +44 (0) 207-729-4884. DJ Andy Wilson in Ibiza: tel. +34-686-459-100.

2. Shop with a groove at the hippie market. During the summer, you can head to Punta Arabí right outside Es Canar on Wednesdays for some retro shopping. You'll find everything from clothing,

jewelry, glassware, and leather, to sand pictures, fake Rolexes, and pottery. A great place to buy treats for your friends.

3. Dress like a diva. So you forgot your gold lamé miniskirt and see-through halter top? You're in luck! Ibiza City has some wicked shopping to satisfy even the most ravenous party girl. Spend a day just touring the shops filled with colorful clothing and swimwear. All the streets are lined with tempting boutiques that sell clothes you would never let your mother see.

4. Repent for your sins at Santa Eulària Cathedral. Just in case you need some redemption, you can go light a candle or say a prayer at Santa Eulària, which is conveniently located in Ibiza City. Besides that, it's a beautiful church with a great history and it's worth a visit even if you haven't sinned. (Yeah, right.)

5. Wake up to wake boarding. Just in case there's a day you don't wake up with a hangover, or a handsome Italian, and want to try something exciting, why not try wake boarding? Experience the adrenaline rush with a fine crew of locals. WakeBoard Ibiza will take you to the best places on the island to try out your skills. www.rent-wake-boat .com.

6. Get privileged. Club Privilege is the most famous club in Ibiza, and it's adored by the glitterati. If you get queasy looking at beautiful, practically naked bodies and majestic dancers draped in rhinestones and feathers, then this isn't the place for you. The club has a hedonistic reputation and features some of the most flamboyant stage shows on the island. This club comes equipped with a massive main room that overlooks a swimming pool complete with an outdoor bar. Tel: 34-971-1980-86 or 971-1981-60.

7. Recuperate. Sneak out to the relaxing "Es Bol Nou" beach Bol Nou, which is perfect for the solo girl who wants to rest her dancing legs and bruised liver. Explore the beautiful sea beds, wade in the warm *azul* waters, and journal about the night before. If you dare.

Alternatively, you can get away from clubbing madness simply by taking a walk in the gorgeous countryside, which is alive year-round. Create your own bouquet of rosemary, sage, jasmine, and colorful wild flowers.

8. The next morning pretend you don't remember. Here are a few of my favorites— that I can remember:

Club Amnesia:

From midnight to 7 a.m., 4,000 revelers pack this well-known club and dance. The place is known for its cream parties. The drink prices are just moderate, in case you have to buy your own. On the road to Sant Antoni; tel: 34-971-19-80-41.

Pachá:

Check out one of the best discos on the island and, by many standards, one of the best in the world. A must! Calle de Barceló 28004; tel: 91-447-0128.

Es Paradis:

If you've never danced while splashing around in water, here's your chance. Don't wear silk here. Calle Salvador Espriu; tel: 34-971-34-66-00.

Mambo Café:

A great place to watch the elite, while enjoying good drinks, light dining, and music. C/ Garijo; tel: 34-971-31-21-60.

Privilege:

This is *the* place for dancing, socializing, and having fun in the true Ibiza way. Considered the best on the island with a capacity of hosting 8,000 gorgeous dancers. Carretera Sant Antonio; tel: 34-971-19-01-60.

Space:

One of the most popular clubs on the island. It is located at the airport and the party takes off at 7 a.m. (What time does your flight get in?) Platja de Bossa (Airport); tel: 34-971-31-40-78.

Teatro Pereyra:

During the day the theater is a low-key café, and at night it transforms into a

---

Café Del Mar

Café Del Mar is famous for stunning sunset views and the gorgeous collection of music played there. Buy one of its CDs before you leave. Visit www.cafedelmarmusic.com.

cool jazz bar. Entry is free. Calle Comte Rosello; tel: 971-304-432; www.teatropereyra.com.

9.   Take a deep breath. Time to detox? Far from the club scene, Ibiza Yoga has two retreats taught by many renowned world-class teachers, both within walking distance of Benirras Beach. They offer a weeklong yoga course designed to revitalize both mind and body in the unspoiled north of the island. Villa Palmas has a Mediterranean garden, a swimming pool, and spectacular sea views. www.ibizayoga.com.

10.   Speed around the island. Mopeds are one of the most popular ways to get around the island. If you have never experienced a moped, this is the place to try one. The island is pretty small, so you'll be able to cover lots of ground in a few hours, have fun, and stop for lunch. Motos Valentin, Bartomeu Vicent Ramón, Eivissa (Ibiza Town); tel: 34-971-30-24-42.

LISBON, PORTUGAL

Victoria revels in Lisbon's beauty.

Why This Place Rocks for Flying Solo

Gently touching the blue Tagus River, Lisbon rests like a sleeping beauty waiting to be woken. After years under the spell of obscurity, Lisbon now rises up like the Phoenix ready to dazzle even the fussiest traveler. It is a generous destination that gives of itself through its extraordinary food, lively social scenes, and remarkable history. And if you are a jet-setter who's forever in search of the next great place, then put Lisbon on your list, before everyone else does.

Portugal perches on Europe's westernmost shoulder, boldly facing the pounding Atlantic Ocean. Because of its position, the country has been peripheral in the minds of the masses. Take advantage before they realize what they've been missing. While the hordes are crowding on double-decker buses to see Big Ben, you can be slowly strolling down twisting alleys of the medieval districts, and as people push their way through the Louvre, you could be riding century-old lifts up and down the steep slopes of Lisbon or enjoying a boat ride on the sparkling Tagus. The fine folks who call *Lisboa* home are just as sophisticated, savvy, and beautiful as their Spanish and French neighbors, but without the characteristic tenacity that can leave some solo sisters feeling sheepish.

It's hard to believe that merely 30 years ago, Portugal was under a tight, fascist government that wasn't into sharing its culture with the rest of the world. Thank goodness that changed in 1974, and it's been all uphill ever since. In 1986, Portugal joined the European Union and has followed up with some fabulous parties, like the MTV European Music Awards, Euro 2004 soccer championship, and the World Expo.

Culture: 4

For you history buffs, plan on learning a ton here in Lisbon. Unlike other better-known destinations that filled the pages of your high school textbooks, Lisbon will surprise you with its secrets. For instance, did you know that Lisbon and Spain share the longest standing border in Europe? You will be blown away with this city's beauty and deep passion for the past. From *fiera da ladra* to fascism, there is plenty to discover here.

Activity: 2

If shaking your booty at night and climbing steep hills during the day sound like a good workout regimen, then you will be set. The only marathon you will be doing here is a gastronomical tour of all the incredibly delicious restaurants in town.

Weather: 3

The summers can get a bit hot and humid; so don't bother bringing your hair dryer. Winter is surprisingly mild, but expect rain in fall and spring. Really, this place is divine, but if you come during the rainy season, be prepared.

Social: 3

This city is working up the global social ladder and is geared to become one of the best party places in Europe. Lisbon's nightlife is like ripe fruit on abundant trees—just pick one and it's sure to be sweet and juicy. It's good to know that most Portuguese keep to themselves, so don't expect to get into the same trouble you did in college.

Lisbon Accessories

Great strides. I love heels as much as you do, trust me, but no one likes to be the tripping tourist who didn't know which shoes to bring. Portugal is an old city, i.e., cobblestones galore. Don't let ancient street-pavers and gravity team up on you. Bring shoes you're steady in.

Speaking of your sneakers . . . When I know I'm going to be walking long distances, I like to bring some talcum powder to sprinkle in my shoes overnight, keeping them dry and comfortable for the next day. Also consider some peppermint foot cream (to be massaged onto your hardworking tootsies, preferably by some *bem parecido* local).

Less is more. You can find anything you need in Lisbon, and the euro will take you farther here than in other European countries.

Peeled eyes. The city is full of unique architectural touches, bizarre statue arrangements and remarkable artistic features. Stay alert or you'll miss them.

Waterproofing. Though Lisbon probably won't see another tsunami like the one that swept over the city back in the eighteenth century, it can get quite wet in the rainy months.

The Top 10 Extraordinary Experiences

1. Listen to fabulous Fado. Depending on whom you speak with in Lisbon about Fado, you are bound to get different answers. They'll all agree on a few things, however. Fado means "fate" and refers to a type of Portuguese music rooted in deep-seated feelings, disappointments in love, the sense of sadness and longing for someone who has gone away, etc. Like the Portuguese version of the blues, Fado makes you sad and lonely in a good way, and no trip to Lisbon is complete without an evening in a Fado house. Kinda like the House of the Rising Sun, I guess. The intimacy of a restaurant or Fado house is the best way of enjoying this music—misery loves company in any language. Here's a list of the best places to listen to this fabulously mournful music:

Adega do Machado, Rua do Norte 91; tel: 213-224-640

Adega Mesquita, Rua Didrio de Noticias 107; tel: 213-219-280

Cafe Luso, Travessa da Queimada 10; tel: 213-422-281

Clube do Fado, Rua de Sao Joao da Praca 92, Alfama; tel: 218-882-694

Lisboa a Noite, Rua das Gaveas 69; tel: 213-462-603

2. Party like a rock star, really. Lisbon has become the *Grande Finale* city for many bands that go on tour in Europe. Just like in *Casablanca*, Lisbon is the last port before they head back to reality. Go out, and revel in the intense nightlife of Lisbon, famous for the quality and sheer diversity of its range of nocturnal nests. Start off with dinner at any of the great restaurants in Bairro Alto and move on from there. Here's a list of some favorite night spots:

Lux, Santa Apolónia; www.luxfragil.com

Buddha Bar, Gare Maritima de Alcântara; tel: 21 395-0555; www.buddha.com.pt

Havana, Doca de Santo Amaro; tel: 213-979-893

Blues Café, Rua da Cintura do Porto de Lisboa; www.bluescafe.pt

Paulinha (Wednesday is "Ladies Night"), Avenida 24 de Julho

Kapital, Avenida 24 de Julho; tel: 351-21-395-71-01; www.kapital.pt

Plateau and Kremlin, Escadinhas da Praia

Xafarix, Rua D. Carlos I; tel: 21-396-9487

Café da Palha, Garcia de Orta gardens; www.cafedapalha.pt

3. Sail away. For you wannabe sailors, the Oceanário de Lisboa's Nautical Centre, located in Doca dos Olivais (Parque das Nações), is a perfect place to spend an afternoon getting acquainted with the water and the fine art of sailing. Play around in a secluded, tranquil body of water on a boat that is less intimidating than, say, a 60-foot sailing yacht. The water park is located in the middle of the Atlântico Pavillion, the Vasco da Gama

Shopping Mall, and the Oceanário. So, after all that hard work of tacking and jibing, you will find a bevy of cafés and restaurants to satisfy that hardy appetite you worked up. "Ahoy, sailor!" Hours (check for each season): daily 9 a.m.–6 p.m.; tel: 21-891-85-32; e-mail: centronautico@oceanario.pt; www.parquedasnacoes.pt, click on "Activities."

4. Stride through history. Walking tours rock. They can be the smartest things to do when you first get into a city. You get to meet a few locals and learn about their town before you decide to go wandering out alone. Also, you meet other travelers, and many times you'll want to make plans together after the tour is over. Lisbon Walking Tours has a bunch of different tours for you. Just make sure you choose a tour that they are doing in English unless you want to practice your Portuguese, French, or Spanish. You can reach them at www.lisbonwalks.com. Here is a list of their historical tours:

Ancient Lisbon. Frolic in the most historic area in Lisbon with a guide who can tell you all about Lisbon's history. This walk includes the Alfama and Castle areas that are famous for being the birthplace of Lisbon as a city.

Medieval Suburbia. You've never seen suburbia like this before. Discover the area that ancient Lisbon first extended beyond its walls as a protected city. You will also enjoy a stroll through the charming neighborhoods of Chiado, the Bairro Alto, and Carmo.

Heart of Lisbon. Dive into the heart of the city and feel the energy of life in Lisbon. See where the ancient city and modernity mix in a cosmopolitan cocktail.

Another tour company you can check out is Lisbon Walks at www.lisbonwalker.com.

5. Go exploring from Alfama to Mouraria. Alfama is one of the oldest quarters in Lisbon and it's worth your while to spend a few hours getting lost in the ancient streets of this area. It has maintained its Arab structure, with its labyrinthine streets, courtyards, and lanes. The Sé (Cathedral) is wonderful, and the Feira da Ladra (flea market) is a must for bargain hunting and searching for that perfect souvenir. Next to Alfama are the quarters of Castelo and of Mouraria. During the Santos Populares (Patron Saints) celebrations, these quarters are packed with music, dancing, and food. Don't miss Castelo de São Jorge, set high on the hill of the same name with some of the best views of the city. At Miradouro de Santa Luzia or Miradouro da Graça (which has a café), enjoy more stunning views. For an instant fix on what Fado is all about, head to the Casa do Fado.

6. Tour Baixa. If you are more of a true solo gal and don't want to join a group, follow this self-guided tour created by the fabulous folks at the Turismo de Lisboa.

Begin in the Praça do Comércio, the great visiting room of Lisbon, opening up generously onto the wide Tagus estuary. Then, take the Rua da Alfândega, passing the Welcome Center of Lisbon. In front, you'll find the Praça do Município; in the center, you can see the ancient city's pillory flanked by the impressive Paços do Concelho (Royal Council Building). Return to the Praça do Comércio and head down the pedestrian street of Rua Augusta (under the triumphal arch), where you can saunter and shop the day away. On Rua Santa

Justa (the final road crossing Rua Augusta before reaching the Praça do Rossio), take a turn to the left and the Santa Justa elevator. Go up to the top floor for some of the best views of downtown Lisbon with the lovely Tagus River in the distance. Head back down and finish your stroll in Rossio, the square that used to be the political and social forum for Lisbon. Now you can eat!

7. Eat your way through Lisbon. Get those spandex pants ready for a movable feast of fresh seafood, grilled meats, delicious cheeses, and rich Portuguese pride served in heaping platefuls of hospitality.

Here are some of the best restaurants in Lisbon:

Tavares Rico:
A place that exudes Old World charm, the restaurant dates to 1784 and is not only the oldest restaurant in the city but also one of the best. The menu features traditional Portuguese seafood, as well as lamb, duck, and beef. Rua Misericórdia 35 rc; tel: 21-342-1112; www.tavaresrico.pt.

Terreiro do Paço:
These are actually two restaurants located on one of the city's main squares, Praça do Comércio. Under the watchful eye of one of Portugal's best-known chefs, Vitor Sobral, the upstairs restaurant, "O Paço," serves up a refined menu of Portuguese-inspired dishes whereas "Terreiro" downstairs offers a more casual dining experience with steak a major feature. tel: 21-031-2850; www.terreiropaco.com.

Bica do Sapato:
Co-owned by John Malkovich and Fernando Fernandes, this is still one of the trendiest places to eat in the city. Av. Infante D. Henrique, Sta. Apolónia; tel: 21-881-0320; www.luxfragil.com/bicasapato/bica_beta.html.

Flores Restaurant:
The trendy restaurant of the new boutique Hotel Bairro Alto is open to guests and visitors for lunch and dinner. Praça Luis de Camões, 8; tel: 21-340-8288; www.bairroaltohotel.com.

Eleven Restaurant:
One year after opening, Eleven was awarded a Michelin star and is one of Lisbon's newest gourmet restaurants. Stylish, Eleven specializes in acclaimed head chef Joachim Koerper's version of Mediterranean cuisine. Rua Marquês de Fronteira, Jardim Amália Rodrigues; tel: 21-386-2211; www.restauranteleven.com.

Água e Sal:
Your mouth will simply water as you go inside and experience the aroma that rises in the air above an old-fashioned charcoal *parrilla* oven, where the chef prepares gourmet delicacies right before your eyes. Oceanário de Lisboa; tel: 21-893-6189; www.oceanario.pt.

8. Muse at a few museums. Get lost in Portugal's remarkable history and their love of fine things. They give other cultural meccas a run for their money with their impressive list of museums and historic sites. Start your day at the Museu de Arte Antiga (Museum of Antique Art). Here, you will find the Panels of Saint Vincent de Fora, one of the most renowned group portraits in the European tradition, and the "Temptations of Saint Anthony" triptych by

Hieronymus Bosch. Two museums should not be missed in the Belém area. The Museu Nacional dos Coches (National Carriage Museum) hosts a unique collection in which three monumental carriages given to Pope Clement XI by the Portuguese Embassy are featured. The Museu do Design (Museum of Design) displays fascinating pieces designed from the 1930s to today. Visit the extraordinary collection housed in the Museum of the Calouste Gulbenkian Foundation and its collection of pieces by René Lalique. Don't miss the works by Amadeo de Souza-Cardoso and Paula Rego, in the Modern Art Centre of this museum. In the Chiado area, one of the city's historical neighborhoods, the Museu do Chiado offers you a tour through Portuguese contemporary art. Get to know Portugal better by getting to know one of its most characteristic artistic elements at the Museu do Azulejo (Museum of Decorative Tiles).

9. Get spoiled with some splendid spaing. A vacation is not complete without a day at a spa getting pampered and beautified for your trip home. Oh, how a diva loves to hear: "You look so rested!" For the ultimate spa experience, head over to the Four Seasons Hotel Ritz, sitting atop one of the seven hills in Lisbon, overlooking the stunning skyline. Enjoy afternoon tea (don't forget the champagne) on the terrace and marvel at the views of Eduardo VII Park, St. George's Moorish castle, the Old Town, and the Tagus River. Bring your camera and ask your waiter to get a picture of you looking like a princess in her palace perched above her kingdom. After tea, flutter over to the spa for a massage and a facial. You will return home glowing. www.fourseasons.com/lisbon.

10. Beach it! Lisbon has plenty of places for you to relax in the sun with your journal. In Cascais, with a more cosmopolitan atmosphere, you can practice water sports such as surfing, windsurfing, diving, and sailing. Costa da Caparica, located in the south bank of the Tagus estuary, is very popular with Lisboetas. For the naturist in you (that means getting naked), head a little farther to Meco. Between Cabo Espichel and the north bank of the Sado River mouth, the beaches face southward. Smaller and often rock-lined, they have on one side the clear blue of the sea and on the other the imposing Serra da Arrábida hills. Take a trip to the beach, enjoy a walk in the hills, try underwater snorkeling, go sea fishing, or feast on fresh grilled fish.

Most Unique Hotels in Lisbon
Belmonte Palace. Beautiful palace; www.palaciobelmonte.com

Pestana Carlton Palace. At the nineteenth-century Valle Flor palace; www.pestana.com

Ritz the Four Seasons. Unforgettable; www.fourseasons.com/lisbon

Lapa Palace. Nineteenth-palatial town house; www.lapa.palace.com

Bairro Alto Hotel. Located in the heart of the trendy Bairro Alto; www.bairroaltohotel.com

LONDON, ENGLAND

Kimberly power shopping
on a chilly London day.

Why This Place Rocks
for Flying Solo

I f you flunked World History 101, here's your chance to redeem yourself, girls. London is packed so full of iconic historic moments that you'll be gasping over "so that's where it happened" sites about every three seconds. Just minutes after arriving in London, you'll understand why the United Kingdom ruled the world for centuries, and the reason this country is called *Great* Britain, and not just Britain. How many places in the world can you go where, in mere minutes, you can walk from the place where two of King Henry's wives lost their heads to the spot where Shakespeare's famous words "To be or not to be" were first muttered?

London is a big, bold city that revels in its heritage and quirky British ways. As leaders of experimentation and fashion, they might take a no-holds-barred attitude with their style, but you won't see them mess with their traditions. Afternoon tea is an institution, the royal family is loved, and pubs are still their social hubs. They might live in the past with their staid customs, but they love to push the proverbial envelope as far as possible.

This is a city of unforgettable images and picturesque scenes. When you're in London, you know it. From the lumbering double-decker buses to the beloved red phone booths, everywhere you turn, you can hear Londoners saying, "Absolutely!" "Brilliant!" "Lovely!" and "Cheers!" The Brits' adoration of London is what makes London such a *lovely* place to visit.

From the ease of the Underground to the unending list of museums, exhibitions, and events to the rolling countryside and its many attractions, you are sure to be very busy during your solo stay. It helps that they speak English here; it's one less thing you need to struggle with on your vacation. *I think this is the perfect first-time solo adventure!*

Culture: 5

London still holds the throne when it comes to opportunities to embark on enlightening journeys into the past. In one week, you could have a solid understanding of both World Wars, a dramatic glimpse into England's traumatic history, and an abridged comprehension of the great English luminaries, such as Shakespeare, Dickens, Austin, Darwin, and my favorite, Princess Diana.

Activity: 2

Fish and chips, meat pies, beers, and freshly baked scones don't go very well with working out. So, put away your running shoes and enjoy London for what it is—a great place to eat lots of really fatty food and hang out in smoky pubs. There are a few parks where you can power walk, but why bother power walking when you can be power sightseeing or shopping?

Weather: 1

Girl, this is England, not Ibiza. You holiday in London for the culture, history, and magnificence of this remarkable city and not because of the climate. It's cold and monochromatic in the winter and chilly in the summer. Make sure to bring a jacket and a few sweaters no matter what time of year you land in London.

Social: 3

Londoners are not rude, but they're pretty reserved and tend to stick with their peeps when they go out. Think herd animals—deer, horses, and sheep. You won't ever get a guy offering to buy you a drink, unfortunately. Your best bet to meet people here is to join a fun walking tour the first or second day in London. You'll meet other travelers who will love to share a pint with you, even if they won't share the bill.

Flying Foreplay

The English love their theater, and so do the million visitors who descend on London every year. Unless you are a rock star, supermodel, or a Royal, the chances of your getting a good ticket to a hot show are slim. So, be in a feature film, or book before you depart.

Check the exchange rate: The Brits love their English pound and it's been pounding the U.S. dollar for the past few years. So, when you check prices, make sure you're reading them in dollars, not pounds. Otherwise, you will be unpleasantly surprised when you get your credit card bill.

London Accessories

Refresh it! They still smoke in pubs and restaurants. So, to avoid stinking up all your traveling clothes, bring clothing spray, rose water, or fabric softener sheets to perk up your stale wardrobe.
Layer it. From the famous London fog to the cozy pubs, you are bound to experience a few microclimates in a day. Dress in lovely layers, darling.
Be antibacterial, baby. It's not that the Londoners have more germs than others; it's just that you will be riding public transportation everywhere you go. After jumping on the Tube to check out Wimbledon, it's nice to dab your palms with some refreshing germ-killing lotion.

The Top 10 Extraordinary Experiences

1. Do a double decker. As cheesy as it sounds, you have to do the "Hop On Hop Off" tour on a double-decker bus. It's the best thing to do when you first get to town because they wind you in and out of London's main attractions over a two-hour period, so you can really get a good feel for its size and layout. The great thing is that you can hop off at any time, check out the sights, and hop back on. During your tour, there's a tour guide who explains all the attractions in detail to you.

2. Take a Bath. Leave the city and head to Bath for a day of pampering and playing. Situated adjacent to the historic Roman Baths (www.romanbaths.co.uk), which date back to A.D. 43, is the state-of-the-art Thermae Spa (www.thermae

Glam

Go get your makeup done free at one of the many makeup stands in Harvey Nichols, and shop Sloan Street looking like the princess that you are.

bathspa.com), which has 20 treatment rooms and natural water baths. Other must-sees in and around Bath are the Postal Museum (8 Broad Street, tel: 0-1225-460333); No. 1 Royal Crescent, a fully restored Georgian Home (tel: 0-1225-428126); and Bath Abbey and Heritage Vaults (tel: 0-1225-422462).

3. Be a shopping Sherlock. Head to Selfridges for a sexy skirt (www.self ridges.co.uk), then over to Harvey Nichols (www.harveynichols.com) for some darling knickers, then strut over to Harrods (www.harrods.com) for everything else! Love markets? Oh, then Portobello Road is the place to be on the weekends (www.portobelloroad.co.uk). Columbia Road Flower Market is one of London's great Sunday markets, selling everything from flowers to furniture (www.columbia-flower-market.freeweb space.com). Carnaby Street is a fabulous area to walk and shop in (www.carnaby.co.uk). The unique department store Liberty is situated at the top of Carnaby Street (www.liberty .co.uk), and for something completely different, Greenwich Market is the place to be (www.greenwich-market.co.uk).

4. Sip some English elixir. Enjoy the British institution of afternoon tea at one of London's iconic hotels. Make sure to dress like royalty—no jeans and tennis shoes allowed! Try the Ritz (www.theritzlondon.com), the Savoy (www.savoy-group.co.uk), Claridge's (www.claridges.co.uk), or Fortnum and Mason (www.fortnumandmason.com).

5. Go see a show. London's theater scene is huge, and there's nothing better than enjoying an evening in one of those big cushy British theater seats. Try the Albery Theatre (tel: 011-44-8700-606621) for the latest musicals. For some Shakespeare, try the Old Vic (www.oldvic theatre.com) or the world-famous Globe Theater (www.shakespearesglobe.org). And for you opera lovers, head to Sadlers Wells (www.sadlerswells.com).

6. Take a walk. For you ladies who are into spooky stuff, check out a walking tour of Jack the Ripper's slashing grounds. For you less morbid types, try out one of the tamer walks like a tour around Buckingham Palace and the Thames River. These are great ways to meet other travelers, too. Check out www.londonwalks.com.

7. Get stoned. Crop circles, aliens, UFO, and Stonehenge. Now that sounds like a perfect day! If you get tired of all that museum hopping and pub crawling, take a bus out to the country and visit Stonehenge.

Harvey Nics

Harvey Nics (as the locals call it) is the place to see and be seen. Check out the restaurant on the fifth floor. The action starts after 7 p.m. Visit www.harveynichols.com.

8. Stroll the South Bank. For an absolutely fabulous afternoon, start at the London Eye, which is the world's largest Ferris wheel, and jump on for an hour-long ride above London. Then stroll down to the Tate Modern gallery for some art gazing, and pop over to Parliament, where you can get more great shots of London in all her glory.

9. Have a pub meal. You can't say you've been to London without chilling in a pub. Remember, the locals aren't that outgoing, so your best bet is to belly up to the bar and chat up your bartender. Pub meals are also best eaten at the bar with a pint of Guinness. The pub loved by the glitterati is Windsor Castle in Notting Hill. Think Hugh Grant, Madonna, etc. Check out www.windsor-castle-pub.co.uk.

10. Meet Mr. Twining. The Four Seasons in the London neighborhood of Knightsbridge offers tea classes with Steve Twining (yup, that's the tea you have in your cupboard) a few times a year. He'll share his tea secrets with you while sipping on a few different flavors. Contact the Four Seasons in London for the dates of Mr. Twining's cozy tea classes.

PARIS, FRANCE

Sara strolling the grounds
of the Louvre.

Why This Place Rocks
for Flying Solo

For you bon vivants, say *"Bonjour"* to Paris, the epicenter of all things wonderful, fine, delicious, and beautiful. Here, in the "City of Lights," everything is possible. From eating the best meal of your life to buying the most beautiful ensemble you've ever worn, Paris is out to seduce and impress. Even small acts here in Paris are completed with perfection. Drinking hot cocoa is an art, and daydreaming at a sidewalk café is skillfully done. The Parisians love it here, and so will you after a few days uncovering all that the City of Lights has to offer.

If you happen to be one of those poor

souls who lack fashion sense and a decent wardrobe, Paris is the perfect place for you to explore your style and create a fabulous new you. Bring your flat hair, weary face, chipped nails, and sad wardrobe, and watch Paris transform you. This city is packed with places that can take your "ho hum" and turn it into "va-voom." That's what Paris loves to do—make things as beautiful as they possibly can be. And if you're already style-savvy, then get lost in the labyrinthine lanes of the Left Bank.

Walking around in the city is like walking a fashion show catwalk. Everyone looks like someone famous. From the way they wear their sexy sunglasses, to the way they hold their fork in one hand and a cigarette in the other, it's all done with sheer excellence. Paris is a dream, a place where you can become whomever you envision, and if you have big dreams, then Paris will fulfill them. Come as a fashion hazard and leave a supermodel—it's all possible! Be warned, it's a city with attitude, and when you go, be prepared to conform to Parisian standards, because Paris won't conform to you.

Culture: 5
Paris is everything you expect it to be. It's an awe-inspiring take-your-breath-away city filled with the best museums, opera, galleries, cafés, architecture, and shopping in the world. Unless you move to Paris, you'll never get the opportunity to experience all the wonderful cultural offerings this city boasts. So when you come, decide what you really want to see and stick with that; otherwise you will get overwhelmed by all the options.

Activity: 1
This is Paris, not Patagonia. So leave your running shoes at home and pack

your stilettos. Looking good, shopping, and dining at trendy restaurants are high activities in Paris. Try not to get caught up in the fact that you'll probably gain a few pounds while there, and if you do, remember it's totally worth it.

Weather: 3
Oh yes, Paris in the springtime. It's splendid, amazing, and the place to be if you want to get plowed down by tourists. It can get chilly in the winter, but summer is nice and warm. It's best not to plan your trip around the weather; instead, plan it around the retail sales and wine season.

Social: 2
Unless you speak French or hang out at tourist hotspots, it's pretty difficult to meet locals. This city is a bit full of itself—for great reasons—but the locals can be annoying and difficult sometimes. You'll definitely need to pack plenty of patience and a phrase book, *a chérie*.

Flying Foreplay

Parlez français. Learn some French before you arrive. This is critical to your success. Even if you only learn a few phrases, the Parisians will appreciate your effort. If you hit the town with, "I only speak English," they are likely to stare condescendingly at you and then walk away. Here are a few phrases to help you out:

A table for one, please. *Une table pour une, s'il vous plaît.*
Thank you. *Merci.*
I don't eat raw beef. *Je ne mange pas du boeuf cru.*

Another glass of champagne, please. *Un autre verre de champagne, s'il vous plaît.*

How much for the haircut and color? *Combien pour la coupe et la couleur?*

Can you make me look like a supermodel? *Pouvez-vous me faire le ressembler à un modèle superbe?*

Know their schedule. The Parisians all leave town the last two weeks in August, so if you visit during this time, none of the darling local eats, shops, or cafés will be open. They'll all be vacationing in Italy or Spain.

Setting Your Scene

Paris is divided into 20 different neighborhoods called *arrondissements*. They start from the center of Paris and move out, like a snail shell. So, you'll want to stay in the first six or so *arrondissements*. After that, they get pretty residential.

1ère. This is in the center of Paris and a haven for tourists. The Louvre, Les Halles, and the Palais Royal are all here.

2ème. This is the financial area and not much fun for exploring.

3ème–4ème. This area is called Marais. It's an energetic, alternative neighborhood. You'll find trendy bars, shops, and restaurants here.

5ème. The famous Latin Quarter. This is the place for the university crowd. The rue Mouffetard is a main thoroughfare where shops, restaurants, and student bars and cafés are scattered about.

6ème. St. Germain. One of my favorite places to stay in Paris. Very chic, but still bohemian and casual.

7ème. Here you'll find the Eiffel Tower and the Musée d'Orsay. This is pretty upscale.

8ème. The neighborhood around Champs-Elysées is filled with shops and tourists, while the area to the east, between the Champs-Elysées and Place de la Madeleine, is less so.

9ème. A diverse residential neighborhood with lots of artistic folks. The Paris Opera is located here.

Paris Accessories

Strolling shoes. The reason Parisian women don't get fat is not because they eat less than we do; it's because they have to walk everywhere! So, make sure you bring a really good pair of walking shoes. (Don't forget your sexy stilettos for those glorious Parisian nights, though.) These shoes need to be able to tackle the serpentine streets of Paris, the colorful cobblestone passages, and the many museums that you plan to conquer. Oh, and can you make sure that they are stylish? No frumpy flats allowed in Paris. Don't even think about wearing running shoes; that's the number one way of looking like a tourist—which is a no-no in Paris.

Map it. At first, Paris seems like a lovely French town that you can easily navigate by following the Seine. Well, you can't. It's huge. So, when you get to Paris, you can pick up a really cheap red map that they sell everywhere. Make sure to get the version that only has the 20 *arrondissements*. You don't need to know anything about the suburbs.

Electronic translator. This is a city where you end up meeting lots of people very quickly and everything you want to do will involve some personal interaction with others. To make things easier for you, you might want to invest in a pocket translator, because if you are massacring the language, at least you can show them what you mean by handing them the translated version of your thoughts.

Pack your accessories. Bring your scarves, hats, and rock star sunglasses—or buy them all when you get to town. The women in Paris dress to kill, so to avoid looking like a lone tourist—dress up!

Read Before You Go

Le Divorce, by Diane Johnson
Paris to the Moon, by Adam Gopnik

Sixty Million Frenchmen Can't Be Wrong, by Jean-Benoit Nadeau and Julie Barlow

Local Magazines in English

Where Paris. This is a great weekly guide with local happenings that you can find at hotels.

This City Paris. This quarterly magazine can be harder to find and the information is not as current as *Where*, but it gives you a good overview of Paris and its culture.

FUSAC. You'll find this publication in cafés around Paris. It's written for the American reader and focuses on American topics.

The Top 10 Extraordinary Experiences

1.   Call Jim. Jim is an American guy who's been living in Paris for the past 27 years. Each Sunday night, he cooks a big meal for the first 20 to 30 people who call him on Friday night. This is a great way to meet expats and others who are wandering through Paris. The dinners are 20 euros, which includes everything. The trick is getting to his place; it's in the 14th arrondissement of Paris. Give him a call and he'll give you directions. Tel: 011-33-1-43-27-17-67.

2.   Get naked. Off the busy walking street of Montorguil, hidden behind a cobbled courtyard, lies a Moroccan bath haven. Take a morning or afternoon and get lost in the world of *Aux Bains Montorgueil*, the Moroccan-hammam-with-a-French-twist spa. Enjoy two hours of pleasure beginning with a leisurely stint in the eucalyptus-infused steam room, followed by a totally naked exfoliation experience at the accomplished hands of Wafa or Fatia, a hot rinse under a waterfall-like showerhead, and a freezing dunk in the gorgeous underground pool. The crowning glory is the Argan oil massage, a totally sensuous rubdown using the highly prized, fragrant oil of the Moroccan Argan tree. After this, you'll be ready for anything. Aux Bains Montorgueil, 55 rue Montorgueil, 75002 Paris; tel: 01-44-88-01-78; auxbainsmontorgueil@wanadoo.fr.

3.   Go to market. The Parisians really know how to sell stuff, especially in their lovely little markets sprinkled around the city. You can really buy anything you want—from a hairy goat head to a one-of-a-kind candelabra. You just have to find it! There are 80 different markets in the city. Try the morning market at Marche Avenue du President Wilson or rue Mouffetard. A popular covered market is Marche Enfants Rouge, and for a real treat, stroll the daily flower market on Ile de la Cité. This amazing market

Baguette Heaven

Go to a bakery at 2 p.m., along with other Parisians, and get yourself a freshly baked baguette.

turns into a bird market on Sundays and is a must.

4. Get beautified. This is where the manicure started, darling. So make sure you don't leave Paris without getting one! Expect it to take way longer than the ones you get at home. After the manicure, get a facial, hairdo, and makeover. Why not get your makeup done at Chanel? They can also let you know where you can get all the other services you need. Chanel, 42 ave Montaigne; tel: 01-47-23-74-12; www.chanel.com.

5. Buy an icon. There is something so wonderful about saying, "Oh, I got this in Paris!" especially if it's something that's so French, so designer, and so colorful. Yes, many designers in Paris cost a fortune, but you can get away with spending around $200 on something that will last a lifetime. My favorite things to buy are shoes from Charles Jourdan (86 ave des Champs-Elysées), scarves from Hermès (42, Avenue George-V), or from Chanel (42 ave Montaigne), or a cool piece of jewelry-cum-cosmetics at Christian Dior (30 ave Montaigne).

6. Be a tourist. Okay, just for one day—or two—you can bundle up, wear your comfy-yet-stylish clothes, and explore the great museums in Paris. Buy a Paris Museum Pass. With the pass, you're prepaid, there's no waiting in lines, and no limit to the number of times you can visit the more than 70 museums and monuments in and around Paris such as Le Louvre, Musée d'Orsay, Arc de Triomphe, Tower and Crypte of Notre Dame de Paris, and Versailles Castle. Check out www.conciergerie .com.

7. Make a wish. In front of Notre Dame, the famous cathedral that's been featured in a ton of movies and cartoons, there is a small, circular, gold plaque that was used as a measuring point to distant destinations. Now, it is a place where you can make a wish. Stand on the plaque, facing Notre Dame, and spin clockwise (very important!) and whisper your wish as you spin around three times, stopping at the same place you started. *Voilà!* Your wish will come true. It worked for me—I got this book published!

8. Bike Versailles. Spend the day at one of the most beautiful spots in France, and make a few new friends, too, as you bike your way through Versailles's majestic gardens. The highlight of the day is the ride through the gardens behind the Chateau. The average Versailles tourist doesn't realize that she can visit only a small fraction of the gardens on foot. On this tour you get to see Marie Antoinette's Hameau and the quiet Petit and Grand Trianons. Fat Tire Bike Tours Paris; www.fattirebiketoursparis.com.

9. Chill with champagne. Paris is not short of places where you can hang and look like a mysterious rock star. Here are a few that both the locals and the glam frequent. You might want to bring something to read or write in; it's all about looking, not talking. But more power to you if you can strike up a conversation with a supermodel.

Hotel Costes—for a fashionable drink. 239 rue St-Honore, 1 er; tel: 01-42-44-50-00

Hemingway Bar—Ritz Hotel—it's the Ritz. 15 place Vendome, 1 er; tel: 01-43-16-30-30

Le Cine

If you want to check out a movie in French, the cinemas on the Left Bank are cheaper on Mondays and Wednesdays.

Kong—Philippe Starck's dream. 1 rue du Pont Neuf 1 er; tel: 01-40-39-09-00

La Belle Hortense—intellectuals and artists. 31 rue Vieille du Temple, 4 eme; tel: 01-48-0471-60.

10. Walk in the steps of Marie Curie. For those women who love femme power, you'll love this self-guided walking tour of Marie Curie's life. She is the amazing scientist who discovered radioactivity, and who said, "Nothing is to be feared, it is only to be understood." You can download a free walking tour at http://hypatiamaze.org/m_curie/curie_walk.html.

PRAGUE, CZECH REPUBLIC

Katerina shines in Prague's
ancient beauty.

Why This Place Rocks
for Flying Solo

----

*P*rague, a fairytale destination, was hidden behind the iron curtain of communism for more than 40 years, but in the past decade this enchanting city has woken up from a sleepy Soviet haze. Now, it welcomes travelers to explore her collection of architectural masterpieces and lavish sites. Prague (Praha), capital of the Czech Republic, is one of the most well-preserved historical cities in Europe and home to some of the most stunning Gothic, art nouveau, and Baroque buildings in the world. From the maze of tiny cobblestone streets that lead you into the poetic center of this bustling medieval town, to the dramatic Prague Castle (Przsky Hrad), there are plenty of awe-inspiring moments for a solo girl to have here.

High above the picturesque town center is the dramatic Castle District, which is separated from Old Town by the calm Vltava River and wondrous Charles Bridge. No matter what side of the river you explore, you can wander for hours, getting lost in the sheer beauty and historical richness of this place. The Czechs are eager to bring Western visitors to Prague and have done an excellent job of creating a destination that is teeming with fantastic restaurants, great museums, good public transportation, and a host of hotels. It's not hard to find a crew of expats living out their artistic and literary dreams in Prague. The cafés, restaurants, and streets are filled with young intellectuals on their cell phones and laptops, carving out their bohemian fantasies of living in Eastern Europe. The size of Prague is very manageable; it is not a huge metropolis like London or Berlin. A good pair of walking shoes, a decent map, and some time to get lost in the streets are all you'll need.

The city hopes to shed memories of its 40-year communist rule by becoming a center for international music. Jazz, blues, and opera are favorites of street performers and musicians during the day, and nightclubs fill the city after dark. The city also attracts international festivals of all persuasions. Wenceslas Square, the site of a century of political turbulence, is now a posh shopping district.

Culture: 5

All literary, history, and art buffs will love Prague. Franz Kafka's dark and paranoid stories, hardly your typical summer reading, give an excellent background into the mood and mysterious-

ness of the city. Hordes of visitors every year crowd the city to have a look at Old Town (Staromestské namesti), Charles Bridge, Old Town Hall, and Tyn Church. Josefov, the Old Jewish settlement, is a heart-wrenching look into this beautiful city's ugly past. The Gallery of Modern Art houses a collection of twentieth-century European art. And you shouldn't leave the city without a tour of Prague castle and its adjacent, maze-like gardens overlooking the city. For a great glimpse into the craziness of communism, spend an afternoon at the Communism Museum.

Activity: 1

Attempting to bike the cobblestone streets can be treacherous, and I would recommend that you avoid it at all costs. Just walking on these streets will kill you if you're not careful. Honestly, this is not a city where you come if you want to work out. This is a city that you come to when you want to get lost in another world. It's a place where you can sit for hours at a sidewalk café and write in your journal or just enjoy the spectacular scenery. The food is heavy and fried, and the beer is always ready to be poured.

Weather: 2

Bitter cold in the winter, hot and sticky with frequent flash storms in the summer, describes most Eastern European destinations, and Prague is no exception. While there will be plenty of time to catch a tan, there will also be plenty of times to stay inside. Consequently, the best season for weather is also the worst time for tourist traffic. Be warned: If you go in winter, you will be very, very cold and it's hard to enjoy a place while you're freezing to death.

Social: 4

Bring your dancing shoes! The people of Prague love music and you are going to need them for Prague's burgeoning nightclub scene. Prague is renowned by many tourists (especially European males) for its bargain-priced beer. While we do not suggest that you rush out to the nearest pub for happy hour, this little factoid makes Prague an excellent place to meet men. Coffee and tea houses are relaxed climates for foreigners to mingle with locals. Most everyone speaks some English, so you might need to talk slower than usual, but you can have some good conversations.

Flying Foreplay

Hotels. Book early if you plan to travel in the high season, which is June through August, because quality accommodations in Prague fill up fast. Stay near Old Town, or on the river. Be aware that the streets in Old Town are narrow and can get very confusing at night. You really need to know how to get back to your hotel room. My favorite hotels in Prague are Hotel Josef (www.hoteljosef.com) and Hotel Maximilian (www.maximilianhotel.com). They were both designed by the amazing Czech architect Eva Jiricna. And Hotel Maximilian has a spa, with floating tanks, that is open until 10 p.m.!

Money honey. The Czech Republic uses the Czech Crown (koruna) as its legal form of currency. Many restaurants, stores, and tourist attractions, however, will allow you to pay in euros. Like all major European cities, low-commission exchange bureaus abound. Make sure to carry cash before a trip, as some hotels or restaurants may not accept credit cards.

Language barriers. You will not find the same amount of English speakers in Prague as you will in other parts of Europe, but it's easy to get around the city knowing little or no Czech. You might want to pick up a phrase book before you go. It's a pretty tough language, so don't expect to master it in a week.

Prague Accessories

Comfy flat shoes. If you don't bring the proper shoes, you will have a miserable time. This is a walking city, but because the roads were built in the fourteenth century—way before Jimmy Choo—walking can be very trying. In some places, it's not even cobblestone so much as cobble rocks.

A good map. This city is a maze and it's really easy to get lost. You'll need a good map that lists all the street names clearly. Because Czech is a difficult language, you can't just assume you're on the right street. One change of a letter and you are somewhere totally different. Also, you might want to stay out of the dark alleys after sunset. Prague is a great place to get lost in during the day, but at night it can get a little bit scary, and walking around looking up at the street signs to figure out where you are makes you a target.

The Top 10 Extraordinary Experiences

1. Get down in Old Town. You're sure to do all those other things that tourists do, like watch the 600-year-old astronomical clock do its amazing act every hour, visit the breathtaking Tyn cathedral, climb to the top of the 200-foot tower of the old Town Hall, and relax in one of the many cafés that litter the square. But wait! Why not party like it's post-communism.

M1—the place of the beautiful people. Masna I; tel: 221-874-256

Alcohol Bar—casual locals. Dusni 6; tel: 224-811-744

Tretters—expats and businessmen. V Kolkovne 3; tel: 224-881-165

Roxy—nightclub. Dlouha 33; tel: 224-826-296

2. Connect with the Cubans. Some Cubans opened a kick-ass restaurant that's filled with expats, ex-commies, and extraordinary dancers and serves the best mojitos this side of the iron curtain. Grab a seat at the bar, a Cuban cigar, and enjoy your night. La Bodeguita Del Medio, Kaprova 19/5 110 00 Praha; tel: +420-224-813-922.

3. Visit the communists. Yes, there is a theme here. I really dig the fact that this place was under the communist rule up until 1989. So, why not check it out and understand what it's all about. For a great introduction to communism, visit the Communism Museum at Na Prikope 10. Ironically, it's above McDonald's and next to a casino.

4. Write on. Okay, here's one more communism-themed activity. Write on the "Lenin Wall" and I'm not talking about John and his peaceful songs. During the communist era, this was the wall where revolutionaries risked their lives to scribble antigovernment slogans. Now you can share a peace-filled thought without worrying about getting arrested.

To get there, go toward the West Bank of the Vltava, cross Charles Bridge, and take the steps on your left side. At the square called Na Kampi, cross and turn right. Phew.

5. Search for ghosts. Meet your spooky host at 7 p.m. under the astronomical clock. From there, you'll be taken on a tour to some of the most haunted spots in Old Town. They will lead you through dark, serpentine alleys while sharing ghoulish stories of tragedy and fear.

6. Go to the ghetto. Take a fascinating and thoughtful tour of the Jewish Quarter, encompassing all sites of the Jewish Museum and the Old Jewish Cemetery, while your guide shares the history of the Jewish community dating back 1,000 years to the present day. Contact Sylvie Wittmann; www.wittmann-tours.com.

7. Get sexed up. For a racy afternoon of decadence, check out Prague's sex machine museum. It is an exposition of mechanical erotic appliances, and we're not talking your usual toaster oven, my dear. There are three floors of over 200 objects and mechanical appliances on view, a gallery of art with erotic themes, a cinema with old erotic films, erotic clothing, and many other things pertaining to human sexuality. They do have a museum shop if you feel compelled to take home some sexy souvenirs. Melantrichova 18; www.sexmachines museum.com.

8. Float away. After all that walking, you'll want to just float away for a while, and the Hotel Maximilian can make that happen with a flotation tank and full-service spa. They offer everything from Thai massages to foot reflexology. It is the perfect haven after a day of shopping and exploring. www.maximilian hotel.com.

9. Explore the castle. A trip up to the castle is worth the long walk. I wouldn't recommend taking a bus tour of Prague. The buses are huge and Prague is so pretty, it's like a Tonka truck touring through Cinderella's palace. If you don't want to do an all-day walking tour to the castle, you can get there by other means, such as a cab or public transport. It is a spectacular place right out of the pages of a fairy tale.

10. Walk with Franz. For you literary buffs and lovers of the absurd, a walking tour of Franz Kafka's life is the perfect way to get into a Prague state-of-mind. This delightful self-guided tour, created by the New York City Library, is free off their website (www.nysoclib.org/travels/kafka.html). And of course, you should be carrying a copy of one of his many "Kafkaesque" novels while you wander through his world.

REYKJAVIK, ICELAND

**Gloria relaxing in Iceland's
Blue Lagoon.**

Why This Place Rocks
for Flying Solo

*I*f riding the edge of life's extremes
is your favorite mode of transportation, then get on the next Icelandair flight heading to Reykjavik.
Because on this small, remote Arctic island, you'll find more than a whale and a
few Vikings; you'll find a culture of people who put *vivre* in joie de vivre. Plan on
submerging yourself in one of the most
soulful, dramatic places on the planet.
From the welcoming harbor of Reykjavik, to the stark, cold glaciers near the
Arctic Circle, you'll always find a kind
person, a mystical folktale, and an amazing view. Make sure to catch your breath
between each.

Iceland is part Scandinavian, part European, part Viking, part saga, and part dream. It's a country of hot tubbing, socializing, and exploring. Don't be surprised if you find yourself daydreaming of trolls and fairies while hiking the lava mounds in northern Iceland; and it won't be the first time someone dozed off in the warm, creamy blue waters of the Blue Lagoon mesmerized by the steam that resembles Thor, god of thunder. Be prepared to experience a profound mystical change after visiting this country. You'll experience what life was once like, both through the eyes of the Icelanders, as well as through Mother Nature, who spares no expense when it comes to showing you what creation looked like before mankind. She'll enchant you with her bubbling pools of mud, steaming geysers, hot pots, and barren lava fields. And by the time you have to leave, you'll be in love with both her and her children, the Icelanders.

Now, just because Iceland is the puffin capital of the world doesn't mean that this place has no nightlife—*au contraire!* Since the sun is out twenty-three hours a day during the summer, this place rocks for midnight socializing, dancing, and hanging out. The people here are more likely to be found in pubs or cafés than scaling the walls of lava that fill this country. So remember to bring plenty of business cards and a little black book, because you'll meet a bounty of incredible Icelanders while adventuring through this magical country the size of Kentucky.

Culture: 3

The Vikings would tell you, while gently pulling your hair, that Iceland is the epitome of culture. But for those of you who find Rome and Paris a tad stimulating, you'll find Iceland a cultural dust field. Yes, the Viking thing is cool, but how many Vikings can you take? They do have a burgeoning art movement and the Icelandic traditions are quite fascinating, but don't expect to find the Sistine Chapel here.

Activity: 5

Girl, you'll be so busy trekking, golfing, exploring, hot tubbing, horseback riding, and swimming that you won't care about having a bad hair day. Icelanders are a very active pack and love to get out and explore their countryside. From searching for hot pots (natural hot tubs) to soak off the day's activities, to four-wheel-driving through rough lava fields and glaciers, you'll always be on the go. Oh, and did I mention the 62 golf courses that this country boasts?

Weather: 1

Ugh! They say it gets up to seventy degrees in the peak of summer, but I wouldn't count on it. Honestly, if you don't like cold weather, you might want to find someplace less exciting to visit. But if you don't mind a thick breeze, random summer snow flurries, and the midnight sun, then definitely head to this crazy, wild place.

Social: 5

Only a complete hermit could leave this country without meeting someone. With a population of only 300,000, Icelanders love visitors. Hell, they already know everyone on the island, so fresh meat is always welcome! Plan on meeting outgoing people who will take great care of you. This place is one of the friendliest destinations I have ever visited.

Flying Foreplay

V isiting such an isolated place takes a bit of planning, and when heading to the Arctic Circle, you might want to take extra care packing. It's not like Iceland is cut off from the rest of the world and you won't find anything there, it's just that most things are imported. So if you leave your to-die-for cozy fleece number at home, plan on spending at least double the price for something not quite as spectacular.

Check the exchange rate. At the time of this book's publication, the U.S. dollar was getting the life kicked out of it by the Króna (which goes by the abbreviations ISK, IKR, or KR). The score is about 1,000 Króna for every 15 USD right now. On my last visit, for example, I ordered two drinks—a Bailey's and a gin and tonic—and my bill was 2,200 Króna. That's $36. So, if you're a big spirits drinker, I would suggest you pick up a bottle for your hotel room—or someone else's room—while you're going through duty-free.

Check the weather. It's called Iceland for a reason. Even though the bars, cafés, and hotels are cozy and warm, the temperature plummets once you step outside. Check the weather before you go, and don't bother going in December, when you'll encounter almost twenty-three hours of darkness, bleak weather, and snow. Unless you like that kinda stuff, plan on going before November or after February.

Websites

This is a Web-savvy destination, and everywhere you go, you'll find a wireless connection—it's wonderful for those who have wireless withdrawal while jet-setting. And with wireless comes websites. Here are a few of Iceland's favorites. Because Icelandic is the mother tongue, it's great to find English sites where you can check out the happenings and social scene *before* you arrive.

www.IcelandReview.com. Surf this English-language magazine on Iceland. It features a plethora of subjects from art, music, and fashion to business, politics, and news, all through the eyes of Icelanders. It's a great place to peer into this fascinating place.

www.Grapevine.is. For a glimpse into the real life of Viks (that's short for people who live in Reykjavik), check out this alternative online magazine. Once you get to Iceland, you can pick up a hard copy every week. Good reading. It lists all the happening clubs, pub, concerts, art exhibitions, and more.

Basic Tourist Information Sites

www.visitreykjavik.is. Find out where to wine and dine in the capital city. Along with eating and drinking, you can find out what's on where. This is a great website for the mainstream traveler, just in case the *Grapevine* is just a bit too avant-garde for you.

www.icetourist.is. This is your basic tourist website, but it's got some good travel information. You'll find statistics, practical advice, and general information about Iceland.

www.dice.is. Another website dedicated to tourism. This site is all about different tours you can take—fantastic if you're not ready to drive cross-country alone.

Setting your Scene

*B*ecause Iceland is a pretty casual country, there's not too much you need to worry about booking before you go. But things are expensive, so you might want to be prepared to spend some hard-earned cash.

Reserve your Rover. You haven't been to Iceland unless you unleash yourself onboard an Iceland Rover. These are Land Rovers on steroids that rip through the countryside, spill into rivers, and jump over lava rocks. If adrenaline is your friend, this is a

must. Before you depart, check out the different tours they offer, and book one before you go; they can take only eight passengers at a time. Included among the tours they offer: Essential Iceland, Volcano Jeep Safari, Volcano Jeep Tour, Mt. Hekla & Hot Springs and Landmannalaugar, Hot & Cold, The Continents Drift Apart, Glaciers & Waterfalls, and Northern Lights & Lobster. They have confirmed departure times throughout the week, so even if you're the only one on the tour, they'll still take you. Oh, and did I mention the two guys that run this operation are *hot*? Iceland Rovers; www.icelandrovers.is.

Buy ahead! Buy all your travel guides and reading material before you go. I made the mistake of buying two fiction paperbacks while I was there for a whopping $60—I could have gotten the same two books online, used, for less than $20 total.

Reykjavik Accessories

Bundle up. Warm clothes, gloves, hats, and clothes that you can layer are a must. Although it's not the coldest place in the world, it can get pretty darn cold. But it can warm up in a flash. This is not Manhattan, so you're okay if you don't bring your Versace cocktail dress and Gucci stilettos. Stick with warm, comfortable clothes. But don't dress like a hillbilly; they do have great style and *dépêche-mode* here due to the strong Scandinavian and other European influences.

Hot to trot. You'll need to keep those tootsies warm, so a nice pair of walking shoes is a must. I prefer boots here, especially wedges or flats. Heels can lead to an early demise if it happens to snow, so bring boots that were made for walking.

Icelandic 101. Almost everyone speaks English in Iceland, so you don't need to know a stitch of Icelandic, unless you head to the remote areas, where you may find it useful to have an English-Icelandic dictionary.

Sweet dreams. If you're visiting in the summer, you might want to bring a sleeping mask for those very bright nights. Some hotels have thick curtains, but don't bank on that. It is definitely surreal going to sleep when the sun's still up.

Diving in. Icelanders love to swim, and one of their favorite social hot spots is the local heated swimming pool. You can find them there even when the snow is falling! Make sure you pack that sexy bikini.

Bring your bottle. If you rely on your after-dinner brandy, you might want to think about buying a bottle before you land. Alcohol is ridiculously expensive here.

Best of the Books

Icelanders, by Unnur Jökulsdóttir and Sigurgeir Sigurjónsson. Forget those wordy, pragmatic travel guides—this one's got pictures! This book is full of photographs of Icelanders in their natural habitat. You have to pick this up in Iceland, though—sorry!

Insight Guide Iceland, by Jane Simmonds. This is a fantastic pretrip read about Iceland's history, culture, and people. It lists lots of off-the-beaten-track trips that make Iceland so spectacular, and

the pictures are great. Get this book if you're not too worried about specifics.

The Rough Guide to Iceland, by David Leffman and James Proctor. This particular "Rough Guide" is certainly the best guidebook to Iceland. It details every section of the country, and has pithy, relevant remarks on accommodations, places to eat, and things to see.

Local Magazines and Newspapers

Grapevine. This is the local weekly for all that's going on in Reykjavik. Find everything from the newest nightspots to the latest bands: who's who, what's up, and where to go. It is the first thing you should pick up (after that hot Viking) when you get to town.

Iceland Review. Just like the website, this hip magazine is a great read when you first get into town. It might be hard finding a copy because it's printed only four times a year.

Atlantica. If you fly Icelandair, the only carrier that can get you to Iceland, you'll have access to this event-filled magazine. It is a great in-flight read (after you finish one of those Icelandic novels!).

The Top 10 Solo Dining Places

You won't be alone long in this social party city. They love visitors, and are more than willing to share a beer with you—expect to pay for yourself, as drinks are expensive and it's not culturally appropriate to buy a girl a drink. Sorry!

- **Vegamot:** the coolest place in town; you'll find Iceland's finest here.
- **Jomfruim:** for a quick open-faced sandwich.
- **Hornid:** a great Italian restaurant that's reasonably priced.
- **Galileo:** is a fabulous place to people-watch, if it's warm!
- **Einar Ben:** for a more restful, upscale dining experience, located on the second floor.
- **Bertel Stofa:** with a fabulous location on the square facing Parliament, and a social center in the summer.
- **Café Paris:** the perfect place to chill with one of those Icelandic Sagas.
- **Café Breeslann:** a hip café where you're bound to run into some famous European.
- **Apotek:** a place so hip it hurts.
- **Kaffinbarinn:** a café that was the resting place for rock stars who were crossing the pond and slipping into Reykjavik for a cold drink.
- **M&M:** in the heart of the city, stroll the aisles for books and CDs, then grab a café and chill.
- **Prikid:** a hip, casual café where you can get a diner-style meal at the bar.

The Top 10 Extraordinary Experiences

1. Try the Golden Circle tour. On this daylong tour, you'll see some of Iceland's most famous natural attractions, including Kerio volcanic crater, the powerful Gullfoss waterfall, the spectacular Geysir hot springs, and the dramatic Pingvellir National Park. See where Iceland held its inaugural Parliament meeting in AD 930, and catch a glimpse of where the earth is ripping apart through volcanic activity. A truly wonder-filled adventure.

2. Swim in the Blue Lagoon. Relax in the amazingly milky-blue mineral waters of the Blue Lagoon for the afternoon. Book yourself a spa treatment or just rest in the therapeutic waters with your face covered in natural silica mud. Lunch here is divine! 240 Grindavik; tel: 354-420-8800; www.bluelagoon.com.

3. Eat like a Viking at the Viking Village. Go to the Viking Restaurant for a traditional Viking feast and an evening of Viking sing-along (didn't think Vikings sang, did you!). They'll pick you up from your hotel room (not by your hair, thankfully) in Reykjavik—or spend the night there; it's also a hotel equipped with wireless Internet access and breakfast. The Viking Village, Strandgata 55, 220 Hafnarfjordur; tel: 354-565-1213.

4. Enjoy lobster and lights. Head for the south coast, away from the lights of the city, and hunt for the Aurora Borealis. Visit the black sand beach for a little taste of Icelandic delicacies at an unforgettable lobster feast at the Fjorubordid restaurant. After this delicious dinner, drive into the night and search for the mysterious lights once again then head back to Reykjavik. This tour is done by Iceland Rovers. www.icelandrovers.com.

If you don't want to do the tour, it's worth the forty-five-minute drive just to eat at the Fjorubordid restaurant. They serve the most delicious steamed lobster tails by the bucket, with potatoes and side dishes that include couscous, grilled eggplant, salad, and hot bread. The lobster bisque is incredible; so are the insane desserts. Fjorubordid, Eyrarbraut 3a, 825 Stokkseyri; tel: 354-483-1550; www.fjorubordid.is.

5.   Fly to Akureyri, drive to Husavik, whale-watch, visit the Phallalogical Museum, and see the puffins. Take a quick hour flight to Akureyri, then rent a car and drive to Husavik. In Husavik take a whale-watching trip (tel: 345-464-2350), explore the Whale Museum (tel: 354-464 2520), visit the only penis museum in the world (the Icelandic Phallological Museum, Hedinsbraut 3a, 640 Husavik; tel: 354-566-8668), and drive out in search of puffins. Stay at Hótel Reynihlíd, Reynihlid, which is a cozy property with a full bar, restaurant, and wireless Internet. 660 Myvatn; tel: 354-464-4170; www.reynihlid.is.

6. Soak in the hot geothermal waters at Myvatn. After all that whale watching and puffin spotting, spend the next day soaking in the healing waters of the Myvatn Natural Baths. Rest in clouds of steam rising up from a fissure deep in the earth's surface and end with a luxurious swim in a pool of geothermal water drawn from depths of up to 8,000 feet. Myvatn Nature Baths, Jardbadsholar, Myvatn; tel: 354-464-4411; www.jardbodin.is.

7.   Tour Myvatn, witness a boiling mud pool, eat at the Cow Shed, and stroll through troll gardens. Drive to Mount Námafjall, where you will find the most incredible pools of bubbling mud. Head to the Cow Shed for a delicious meal of fresh milk, homemade mozzarella and feta cheeses, and *skyr* (Iceland's version

of yogurt)—if you're real lucky, the owner, Ólöf, will have just baked some warm *hverabraud* (sweet rye bread) using only geothermal heat from the local lava fields (Vogafjós Café, 425 Vogafjós, 660 Myvatn; tel: 354-464-4303). After your wonderful meal, visit Dimmuborgir (that's "Dark Citadels" in Icelandic), where you can spy on dozens of trolls petrified in action after partying too much and getting frozen by the sun.

8.   Chill at the ice bar with a shot of Black Death. Brennivin is the national libation of Iceland, and it means Black Death. Sometime in the fourteenth century, the black plague killed between one-half and two-thirds of Iceland's population. And if you have too many shots of this poison, you just might keel over and die, too. Visit the Icebar at Kaffi Reykjavik for a shot of Brennivin. There you'll find the bar a toasty −5°C; the shot glasses are made of ice. Kaffi Reykjavik; Vesturgata 2, IS-101 Reykjavik; tel: 354-552-3030.

9.   Visit the Viking Saga Museum and have dinner at Pearl. Arrive early evening to tour the impressive Saga Museum, which depicts the two hundred centuries of Icelandic history. There you can learn much about how Iceland was settled and became the country it is today (Saga Museum, 354-511-1517, www.saga museum.is). Head up to the Pearl restaurant, where you'll enjoy a 360-degree view of Reykjavik while dining on some of the finest food in the country. The room revolves 360 degrees every two hours (105 Reykjavik; tel: 354-562-0200; www.perlan.is).

10. Play a round of midnight golf. Play the world's northernmost eighteen holes at the Akureyri Golf Club (Jari, 600 Akureyri; tel: 354-462-2974; www.golf.is). Putt and swing while surrounded by stunning views of local mountains and fjords. Each June, golfers from around the world come to the thirty-six-hole Arctic Open International Golf Tournament, with three days of golf games running well past midnight. The tournament is open to all men with a handicap of 28 or below and women with a handicap of 24 or below, as long as you pay the $350 entrance fee. Contact Britannia Golf (tel: 804-346-8714; www.britanniagolf.com) to join the tournament.

ROME,
ITALY

Nicole feeds the pigeons in the
Piazza San Marco in Venice.

Why This Place Rocks
for Flying Solo

*I*f you've fallen in love with Fellini's
La Dolce Vita or Audrey Hepburn's
Roman Holiday, why not experience the magic of Rome live and in person? Because to truly experience the
crazy passion of this ancient city packed
with Vespas and Versace, you need to do
it while sipping an espresso in the heart
of Roma. It's a city that dazzles you with
its fashion, style, and beauty at one moment, then suddenly transports you to
historic sites of contemplation to garner
your respect for its long, eventful past.
When it comes to the Chianti cup of the
Romans, it's not half full, it's spilling
over, dripping off the sides, and the Ro-

mans are always there, smiling, making sure that they drink every last drop. This is a place of boisterous conversations, delicious food, beautiful people, and rich culture. You want it all? Come to Rome!

As for the Romans themselves, they know how to live and love, flirt and eat—usually, all at the same time. Romans love life, good food, and fast cars. Almost any wild thing you do can be justified with a shrug of your shoulders and a "Hey, when in Rome . . . !" And once you visit Rome, the word *romantic* will conjure fantastic memories of your time devouring the incredible sights and drinking in the energetic scene.

For you darlings who want to venture out to the countryside of Tuscany or even to Venice, it's easy because Italy is a fairly small country. Florence, the birthplace of the Renaissance, Michelangelo, Dante, and DaVinci, is a quick train ride from Rome. Spend a few days eating your way through Tuscany and head up to the picturesque town of Venice for some shopping and gondola riding. In Venice, fall in love with colorful Murano glass, or delight in the delicate handmade lace that was the envy of all Europe for hundreds of years.

Culture: 5

The Italians invented the Ferrari, the Lamborghini, and the pizza. Surely they must have invented culture as well. Centuries-old ruins lounge amid erect, modern buildings, ancient and modern coexisting like lovers on a warm Sunday morning. It's easy to stumble across antiquity while you're walking to get an espresso. Romans embrace their past and allow it to seep into their everyday life. You'll find modern art galleries sprinkled alongside classic painting masters in museums. After hitting the main sights, be sure to step off the well-worn path that circumnavigates Rome. You'll be rewarded with lesser-known cultural wonders.

Activity: 2

The only thing that's going to get your heart racing here is the gorgeous men. This is not the city to visit if you want to hike, bike, or Rollerblade—you might end up killing yourself on all those cobblestones. But if sitting in a café, reading a novel while watching beautiful people stroll in and out of shops and restaurants is your moda, then this is the place for you.

Weather: 3

Rome can get a bit chilly in the winter, and in the summer the days are as warm as lattes. Days in August can get uncomfortably hot, and touring the city at noon can feel like Dante's Inferno. It's a great place to show off your savvy style sense, so work with the weather. In winter, bring your fur; in summer, bring your sexy ensemble.

Social: 3

Venturing out alone at night in Italy can be tricky. Men are rarely aggressive, but frequently attentive to the solo female, and can go too far in lavishing unwanted (and vocal) attention. It is essential to follow good common sense; Rome is a lovely city but a city nonetheless and you shouldn't find yourself walking alone in the dark. Italians make friends fast and are very welcoming—just remember to trust your instincts and learn to say "Hit the road, buddy!" (*"Vai via, ragazzo!"*)

Flying Foreplay

*B*ecause Rome is a major metropolitan city with plenty to keep you busy, you won't need to plan much before you go. Research the different areas of Rome and try to stay close to the center by Piazza Navona, the Spanish Steps, or Campo di Fiori. You'll be close to great shops, restaurants, sights, and transportation. You want to stay somewhere central enough that you can walk back to your hotel after a day of sightseeing. Taxis are pretty trustworthy,

so if you do stay a bit farther out, make sure to keep a card on you with the name and address of your hotel. Don't expect the cab drivers to speak English.

Those Italians love going on strike. Sometimes the strikes last only a day; other times they can go on for weeks. Check to make sure that no one is striking. It's usually the train workers who like to strike. So if you're planning to take a lovely train ride out to the country, make sure you'll be able to get there.

Read Before You Go

Angels and Demons, by Dan Brown
Eat, Pray, Love, by Elizabeth Gilbert
Many of the books in the New Testament—the Book of Romans is a good place to start
When in Rome, by Ngaio Marsh

Rome Accessories

A great map. People have been living in Rome for thousands of years, filling every nook and cranny of the city with interesting and confounding sights and

For Free

For the girl on a budget, here are some free attractions: Roman Forum, Pantheon, views from the Pincio, the Gianicolo and the Capitoline, Trevi Fountain, Bocca della Verità, St Peter's Basilica, every church in Rome (amen!), Sistine Chapel and Vatican Museums on the last Sunday of the month, and walking through Villa Borghese or Villa Doria Pamphili parks.

buildings. You'd be missing out if you walked blindly around. Let a good map point out the fascinating things you might otherwise pass right by.

Fabulous threads. This is a city of style, and looking like a frumpy tourist is not going to cut it here, especially when traveling solo. Leave the tennis shoes at home and pack some comfortable, sexy wedge boots or spicy-hot trendy sports shoes (think pink and orange Pumas). This is a walking city, so you don't want to wind up spraining your ankle.

Italian phrase book. Many Italians speak some English, but it's always helpful to know some of the basics before you go. Here are a few to get you started:

How much is that? *Quanto costa?*

I don't understand. *Non capisco.*

What is your name? *Come si chiama?*

Please take me to the train station. *Prendami prego alla stazione di treno.*

I heard Italian men kiss well. *Ho sentito bene il bacio italiano degli uomini.*

You're not married, right? *Non siete sposati vero?*

The Top 10 Extraordinary Experiences

1. Knock your socks off with an espresso at Tazza D'Oro. This truly Roman café just off the Pantheon's piazza has the best coffee in Italy. With long bars for perching, you can drink espresso until your legs give out, and you might want to. If the day is too hot for coffee, enjoy a refreshing coffee *granita*. Bring back a bag of this coffee as a gift; it will immediately establish you as a coffee guru among your friends and family. Tazza d'Oro Coffee Bar, at the corner of via di Pastini just off Piazza della Rotonda via degli Orfani, 84; tel: +39 06-678-9792.

2. Get ruined at night. Discover some of the most famous monuments of the Eternal City in the dark. Some of the sights that will be illuminated for your pleasure include the Coliseum, St. Peter's, Trevi Fountain, Via Veneto, and Piazza Navona. Check out www.viator.com for more details.

3. Meet Angels and Devils. Based on a Dan Brown novel, the Angels and Demons Walking Tour will lead you through a fascinating network of mysterious, hidden symbolism and forgotten tales. Experience an incredible journey, at the end of which you will discover the Illuminati and their secrets. Follow the Path of Illumination and understand how to solve the many puzzles and enigmas that await. www.nerone.cc.

4. Wave at the Pope. The divine, the devout, and the just plain curious will enjoy a trip to the Vatican and its museums. Schedule your trip to coincide with a Sunday mass, or a papal appearance and get a chance to see the new guy.

5. Shop like an Italian princess. Rome takes its status as capital of fashionable Italy *molto* seriously. The shopping strip that sprouts from the Spanish Steps can hold its own with Paris and Milan, boasting haute couture in condensed but long pedestrian avenues, Via Condotti and Via del Corso. Say *buongiorno* to Gucci, Prada, Furla, Dolce & Gabbana, Versace, and all their friends. The devout shopper will organize her trip around sale season, or *saldi*, in January–February, and then late summer.

6. Hear the pagan call at the Pantheon. Formerly a pagan temple, the Pantheon (Greek for "all gods") is one of the most intriguing buildings in Rome. A giant hole (oculus) in the center of the immense dome leaves the one-room temple open to the elements year-round. The informed visitor can tell time by the placement of the broad beam of sunlight that travels slowly around the interior on a clear day. The first king of Italy lies buried here, as well as his daughter-in-law, Queen Margherita, who is purported to have commissioned the first modern pizza. She championed a pie with tomatoes, mozzarella, and fresh basil to represent the colors of the Italian flag: red, white, and green. Say a word of thanks at the tomb of this woman, the original Pizza Diva.

7. Toss a coin in the Trevi Fountain. Little did you know, the way in which and the quantity of coins you throw in this gorgeous Baroque fountain can have momentous consequences on your fate.

One coin over your right shoulder means you'll be engaged within the next year. Two over your right mean you'll be married. But beware! Two over your left means you'll be divorced in the year. Play it safe: One over your left shoulder (back toward the fountain) means you'll return to Rome someday. This has worked unfailingly for me many times. If you are feeling especially diva-esque, frolic around in the fountain, La Dolce Vita style. Do it fast, though—the guards have met your kind before.

8. Take the train to Florence. Two hours of gorgeous Tuscan scenery is the only price (plus ticket cost, of course) of a lovely train ride north to Florence. This is a city of art, and it's a crime to miss the Uffizi, which holds the genuine masterpieces of Western civilization such as Botticelli's *Birth of Venus* and Michelangelo's *Tondo Doni*. Be sure to reserve tickets ahead of time and skip the endless lines that crawl around the block. (Reservations can be made online at www.virtualuffizi.com/uffizi.) Dinner in the brick-lined Francescano is a must; their squash ravioli is fittingly divine. Reach deeper in your pocket and find Acqua al Due, renowned for their bistecca al mirtillo, or blueberry-topped steak. It's as delicious as it sounds preposterous.

Uffizi, Loggiato degli Uffizi, 6—Florence; tel: +39 055-238-8651-652

Francescano, Largo Bargellini 16, Piazza Santa Croce, Florence; tel: +39 055-241-1605

Acqua al Due, Via dela Vigna Vecchia, 40R; tel: +39 055-28-41-70

9. Voyage to Venice. After a few days in Florence, catch a train to Venice and explore her many canals via foot and by gondola. Meander through the itty-bitty shops that line the narrow canal pathways and treat yourself to something fabulous. Eating out in this charming city is a breeze, but stay away from the fish; it tastes like sewer water. Go to Harry's Bar and order a Bellini and a bowl of pasta. If heaven were on earth, you'd find it in Venice. Harry's Bar, San Marco 1323 Calle Vallaresso; tel: 041 528-5777.

10. Dance and flirt with the locals. If you're up for a big night out of flirting, dancing, and mingling, try one of these hot spots.

Alien is one of the hot spots. The decor is like a set from a science fiction film, and yes, chicks dance on raised platforms. The music is a mix of house, techno, and hip-hop, although one of the two dance areas also features 1970s and 1980s revivals. Via Velletri 13; tel: 06-841-2212.

Piper has been around for decades but reinvents itself regularly and appeals to all tastes, depending on the night. It plays house and underground music on Friday and Saturday. Its gay night "Stomp" is on Saturday and there's live music on Thursday. Via Tagliamento 9; tel: 06-841-4459.

In the Ostiense area near the Basilica di San Paolo Fuori-le-Mura is Goa. It's decked out in ethnic style, with comfy couches to sink into when your feet need a break from the dance floor. The bouncers rule—you might not get in if they don't like the look of you. Tuesday is "Gorgeous Goa Gay" night. On Wednesday, it's "Marrakesh," where Eastern atmosphere meets Western sounds. Via Libetta 13; tel: 06-57-482-77.

Black Out Rock Club in the San Giovanni area is home to punk, rock and indie music, with occasional gigs by British and American punk and rock bands. Via Saturnia 18; tel: 06-704-96-791.

Bush in Testaccio has a reputation for its excellent DJs, especially on Thursday, which is hip-hop, R&B, and soul night. Via Galvani 46; tel: 06-572-88-691.

Appealing to a slightly older, wealthier (and some might say less than cool) clientele is Gilda near Piazza di Spagna, which has plush decor, state-of-the-art lighting, and a huge dance floor. Despite all this, it has a sterile, formal atmosphere—not helped perhaps by the dress code, which requires jackets. Via Mario de' Fiori 97; tel: 06-678-48-38.

Jackie O is a similar joint, with a pricey restaurant tacked on for good measure. Both are good for politician and celebrity spotting. Via Boncompagni 11; tel: 06-42-88-54-57.

ST. MORITZ, SWITZERLAND

Lucia frolicking
in the snow of St. Moritz.

Why This Place Rocks
for Flying Solo

"Darling, I can't join you this holiday season, I'm off to St. Moritz!" Yes, all the iconic images of *savoir vivre* that swirl around your head about this posh resort town are true. With a reputation of catering to the rich and famous, St. Moritz is the mini-Manhattan of Chanel and Armani in a dreamy postcard-perfect lakeside setting. St. Moritz's legacy of welcoming travelers dates to the Middle Ages, when the area's mineral springs lured hearty pilgrims over the mountain passes. Today St. Moritz is almost exclusively a winter vacation destination drawing princes and presidents with its *champagne climate*, which refers to both the average 322 days of sunshine a year, as well as St. Moritz's abundance of bubbly! Kings and queens, Hollywood starlets and the nouveaux riches clamor to be associated with St. Moritz, and the place gladly responds, turning on the dazzle all winter long with an endless round of galas, celebrations, and spectacles centered on the frozen Lej da San Murezzan Lake, including horse racing, polo, and cricket on ice.

St. Moritz is a destination you need to embrace like a genuine jet-setting princess. It's expensive, the landscape is extraordinarily beautiful, the community is first-class, and the champagne is always ready to go. If St. Moritz calls to you, as it does many high-class socialites who enjoy high-altitude networking, then pack your Versace ski suit in your Louis Vuitton and get ready for a week of mixing and mingling with society's finest.

Culture: 1
The buzzword is *couture*, not culture. The only date they care about here is on the wine bottle that is about to be corked in front of a cozy fireplace or in a chic venue.

Activity: 5
St. Moritz is definitely for the wealthy and healthy. This place is brimming with an endless list of activities you can do on the snow and ice. From bunny slopes to threatening double black diamonds, even the most extreme athlete will be challenged. If you suffer from any serious injury, you can still enjoy the legendary *après-ski* cocktail hour at any time of the day.

Weather: 4
St. Moritz gets more winter sunshine than any other Alpine resort. But it is still frosty and cold, so prepare to pack all your cozy, high-style pieces lined in real fur. If you decide to take advantage of their summer festivities, still bring warm clothing; it is nippy all year-round.

Social: 4
You come for the people, the social scene, and the nightlife. It's a place that thrives on seasonal business, so make sure you are here between December and March, or June to October. Other times of the year are dead.

Flying Foreplay

*I*f you just got your mink out of storage and plan on strutting around in St. Moritz between December and March, then you better book everything you want to do before you depart. There are a host of jet-setters also planning to descend on this winter playground, and it's first come, first served—unless you've got loads of cash. **St. Moritz Accessories.** First, pack your

---

Mother Tongue

Rhaeto-Romansch is the native language in St. Moritz. It was recognized on February 20, 1938, as Switzerland's fourth national language.

best "I deserve to be here" attitude, because you can get overwhelmed by all the beautiful people in St. Moritz.

Fur for sure. You won't find many PETA members up here, so pull out that fox, mink, rabbit, chinchilla, lynx, coyote, and/or beaver.

Layers and layers. The 322 days of sunshine mean that the weather is often surprisingly warm, even in the winter (in fact, often most of the snow on the ski slopes is man-made). You should dress in layers for easy removal when it warms up.

Dress for success. Hit the designer shops before you hit the slopes. Pack your prettiest Prada purse and your most daring Dolce & Gabbana dress; this is one place where the name of the game is the label on your lapel.

The Top 10 Extraordinary Experiences

1.   Stroll St. Moritz for the sexiest styles. Not into skiing, how about shopping? On the steep incline of via Maistra, and at the legendary Badrutt's Palace, near the corner of via Serlas, you'll find boutiques for Gianni Versace, Prada, Jil Sander, Bulgari, Hermès, and Louis Vuitton, as well as enough upscale boutiques for Swiss watches and jewelry to outfit a princess. And if it is well-designed sports equipment and sexy ski fashion you want, strut over to Boom Sports, via Tegiatscha; Corviglia Sports, via Maistra 21; and Ender Sport, via Maistra 26.

2.   Relax. You are likely to feel the altitude and alcohol when playing in the Alps. And your head and body (and liver) will be crying out for a reprieve. Enjoy some R&R after all your S&S (shopping and skiing)—find a nice, quiet spa and spend the day in total bliss. Here are a few:

Health Spa Center (Heilbad Centrum), Plazza Paracelcus, next to the Kempinski Grand Hotel; tel: +41 (0)81-833-30-62

MTZ Medical Therapy Center Spa, Plazza Paracelsus 27500 St. Moritz; tel: +41 (0)81-833-30-62

Other telephone contacts for massages and spa services:

Carlton Hotel	+41 (0)81-836-70-00
Crystal Hotel	+41 (0)81-836-26-26
Kulm Hotel	+41 (0)81-836-80-00
Noldapark Hotel	+41 (0)81-833-05-75
Waldhaus am See Hotel	+41 (0)81-836-60-00
Randolins Hotel	+41 (0)81-830-83-83

By the early sixteenth century, the "healing waters" of St. Moritz were so famous for their power that Pope Leo X promised full absolution to any Catholic who bathed in the springs. Amen!

Europa Hotel	+41 (0)81-839-55-55
Christoph Mosimann	+41 (0)81-833-03-30
Gut Training Dorf	+41 (0)81-834-41-41

3. Blast on a bobsled. St. Moritz has the world's only natural ice bobsled run, and you can go for a spin on it. Some of the events that take place here include Swiss and European bobsled world championships. You can watch the races for 5 Swiss francs or tear down it yourself if you ride with an experienced pilot. Make sure to get your picture taken. You'll also get a certificate of completion. Olympic Bobsled Run, via Maistra; tel: +41 (0)81-830-02-00. Make reservations!

4. Try some chocolate. A trip to Switzerland wouldn't be complete without indulging in some famous Swiss chocolate. Located inside the Hauser Hotel is an over-the-top confectionary shop. Between bites of mouthwatering chocolate, watch the master confectioner use the finest Swiss chocolate to create truffles and seasonal specialties. And if you're nice, he might even let you try your hand at covering some delicacies with chocolate. And they even offer free tastings! Heaven.Via Traunter Plazzas 17; tel: +41 (0)81-837-50-50.

5. Take the slow train to the top of the world. Marvel in the stunning beauty of the Alps while riding on the Glacier Express. It's a 7½-hour ride through 91 tunnels, over 291 bridges, at 6,668 feet in the clouds. This Switzerland Scenic Train connects St. Moritz to the other famous Swiss ski resort of Zermatt. Experience this memorable way of traveling from the eastern to the western Swiss Alps. Book this before you go! It sells out during the high season! 877-237-2887; www.raileurope.com.

6. Meet the Matterhorn. St. Moritz could be described as Disneyland for grown-ups, and it would not be complete without a ride on the Matterhorn. If you take the Glacier Express to Zermatt, then ride the Gornergratbahn, you'll cruise along the highest open rail system in Europe. The railway line is only five miles long, and when you reach Gornergrat, you get to visit the observation terraces with stunning views of Matterhorn and Monte Rosa and glaciers. Bundle up! The ride is in an open-air train. Tel: 877-237-2887; www.raileurope.com.

7. Hike to Pontresina. For you die-hard hikers, spend a day hiking to Pontresina. You'll hike past the daunting Olympic ski jump and towering glaciers. You get to experience the splendor of the Alpine Valley and view the peaceful Hahnensee Alpine Lake, then end at charming Pontresina. Plan on walking for a minimum of six hours.

8. Saunter through the Segantini. The museum in St. Moritz was built in 1908 and is dedicated to the painter Giovanni Segantini, who spent the last five years of his life in Engadin (the area around St. Moritz). The building itself is a work of art, and the art collection is breathtaking. It is a great escape from all the socializing you'll be doing. Open Tuesday–Sunday 10 a.m.–noon and 3–6 p.m. Closed Mondays. Via Somplaz 30, St. Moritz; www.segantini-museum.ch.

9. Get educated about Engadin. At the Engadin Museum, you can learn about the old way of life, before this area was all about putting on the ritz. The museum is packed with displays of furniture, tools, and pottery from the past few hundred years. Artifacts from the Bronze Age, when Druids lived in the land, are also on display, including the 3,000-year-old encasement of the spring of Mauritius. It is said that St. Moritz is located on a former "mystic place" of the Druids. Open June–October, weekdays (closed Saturday) 9:30 a.m.–noon and 2–5 p.m. Sunday 10 a.m.–noon; December–April, weekdays (closed Saturday) 10 a.m.–noon and 2–5 p.m., Sunday 10 a.m.–noon. Via dal Bagn 39, St. Moritz, Graubünden; tel: +41 (0)81-833-43-33.

10. Navigate the nightlife. Just when you thought it was safe to go to bed, the pulse of St. Moritz nightlife seizes you! Before you know it, you're out the door, clad in your finest threads, hair coiffed, and ready to dance the night away. Here are a few options for you social bunnies:

Hotel Schweizerhof. You'll find three different bars offering an endless selection of nightlife options that range from the quiet to the boisterous. Via dal Bagn 54; tel: +41 (0)81-837-07-07.

Vivai's Disco. Intimate and always buzzing, this place has a DJ as well as live music depending on the night. Expect to pay an entrance fee, or flirt if there is a man at the door. Hotel Steffani, Somplaz 1; tel: +41 (0)81-836-96-96.

King's Club Disco. Expect to see a few rich and famous lounging about, along with some wannabes. The venue is as beautiful as the people. Badrutt's Palace Hotel; via Serlas 27; tel: +41 (0)81-837-10-00.

ST. PETERSBURG, RUSSIA

Oksana catching a ride
in the Hermitage.

Why This Place Rocks
for Flying Solo

*H*ome of the ornate Fabergé egg, the grand Hermitage, and the iconic White Nights, St. Petersburg is a cosmopolitan jewel dazzling in the midst of a vast northern wilderness. For the solo sister who wants a little depth and substance to her getaway, St. Petersburg will definitely give you that, along with 500 bridges and 150 imperial palaces.

The city was built three hundred years ago by Peter the Great because he wanted a marvelous metropolis that would outshine any European destination. It was his goal to create a place where the Western elite could enjoy the

Watch the Bridges

Between April and November, the 500 drawbridges that connect the city go up at 2 a.m. and come down at 5 a.m., so make sure if you're out partying like a Russian princess, you're on the right side of the river.

beauty and culture of the East. He succeeded in building what is known as the "Venice of the North" and the "Paris of the East." Glorious architecture and unrivaled art galleries line the wide, regal streets of St. Petersburg. And around every corner lies something intriguing to experience. Sometimes it is truly spectacular, but other times it could be an unbecoming remnant of the communist Soviet Union—you never know. Like a mysterious hero in a Russian novel, the city strives to portray a splendid vision of the future while struggling with its tumultuous and somewhat torrid past.

Culture: 5

Much like the finest cities in Europe, St. Petersburg revels in its history and well-kept bounty of art and literature. Empress Catherine the Great, wife of Peter, figured that if she could not live in Italy or France, she would bring the countries' finest works to her not-so-humble abode. She called it the "Hermitage" because it was her private (hermit) retreat, even though this home-shopping diva soon outgrew her chambers with all the masterpieces she acquired, and when I say home-shopping, I mean that she bought whole collections from nobles' homes! Now that the czars are history, you can spend days (it would take you years!) strolling through the Hermitage ogling the fantastic art, regally appointed rooms, and literary collections housed there.

Activity: 1

A Russian once told me that sports were for the bourgeoisie. Now that you know, don't expect to find many leisure sport activities. But with all the vodka drinking and caviar eating you'll be doing, why would you want to work out anyway?

Weather: 3

In the summer the city bursts with life and sunshine—up to 21 hours of it during the summer solstice. Frenzied festivals take over the streets and the population ex-

The Russian Renaissance

Russian ballet made its graceful debut in this fine city, and Tchaikovsky dreamt up *Swan Lake* and *Sleeping Beauty* here.

plodes with foreign partygoers. But please don't confuse sunshine with warmth. You will still need that sweater, and possibly umbrella, well into the summer months. And come winter, you might as well poke your eyes out it's so cold and dark.

Social: 3

Russians won't smile at you on the street, but get them into a bar and the notorious Russian vigor begins to pour out as quickly as home-brewed vodka. You can catch concerts and dance performances, but the interactive social life of St. Petersburg occurs in the many clubs and bars scattered around the city. The best way to get a taste of authentic Russian social life is to befriend a local; the impersonal chill you get from strangers quickly transforms into unbelievable hospitality and warmth. Russians can be some of the most welcoming and gracious hosts in the world, if they trust you. Years under communism made Russians suspicious of outsiders, but once you overcome this stigma, you'll be slapped on the back and handed a shot glass like you're an old family friend.

Flying Foreplay

*T*hose lovely Russians don't make it easy for a foreigner to waltz across their borders.

You'll need a tourist visa for any length of stay, and this is not just a formality. Russian border guards live up to their stern reputation, and no amount of eyelash batting will melt their iron curtain.

Carry your passport. Always carry your documents around with you. It is legal for the police to stop you at any time to check your visa and passport, and no matter how cute your fur stole is, they are allowed to bring you to jail until you can prove you have the right documentation.

Book your bed. Be sure to book accommodations beforehand if you are planning to visit during the White Nights. The normally bustling city overflows with visitors who plan to revel in the celebrations of the midnight sun.

Read Before You Go

The Amber Room: The Fate of the World's Greatest Lost Treasure, by Adrian Levy and Catherine Scott-Clark

Crime and Punishment, by Fyodor Dostoyevsky

Lost Splendor: The Amazing Memoirs of the Man Who Killed Rasputin, by Prince Felix Youssoupoff

Peter the Great, by Robert K. Massie

War and Peace, by Leo Tolstoy

St. Petersburg Accessories

W hen admiring the glorious beauty of this city, it's easy to forget that you need to pack a few extra items that could make or break your trip.

Bite back. Bug spray if you're going in the summer. St. Petersburg used to be a swamp, and these insects haven't gotten the memo that bug bites aren't in this season.

Pack cash. Keep a couple extra rubles in your pocket: The Russian government charges a nominal fee to use your camera and video inside various palaces and museums in St. Petersburg. Also, don't forget to spend every last ruble you exchange in St. Petersburg! The ruble is totally valueless outside the country, so don't expect to change them back for your own currency once home. They will become souvenirs whether you like it or not!

Pills, please. Make sure you have any prescriptions you need. In fact, have a backup supply handy. Certain medicines are difficult to get, so if you think you might need something like motion sickness medicine or your faithful painkiller, better bring it.

Keep it close. Pickpocketing is a reality in St. Petersburg, so make sure to keep your belongings very very very close to your body—if not on your body. Make sure any purse you bring has a very sturdy zipper. Sorry, no gaping Gucci bags here.

Tissue issues. Whether it's for snuffling noses in the cold or toilet paper insurance in the sketchy public toilets, those little packs of tissues will be your best comrade.

The Top 10 Extraordinary Experiences

1. Walk with Peter. I think the *best* way to meet other travelers when going solo is to join walking tours. And in St. Petersburg, Peter is the guy to see. His tours are in English and he offers a pretty impressive selection. Here are just a few to choose from:

- The Original Peter's Walking Tour: Duration 4–5 hours
- Peter's Top Five St. Petersburg Walking Tour: Duration 3 hours
- WWII and the Siege of Leningrad Tour: Duration 5–6 hours
- Peter's Revolution Tour: Duration 4 hours
- Peter's Communist Legacy Tour: Duration 3 hours
- Rasputin Walk: Duration 4 hours
- Dostoyevsky Walk: Duration 3 hours
- Peter's Food Tour: Duration 4 hours
- Peter's Slums Walks: Duration 3 hours
- Dostoyevsky Pub Crawl: Duration 3.5–4.5 hours
- Petrogradsky Pub Crawl: Duration 3.5–4.5 hours
- Lenin's Secret Walk Pub Crawl: Duration 3–4 hours
- Big Night Out Tour: Duration flexible
- Peter's Bike Tour (runs late April through early September): Duration 3.5–4.5 hours

If you see nothing else on your visit, definitely stop inside the mind-blowing and jauntily named Church of Our Savior on Spilled Blood. And make sure Peter takes you to Peterhof! info@peterswalk.com.

2. *Na zdorovje!* It's a toast meaning "to your health," not "get the aspirin ready," though the difference is negligible. So, when you're in the country that invented vodka, you've got to check out the world's only vodka museum. After learning about vodka's infamous past, head to the museum's restaurant called Tractir.

You'll get to sample some yummy Russian dishes prepared according to their official Cook Book published in 1887. This cozy underground restaurant also offers an excellent choice of vodkas. Why not splurge on some sturgeon and salmon caviar with your vodka tasting? Tasting sessions are very popular, so book in advance at reservation@vodkamuseum.ru. 5 Konnogvardeisky bv., St. Petersburg, Russia; tel: 812-312-91-78; www.vodka museum.ru/english.

3. Sweat it out! Drink too much vodka and need some detoxing? Banyas or Russian bathhouses (saunas) are an interesting cultural experience, particularly if you enjoy being beaten by birch branches. Here's a list, but check with your concierge before you book your banya.

Banya-de Luxe na Kryukovskom kanale; Russian banya (English-speaking), 29, Kryukova Kanala nab., Metro Station Baltijskaya; tel: 114-38-57

Banya na Vasiljevskom; Russian banya and sauna (English-speaking), reservation required with Russian cuisine provided upon request, open 24 hours; 20th line of V.I., 9, Metro Station Vasileostrovskaya; tel: 320-54-54

Mytninskie Banya; Russian banya and sauna, public and private rooms; 17/19, Mytninskaya Str., Metro Station Pl. Vostaniya; tel: 271-71-19

NEPTUN, Sport & Banya Center; Euro-style (English-speaking), open from 8 a.m. to noon, reservation required, includes café and room for rest; 93, Obvodnogo kanala nab., Metro Station Pushkinskaya; tel: 324-46-96

Pushkarskie Banya; Russian banya and sauna, private rooms, 200–450 rubles per hour, open 24 hours; 1, Tchajkovskogo Str., Metro Station Chernyshevskaya; tel: 272-39-61

Smolninskie Banya; Euro-style, public and private rooms; 7, Krasnogo Tekstilshika Str., Metro Station Pl. Vostaniya; tel: 110-09-50

Tureckie Parnye; Turkish banya, private room, café included, reservation required, Dekabristov Ul., 34, Metro Station Sennaya; tel: 114-03-89

Usachovskie Banya; Russian banya and sauna, public and private rooms, 12, Makarenko per., Metro Station Sadovaya; tel: 114-34-47

Volna, Sport & Banya Center; Russian banya and sauna, public and private rooms, café included; 221, Obvodnogo Kanala nab., Metro Station Narvskaya; tel: 251-52-08 (public rooms), tel: 251-81-73 (private rooms)

4. See them dance. Traditional Russian dances are a flurry of color and a swirl of sheer athletics. Find a folkloric dance group—for example, the High Lights of St. Petersburg dance troupe, which usually performs in the best dance halls of the city (www.globe-tour.ru/en/entertainments.htm). And of course, do *not* miss the opportunity to see the Bolshoi or Kirov ballet companies perform in their Motherland. See young, gorgeous dancers in positions you never imagined, and then wonder why Carrie let boyfriend Baryshnikov get away!

5. Stroll the Nevsky Prospekt. Nevsky Prospekt is known as St. Petersburg's Fifth Avenue or Champs-Élysées. This is where everyone goes to see and be seen. Spilling over with street vendors by day and a promenade of both who's who and lovers in St. Pete's by night, no trip is complete without pounding your heels down Nevsky.

6. Give yourself the heebie-jeebies. The eerie, tragic story of Rasputin, the mad Siberian monk who was advisor to the royal family, is recreated in the Yusupov Palace. Rasputin was accused of treachery, and as punishment he was first poisoned, then shot, then stabbed, and when that didn't work, he was ultimately shoved into the frozen Neva River, finally succumbing to exposure. A freaky wax-figure tableau recreates the scene. Trust me, it's a guaranteed goose-bumper; if not, you can enjoy the camp factor of the wax museum dedicated to the most eccentric and (almost) indestructible figure in Russian history.

7. Join the ice follies. If you have traveler's insurance and are in St. Petersburg in the winter, you might want to practice your triple jumps and midair splits on one of the many ice-skating venues throughout the city. In the winter, skating is free on most canals, but in the summer you'll have to pay to ice-skate. Here's a list of rinks if you're not up for ice skating on the canals.

Babushkin Park, outdoor rink; Pr. Obukhovskoy Oboroni 149; tel: 715-71-91

Central Park of Culture and Leisure, outdoor rink, admission free; Elagin Island, Building 4; tel: 430-09-11

Ice Palace (Ledovy Dvorets), indoor rink; Pr. Piatiletok 1; tel: 718-66-20

Signs

At the old schoolhouse at Nevsky Prospekt No. 14, there is a blue sign with white letters referring to the siege between 1941 and 1944. It states: *Citizens! This side of the street is the most dangerous during artillery bombardment.*

Ice World (Ledovy Mir), outdoor rink; Pr. Aptekarsky 16; tel: 234-65-42

Khimik Stadium, 24-hour outdoor rink; Rublevskoe shosse 9; tel: 526-76-21

Kirov Stadium, outdoor rink; Yuzhnaya doroga 25; tel: 235-70-15

SKA Sport Palace, indoor rink; Ul. Zhdanovskaya 2; tel: 237-00-73

Spartak, indoor rink; Ul. Butlerova 36; tel: 535-28-55

Tavrichesky Garden, outdoor rink; Ul. Kirochnaya 50; tel: 272-60-44

Victory Park (Moskovsky Park Pobedy), outdoor rink; Ul. Kuzhnetsovskaya, Building 25; tel: 388-32-49

8. Visit Voltaire's library. If you are a fan of the French philosopher Voltaire, then don't bother going to France to see his original masterpieces. They are all at the Hermitage in St. Petersburg, along with other French masters like Matisse, Monet, and more. Besides her love of horses, Catherine the Great loved Voltaire. So, when he died, she bought his whole library of works. Beyond the impressive works of the witty philosopher, you can see over 300,000 original pieces of art and palatial interiors within the grand, marbled halls of the Hermitage. Keep an eye out for the Peacock Clock in the Pavilion Hall—if you time your visit right, you can see the peacock spring to life at 5 p.m. each Wednesday. www.hermitagemuseum.org.

9. Experience White Nights. You saw the movie; now you can experience the odd sensation of being in a bustling city when the sun barely kisses the edge of the tallest building, then rises again. At first, it can be a bit difficult to sleep, but after a few shots of vodka, you will sleep as sound as a *matrioshka* doll. If you love the arts, then visit in May or June and take advantage of the month-long White Nights festival. Spend the

Get Glam in the Former USSR at Versace

The Gianni Versace Haute Couture Boutique is located at 39 Nevsky Prospekt on the grounds of a large park adjacent to the Anichkov Palace. Statues of Roman legionnaires guard the store.

bright evenings attending the opera, ballet, or classical music performances. The festival features Russia's greatest choreographers and composers. And if you are not into the finer cultural acts, that's okay, because the whole city is buzzing with music and dance performances in small theaters, parks, and courtyards.

10. Feast on caviar good enough for a czar. The Grand Hotel Europe, in the heart of St. Petersburg, is considered to be one of the best hotels in the world. They offer some fabulous three- to seven-day packages, as well as a list of impressive guided tours. If you want to really do St. Petersburg like a princess, rest your head here. And don't forget to spend an afternoon in their famous caviar and champagne bar, where you'll dine on the best caviar in the world. If your palate prefers vodka, then you'll be more than impressed with their endless list of vodkas to choose from. Nevsky Prospect, Mikhailovskayas Ulitsa 1/7; St. Petersburg; tel: +7-812-329-6000; www.grandhoteleurope.com.

STOCKHOLM, SWEDEN

Charlotta chatting on Djurgardsbron Bridge.

Why This Place Rocks for Flying Solo

S himmering like a diamond in the dazzling Baltic archipelagos is the city of Stockholm. This crowning jewel of Sweden is ingenuously built on 14 unique islands connected by 57 bridges. Quintessentially Scandinavian,

Stockholm is a divine destination for a solo sister. Rich in culture and absolutely pristine, Stockholm is blessed with some of the most beautiful people in the world.

Undoubtedly one of the most attractive cities in Europe, Stockholm is a magic mix of Viking lore, Swedish hospitality, and unadulterated beauty. Swedes are famous for their remarkably friendly nature, which is just what you need when vacationing alone. Jampacked with museums, incredible boutiques, and the remnants of a proud Viking culture, how could you not love Stockholm?

Stockholm is home of ABBA, IKEA, the smörgåsbord, the Nobel Prize, Absolut Vodka, Swedish massage, Greta Garbo, and Ingrid Bergman. Stockholm is small enough to explore on foot, but big enough for a boatload of Swedish fun. In the summer, days go on forever, with plenty of time to explore the islands in the morning, chill out at an ice bar in the afternoon, and finish the day techno dancing under the midnight sun.

Culture: 4

In one afternoon, you can visit a restored sunken Viking warship (complete with original crew members skeletons) at Vasamusset, then listen to Martin Luther King's 1964 acceptance speech at the Nobel Museum not far away, and step back in time with a stroll down the narrow alleys of Gamla Stan. If you want culture, Stockholm will fill you up.

Activity: 2

If you are a runner, then Stockholm will be dreamy, because during the spring and summer, you can easily jog around the city. In winter you can practice an endless list of sports that have ice and snow involved. But it's freaking freezing in the winter. As for activities during the few warm weather months, Swedes prefer to lounge in the sun like lizards. Think of this vacation as your time to connect with your inner diva and book yourself a Swedish massage.

Weather: 3

The summers in Stockholm are so divine that even the sun doesn't want to miss any of the fun. During summer, the sun never sets, it just kisses the horizon and peaks back up to start another glorious day in Sweden. The sun makes up for all that partying in winter. From November to February, words like *bleak*, *freezing*, *blackouts*, *blizzards*, *dark*, and *harsh* fill the weather reports.

Social: 4

There are more single-person households in Stockholm than in almost all of Europe. What does this mean for your Swedish social experience? As a solo sister, you are sure to find people to party with, whether it's a tango dance partner at La Cucaracha (Bondegatan 2 116 23) or karaoke backup singers at Kicki's Bar & Cafe (Kungsgatan 54 111 35). Get ready to be a serious *värsta brud* (foxy chick).

Flying Foreplay

There are three airports that serve Stockholm: Bromma, Skavsta, and Arlanda. Most likely you will land in Arlanda, which is only thirty miles from town. You can catch a train every 15 minutes from Arlanda to Stockholm; it's easy and the cheapest way to travel. So no need to book a driver or rent a car.

Watch the weather. Stockholm is blessed to have four seasons, but Mother Nature might have other plans. Make sure you check the weather before you depart, so you can pack accordingly.

Speak some Swedish. *Berlitz Swedish Phrase Book* is a great book to have. It lists words as well as important phrases.

Before you go, check out this clever and useful blog: How to Learn Swedish in 1,000 Difficult Lessons (http://francisstrand.blogspot.com). Authored by Francis Strand, an American magazine editor living in Stockholm, the site gives unique cultural tips, personal expat anecdotes, and a long list of Swedish words and phrases. For example:

My true love. *Min stora kärlek.*
I'm better-looking naked. *Jag är snyggare naken.*
And what language do you use in bed? *Och vilket språk använder ni i sängkammaren?*
I've actually become a Swedish citizen. *Jag har faktiskt blivit svensk medborgare.*

Read Before You Go

Stockholm: City of My Dreams, by Per Anders Fogelstrom

Stockholm Accessories

*P*ippi Longstocking knew what was up (her story was written by a Stockholmer). Bring your long underwear in the winter; you'll be glad for the added protection under your clothes. Don't worry, the Swedes make sleek versions for those who don't want an extra layer of bulk.

The Top 10 Extraordinary Experiences

1.   Be an Absolut ice princess. Bring out your inner ice princess and grab a quick shot of Absolut at the ice bar. The Absolut Icebar is the world's first permanent ice bar, and it is in the heart of Stockholm. The interior is kept below freezing all year round. All of the interior fittings, including the glasses, are made of pure, clear ice from the Torne River in northern Sweden. They will supply you with a lovely silver parka to keep you warm between vodka shots. It's not very cozy and you won't find any locals chilling here, but if you've never been into an ice bar before, then you've got to do it. Make sure to get a picture of you downing a shot in a glass made of ice. Nordic Sea Hotel, Vasaplan 7, Box 884, SE-101 37 Stockholm, Sweden; tel: +46 (0) 8-50-56-30-00; www.nordicsea hotel.se.

2.   Have sweet ice dreams. Now, if you really loved your ice shot and want more, then you can take a plane to Jukkasjärvi, which is the home of the ICEHOTEL. Jukkasjärvi is in northern Lapland and about 150 miles above the Arctic Circle. Brrrrrrr.

The direct flight from Stockholm Arlanda to Kiruna Airport is about an hour and a half. SAS has flights daily. Scandinavian Airlines System, SAS;

www.scandinavian.net; Fly Nordic; tel: +46(0)8-52-80-68-20; Hemsida, www.fly nordic.com.

It is a beautiful trip by train, but it takes forever. Traveling time from Stockholm Central Station and Kiruna railway station is estimated at about 16 hours (Rail Connex, www.connex.se). The lovely folks at the ICEHOTEL will meet you either at Kiruna Airport or Kiruna railway station. Make sure to book your transfer in advance, so they know to pick you up. You can also travel by snowmobile from Kiruna Airport and travel like one of James Bond's snow bunnies. ICEHOTEL AB, 981 91 Jukkasjärvi, Sweden; tel: +46 980-66-800 or toll-free within Sweden: 020-29-14-33; www.icehotel.com.

3. Experience museum madness. In a city with more than 70 museums, you'll be begging the Stockholm city council to give you just a few more opening hours. No need to twist their arms; October 1 is Museum Night in Stockholm, where half of the museums remain open way past visiting hours to make sure that you see every last Viking artifact and Nobel Prize memorabilia item on your list. www.museinatt.se.

For a complete list of museums visit www.stockholmtown.com, where you can decide which ones you want to tackle.

4. How Nobel it is. Every year on the anniversary of Alfred Nobel's death, prizes are awarded in his honor and distributed in Stockholm. Take advantage of this opportunity to hear the winners give lectures on their areas of expertise, or get a more detailed perspective at the Nobel Museum. Want a closer look? Go to Stockholm's City Hall, which is not only one of Sweden's most architecturally interesting buildings, but also the site of the annual Nobel Prize Banquet. After the banquet, guests climb the glorious City Hall stairway to dance the night away in the Golden Hall. If you don't manage to win a prize, you'll have to settle for a guided tour, held daily. Tel: +46 8-502-290-58; www2.stockholm .se/cityhall.

5. Go go the archipelago. If you wanted to visit all the 24,000 islands in the Stockholm archipelago, it would take you 65 years if you visited one every day! Here's the lowdown, so you can jet over to the best and skip the rest. The closest destination is the charming archipelago town Vaxholm; you can take a tall ship over for the day. If you like walking, fishing, or taking a winter dip followed by a sauna, you may be tempted by Finnhamn and Möja, which lie a bit farther out. The island Sandhamn is known for its cultural heritage, restaurants, and regattas and has several small hotels. For more details, visit www.stockholmtown.com.

6. Be glam on Gamla Stan. Strolling through the narrow cobblestone alleyways of Gamla Stan (Old Town) is like a magnificent journey into the past. Tall, weather-worn buildings line the streets, and soaring spires tower above you as you wind through walkways built over 700 years ago. Dress up and bring your camera; you'll have to ask passersby to take your glam shot, but it will be worth it! Imagine what your friends will say about your Christmas card picture—ooh la la! Gamla Stan is actually one of the 14 islands that make up Stockholm and it's home to the Royal Castle and Storkyrkan (the big church), Tyska Kyrkan (the German church), and StorTorget (the big square). Check out Mårten Trotzig's Alley; it is a charming and very narrow alley about 35 inches across. Head to StorTorget, where you will find an impressive selection of cozy restaurants and cafés, and during the summer you can grab a seat on a bench and listen to impromptu musicians and street performers. Beware, many places close during July.

7. Sing and drink, drink and be seen.
The Opera House was originally built in 1787, and the Operakällaren restaurant opened its doors at the same time. Since then, it has been *the* place in Stockholm to see and be seen. This is a venue gilded with gorgeous socialites who parade through the bar like fashion models. You are sure to meet a few international jet-setters who enjoy an après-opera cocktail or a sparkling glass of champagne. The bar is the place to be, and you can order from a small menu. If you want the full-on dining experience, make reservations at the restaurant. There you will be treated to a gastronomic extravaganza by some of the best chefs in Sweden. Operakällaren and Opera Bar, Karl XII Torg; www.opera kallaren.se. The Royal Opera; for a current program, check www.operan.se or www.ticnet.se.

8. Stroll Skansen.
Skansen is a great place to spend an easy day of wandering and learning about Sweden's rich past. The park is the oldest open-air museum in the world, and it even has a zoo with Scandinavian wildlife you won't meet in the local bars. You will also find an interesting re-created village of edifices dating back from the eighteenth and nineteenth centuries. It is located on the island of Djurgården, a royal park near the center of Stockholm. Sounds a bit corny, but it is an endearing look at old-time Sweden. If you are crazy enough to visit Stockholm in the winter, Skansen is also the site of one of Stockholm's best Christmas markets held on the three Sundays before Christmas. You can enjoy Swedish treats including *lussebullar* (saffron buns) and *glögg* (hot wine drink). www.skansen.se; e-mail: info@skansen.se.

9. Hop on and cruise away.
You've got to love a city that offers a Hop-on Hop-off sightseeing tour on a thirties-style open wooden boat. It makes touring a city in a bus seem oh so tawdry. The darling boat stops at Slottet (Royal Palace), Nybroviken, Vasamuseet, Gröna Lund, and Slussen/Gamla piers. You can get on and off at your leisure.

The tour starts June 4 and runs throughout the summer. One of the bonuses is that the tickets are valid for 24 hours. www.stockholmsightseeing.se.

10. Volley with the Swedes.
Stockholm in the summer is a haven for buffed

bumpers and setters just waiting for a traveling chick with a wicked serve. It is common to just go up to a group (preferably a team of drop-dead gorgeous blond Swedish men) and ask if you can join in the fun. This is a great way to meet a new set of friends, get some exercise, and enjoy a bit of sun. Don't be surprised if they take quenching shots of vodka between sets—it takes the competitive edge off. Nets are set up throughout the city in parks and on beaches, but you can find permanent courts at these two sites:

Rålambshovsparken Smeduddsvägen, 112 35 Stockholm; tel: +46 8-618-62-91

Kampementsbadet Sandhamnsgatan, 115 40 Stcokholm; tel: +46 8-661-62-16

TURIN, ITALY

Heidi savoring her solo moments
the Italian way.

Why This Place Rocks
for Flying Solo

Once upon a time, there was a stunning kingdom tucked away between the dramatic Swiss Alps and the glamorous Mediterranean seaside. In the second century, this piece of rural heaven was named Turino by the Emperor Augustus, and today it's known as Turin, Italy. For centuries, the locals have taken pleasure in Turin's impeccable beauty, torrid history, divine wines, and delicious cuisine, and now it's your chance to indulge in its richness—one delectable experience at a time.

Off the beaten path and not listed in

Vermouth 1786

The liquor shop below the Porticoes of Piazza della Fiera (now Piazza Castello) on the corner with Via della Palma (now Via Viotti) had an apprentice named Antonio Benedetto Carpano from Bioglio Biellese. He loved the extrafine qualities of moscato wine, and decided to create an aromatic wine by adding spices and herbs according to the dictates of the monks of his native valley. This was how vermouth was born.

most guidebooks as a "must-see" (although it should be!), Turin is a sophisticated region that offers all the delights that a solo jet-setter seeks out—from shopping to spa-ing, eating and drinking. Whatever you love to do, you can find it in this itsy-bitsy region of Italy. Less than an hour from Milan, it's the fashion capitol of Prada, Armani, Tod's, Fendi Gucci, and Mui Mui, to name a few. And around an hour from the *azul* waters of the Mediterranean, it's the home of some of my favorite things: Nutella, Vermouth, white truffles, and Fiat sports cars!

If you enjoy getting lost in a culture without the onslaught of tourists and peddlers, then seriously consider Turin as the next spot on your holiday calendar. Settle into the local pace, experience a truly quintessential Italian city, and explore some of the most beautiful landscapes in Europe. Turin is your launching pad into the Alps, the Mediterranean, Milan, and the wonderful Piedmont region. To fully enjoy this adventure, plan on taking day trips outside Turin.

Culture: 5

If you think you've heard of Turin before but can't place it, I'll give you a hint: Remember the Shroud of Turin, the supposed burial cloth of Jesus Christ? This single most studied artifact still resides in the city, along with some impressive collections of art and stolen artifacts from Egypt—dating back two thousand years. Strolling through Turin is a history lesson in itself with its renaissance architecture, ancient piazzas, and long, theatrical archways.

Activity: 3

Turin's geared more for those who want to watch sports than play them, but seek and ye shall find. There are golf courses, tennis courts, swimming pools, and in winter, ski slopes. A great way to see the city is to cruise via bicycle along the 50 miles of cycle paths that flank the Po River.

Weather: 2

It might be close to the Mediterranean sunshine, but not close enough to bask in the warmth of the region. Bring a jacket no matter what time of year you visit. The hottest months are July and August, which can heat up to a nice 80 degrees, and the chilliest are December and January, when temperatures hover around freezing. High season is autumn because of the wine and truffle festivals throughout the Piedmont region.

Social: 2

It's often said that Turin is the most French city in Italy or the most Italian city in France. While Turin lacks much of the enveloping warmth (social and climate-based) of southern Italy, it's still worth a visit just to sample the wonderful food and glorious landscape that surrounds Turin. Some people, including other Italians, find the residents of Turin snobbish, unfriendly, and somewhat distant. So don't expect your typical Roman love fest here.

Flying Foreplay

Check the weather. It may be quite tempting to bring that wispy summer dress you've always pictured yourself jetting around Italy in, but Turin gets snow in the winter and you'll be one chilly chick if you don't pack appropriately.

Read Before You Go

Among Women Only, by Cesare Pavese
For Solo Violin: A Jewish Childhood in Fascist Italy, by Aldo Zargani
Nietzsche in Turin: An Intimate Biography, by Lesley Chamberlain
Shroud, by John Banville

Turin Accessories

Instant Italiano. Turin is less tourist-oriented than many Italian cities, and many of the locals do not speak much English. So bring that pocket dictionary or electronic dictionary when you visit.

Appropriate apparel. Just like anywhere in Italy, pack some nice clothes unless you want to stick out as a foreigner. Italians really do dress well, even when they are wearing casual clothes.

For You Chocolate Lovers

Visit Peyrano-Pfatish and Gobino, the two most famous chocolatiers in town. One of the city's icons is the Gianduiotti chocolate, a mixture of Tonda Gentile delle Langhe hazelnuts and cocoa. These two ingredients were combined during Carnival season and you might recognize the flavor as Nutella.

The Top 10 Extraordinary Experiences

1. **Hunt for treasure.** In the rest of the world, it's called "junk," but when you find it in Italy, it's called "a rare treasure!" You can find an endless inventory of "treasures" in the many stalls of the bohemian flea market called Mercato del Balon, held every Saturday at Piazza della Repubblica. For truly magnificent Italian antiques and artwork, visit the Gran Balon, which is held at Porta Palazzo the second Sunday of every month. If you're looking for some fun, cheap clothes, check out Mercato della Crocetta, at Largo Cassini. At Porta Palazzo, Europe's largest open-air market, wander through the stall of fresh produce and food from the famous Piedmont region. This market is open Monday through Saturday from 6:30 a.m. to 1:30 p.m. and Saturday from 3:30 to 7:30 p.m.

2. **Pursue Piedmont.** Piedmont's iconic epicurean pleasures can be at the tip of your tastebuds in Turin. One of the most famous darlings from this region includes the elusive white truffle from Alba, also called *countryside caviar*, which costs about $10 per gram, almost the same as gold.

   Other regional specialties include *agnolotti* (ravioli-like pasta filled with beef or lamb), *bollito misto* (a variety of boiled meats), and *gianduiotto*, a luscious blend of chocolate and hazelnuts (think Nutella). To find local treats, try Platti for desserts, Pfatish for unreal chocolates, and Porto di Savona for an intimate, traditional dinner.

   Platti, Corso Vittorio Emanuele II, 72—Via Nizza, 280 10128—Crocetta; Open Monday–Sunday 7:30 a.m.–1 a.m.

   Pfatish, Via Sacchi, 42; tel: 011-56-83-96-2

   Porto di Savona, Piazza Vittorio Veneto, 2—10123—Centre; Open Wednesday–Sunday 12:30–2:30 p.m., Tuesday 7–11 p.m.

3. **Party like Dante.** The Divina Commedia is a fiery pub with three floors: Inferno, Purgatory, and Paradise. Set the scene with a bit of devilish behavior and pick the level of your divine judgment. Via San Donato, 47—Via Livorno, 60 10144—Campidoglio; Monday–Sunday 7:30 p.m.–2:30 a.m.
   Other noteworthy venues:
   Beach. A beautiful space on the edge of the river that draws a younger crowd; www.thebeachtorino.it
   Giancarlo. A bar south of the bridge that attracts Turin's alternative crowd. Things are generally at their liveliest from 11 p.m. to 2 a.m.
   Hennessey. One of the most popular discos and trendiest venues; Strada al

traforo di Pino, 23; tel: +39-01-18-99-87-33

4. Check out the Museo Nazionale del Cinema.
A visit to Turin's most popular museum is a must. The museum itself is architecturally stunning and located in the Mole Antonelliana, a towering nineteenth-century landmark. Take a mesmerizing multimedia tour of Italian cinematic history, which was founded in Turin! Many popular film genres—for example, love, war, history, and Italy—are illustrated with original movie clips. If the line is not too long, be sure to ride the elevator to the roof, where you'll be treated to a gorgeous view of the city. Museo Nazionale del Cinema, Via Montebello 20, just east of the Giardino Reale; tel: 011-812-56-58 (info); hours: Tuesday–Friday and Sunday 9 a.m.–8 p.m., Saturday 9 a.m.–11 p.m.; www.museonazionaledelcinema.org.

5. Savor Savigliano.
Imagine strolling through serpentine paths lined with baroque palaces and medieval treasures, feasting on Italian food and drinking local wine. You can do this all through Italy, but one of the most charming, picturesque places to enjoy "all things old-world Italian" is in the beautiful town of Savigliano. Its town center is the gorgeous square of the Piazza Santa Rosa, surrounded by shops, protected by a medieval tower, and ornamented with scores of grand palaces. Just 33 miles south of Turin, you can spend the day in this Italian paradise. It's an easy trip because of the two to four trains per hour that can whisk you to a piece of heaven.

6. Ski like an Olympian.
If you visit in winter or spring, then head up to the largest ski areas in Italy called the Milky Way or Via Lattea in Italian. There, you get to slice through more than 350 miles of snow-covered runs equipped with ultramodern lifts (thanks to the Olympics in 2006). Luckily, you don't have to be a gold medal skier to enjoy the slopes; sometimes it's more about the way you look than how fast you can ski. So make sure to pack that Gucci ski suit, and Bvlgari sunglasses for those après-ski socials. www.vialattea.it and www.montagnedoc.it.

7. Judge for yourself.
Go to the Cathedral of San Giovanni and see (they claim) the Holy Shroud—possibly the most well-known and controversial relic associated with Jesus. Unfortunately, you can't see the real shroud for another 20 years or so, because of its frail state (or because the Vatican wants to keep the myth alive). But you can see the copy that's on view in front of the main altar. Piazza San Giovanni.

8. Visit the royal digs.
No great European city is complete without a palace or two, and that's true for Turin. The palace Veraria Reale is Turin's crown jewels of royal residences. A seventeenth-century marvel that France's Louis XIV copied when he built Versailles a year later, it includes a main palace, parks, stables, an equestrian center, and a hotel. Take the train or bus. It's about three miles northwest of town. Piazza della Repubblica 4; Tuesday, Thursday, Friday without appointment; Monday, Wednesday, Friday with appointment; tel: 39-11/459-3675.

9. Eat, drink, and tram it.
Clatter along old town Turin in a tram from the thirties while sipping cocktails and listening to soothing saxophone tunes. Choose from

The Bus

Take the hop-on/hop-off Turismo Bus Torino, which offers a running narration as it shuttles between more than a dozen stops around town. Once you've gotten your bearings, you can jet around easily like a local.

two different tours: enjoy the hour-long cocktail party tour, or go for the dinner tour. Both are fabulous for meeting fellow travelers and a few locals who can give you tips on Turin. www.somewhere .it/eng.

10. Go down. Beneath the hectic and bustling city of Turin lies a mysterious and unknown world where time stands still. Tunnels of the citadel and the subcellars of the baroque palaces can be explored on this thrilling tour, which takes you into an air-raid shelter and the royal ice depots of Porta Palazzo. Piazza Vittorio; Wednesday and Friday, 9:30 p.m.; www.somewhere .it/eng.

VIENNA, AUSTRIA

Victoria shopping at Naschmarkt in Vienna.

Why This Place Rocks for Flying Solo

*I*f you ever wanted to be a member of the von Trapp family, twirling on mountaintops in a frilly dress, then Vienna is a great place to live out your fantasy. And if you want to find your own gorgeous Captain von Trapp in one of the many chic nightclubs or bars, then Vienna will provide you with plenty of delicious entertainment. While this charming city is still home to the Vienna Boys Choir and Mozart memorabilia, they're not why the young Euro-hipsters flock to this place. We're talking Vienna boys at the bar and more art than you can handle in a week. This place has gone from high society to

The Perfect Princess

Elisabeth, or "Sisi," one of the last Hapsburg empresses, was the supermodel heiress of the nineteenth century. The girl had hair past her hips and loved writing poetry. Filled with wanderlust and bored with the Austrian countryside, she frequently traversed the empire, namely the Greek islands and the Adriatic coast. Besides her penchant for wandering, she enjoyed traveling under false names. Like a true woman of the world, she came back from one of her many sea voyages with an anchor tattooed on her shoulder. (At least it was not the name of some Greek guy she rendezvoused with in Mykonos.)

high-end scene. Because of its central location—right in the center of Europe (some say the world)—this destination is teeming with Europhiles who are all about enjoying Vienna's decadence. And if you still want to experience old Vienna, you'll be delighted by this town's meticulous preservation of the past. Still, it doesn't hurt that the guys are hot.

Culture: 5

Girls, the only place you'll find more culture is in a cheese factory! From odes to Mozart to opulent museums bursting with priceless artwork and chandeliers, you fine-art junkies will get your fix. Just strolling the streets of Vienna is an art history lesson. You can't turn a corner without encountering some amazing historical site or tribute. Even the city's modern art is steeped in tradition. And for you music lovers, Vienna will woo you with her many nights of musical serenades for the public.

Activity: 3

Carbo-loading is the main activity here. I'm talking about marathon café-sitting,

endurance wine-tasting, and schnitzel-eating sprints. If you need to burn off that apple strudel, then the Prater—a lovely, flat, 5-kilometer park just north of the city—is the place to be. And for you die-hard hikers and skiers, the nearby slopes of Salzburg and Innsbruck await you.

Weather: 3

Let's just say that you're going to Vienna for the lavish architecture and captivating art and music. You can leave your tank tops at home, along with your bikini. Do bring your camera to capture the gorgeous landscape, mesmerizing buildings, and intricate gardens. What Vienna lacks in tepid weather it makes up for in sheer beauty.

Social: 4

The social citizens of Vienna care more about the local scene than the temperature. With cafés scattered throughout the city and a vibrant nightlife and music scene, it would be impossible for you not to find something to do in this enchanting community. Although English is not the mother tongue, you're sure to find some Austrians who speak the Queen's English.

Flying Foreplay

Pre-Opera. Book your opera tickets to the Staatsoper (Vienna State Opera) before you leave for your trip. If opera is your scene, you know that Vienna is the Mecca of opera, and this venue is the Taj Mahal of opera houses.

Run away. Unless you are coming in for the Vienna City Marathon or the Danube Island Festival, you might want to avoid those very popular dates in May and June. The charming city turns into a circus, and you might miss the legendary quaint beauty this place is known for.

Weather check. Check the weather. If you don't own a fur coat and don't care much for snow, then you might want to visit in the spring or summer. Autumn can be a beautiful time to watch the colors change, but you might get rain and a few light snowfalls. And if you want to capture that perfect iconic scene for your holiday card, then winter is the time to come.

Vienna Accessories

Stay wise. Pick up a Streetwise map of Vienna. The map covers the most important areas, from Gürtel LandStrasse to Schottenring. It helps you find the usual suspects, like museums and parks, and comes with a handy-dandy mass-transit map. Lucky for you, it's laminated for those crazy nights outs, and easily fits into your Chanel or Prada bag.

Get wet. Bring that umbrella. Mother Nature enjoys showering her love on Vienna. Even if you plan on jetting over in the summer, come prepared for a bit of rain.

Shoe sense. Unless you're attending one of the many over-the-top fêtes during ball season, you might want to think about packing comfy—yet sexy—walking shoes in lieu of those four-inch, rhinestone-studded Manola Blahniks. Unfair, I know, but between the cobblestone streets and beautiful parks, you won't need them, darling. But *don't* take this suggestion as an excuse to bring your sneakers—the locals are incredibly stylish and appreciate those who also present themselves well.

Fabulous Flirting

Bermuda Triangle and the Spittelberg Quarter. This strip of tiny, winding alleys got its name from the mysterious triangle in the Atlantic, where ships and airplanes disappear without a trace. You, too, can disappear for a while in one of the many nightclubs and late-night cafés.

Try a "Beisl Tour" or "Pub Crawl." Check out Spittelberg, the revitalized Biedermeier quarter. You'll find plenty of hip haunts surrounding the Amerlinghaus event center. Spittelberg is always in season: in winter, inhale the tempting aroma of hot punch and stroll the Christmas market for traditional Austrian gifts. In summer, the place comes alive with cafés that bloom like the flowers decorating the city.

Pretend you're twenty. For you girls who like chilling with the younger crowd, head to the districts of Josefstadt (8th district) and Neubau (7th district). Night spots like the Blue Box, Pulse, Café Jenseits, ¡más!, and Miles Smiles line up like the von Trapp children.

For those who just can't let go of the sixties . . . Near the University and the Naschmarkt area you'll find beatnik bars harkening back to the student revolts of the 1960s. Lounge around and listen to the music of Hendrix, Dylan, and the Stones.

Spring over to Copa Cagrana. On the Danube's shoreline, near the Reichsbrücke bridge, you'll find an enclave of bars, restaurants, cafés, and beach discos between May and September only.

Danube Island Festival. More than two million music lovers flock to the Danube Island for Europe's biggest 72-hour dance party. Admission is free, and there are more than 20 stages on 19 different islands in the Danube with music from around the world.

Muse about at the music and film festivals. In the summer, City Hall morphs into an entertainment extravaganza, with big-screen showings of concerts and opera performances. Fortify yourself with snacks from one of the many food booths nearby.

The Top 10 Extraordinary Experiences

1.   **Sip away.** Sip a local wine at one of the local *Heurigen* (wine taverns) in the Viennese wine country on a warm summer night. Vienna is the only capital city that grows its own wine, and these small, typically family-run *Heurigen* serve traditional Austrian food to complement their varietals.

2.   **See the opera.** The magnificent performances at the Staatsoper *always* sell out, so buy tickets at least a month ahead of time. If you're just breezing through, standing room tickets can be bought the night of the performance for a couple of euros. The shows can be experimental and edgy as well as classical, and the best opera singers in the world are drawn to Vienna. Everyone dresses to the nines . . . don't be the American tourist in jeans!

3.   **Stroll the gardens of Schönbrunn.** This summer estate of the Hapsburgs contains acres of well-manicured gardens and shrubbery, preserved almost entirely in their original layout. This is where the royalty came for their clandestine

rendezvous, smooching in the labyrinthine pathways and garden nooks. Arrange your own empress-like tryst—or simply enjoy the leafy promenades and spurting fountains.

4. Take a day trip to Salzburg. The train will take you straight to the tiny town that gave birth to Mozart and *The Sound of Music*. A hearty walk up to the fortress that overlooks the city provides stunning views, as well as access to the same mountain meadows Maria danced around in! Wear a skirt and wide-brimmed hat—this will give a great effect when you're twirling around hollering about the hills alive with the sound of music. Get back before sunset—the nightlife was probably at its prime when Mozart was pounding the keys.

5. Catch a movie at the Rathausplatz. Films of musical and dance performances are projected on a huge screen on the neo-Gothic City Hall all throughout the summer. The square in front of City Hall is lined with stands representing Vienna's finest restaurants and almost every type of national cuisine. These are no hot dog stands—delicious salmon and wok vegetables can be found alongside grilled tofu over sun-dried tomato faro salad. More people come for the food, drinks, and bustling scene than to watch the operas projected on the imperious building behind them, but it provides an appropriate background for this thriving Vienna social scene.

6. Explore the new MuseumsQuartier. Converted from the imperial stables, the MuseumsQuartier is a newly installed grouping of three fabulous museums: the Leopold, the Museum of Modern Art, and the Architectural Centre Vienna. The inner courtyard is filled with toothpaste-pink benches and a handful of cafés, perfect for relaxing after museum fatigue sets in. Performances, organized and impromptu, are held in this inner courtyard, ranging from jazz festivals to juggling to fire throwing.

7. People-watch in Stadtpark under a linden tree. The city park of Vienna is small and vibrantly green, carpeted with colorful flowers in intricate patterns. Johann Strauss held his rollicking waltzes in the gilded building at the foot of the park, and a golden statue of him stands perpetually ready to start playing on his shining violin. Buy a hunk of fresh bread at the local bakery (Anker and Ströck are just down the street) and a slab of cheese, park yourself in the soft shade of a willowy tree, and people-watch to your heart's content.

8. Interpret your dreams as you walk the Ringstrasse. Freud did it every day to clear his head; it could do wonders for you, too. Emperor Franz Josef replaced the fortress wall that surrounded the old city center with this tree-lined street in the late nineteenth century. Its circuit brings you by the blue Danube, the Kunsthistorisches Museum, the Natural History Museum, and the sprawling Volksgarten with its gorgeous Butterfly House. There are plenty of tiny cafés and wine bars where you can stop and refresh yourself as you make the walk around. It'll take about an hour to walk it; it may take longer to mine your subconscious.

9. Drink coffee under an assumed identity at Café Central. The elegant café is still decorated as it was when the best of Viennese minds would come here to debate the pressing issues of their time. Order a *mélange* (basically a latte) and enjoy live music, well-uniformed and attentive waiters, and the gaudy decor. People might mistake you for an orphaned heiress soul-searching over a warm drink, or a comely vagabond plotting her next scam. Sample the large variety of pastries and cakes, but beware the *Kaisermelange*, a black coffee drink mixed with cognac and egg yolk. Some delicacies are best left to locals.

10. Dance till you're dizzy at a ball. The height of the Viennese ball (or *Fasching*) season is between Christmas and Lent, and the city's largest venues transform into elaborate fantasy settings for the themed dances. The most elegant ball is held at the Hofburg Palace, but the Opera House puts on an especially stunning event, extending the performance stage to cover the entire theater and coating everything in fresh flowers. The parties are known to last well into the wee hours—plenty of time to fill your dance card with tuxedoed waltzers.

BALI, INDONESIA

Lucienne embraces the beauty
at Hotel Tugu.

Why This Place Rocks
for Flying Solo

C lose your eyes and imagine a
dreamy destination with sea salt
kisses and nutmeg embraces. A
place where temples rise to the sky and
monkeys scamper to come greet you.
Picture a place far enough away from
your real life that you finally feel you are
on vacation. Take a deep breath and get
ready to go to Bali, Indonesia. The island of Bali is a single shimmering star
in the Asia archipelago that consists of
over 16,000 islands. Bali is not the
biggest island—it's only 90 miles from
east to west—but it is definitely the
brightest when it comes to being a fabulous place for solo sisters. Its tiny size

Lovin' Lovina

This renowned beach is located about 60 miles north of Kuta Beach. It's famous for its early-morning dolphin-watching boat trips.

means you can hike an active volcano, lounge on a black sand beach, trek through a luscious rain forest, and be back at the hotel for lychee martinis by sunset.

Long established as a magnet for international travelers, Bali has a plentiful supply of lodging and tour groups, enough for the solo girl on the move to be picky about where she stays and what she sees. From five-star accommodations at resorts like the Ritz and Four Seasons, to secluded huts in the jungle, you are sure to find that special place for you. And oh, what you'll see! The natural setting alone is enough to enjoy for a lifetime—sinuous banyan trees dripping with strands of pink bougainvillea; sacred temples carved from black coral rising out of mangrove forests and decorated with fiery hibiscus; heavy white magnolias competing with blooming wild jasmine for bright sunlight. Transparent water that beckons you to dive right in and elusive rainbows that dance from waterfall to waterfall. Tuck an orchid behind your ear and inhale the beauty of Bali.

Culture: 4

The Balinese practice an interesting religion called Agama Hindu Dharma. It is an exotic blend of Hindu, Buddhist, Javanese, and indigenous beliefs. And everywhere you turn, you'll encounter this gentle way of life. Bali's dance, its

music, and its *wayang* theaters are marbled with religion and folklore. You don't need to find a museum to learn about Bali's culture; just walking down the street is a colorful interpretation of Bali's deep spiritual connection and affection for nature.

Activity: 4

Bali is an island, which means the best activities you'll find here are mostly water-oriented. You can ocean raft, surf, dive, and snorkel your heart out, or at least until it's time to refill your cocktail. Whatever you do, get underwater at some point. Otherwise you will miss the marine Technicolor dream of reef fish, pastel coral, and moray eels. Once you are sufficiently waterlogged, you can stay grounded and enjoy hiking up and paragliding down an active volcano, bungee jumping, golfing, or biking.

Weather: 5

There are two seasons in Bali, dry and hot (April–September), and rainy (October–March). Any time you go it will be nice and toasty. But if you plan on scaling a volcano, make sure you pack a light parka because it tends to be cool up there.

Social: 4

Bali is not a large island, but your social options run a full spectrum. Thrill-seeking party girls should head to

Keep your ears tuned to the word on the street. Full-moon beach parties and body-painting parties are advertised only by flyers and through word of mouth. Expect the nightlife to get going around midnight. Clubs and bars won't start filling up until after the clock strikes twelve.

the Kuta area, where you can find lots of Australians as well as clubs such as the Peanuts Disco, Mama's, Bounty Ship, and the Poco Loco. If those names don't give you a sense of the scene, suffice to say it can be like Spring Break uncensored. A girl traveling alone is guaranteed to find some party pals in Kuta Beach, if she's prepared for a little noise and debauchery. For those seeking a more peaceful getaway, go inland to Ubud, which is known to be more laid back. While still fairly populated, the emphasis here is on batiks and cafés instead of short skirts and shooters. To go farther off the beaten path, traveling around the southern coast will provide more immersion.

Flying Foreplay

While we associate New Year's with fireworks and celebratory shouts, the Balinese start their year in silence. Nyepi Day, the Balinese day of silence, marks the New Year, and the island goes quiet with reverence and meditation. Hotels are exempt from Nyepi's demand for silence, but most public streets and beaches are closed off. Check which day Nyepi falls on before planning your trip—if you find yourself there on the day of silence, stay inside and join the island in a thoughtful and peaceful time.

Passport, please. With all the jet-setting you do, keeping track of your passport's date of expiration is not something you think about as much as shoe shopping. But in Bali they require that your passport is valid for the six months after your arrival. If not, they won't let you into the country.

Lights, camera, action! Be forewarned that you will need to declare your cameras, videos, computers (you should be leaving them at home anyway!), and any other expensive electrical devices you bring to Bali. They want to make sure you take them out as well, so expect to be questioned at customs in both directions.

Big buys. Bali is famous for its fantastic furniture buys. And if you think there is a slight chance you are going to buy furniture while vacationing (now that's what I call multitasking!), measure your space and get a good sense of what will work in your home. The last thing you want is to get overwhelmed by all the choices and pick something that ends up not fitting through your tiny doorway, or next to your fabulous new bed.

Read Before You Go

Eat, Pray, Love, by Elizabeth Gilbert
Island of Bali, by Miguel Covarrubias
A Little Bit One O'clock, by William Ingram

Bali Accessories

You can buy most of what you need there and for a fraction of the price at your local mall. Leave room in that suitcase for some beautiful *batiks* for your mom, shiny silver bracelets for your sister, and corny coconut-shell souvenirs for your boss.

Wrap it. Hands down, the best thing to pack is a sarong. Not only will this allow you to enter temples in respectful garb, but also in a pinch it can function as a towel, a shawl, a bathrobe, a skirt, or even a bag. It is the essential multipurpose item for a Bali adventure. And if you don't own one, you can buy one there!

Cover it. Even though temperatures can get superhot, it's not supercool to dress skimpy on the island. Some locals might even consider it offensive. Where do you think you are—Ibiza? Be sensitive and cover that hot bod with some breathable, cool cotton clothing.

Fan it. A folding fan in your purse is great portable air-conditioning. Sure, you could use a random piece of paper, but try to think: What would Audrey Hepburn do?

Top it. The sun shines bright in Bali: bring a hat (or buy one there) and avoid those nasty squinting lines. I don't need to mention sunscreen, right?

The Top 10 Extraordinary Experiences

1. **Let your inner goddess glow.** Always wanted to learn how to surf, but were too embarrassed to try hanging ten

around buff, tan surfer dudes? Well, now you can let loose at Surf Goddess Retreats! Yup, it's a women-only surf camp. Here the activities are endless: you can learn how to surf, go on a *surfari*, practice yoga, and end your days with a relaxing massage. Heaven on earth. Lovingly referred to as the Surf Goddess Sanctuary, the camp is located in a secluded Balinese village surrounded by rice paddies and the ocean, a world away from the island's tourist hub. About 80 percent of the women on the retreats are solo travelers and new to surfing. A typical day includes Goddess Brunches, Goddess Surfs, Goddess Bliss Outs, and ends with, you guessed it, Goddess Dinner. Amen! www.surfgod dessretreats.com.

2. Boogie Balinese-style. The traditional dances of Bali are a sinewy, sensual combination of bhangra and hula, creating a hypnotizing and graceful display of Indonesian culture. As soon as you see the elegant dancers, bedecked in the traditional colorful sarongs, headdresses, and sashes, you will be wishing you could be wearing one of those silky, multihued sensations. The easiest way to do this is through Balinese dancing lessons offered at a few resorts and hotels, including the Matahari Beach Resort. For those willing to delve a little deeper into the nuances of Balinese dance, contact the Yayasan PolosSeni (Foundation for Pure Art) near Ubud, where you can schedule serious dance classes. This isn't your typical slow, slow, quick, quick, slow.

3. Head for the hills. Though Bali is known internationally for its beaches, you might remember it for its sacred mountains. Explore Bali's highest peak at Mount Agung, which Balinese folklore believes is the center of the world. In fact, all the temples on the island point toward this mountain. Mount Batur is more accessible, and has a water-filled crater (Lake Batur) that you can splash and swim in or hike around. Don't be surprised if you see steam rising from the craters of Mount Batur: it is an active volcano you're playing on, darling. You might even catch a group of Balinese in religious procession to make peace offerings to the mountain. They keep their spiritual fingers crossed that the beautiful giant won't erupt again anytime soon.

4. Learn Balinese cooking. Expert chef Heinz von Holzen, who earned his culinary stars at the Bali Ritz Carlton, takes you on a fun and eye-opening journey to the local vegetable and fish market, where you'll gather fresh ingredients before heading to his restaurant, Bumbu Bali. Then the chopping begins as he guides you through your cooking lesson. By the end of the day, you'll have an impressive list of Balinese recipes to add to your cuisine repertoire. Balinese favorites include Ayam Pelalah (shredded chicken with chilies and lime), Pesan be Pasih (grilled fish in banana leaf), and Be Sampi Mebase Bali (braised beef in coconut milk). Are you hungry yet? www.baliguide.com/balicooking.

5. Engage in some international negotiation. You'll notice that not many items in Bali have a fixed price tag on them—this is because the cost adjusts depending on who is asking. It is standard and expected to haggle a bit for your purchases, and a good rule of thumb is to offer a third of the original quoted price and work your way up. Try out your bargaining skills in the Kumbasari market in the capital of Bali, Denpasar. The able negotiator can get everything from artifacts and textiles to fruits and vegetables at a great price. This is the perfect training ground to improve your assertiveness skills, as well as pick up a few handsome souvenirs. You should also leave your Louis V. handbag at home—the more bling you've got, the higher the price. Dress casual and low-key for the best bargaining power.

6. Buy a silver lining. Every girl should accessorize her ho-hum wardrobe with original pieces she buys while holidaying overseas. And when it comes to impressive silver, the Balinese have got it down to a fine art. The best place to score great pieces is in the southern village of Celuk, where the villagers have developed a serious silver and gold niche. In fact, almost every house in Celuk has a small silver-and-gold-working studio. You'll find many galleries and studios with shining collections of local work, as well as jewelry makers happy to create pieces to your liking. This is your chance to have your dream piece made—go for it!

7. Watch artistic elephants at work. Darling, Van Gogh was so last century; it's all about animal art this year! And if

Silver and Gold

Balinese cultural traditions come to life in the jewelry—silver snake bracelets represent the vipers that guard the temple Tanah Lot, and the batik patterns that so beautifully decorate fabrics are transferred to long ceremonial hairpins.

you want to see some four-legged folk painting like pros, head to the Bali Elephant Safari Park, where a group of Sumatran elephants have learned to paint. These aren't your typical struggling artists: these elephants have had their work displayed in international venues, including the Australian Museum of Contemporary Art and Christie's auction house. Besides watching painting sessions, you can also ride the elephants (not all of them paint) through the nearby Taro forest. www.baliadventuretours.com.

8. Follow your nose. Tired of schlepping your beau's bags around when you go on vacation? Sick of doing what everyone else wants to do when you are on holidays? Not anymore! Aroma Tours offers a magical week of renewal with other women. Dive into a nurturing, nourishing week of indulgence in the lush island paradise of Bali. Here you get to focus on emotional renewal, inner healing, while discovering new ways of bringing richness and splendor to your relationships. No men to bug you here, princess. The healing week is designed for busy women who enjoy relaxation, pampering, harmony, and resting. Your week is filled with traditional Balinese massages, relaxing yoga, meditation, and aromatic facials. Aroma—

take me away! www.aroma-tours .com/bali-women.htm.

9. Try some humming and ommming. If you happen to be staying in Ubud or Denpasar, you can take advantage of free Raya Yoga Meditation classes. Imagine the wonderful sense of peace you will feel after spending time in meditation and contemplation in one of the world's most beautiful islands. When you are in Ubud, call 976-206 for the time and locations. There are also free lessons every Monday at the Denpasar Meditation Shop; tel: 237-260. At the Bali Osho Information Center, you will find all the details about the daily classes. If you get hooked, they also sell meditation books, tapes and videos; tel: 423-595.

10. Get wet and wild. Oh yeah, you say that you know how to white-water raft, so here's your chance to really prove it. Bali International Rafting will take you on a crazy ride down Bali's Telaga Waja River. Your adventure starts at the foot of the majestic volcanic mountain Gunung Agung. Oh, did I mention the views from your boat are incredible? Imagine racing past tropical waterfalls amid enchanting gorges and beautiful padi terraces, all at an exhilarating speed. This is a ride you will never forget. www.welcome.to/balirafting.

To the Bat Cave!

Find Goa Lawah in southeastern Bali, a temple that was established a thousand years ago, with at least as many fruit bats hanging from the ceiling.

BEIJING, CHINA

Allison promoting peace on the
Great Wall of China.

Why This Place Rocks for Flying Solo

We all know the Wall is great, but there are a lot of other great things in Beijing. Beneath the watchful eye of Chairman Mao lurks a tremendous thriving nightlife. Of course there are acrobatic shows, dinners of duck, and unmatched places of historic and political importance. Some parts of Beijing are grand and official like Tiananmen Square. But there are quiet, small things like the quick sound of bicycle bells on city streets and mazes of modest houses separated by old alleyways called *hutongs* nestled behind monuments.

It's no secret—Beijing wants you to

The Olympics

The 2008 Summer Olympics are already starting to transform the city. Totally mind-blowing architectural plans are in the works to drown out the drab with shocking forms. To their credit, Beijing high-ups said, "Go for it!" to famous international architects who can't get enough of this carte blanche action. A new Beijing is about to be unveiled for the world to see. Check it out at http://en.beijing2008.com.

hear the big things, like the grand marches of the guards as they lower the flag in Tiananmen Square. A vast ideological pride is apparent and well deserved by this ancient culture still able to roll with the times. Now is an exciting time to visit Beijing—its people are in transition and are spreading their economic wings and managing to rustle a few feathers of the superpowers. A consequence of all this modernization and economic power, and you didn't hear it from me, is an insane array of cheekily flaunted pirated goods. Knock-offs to knock your socks off. And why are they so good? Because we taught them how to make them! We're the ones who outsourced our goods, and they're the ones outsourcing our corporate secrets.

Whether you make purchases in a silk market or black market, the best thing about shopping in China is bargaining, so don't be shy. Fierce negotiations are fun! A good rule of thumb is to hack the offered price in half—the true price probably hovers around there. You'll think you're watching *General Hospital* with all the dramatic gesticulations that ensue from your chosen vendor, but you're definitely earning street cred by not being a gullible tourist.

Culture: 5

Beijing is all about culture—ancient, adaptable, and awesome. The Cultural Revolution destroyed much of Chinese culture, yet China is as fascinating a culture as ever. A waking dragon of an economy, the Chinese edge is the sheer size of its workforce and the shrewdness of its policymakers. The backdrop to all this prosperity is thousands of years of straight-out-of-a-textbook history. You'll have to pinch yourself with chopsticks to convince yourself that you are actually here. You've come a long way, baby!

Activity: 2

Besides the gym in your hotel and a bicycle ride around town, Beijing offers athletic activities like hiking along the Great Wall. But dusty air, smog, and intermittent sand storms make sustained activity a bad idea for most, especially the breathing-impaired among us who might suffer from asthma or emphysema. You should be fine for the first few days of your trip (bring your meds!) if you time your visit well, but I wouldn't recommend going all out every single day.

Weather: 2

Unbearably hot summers and sandstorms off the Gobi Desert make Beijing

Powdering One's Nose

Toilet paper and hand sanitizers are your best friends in China, and you won't want to go anywhere without your best friends. One of the most intense experiences you have in China might be in the public facilities. Not those of big hotels and upscale restaurants, but be prepared for the state of affairs in train stations and more rural bathrooms (near the Great Wall at Simatai, for example). Western sit toilets are hard to come by. Luckily squatting over a hole in the ground is good for the hamstrings.

a little tough for weather. While parts of the world enjoy April showers, spring means near dustbowl conditions in Beijing. The winter is very cold and brings with it the weird phenomenon of static electricity that bites the dry air. Autumn is the best time to go, and early spring (March) is the next best time to visit.

Social: 2

The Chinese are expressive and eager to engage, especially when trying to sell you something, but their in-your-face style may take some getting used to. The way that personal hygiene is practiced on the streets makes for some interesting cultural interactions, too. The most reflex-worthy among us are destined to always get out of the way before the spit flies. Think of public sidewalks as part handkerchief, part toilet, and part spittoon. The dust, sand, and smog-forced buildup of phlegm is understandable, but managing it in public is not for most visitors.

Flying Foreplay

Know Your History

Your visit will only be complete with a good foundation of history and culture.

Only then will the landscape of this ancient culture become three-dimensional for you. What was the Cultural Revolution? What did China do to thwart invading Huns? What indispensable modern products were first invented here? What is so forbidden about the Forbidden City?

Movie Musts

See before you go:

- *Beijing Bicycle*, showcasing everyday life
- *The Last Emperor*, to learn about the last days of the Forbidden City
- *Shaolin Soccer*, which just rocks!

Read Before You Go

China for Women: Travel and Culture, part of the Feminist Press Travel Series, edited by Anne Gertslacher

The Kitchen God's Wife and *The Joy Luck Club*, by Amy Tan

Red China Blues: My Long March from Mao to Now, by Jan Wong

The Search for Modern China, by Jonathan Spence

Beijing Accessories

Patience is a virtue; so is standing your ground. The stampede of billions of souls will overwhelm you. There are only so many train seats and bus seats. Only so much asphalt between you, a hundred bicycles, and a huge, diesel-spouting bus. Be patient when the time is right, and push back against the sea of humanity when the situation calls for it. Queue is not a letter in the Chinese alphabet, so harness the lightweight boxer within and muscle your way to the front. It's your turn when you make it your turn, you know? Stick up for yourself! No one else will.

The Top 10 Extraordinary Experiences

1. Rent a bike for the day and catch the rattle and hum of the cycling streets. Everyday life in China will unfold around you. The din of seat-to-seat chatter is the ultimate play list for your adventure. Here is a man carting hay; here are four people piled high on one rusty bike. You stumble onto a group of kite flyers. You encounter a sudden park. How wonderful! It sure beats walking—especially because state-sponsored squares encompass multiple city blocks, making walking just the tiniest bit frustrating.

2. Let Roger Moore guide you through the Forbidden City. Roger Moore narrates the English audio tour of the Forbidden City, and who better to whisper in your ear about the architectural delights? His smooth commentary is in direct contrast to the enormous Imperial complex that surrounds you. Calmly you walk with 007 as he intones in perfect Londonese about the lovely items you pass. Isn't it *fabulous*? Yes, it's fabulous to have your history shaken when you're stirred. But don't dawdle, Bond girl, if you want to make time for the garden at the far end of the Forbidden City. Its twisting trees and small-scale mountaintop temple are *mahhhvelous*. Afterward, bid adieu to Mr. Moore and cross beneath the street to a park on the opposite side. You'll see a path leading up a hill. Follow it to the top, where an exquisite vista of the entire Forbidden City awaits you. And it's free.

Beijing DJ

The Centro Bar and Lounge at the Kerry Centre Hotel in Beijing is a very hip place to sip cocktails. It's so hip that British DJs love to spin here. From Britain! Centro was proud to host such a groundbreaking event when song sets from Brighton lads zoomed over a dedicated broadband connection. So if you're sitting in the lounge and decide you want to request your favorite song, you might have to e-mail the DJ. No. 1 Guanghua Road, Chaoyang District.

3.   Climb that Great Wall. If you want to grab a Starbucks coffee at the only human-made marvel visible from space, then by all means stay on the tourist trail and visit Badaling. However, if you want to challenge yourself on an intense hike across this crumbling majesty, then head to the outer edges of the Wall, where the tourists will be fewer and you can hear the distant howl of desert winds across the empty plains. Wait, is that the faraway call of Mongol hordes? The hike from Jinshanling to Simatai is not for the faint of heart. But this very difficult endeavor is well worth it for the quality time between you and history. Local villagers appear out of nowhere to help you over the rough spots and show you how to circumvent the worst parts. You don't have to pay them but maybe you want to buy the Great Wall book they sell? The first time they help you out of a crumbling parapet, you'll want to name your children after them.

4.   Join Suzie Wong for a drink. The World of Suzie Wong Club affords foreigners the ability to meet and mingle with multinational minions. Curious to see how the entire corporate world is trying to get a piece of the action in China? You'll clink glasses with a Scandinavian mobile phone executive and a Tongan ambassador's niece. Make even more friends at the Sanlitun nightlife district full of very cool bars and clubs. Suzie Wong's, 1A South Nongzhanguan Lu, West Gate, Chaoyang Park, Chaoyang District, Beijing; www.suziewong.com.cn.

5.   Experience Peking duck to die for. The most famous and oldest Peking duck restaurant is Quan Ju De. In addition to the classic, soft bun and hoisin sauce recipe, indulge in all kinds of duck dishes like sweet and sour duck. Li Qun Roast Duck restaurant also gets high praises. Less touristy and located in a hard-to-find hutong area, this only adds to the authentic experience. Whatever the hottest restaurant of the moment is, definitely don't deny yourself this culinary experience. Sure, you can find Peking duck at home, but it will be a lot more expensive and will probably be missing that *je ne sais* quack. No. 14, Qianmen West Street; tel: 86-10-6304-8987; www.quanjude.com.cn/defult.html.

6.   Say hello to the hutongs. In stark opposition to the largesse of monumental architecture, the humble hutongs hunker down behind the Forbidden City and Tiananmen Square. Quiet dwellings all, these gray row houses are centuries old in most cases and are organized in a labyrinth of alleyways. While the big stuff is all about the state as a whole, the hutong represents microcosmic life. If you don't get totally lost, there is something comforting about wandering through or cycling around these gentle groupings. I think it's the scale of things. A visit to Beijing's famous hutongs should be near the top of your list because they might not be around forever. With all the development going on, who knows if they will ultimately be preserved?

7. See giant pandas at the Beijing Zoo.

Who wants to miss out on this local VIP? The cuddly panda softens hearts from all continents. Its power as a symbol is undeniable—it is the World Wildlife Fund's logo and a powerful diplomatic tool for the Chinese government. The problem that all this panda propaganda presents is that the panda doesn't like change. And it particularly doesn't like to move. Munching bamboo in the high hills of China, the poor animal suddenly finds itself in the go-go-Gidget California sunshine penned in with a beach babe and urged to make panda porn for the world to see. Thus, the world's most adorable animal faces tough times ahead. But at least at the Beijing Zoo, the cuddly panda enjoys a seminative habitat and can at least order bamboo off the menu in its native tongue. Beijing also boasts the largest inland aquarium in the world. No. 137, Xizhimenwai Avenue, Xicheng District.

8. Don't miss Mao. It's not the very best, most fun thing in the world to do—

waiting in a long but quick line and filing through a mausoleum on a sunny day—but it is certainly unique to Beijing. And who doesn't like a challenge? You may very well miss Mao's Mausoleum if you're not careful. It is open at bizarre and random times throughout the day. But because he is the ideological architect of so much that you see and experience in Beijing, it would be a shame to come all this way and miss this famous, er, corpse. Located in Tiananmen Square, all you have to pay is your respects.

9. Shop at the Xiushui Silk Market and Wangfujing Road. Shop till you drop along Wangfujing Road and knockoff-filled Xiushui Silk Market. Wangfujing has an especially wild night market where you can buy fried scorpion skewers (I forget—do you eat the stinger?) and other fascinating delicacies. You will recognize some stores (TCBY) and become captivated by others. Keep your eye out for cheap foot massage places. You haven't lived until you've had a foot massage in China. Xiushui Silk Market is full of treasures and trinkets. Again, the fun of shopping here is the fierce negotiation games. And just when you think you're getting ripped off for a set of chopsticks or a teapot, just remember that your poor tourist friends in Japan are paying ten times the price. Value is probably the universe's most relative concept!

10. Fly to Shanghai! It's the Paris of Asia with its old French and British colonial architecture and wide riverside promenade called the Bund. Take the campy-narrated tourist tunnel ride underneath the Huangpu River from the Bund to supermodern Pudong, where the Pearl TV Tower and mile-high Grand Hyatt Shanghai live. Have a drink at Cloud 9 on

the hotel's eighty-seventh floor. Spend a remarkable afternoon at the Shanghai Museum in their jade and furniture rooms, and please don't miss the costumes in the minority nationalities' art hall. Be sure to have a cup of oolong tea at the museum café. Have fun shopping and bargaining at YuYuan Market, and finally set your sights on the awesome Maglev that will zip you back to the airport in 8 minutes, versus a 45-minute cab ride from the middle of town.

BHUTAN

Peggy trekking through the
Kingdom of Bhutan.

Why This Place Rocks
for Flying Solo

*E*very woman, especially you, deserves a trip of a lifetime. A journey somewhere so profound that the experience is like alchemy for the soul. Expect an adventure into Bhutan to transform your rusty thoughts into golden memories of temples and prayer wheels.

Out of a fantasy with real places called "The Dragon Kingdom," "Mountain of the Goddess," and "Tiger's Nest," how could you not feel like a mythical princess on an enchanting voyage into the exhilarating unknown? The country has been cautiously guarded for centuries, creating a land that's not quite of this world, where thunder lizards roam, clouded leopards purr, and one-horned rhinoceroses dream. Nestled between Tibet and India, Bhutan's rich culture has been able to gently roll with nature, unhurried by modernity and the Western world. Bhutan is still a kingdom of lotus-flower-painted houses, cliff-dwelling monasteries, and a true haven of peace in a world that has raced by.

Tourists were allowed into this remotely isolated kingdom only recently, and just like a hot venue in New York, Bhutan is careful about who is let in and maintains strict rules about how visitors conduct themselves. For example, you are not allowed to roam the countryside like an Asiatic elephant; you are required to have a guide or be on a guided tour. Visas are mandatory for everyone who visits, along with a base rate of around $200 a day that needs to be prepaid before you enter Bhutan. Like an all-inclusive resort, the fee typically covers transportation, meals, lodging, entertainment, and your tour guide. The wonderful thing about this kind of traveling experience for a solo sister is that you get to band with other journeyers and participate in like-minded adventures. Festival tours, biking tours, nature tours, even textile tours are offered to make sure that you get the most out of this carefully preserved nation.

Culture: 5

Bhutan is one of the few countries to have never been colonized so their culture is unique and untainted with foreign influence. Within Bhutan, there are around nineteen distinct dialects spoken, a result of the natural geologic barriers that have kept communities secluded from one another in an already isolated nation. It's not like they can jump on a yak and cruise onto another village—getting around here is hard work. They teach English in the schools as the primary language, so you might find yourself deep in conversation with a young monk while visiting a monastery. It's also a good reason to be mindful of what you are saying!

Activity: 4

This is the land of trekking, and the extreme mountainous regions will have you pausing for breath walking to and from lunch. If you're not a hard-core hiker, you

All-Inclusive

Visiting Bhutan is like going to an all-inclusive resort! High season is about $200 a day per person. Low season is about $150 per day. Low season is only July and August, the rainiest months of the monsoon. These minimum daily rates include accommodations on twin sharing basis, all transfers and sightseeing within Bhutan, all meals, and one riding pony. Your price also includes a dear soul who wakes you up with hot chocolate and a basin of warm washing water so you can pretend you're taking a bubble bath. All entrance fees into the museums and monuments are also covered. Each hotel charges an additional fee.

can be a pioneeress of Bhutan's growing river-rafting industry. The national sport is archery, so you can always try a bit of aiming and shooting. Basically, you need to be in good shape to come here.

Weather: 4

It's the Himalayas, darling. You are not coming here to get a tan. Bring lots of layers and check with your chosen travel guide about the items you need to bring to keep you comfortable. Because of all the microclimates, the weather will differ depending on where you decide to explore. Oh, did I mention monsoon season runs from June to September?

Social: 2

Don't expect much bhooty shaking in Bhutan. This is a land where you'll hear monks chanting and the whisper of blue poppies blooming, not "Make that a double margarita!" In a country where more than 90 percent of the people live on subsistence farming, you are not going to find swanky restaurants or killer clubs on every corner. This is not to say that you won't meet amazing people, both locals and fellow travelers, but know that your social life will be more along the lines of a heated chat on a trek than a steamy dance in a club. Bhutan does have a few discos in Thimphu but they dance in groups of five or six people so everybody gets to dance together. It's a little difficult to crash a circle but it's great when they invite you in and they do.

Flying Foreplay
- - - - - - - - - - - - - - - -

Y ou are about to enter a true kingdom, festooned with real royalty. But that doesn't mean you will have all the luxuries worthy of a princess. So, be prepared for some real big culture shocks (no Starbucks or fast food here).

Plan ahead. Though it's possible to get a visa with as little as two weeks' notice, the Bhutan government prefers three months'. They let in only a certain number of visitors every month; so don't buy your ticket until you get your visa. You can buy your ticket only through an agent who can arrange your visa clearance. It usually takes at least three months in advance to purchase a ticket as they have only one national airline that flies into the country and it is usually booked 3–5 months in advance. It would be a shame if you got the ticket but no visa: all packed up and nowhere to go . . .

Leave home without it. Credit cards won't do you much good in Bhutan. How many *dzongs* have you seen with ATMs? You can use credit cards in a few hotel gift shops and a couple of shops in Thimphu. Generally, you can bring a combination of clean crisp bills larger than $5. If they have a minuscule tear, they won't be accepted by the Bank of Bhutan or by anyone else. Don't bother with $1 bills, because the banks don't accept them.

Kick the habit. Are you really still lighting up? Oh fine, I'll admit it has a certain husky, Bridget Bardot appeal . . . but I digress. Bhutan has a strict "no smoking" policy for the entire country. If ever you needed a reason to quit, here it is!

Read Before You Go
- - - - - - - - - - - - - - - -

Beyond the Sky and the Earth: A Journey into Bhutan, by Jamie Zeppa

Bhutan: Land of the Thunder Dragon, by John Berthold

The Blessings of Bhutan, by Russ and Blyth Carpenter

So Close to Heaven: The Vanishing Buddhist Kingdoms of the Himalayas, by Barbara Crossette

Bhutan Accessories

*W*hat you bring depends entirely on what you are going to do and what time of year you visit. Which one are you?

- **Trekking Tina**: sturdy shoes, a sleeping bag, air mattress, reusable water bottle, and warm clothes.
- **Bird-Watching Betty**: binoculars, digital camera, your pointing finger.
- **Festival-Chasing Freda**: brimmed hat to protect you from the sun, quick speed film that will capture bright colors, a basic knowledge of local customs.
- **Monastery-Loving Mona**: layers for the high-altitude buildings, a respectful demeanor, some research under your belt (only turn prayer wheels clockwise!).

The Top 10 Extraordinary Experiences

1. **Journey to Druk Yul (3 days).** Enjoy a breathtaking flight over the great peaks of the high Himalayas into the Dragon Kingdom's airport. Drive to picturesque Paro Valley and relax in your chosen hotel. Sightseeing includes the old fortress of Drugyel Dzong, the Fort of Drukpa Victory, Ta Dzong, the National Museum, the Fortress of the Heap of Jewels, and the "Tiger's Nest." On a clear day you can see the majestic Mount Jhomolhari (Mountain of the Goddess). It is a dramatic rock formation that punctures the sky like an exclamation point. If you happen to be here during a Saturday or a Sunday, you can visit the market where the locals go to buy their food for the week. The crowded stalls sell great items you can bring back to your friends like yak tail dusters, butter teacups,

and turquoise from Tibet. Bhutan Tourism Corporation; www.kingdom ofbhutan.com.

2. Mystical Western Bhutan (7 days). This is a great tour if you want to experience the vastness of the Himalayas and peek inside a few Buddhist temples. Visit Wangdue Valley, the gateway to Central and Eastern Bhutan. En route to Punakha, you will pass the Semtokha Dzong, which was built in 1629. You get to visit the holy Punakha Dzong and monastery that was built by Lama Drukpa Kueeley, known as the Divine Madman for his outrageous thoughts on faith and sex. Bhutan Tourism Corporation; www.kingdomofbhutan.com.

3. Gasa Hot Spring Trek (9 days). Imagine sitting on the top of the world in a steaming hot spring. The Gasa Hot Spring Trek is one of the easier treks in Bhutan. This is a walking tour that will keep you on your feet most of the day. Be warned that—there's no charming way to put it—from April to September there are lots of leeches en route. They love the warm and humid climate of Punakha Valley, and if you have a problem with bugs, you might want to try this trek when it is cooler outside. Department of Tourism, Post Box 126, Thimphu, Bhutan; tel: (975) 2-323251; dot@tourism.gov.bt; www.tourism.gov.bt.

4. Testosterone-Free Treks (6 days or 21 days). Join Peggy Day on one of her testosterone-free treks that take women on expeditions sans the men. She does two trips a year. A Personal Introduction will take you on a vigorous tour that introduces you to the Bhutan she has grown to love during her 25 years trekking the rugged terrain. This adventure happens in spring and is a six-night high-altitude trek (13,400 feet is the highest campsite) where you ride through Bhutan in a horse caravan. The second is the mother of all treks, the 21-day Wild Lunana or Snowman Trek, which happens in October. This is chick-only trekking at its finest! Peggy Day—Day Treks; mizday@hotmail.com.

5. Celebrate good times. Those Bhutanese love a good party. If you are in the country when a festival is happening, make it a priority to check it out. The Buddhist festivals, or Tsechus, are huge events filled with colorful dancers and music. The Tsechu is a specific kind of festival in honor of Guru Rinpoche, the saint who brought Buddhism to Bhutan and the Himalayan world. Tsechus take place throughout the country in every district at different times of the year. The smaller Tsechus are often more interesting as visitors get a close and better perspective of a local festival. The Department of Tourism maintains a list of Tsechus, locations, and dates for the year. Apart from the main Tsechus in every district, folk festivals exist on a smaller, community scale that provide a fascinating insight into local beliefs.

6. Bike Bhutan (18 days). This amazing biking tour is definitely for you biking babes who can ride around 20 to 30 miles a day. You will be covering some of the most amazing landscape in Bhutan. Seeing it from the seat of your bike is an unforgettable experience. Most nights you will be staying in hotels, but there are a few nights that you will be sleeping in tents. At each stop, you can spend the rest of your day touring sites, visiting museums, and hanging out with the locals. Mountain bike safari with Footloose Adventures; www.footloose adventure.co.uk.

7. Magical Bhutan (10 days). Think Iron Woman! Discover Bhutan on this "multiadventure" trip. The trip includes hiking to the beautiful Tiger's Nest Monastery, the stunning six-day Druk Path Trek, rafting the turquoise waters of the Po Chhu River, with optional mountain biking and rock climbing. The highlight of this adventure, the Druk Path Trek, follows a high ridge line with stunning Himalayan views. The Druk Path is an ancient trekking route, formerly used by villagers traveling from valley to valley. Along the Druk Path you'll visit an ancient dzong still inhabited by monks, meet yak herders in high summer pastures, and camp by mystical lakes full of mountain trout. Your fabulous Bhutanese guides will also take the group to amazing temples and cultural sites. Mountain Spirits Adventure Travel; www.mountainspirits.com.

8. Tour the Thimphu Festival (9 days). Your first night is spent in Paro, where you can enjoy the day exploring the city. The next four days you'll spend at the famous Thimphu Festival. On Day 5 the tour heads to Wangdi across Dochula Pass (10,500 feet) to the valley of Wangdi Phodrang and Punakha. On Day 6 the group travels to Gangtey and Phobjikha valley, declared as the first ecotourism destination of Bhutan. This valley is the winter home of rare and endangered black-necked cranes, which migrate to Bhutan from Tibet. You can check out some of Bhutan's wildlife here, including wild boars, barking deer, Himalayan black bears, red foxes, and leopards. On Day 8, you hike to Taktsang Monastery view point. Taktsang means "Tiger's nest," and it is built around a cave where they believe Guru Rinpoche meditated, clinging to a cliff at 3,000 feet above the valley floor. For the locals, this is a place of pilgrimage, and for us tourists, the view of the monastery is overwhelmingly spiritual. The legend says that Guru Rinpoche flew to the site of the monastery on the back of a tigress from Tibet and meditated in the cave there for three months. On Day 9, you head back home with a suitcase of unbelievable memories. Thimphu Festival Tour Package, Services International; www.bhutantravelinfo.com; arrive September 1.

9. Somewhat Luxe Treks (3 to 25 days). Bhutan is no Monte Carlo, but the folks at Asia Transpacific do what it takes to give you the most comfortable trekking experience possible. Their guides are stellar, as are the yaks and ponies they use on their trips. For a truly terrific trek, try:

- **Bumthang Cultural Trek:** 3 days, easy. Winds through low-altitude terrain.
- **Druk Path Trek:** 4–6 days, moderately strenuous. A wonderfully scenic high-altitude walk taking you past remote alpine lakes and yak herders.
- **Chomolhari Trek:** 9 days, strenuous. Altitude reaches 16,000 feet! This trek goes through Jigm Dorji National Park, which surrounds sacred Chomolhari Peak.

- **Snowman Trek:** 25 days and ridiculously strenuous! The jewel of Himalayan trekking and a must for crazy people who like snow.

Asia Transpacific Journeys; www.asiantranspacific.com.

10. Only Uma. Not into trekking or rafting or biking? How about spa-ing? Then Uma Hotel has got you covered. This 5-star resort in Paro is a must for you jet-setting divas who are always on the hunt for the best places in the world to escape to and get pampered in (and run into celebrities who are also trying to get away from the paparazzi). The hotel features yoga and Asian-inspired therapies devoted to both your body and your spiritual well-being. The food is top-notch and an integral part of the sacred experience here. The rooms are over the top: the way I see it, why should I sleep in a tent next to yaks? Give me Egyptian cotton, sweetheart, and book me in for a deep-tissue massage, honey. Included in your price are:

- Two guided day walks with picnic lunch taking in the highlights of the Paro Valley, including Taktsang "Tiger's Nest" Monastery, the National Museum, Drukyel Dzong, and a visit to the temple of Kyichu Lhakhang
- One COMO Shambhala massage
- Airport transfers in Bhutan
- Daily government royalty

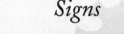

Signs

Good news! Most city signs are in both Drongka and English.

- Arrangement of visa
- Departure tax
- 10 percent sales tax and 10 percent service charge

Outdoor activities, private guides, and private air transfers are available at an additional charge. Uma Hotel—Paro; www.uma.como.bz.

HONG KONG, CHINA

Chiara styling under Hong Kong's skyline.

Why This Place Rocks for Flying Solo

S o, you've mastered shopping in Paris, Rome, New York, and London. Well, then, young grasshopper, you are ready to tackle the awe-inspiring shopping in the world's biggest marketplace, Hong Kong. Hong Kong is for you if you are ready to experience the buzz of a destination that is completely foreign, while still being able to order dinner in your native language. Formerly occupied by the British, more than one-third of Hong Kong's seven million residents speak English, making it easier for a female traveler to navigate the busy urban scene by herself. Though densely populated, Hong Kong is one of the greenest cities in Asia, leaving plenty of room to discover the 260 islands that have been enchantingly preserved with their unique traditions. Hong Kong proudly boasts its colorful blend of Chinese heritage with a twist.

Adding new meaning to the term *Asian fusion*, you'll recognize the British influences from the double-decker buses that drive on the left to the Marks & Spencer department store in the Central district. Whether you're searching for designer duds from upscale shops or bargains from open-air markets, indulge your penchant for perusing in Hong Kong. But be forewarned: Hong Kong is not like home with chopsticks—prepare to elbow your way through crowds, get lost in a sea of people, and wrestle over tables at local noodle shops. Night owls will embrace the energy that emanates from the throngs of people who spill onto the neon-lit streets and sidewalks as soon as the sun sets. And if you crave some serenity, the outlying islands are just a ferry ride away. Spend some time in this global gem and discover why you'll want to come back.

Culture: 5

Hong Kong has been a gateway between the East and the West for centuries. This dynamic role has infused the city with an eclectic electricity that comes through in the culture, plentiful festivals, architecture and everyday life. Nestled up against soaring steel skyscrapers, tiny temples are illuminated with flickering candles. Urban sprawl casts shadows on lush, rolling hill and parks where locals find solace in their crazy lives. This is a city that mingles 5,000 years of Chinese heritage with more than 150 years of British colonial influence in a spicy brew. It's a city of juxtapositions. The city strives to share its traditions and warm hospitality with foreigners, offering cultural instruction in anything from Chinese cake making to Cantonese Opera appreciation.

Activity: 4

The geography of Hong Kong lends itself to myriad active pursuits: the territory that surrounds the city includes acres and acres of protected open country, rocky coastlines, hidden coves and barren mountains. You can look for sharks as you snorkel in Lobster Bay, hike along the Dragon's Back ridge, seek gray herons at Mai Po Marshes Nature Reserve, or mountain bike through green forests with glimpses of sparkling ocean. Spice it up with a round of kung fu, offered for free every Sunday afternoon at Kowloon Park, and then cool

The Escalator

Hilly Hong Kong is hard enough on the hamstrings without all your shopping bags, so why walk when you can ride? Meet the world's longest outdoor escalator! You can go from Central Market through the Western District and halfway up the Peak without moving more than your head to see the view. The escalator goes down to Central until 10 a.m., and then goes upward the rest of the day.

Don't Rent a Car!

At best, you'll sit frustrated in traffic for hours, and at worst, you'll end up in a rental car sandwich. The public transportation is great.

down with some tai chi. Between these options and you ladies who will work up a sweat store-hopping, Hong Kong is a playground for the active solo sister.

Weather: 3

During the summer, the sweltering heat and humidity can be suffocating. But if you plan on ducking into the air-conditioned shopping malls to cool off, be sure to pack a sweater. The temperature extremes may leave you shivering while you shop. Visitors flock to Hong Kong between September and March, when the weather is just right.

Social: 4

Hong Kong is called the "City of Life" and you can feel its pulse beating when the sun sets and the bright neon lights illuminate the city streets. You can really feel the energy of this urban paradise in the hot and humid summer months when it's significantly cooler in the evenings. Night markets abound, and if you enjoy late-night dining, you'll love Hong Kong.

Flying Foreplay

*H*ong Kong is ready to daze and dazzle you, inspire and empower you. This is a place you visit once you have experienced other successful solo voyages. On a scale of 1–10, 1 being a very easy solo trip, Hong Kong is up there, rating a 7–8. Don't let the intensity scare you; just know before you go that it's going to take a bit of time getting used to the frenetic pace and sensory overloads.

Passport, please. Check your embassy for visa regulations. As always, make sure your passport is valid six months *beyond* your planned arrival date.

Party planner. If possible, arrange to stay in Hong Kong during one of the big festivals, such as Chinese New Year or the Dragon Boat Festival. The already vibrant city kicks into high gear during these ornate events.

Don't get scared, but . . . Immunization against cholera, diphtheria and tetanus, hepatitis A and B, polio, rabies, and typhoid is something you should think about before you go. Ask your doctor first.

Tummy protection. Bring some medication for digestive ailments. Educate yourself on health risks but don't let paranoia rule. It's great to be adventurous but not if your souvenir is a case of dysentery.

Read Before You Go

The Great Fire, by Shirley Hazzard
Kowloon Tong: A Novel of Hong Kong, by Paul Theroux
The Language of Thread, by Gail Tsukiyama

Night of Many Dreams, by Gail Tsukiyama

Noble House and/or *Tai Pan*, by James Clavell

Hong Kong Accessories

Layers. In the summer, the hot and sticky weather outside is countered by overzealous air-conditioning inside most of Hong Kong's stores and buildings. Peel your sweater off or put it on, depending on the drastic and immediate temperature changes.

Space, sweetheart. You are coming to shop, right? So you better bring plenty of extra space in which to pack your treasures or plan on buying more travel bags while you are there. Perhaps a set of faux Louis luggage?

Invest in an Octopus card. It's a debit-style ticketing system for the Mass Transit Railway (MTR). Add money to your card, which can also be used at convenience stores to buy water and snacks. www.mtrcorp.com/eng/train/octopus.html.

The Top 10 Extraordinary Experiences

1. Temple of scents. Man oh man, this place smells good! Man Mo Temple is Hong Kong's oldest and most revered temple, and it's named after Man (not the opposite of woman), the god of literature, and Mo, the god of war. You can easily find the temple with your nose because of the giant incense coils that hang from the ceiling. They are bought by patrons seeking personal fulfillment; you might want to get one for yourself. www.discoverhongkong.com.

2. Free junk. Set sail aboard an authentic Chinese junk for a 360-degree view of Hong Kong's extraordinary skyline and glittering harbor. Originally owned and manned by Chinese fishermen, the Duk Ling is typical of the junks that used to crisscross Hong Kong's waterways 150 years ago. And the best part is that the kind folks at Discover Hong Kong offer these cruises for free! Kowloon Public Pier, Tsim Sha Tsui, Kowloon; visitor

The Power of Seven

Prices are expressed in Hong Kong dollars. Simply divide by 7 to get a rough estimate in U.S. dollars.

hotline: +852-2508-1234; Thursday 2 p.m. and 4 p.m., Saturday 10 a.m. and noon.

3. The doctor's in. Learn some Chinese secrets to keep in your bathroom cabinet. On this free tour, you will get some basic knowledge about traditional Chinese medicine such as the concept of yin and yang and the uses of some typical herbal medicines. 2/F, 152–156 Queen's Road Central; Central, Hong Kong; free! every Wednesday at 2:30–4 p.m.

4. Get jaded. Pop over to the Jade Market in Yau Ma Tai and get yourself some jade charms and jewelry, because diamonds are so last century, princess. The brilliant green stone is associated with long life and good health and we all want more of that. The Jade Market is located on Kansu and Battery Streets in Yau Ma Tai. You'll find around 400 stalls selling a wide range of jade pendants, rings, and bracelets, carvings and ornaments. Remember—haggle, haggle, haggle!

5. What's dim sum? Won't know till you try sum! *Dim sum* in Chinese means "to touch the heart" and it is a yummy collection of wonderful, mouth-watering snacks served in steaming bamboo baskets. When you are in Hong Kong, the menus at the great dim sum places will be in Chinese, so go to www.discoverhongkong.com/eng/gourmet/dimsum to create your own dim sum menu to print out and bring with you to restaurants, where the waiters may not speak your language. No dim sum surprises for you!

6. Sip with Mr. Ip. Enjoy a free Tea Appreciation Class with Mr. Ip, a professional tea man. He will introduce you to Chinese tea and the complex rituals involved in drinking it. You will get to sample an impressive variety of tea, learn how to properly prepare tea, and get a lesson in tea-drinking etiquette. Lock Cha Tea Shop; G/F, KS Lo Gallery, Hong Kong Park, Admiralty, Hong Kong; tel: +852-2801-7177; free, every Thursday at 4–5 p.m.

Other than steaming cups of jasmine, chrysanthemum, and oolong tea, Hong Kong is a hot bed for cool drinks. Bubble tea comes with pearl-size tapioca, hence its other name, pearl milk tea. Skip Starbucks (yes, you'll spot the ubiquitous Seattle-based chain here) and check out Hui Lau Shan, a Hong Kong chain that specializes in mango drinks and desserts. Try the fruity concoctions—your taste buds will thank you. Tip: If you can't remember the name *Hui Lau Shan*, just look for the red storefronts with brilliant gold characters.

7. Pretty in pink. Pink panthers, pink flamingos, and now pink dolphins. If you

Tips

Most restaurants include a 10 percent service charge on the bill, but waiters will expect your loose change.

love wildlife, then this is a sight you won't want to miss. In Hong Kong, they have real-life pink dolphins that are indigenous to the area. Hong Kong Dolphinwatch has three trips a week out to Hong Kong harbor to view the dolphins. www.hkdolphinwatch.com.

8. Try tai chi. Mr. Ng is one of Hong Kong's best-known tai chi masters, and he has been making the art of tai chi easily accessible to Hong Kong's visitors through this very popular—and free— class. Tai chi is made up of a set of graceful movements that help to balance your yin and yang (don't ask me what they are!). Expect to feel peaceful and calm after his classes. Free, every Monday, Wednesday, Thursday, and Friday 8–9 a.m. Visitor hotline: +852-2508-1234.

9. Mix it up in Macau. Since you're just a famous Star Ferry ride away, it'd be a shame not to stop by this region that was declared a Portuguese colony in 1849 and returned to Chinese rule in 1999. If casinos aren't your thing, head for the Space Needle–esque Macau Tower. As you step onto the observation level's glass floor and look about 732 feet down, vertigo will likely make your head spin— in a good way, of course.

10. Fixate on Five-Star Felix! Become a diva for the night and treat yourself to dinner and drinks at Felix, one of the most prized restaurants in town. Located in the Peninsula Hotel, one of the best hotels on the planet, Felix stuns with its Philippe Starck interior, city views, hob-nobbing bar scene, and to-die-for restrooms whose floor-to-ceiling windows allow one to powder one's nose in the throes of decadence. Reservations required!! If you are more of a daytime Diva, then treat yourself to a gorgeous high tea at the hotel. Go to http://hongkong.peninsula.com.

TOKYO, JAPAN

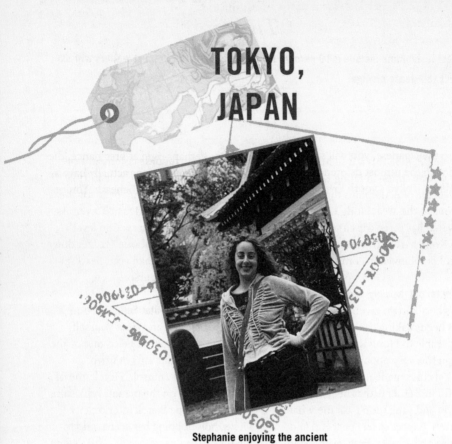

Stephanie enjoying the ancient
and modern in Tokyo.

Why This Place Rocks
for Flying Solo

M ega people, mega places,
mega technology, and mega
safe! That's Tokyo in an
edamame shell. Unlike the world's
other megalopolises, Tokyo keeps it
clean and efficient—a 4:07 train is a
4:07 as the crane flies. But hidden
among the neon buzz of Shibuya and
the futuristic gadgetry of Akihabara
lies another city—ancient, spiritual, and
inscrutable. The world's second hottest
economy, when the day is done for its
dedicated army of *salarymen*, you'll
find the thin screen of modern life
slides open to reveal a second sensibil-
ity: a tea ceremony here, a Zen garden

there. At once a superpower and super-steeped in tradition, Tokyo is nothing if not contradictory. So don't expect to understand everything at first glance. Let confusion wash over you like the autumn mist. Even if you think you know, you don't know. Which is exciting!

While you will always be an outsider, a *gaijin*, to the Japanese, you will still be treated with the utmost deference if not indifference. Tokyo's youth love to have their picture taken, and if you ask politely, they will always greet your lens with a giggle and two fingers held up in a peace sign. Groovy, dude-san. Aside from these interactions, which you must carefully initiate, the populace won't run up and give you a bear hug. You might not become thick as thieves with the Japanese, but you won't be ripped off by thieves, either. Bigger than New York City but safer than Watertown, South Dakota—talk about the ultimate in urban planning! Why not walk the streets alone at four in the morning just to see what safety feels like?

Culture: 5

Temples to both Buddha and Sony exist side by side here, and do expect to gawk one minute at the octagonal crosswalks of Shibuya and the next minute at a Shinto ritual festival you happen to stumble upon. Half the fun of traveling here is learning the unique social mores and trying to turn Japanese for the duration of your stay. Perhaps rigid at first glance, the customs and conventions actually have a graceful rhythm hidden beneath. You're not in Kansas anymore, and that's a good thing. It's okay if you make mistakes—the locals know you're new here—but think of all the mung bean brownie points you'll earn if you catch on to things quickly!

Activity: 3

Speed walking is an Olympic sport, right? And even though your supermodern Western hotel will probably have a gym, you will be too tired from being on your feet all day to visit it. Believe me, you will walk like you have never walked before. The metro stations are their own little

Manners

The Mama-san of Manners is alive and well in Japan! Just about one of the worst things you can do is stroll around someone's house in the slippers used only for the bathroom. Not to mention blowing your nose in a restaurant. Stashing your chopsticks upright in your rice bowl denotes death. And for the love of Sumo, please don't try to shut the taxi door yourself! The automatic doors are controlled by your white-gloved driver, who will get supremely annoyed when a *gaijin* like you dares to slam them. When exchanging business cards, hold the proffered card in both hands and treat it like pics of the grandkids as you stare at it for a full minute lavishing compliments. Oh, and be sure to slurp your noodles.

obstacle courses with multiple layers of stairs and escalators. Climbing seven sets in one trip is not unheard of. Just remember—Tokyoites drive on the other side of the street, which means that you will definitely get a disturbed glance if you are "standing" on the "walking" side. For the supersporty diva, if you have timed your trip right to enjoy the several weeks of good weather here, a gorgeous jogging path around the Imperial Palace awaits you. I do not, I repeat, do *not* recommend renting a bike and riding around Tokyo. You will surely be killed. Did I mention that you'll be walking a lot?

Weather: 2

You've got to hit this one with supreme Japanese precision. There are a handful of weeks in the spring that are utterly spectacular. Plan your trip by the elusive cherry blossom and you should be in weather heaven. Again in the fall, the shocking and fiery display of changing maple leaves awes for a few weeks. Otherwise it is horrendously muggy in the summer and depressingly cold and rainy in the winter. If you are a ski bunny, however, you will delight in the fact that there are ski slopes close enough for a day trip; just grab some skis and jump on a train! The other great thing about winter in Tokyo is that the air is clear enough to spot Mount Fuji.

Social: 2

This is not Rome, darling. Men won't proclaim your beauty with cat calls. In fact, you might feel that you go entirely unnoticed. No, you didn't catch the ugly virus on the plane over, I promise. It's just that this is not one of the world's more demonstrative cultures. The upside of this surprising state of invisibility

---

Sex and Sensibility

Love those love hotels! Young adults just can't afford to live on their own, and most businessmen can't put their mistresses up in an apartment. Enter the love hotel. They offer rooms rentable by the hour or night, but forget everything you know about seedy motels. Picture castle-shaped buildings filled with adult romper rooms decked out with private pools or cave and dungeon decor. Discretion is the Mama-san of invention here, which is why there is no human reception desk. Too shameful! You simply select your room from a panel of vending machine photos, drop in your money, and out pops a key. You *have* to poke around Love Hotel Hill sometime to see this cultural quirk. But please don't ogle the different room photos for too long—love hotelers will be too embarrassed to approach the panel with you there. Time's a-wasting . . .

Shibuya's Love Hotel Hill (Dogenzaka) and specifically the P&A Plaza—Shibuya-ku, Dogenzaka 1-17-9; tel: (03) 3780-3211.

is an inspiring aesthetic of understatement. Which equals fabulous furniture shopping. And who knows—for those of us hijack-a-room-with-our-presence sorts, it's kind of nice to move in the shadows once in a while.

Flying Foreplay

Yen today, gone tomorrow. One thing that is not fascinating and charming about Tokyo is its prices. Talk about expensive! I've paid twenty dollars just for noodle soup. And there isn't really a good way to circumvent the high-priced system. Bulk metro cards offer zero discounts—they just expedite your travels. And speaking of travel, it is basically the same price whether you want to fly, take a train, or rent a car and drive around the country. Trains and flights are expensive, but if you rent a car, you will be faced with hundreds of dollars in tolls. There's even a Virgin movie theater in Roppongi Hills that charges thirty dollars for first-class seating complete with a private bar and blankets for your plush seats! That means, you've got to pay to play here. Do save up for this once-in-a-lifetime trip.

Do not expect to shop for clothing unless you are a size 0. Shop for gorgeous art and antiques; shop for amazing sake. But do not expect to shop for clothing unless you are a size 0. And even if you are a size 0, do not expect to be able to buy bras or shoes. You are simply too big for their britches. We all are. Especially our menfolk. Just forget picking up clothing for the men in your life—nothing will fit them. Not even a pair of boxers! How about a nice kimono robe instead?

Read Before You Go

Western Writers
Ambassador Strikes, Murder at the Tokyo American Club, and *Murder at the Tokyo Lawn Tennis Club,* by Robert "Bob" Collins

Shogun or *Gaijin,* by James Clavell (or rent the *Shogun* miniseries)

Tokyo Suckerpunch and *Dreaming Pachinko,* by Isaac Adamson

You're a Rock Star Everywhere You Go!

Who doesn't love the ecstatic greetings of every single waiter, chef, busboy, and dishwasher the minute you walk into most restaurants? What they are happily yelling your way is, *"Irrashaimase!"* which will sound like "Shy massay" to you. It means "Welcome." You'll hear this in stores, too. If you want to be an even bigger rock star, get to department stores right when they open and experience an Orphan Annie moment as the entire staff bows to you. Don't disappoint them by forgetting to take the shoes off your extolled feet before you step into the dressing room.

The Ultimate Convenience

Send your bags to the airport ahead of time! With your bags bursting from all that shopping, who wants to lug luggage to the airport? Especially since the budget-minded beauty will be hassled enough as she makes her way by metro or bus to the airport to avoid inhuman private taxi rates. And because Tokyo is so wonderfully safe, you can absolutely rest assured that your luggage will be there waiting for you as promised. Inquire with your hotel's concierge.

Japanese Writers

Anything by Banana Yoshimoto, such as *Lizard* and *Kitchen*
The Tale of Genji, by Lady Murasaki Shikibu

Tokyo Accessories

Walking shoes that slip on and off. In this city, you will walk like you've never walked before. You will make discoveries around every new corner, and yes, you'll probably get a little lost. You won't be in a taxi because they are very expensive and have no better sense of direction than you do. Not even their copious, in-car GPS systems can help them find an address in a city bereft of street names. And subway stops always seem to be about four miles from where you actually want to go. But here's the thing—you'll undoubtedly be made to remove your shoes at all temples and other surprising places, and who wants to tie and untie their Pumas twenty times a day? Plus, there are scant few places to actually sit and deal with your oh-so-Western shoestrings.

Amazing Local Rags

Metropolis, a magazine put out by the *Japan Times*, is a cover-to-cover must read, especially for festival and event information. www.metropolis.japantoday.com; www.japantimes.co.jp

The *Tokyo Weekender* is the Bible of English-speaking expats. The *Partyline* society chat is especially fun to read. www.weekender.co.jp.

Fabulous Local Tour Guide

*T*okyo DayTripper tours let you in on a truly local secret! These custom, individual and group tours offer every experience from learning to wear a kimono to checking out Tokyo's café culture and hidden temple gardens. www.tokyodaytripper.com.

The Top 10 Extraordinary Experiences

1. Visit a sumo stable. Stables are for horses, you say. Well, I say they are for all

Ahhh . . . Heated Toilet Seats

Technology does not get any more sublime than this. And warming your tushy is the least of what these contraptions can do! The first time you encounter the motherboard of a heated toilet, you will be astonished, if not a little frightened. All those buttons and pictorial directions—what if you accidentally hit the eject button? In addition to doubling as a bidet, heated toilets can primly mask any unladylike sounds with a selection of flushing noises and in some cases music. When you are finished with your delicate ablutions, you'll need a primer course on how to work the auto hand driers. Stick both hands in and take both hands out. That's what it's all about.

large mammals, and sumo wrestlers are no exception. Seriously, the places where would-be sumo *yokozuna* (champs) live and train are called "stables." Catch a training session some morning! Then see the behemoths battle in one of two annual grand sumo tournaments in Tokyo. Buy cheap tickets and get to the match early to enjoy other people's good seats. A sumo tournament lasts all day, and the champions don't make an appearance until the end of the day. Neither do most of the fans. So come early, take your shoes off, order a hot pot of tea, and sit up close to the ring. Visit www.sumo.or.jp/eng.

2. See the Tsukiji Fish Market at 5 a.m. while you're still jet-lagged. Five a.m. is about the best time to go, and if you're like me, for the first couple nights you'll be up at that time anyway. If you think you've had good sushi before, think again. One taste of fresh-from-the-market sushi from any of the many nearby stalls (open from about 4 a.m. till 1 p.m.) will prove you raw-ng. This is also a great area to find reasonably priced ceramic wear and chopsticks.

3. Learn fashion from the Harajuku girls. If you see nothing else in Tokyo, you absolutely must take a Sunday stroll through Takeshita-dori! This is where fashion-forward teens hang out and show off their fad-ulous ensembles. Will they be dressed as Catholic schoolgirl twins? Will they be fake-tanned to the point that they resemble American hip-hop artists? You never know until you go. The street is as fun a market as you've ever seen with teen-trendy shops filled with trinkets and cheap-for-Tokyo fashions. The footwear will especially blow your mind—you've never seen so many renditions of the sock in your life! And you thought leg warmers died in the eighties. Think again! Harajuku Station, Yamanote Line.

4. Board a bullet train to Kyoto and Hiroshima. Sleek, safe, and yes, expensive, bullet trains are nonetheless de rigueur for travel around Japan. And you simply must go to Kyoto. On the way to this majestically historic city, an awesome view of Mount Fuji will unfold before you. Be sure to have your camera ready. Kyoto is living history preserved—barely a shingle was lost in the war compared to napalm-decimated Tokyo. Here you must visit Gion, the geisha area. Keep an eye out for geishas boarding their customary rickshaws en route to private appointments. Stay on the train a bit longer for an afternoon in Hiroshima that you will never forget. This is an easy day trip from Kyoto and a place that everyone should see. A deeper understanding of Japan and humanity itself can only come from a walk through the Peace Memorial Park and a glimpse of the burned-out cupola of the A-Bomb Dome.

5. Have a *hanami* in Aoyama Cemetery.

Tokyo changes its tune the time of year when the magic pink snow of flowering cherry blossoms falls on the city, calming the hearts and minds of Tokyo's harried masses. When the flowers fall, so do the walls that guard Tokyoite souls. A week ago, you would have been wholly ignored, but this week you are beckoned and cheered and invited to join picnics! One of the very best places for a festive *hanami* (flower viewing) is the Aoyama Cemetery. Graves gush with pink petals,

and street vendors happily hawk octopus on a stick—why not take pause by a mausoleum, crack open a seasonally pink beer can, and revel in your pulse for a while? You can analyze the symbolism all you like—how life is as fleeting as the ephemeral cherry blossom, etc., but I say pour some more sake into my cup and toast with me, *Kampai!*

6. Have tea or champagne at the hotel where *Lost in Translation* was filmed. The

first thing you will ask yourself as you sit at the bar sipping Dom champagne by the glass and smoking a Monte Cristo cigar is, why on earth were Bill Murray and Scarlett Johansson so miserable in that movie? This hotel frickin' rocks! The Park Hyatt boasts gorgeous views of Tokyo and beyond from its now famous New York Grill on the fifty-second floor. At night, the nocturnal city pulses in neon all around you as you sit listening to great live jazz and chuckling every time you order Suntory. If you are not a night person, indulge in a fashionable and dramatic high tea at The Peak Lounge on the forty-first floor. You'll delight in this

Odaiba

Across the Rainbow Bridge is a crazy little artificial island in Tokyo Bay called Odaiba, home to a Statue of Liberty knockoff that faces inland. Odaiba boasts an entire mall of just restaurants, the Mega Web Toyota showroom complete with virtual reality games, Venus Fort mall that looks like it came from Las Vegas, a Ferris wheel, and other huge and strange attractions. It's well worth the visit if only to ride an elevated train across the Rainbow Bridge and stand on the small beach looking back at the city skyline, in the opposite direction of Lady Liberty's gaze.

traditional English high tea with a Japanese twist! Park Hyatt Tokyo, 3-7-1-2 Nishi-Shinjuku, Shinjuku-Ku, Tokyo, 163-1055 Japan; tel: (03) 5322-1234.

7. Visit the Mori Arts Center in Roppongi Hills. The Mori Art Museum is one of the most exciting modern art galleries on the planet. Not only will you see some wacky and wild avant garde installations, but what is also on display here is Tokyo itself from a lofty 360-degree observation deck. Together in one ticket, the Tokyo City View and Mori Art Museum promise a perfect outing. On a clear day you can see Mount Fuji, and every day you can challenge the way you think and the way you look at Tokyo, literally.

Tip: If you know your Louis Vuitton logo history, you'll recognize the look of the Roppongi Hills's logo in an instant—it's Japanese pop artist Takashi Murakami! The Mori Art Museum gift shop is filled with fun Murakami items that make great presents.

8. Forage for food in a department store basement. Beneath floor after floor of international designers and too-small clothing hides a food court for immortals where *oishii* (delicious) treats await you. Come hungry—as long as you can't fit into those clothes upstairs, you might as well indulge! Here the pantheon of global cuisine awaits your choices. Is it time for European chocolates and croissants? Green tea? Sushi and sausage? Takashimaya Times Square offers the ultimate foodie foodtopia. Yummy jelly donut pastries! Wait—that's not chocolate filling . . . mung bean paste??

9. Onsen in the skin you're in. Onsens are Japanese therapeutic mineral bath-houses built on top of natural hot springs. Just thank Japan's angry topography for all these rejuvenating spas. Wonderful for your body both inside and out, just stick to these two simple rules and you'll be fine: Wash yourself before you get in the water, and don't be shy. In the women's area, you will be given a "towel" the size of a washcloth. Strip, stash your clothes, and take your key with you to the nearest washing station. This stage is crucial. Scrub, sister, scrub! Sit down on that tiny plastic stool, lather yourself up, and rinse well. You are now ready to hit the hot mineral pools where you realize what the tiny towel is for—you see wet ones cooling women's foreheads. Definitely try all the different pools and their mineral mixtures. Some are individually sized buckets and others look like lap pools. But all are serenely landscaped and perfectly clean. Don't miss this truly Japanese tradition.

10. Visit Asakusa's Senso-ji Temple. Pronounced "ah-sock-sah," this is a very special temple in Tokyo. Countless celebrations and festivals radiate from its famous red-lantern entrance with flanking formidable gods. This is one of few prewar structures left in Tokyo, and there are many legends about why this temple survived the fires when everything around it was burning. The wide pedestrian avenue leading up to the temple overflows with tons of vendors' stalls selling snacks and toys and lots of fun souvenirs. There is one stall dedicated to all things cats, another to beautiful hair clips and adornments. This is a great place to find irresistible presents for yourself and others at home. In springtime, venture behind the temple to find *sakura* (cherry blossom) ice

Disneyland

When we think of our dearly exported Disneylands, we think of troubled Disneyland Paris, right? Well, there is one Disneyland abroad that absolutely thrives, and that is Tokyo Disneyland. Its attractions are so state-of-the-art with such attention to detail that they rival anything in Orlando. And they have something here that you don't have—Tokyo Disney Sea. Call me crazy but I think this is a hysterical outing. In the Mediterranean Harbor, you'll swear you've teleported to Venice. And Jumpin' Jellyfish in the Mermaid Lagoon is seriously trippy—breathtaking, automated jellyfish rise and fall in a whole undersea environment that is the aquarium that Willy Wonka must have built. Just be sure to come on a rainy weekday afternoon—the crowds can make a Mickey Mouse out of us all. Venture to www.tokyodisneyresort.co.jp/index_e.html.

cream in the surrounding shops. Nearby is also a water taxi station and a view of the controversial Philippe-Starck-designed Asahi Beer Hall—a supermodern building with a golden flame or something on top. Most call it the "golden turd." 2-3-1 Asakusa, Taito-ku Asakusa Station.

THAILAND

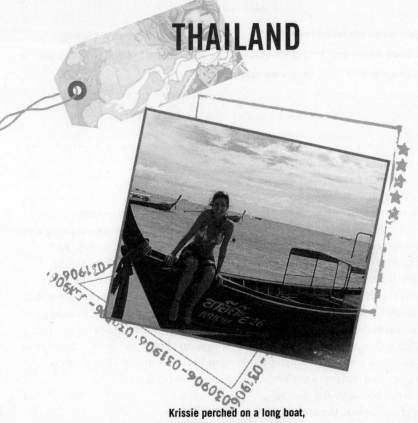

Krissie perched on a long boat,
floating on Railay Beach.

Why This Place Rocks
for Flying Solo

Tucked among the Southeast Asian nations of Burma, Laos, Malaysia, and Cambodia rests the tiny Kingdom of Thailand. It's a gentle nation that prides itself on being known as "The Land of Smiles." This is a beautiful place where playful dolphins swim with sheer delight in the warm Andaman Sea and gray elephants tromp through Khao Sok rain forest freely. It is a country of contrasts as well, with Bangkok's seedy reputation holding strong as Thailand's more respected sports like scuba diving, white-water rafting, and sailing take center stage.

Your Base

Bangkok is the hub for many Asia and Australasian flights, so if you are thinking about flying somewhere for a quick getaway like Bali, Bhutan, the Maldives, or India, make Bangkok your base. Go to www.thaiair.com.

It's all here for you in Thailand. From nonstop shopping to decadent spa-ing, this is a place where you *can* have it all. And for a fraction of the price you would pay at other popular destinations. As for the solo sister, Thailand is a delight. It is a country of cooperation, where politeness is rule number one and respect is always given. Know that you will feel safe here, even though it is a country far away from home. Because tourism is a priority in this nation, you can be sure that English will be spoken everywhere you go. So, if you are ready for an adventure in a place that is close to perfect, where you can buy anything you can imagine, give Thailand the opportunity to wow you.

Culture: 5

Snugly nestled between four different countries, Thailand has created its own rarefied culture by integrating traditions from its neighbors. Buddhism plays an essential role in this country, and there really isn't a separation of church and state. Each area of Thailand boasts its own unique cultural slant. In northern Thailand, the long-necked Indians thrive; in Bangkok you can still catch night shows that will make your head spin; and in southern Thailand you can get lost in the transparent waters of the Indian Ocean while watching local fishermen cast out their rudimentary nets.

Activity: 5

How about some white-water rafting, trekking, mountain biking, canoeing and kayaking, fishing, wind surfing, rock climbing, Jet-Skiing, wakeboarding, walking, bird-watching, and butterfly chasing! Phew, I'm tired just writing that! For you hardcore athletes, Thailand won't let you down, and as for you ladies who want to lounge—go at it! Lounge to your heart's content—the spa options are endless here.

Weather: 4

Thailand has only two seasons: the rainy season (May to October) and the hot season (November to April). Try to avoid Thailand in September and October because they are the wettest months. The best time (but most crowed) to visit is from November to February.

Social: 4

You can easily hook up with a band of tourists from Europe or chill by yourself on a pristine beach. Another option is to join a tour with other travelers from around the world. Of course, tours are the perfect solution for you solo virgins. Let a team of professionals set up your itinerary for you, and all you have to do is show up at the Bangkok Airport!

Flying Foreplay

Thailand is a relatively small country, but it's packed with a ton of things to do—from elephant rides to shopping in night markets. Research the places and activities you want to visit before you board your aircraft so you'll know how to coordinate your visit. No need to buy your local airline tickets to specific destinations in Thailand before you leave home. Many times they are cheaper in Thailand. Also, you might meet up with a fabulous group from Australia (or just one fabulous man from England on holiday) and your plans might change.

Things to know. You really should not spend all your time in Bangkok. Thailand has so much to offer, so plan on visiting at least two other destinations like Phuket and Chiang Mai. Keep Bangkok as your base. Many of the hotels will store your excess luggage for you, and better yet, Bangkok International Airport has lockers that you can rent for around $2 a day. So, when you come back from your adventures, bag your bootie at Bangkok and jet off to your next locale with your sarong and swimsuit.

Plan on shopping. Let your inner consumer run free in Thailand. Everything is so darn cheap here, you'll be kicking yourself if you return home

Visas

If you think you might hop a flight over to Bali, Vietnam, Laos, Malaysia, or Cambodia, take two extra passport photos with you. You will need them for your visas.

empty-handed! If you do plan on buying large items that won't fit in the overhead compartment, think about flying business or first class because they don't have the same tight weight restrictions as they do in economy class.

Tuk-tuk tricks. At many of the tourist spots, you will find tuk-tuks ready to serve you for a ridiculously low price. Beware because many of them will want to take you on a "tour" of Bangkok to "show you very good prices." If you are up for a crazy ride into the heart of Bangkok, a tuk-tuk ride can be fun and informative. But expect to stop by at least three shops selling everything from custom-made silk suits to gold jewelry. This is how the tuk-tuk drivers pay for gas.

Read Before You Go

Anna and the King of Siam, by Margaret Landon (the novel that inspired the musical *The King and I*)
Siddhartha, by Hermann Hesse

Thailand Accessories

B efore my trip to Thailand, I asked my girlfriend Krissie (who just got back from three glorious weeks

alone there) what I should bring. She said, "Bring a few bikinis, some feminine products, and condoms. Anything else you want, you can buy it there." She was right!

Play it safe. Even if you don't think you're going to have your period, still bring some tampons. This is one place where you shouldn't compromise. Especially if you plan on spending time in the water, you want to know you are covered. As for condoms, if you are single but don't plan on hooking up with anyone, again play it safe. Thailand is packed with gorgeous European men and why ruin that oh-so-perfect moment because you did not bring protection. Girls, it's time to be proactive with your prophylactics!

The Top 10 Extraordinary Experiences

1. Take nine days to well-being. Unlike some vacations, where you need a vacation after your vacation, this trip is all about healing and restoration. The fine folks at North By North East tours offer a nine-day tour of Thailand that will leave you healthier, happier, and more relaxed than you've been in a long time. The package smoothly blends Thailand's world-renowned traditional massage, a long heritage of natural health treat-

Hat Rawai

Hat Rawai is about 10 miles from Phuket and is home to a well-established community of Chao Le people, who are sea gypsies.

ments, the art of meditation, and yoga with beautiful scenery. This trip is all about reviving your body and soul. From jet-lag massage to steam baths, you will be floating home on the tenth day. The best part is that you still get to see all the incredible sites in Bangkok and all the way up to Chiang Mai! www.north-by-north-east.com.

2. Shop is a verb in Bangkok. Get ready for a cardio cash-spending workout, because when it comes to bargain shopping, there is no place like Bangkok. Armed with a roll of cash, a Camelbak filled with bottled water, and a pair of very comfortable shoes, you are ready to conquer the shopping beast. From Chatuchak (Kampaengpet Road) weekend market to the very glitzy high-end mall Siam Paragon, you will have no shortage of shopping selections. And just when you thought you had all the shopping you can take during the day, Bangkok pulls out the razzle-dazzle and sets up shops at night. Sometimes night markets are more comfortable to stroll around after the sun sets and the air cools. Try Suam Lum Night Bazaar (Wireless Road) for everything from candles to crystals. For you darlings who love fabulous fakes, head to PatPong night market and ask to see what they have "in the back." If you prefer to shop in an air-conditioned building hit MBK for bargains, and for you rock stars who

want Hermès and Chanel for reals, you'll hit pay dirt at Gaysorn Plaza (999 Ploenchit Road). Many of the better hotels offer personal shoppers. This is the best way to bargain because they do all the negotiating for you! When you book, ask if they offer personal shoppers.

3. Spend one night in Bangkok. You remember the song, "One night in Bangkok makes a hard man humble." And if you ever wondered what that song was about, then take a walk on the wild side—Bangkok style. Head to Patpong Street, where the street transforms into a throbbing scene of massage parlors, sex shops, go-go bars, and strip clubs. Because the area is also a tourist trap, you will feel safer than you'd expect on a street seeping with raunchiness. You will also find reasonably refined venues, but for the most part, this is a place you walk through and don't stop. You might also come across darling young ladies roaming the streets, but don't be fooled because chances are these are guys. Thais call them *kra-toeys*; we call them transvestites.

4. Chill in a tree in Phuket. Congratulations! You have made it all the way to the other side of the planet. Don't you think you deserve 5-star treatment along with a few days of sheer pampering? I think so, too, and that's where Banyan Tree Phuket comes in. Banyan Tree Phuket is

Go Nuts! Methee Cashew Nut Factory

Located at Tilok Uthit 2 Road in Phuket, this factory serves up extremely delicious cashew nuts in a variety of ways: plain, fried with garlic, fried with chili—you name it. You can also see the factory, where every nut has to be cracked and opened individually using a special press. That's why these nuts are so darn expensive.

an oasis of peace and tranquility, a place where you don't have to lift a finger except to order another Mai Tai. This resort is so out-of-this-world that it has earned the honor of being voted the "World's Best Spa Resort" by readers of *Condé Nast Traveler* and the "Best Resort Hotel in Asia" by the *Asian Wall Street Journal*. My solo stay at this resort was the best days of my life! Banyan Tree Phuket, Laguna Resort, Thailand; tel: +66 (0)76 381 010-7; www.banyantree.phuket.com.

5. Viva vegetarians! Phuket Vegetarian Festival is held every October, and if you are a vegetarian, you won't want to miss this spectacular event. The afternoon before the festival begins, a pole at each temple is raised, called the *Go Teng* pole. They believe that the gods will come to earth via these poles, and lighting these poles with lanterns signals the gods that they are ready. Parades, bladed ladder climbing, and fire walking are all part of the fun. It can get pretty crazy because, throughout the festival, fireworks and drums take over your senses. The Thais believe that the louder the noise the better, because the constant clamor drives away evil spirits. www.phuketvegetarian.com.

6. Take Thai Cooking 101 in Chiang Mai. Imagine how popular you are going to

be once your friends realize that you know how to whip up their favorite Thai dishes! After a day or two at the Four Seasons' Chiang Mai Thai Cooking School, you'll be able to throw together dishes like *Gaeng Kheo Wan Gai* (green curry with chicken) and *Pla Nin Laad Prik Bai Horapa Basil* (fried fish with chili). You don't need to be a guest of this posh resort to enjoy a day of shopping for fresh veggies and learning how to cook like a pro. After all your hard work, you get to feast in the beautiful pavilion with the other students. Simply call and see if there is room. Four Seasons Resort Chiang Mai, Mae Rim-Samoeng Old Road, Mae Rim, Chiang Mai 50180; tel: 66 (53) 298-181; www.fourseasons .com/chiangmai, cookingschool .chiangmai@fourseasons.com.

7. Monkey around in Chiang Mai. When it comes to animals, nothing is as adorable as monkeys. And if you spend some time in Chiang Mai, then you can't miss the little rascals at the Monkey School. Yup, it's here where they learn their ABC's and train to pick tamarinds, ride bikes, and smile for visitors like you. Remember to take your camera so you can get a shot of you monkey-ing around with the natives. But whatever you do, don't feed the monkeys. Chiang Mai's Monkey School, 296 Moo 1, Mae

Try Durian

This thorny green fruit weeds out the weak with its terrible smell. But if you can survive the aroma, the delicious taste is your reward.

Rim-Samoeng Road, Mae Raem area, Mae Rim District, Chiang Mai; tel : 053-298818 or 053-860547; www.chiangmai-chiangrai.com/chiangmai_monkey_school.html.

8. Visit the long necks and ride an elephant in Chiang Mai. A visit to Chiang Mai should be on your list of places to visit while in Thailand. And if you only go overnight, then this is the perfect day trip. The tour starts at 8:30 a.m., when you are picked up from your hotel. The first stop is the elephant camp, where you take an elephant ride to one of the hill tribe villages. The hour-long ride takes you through some remarkably lush forest scenery and along a picturesque river. After lunch go for a ride in a bamboo raft down the river enjoying the brilliant fragrant flora, roaming elephants, and glimpses into lychee groves. After the raft ride you will head to Padong, which is the village of the "long neck" tribe. All this, and you'll be back at your hotel in time for cocktail hour. You can book this tour through any tour operator once you get to Chiang Mai.

9. Rally at Railay Beach. Finishing your trip on an intensely warm and brilliantly beautiful beach is the perfect finale. So after all that shopping, hopping, rafting, and cooking you've been doing for the past week or so, don't you think it's time to relax and work on your tan? As with every place you visit, there is a vibe that sets this destination's tone. Some beaches are for lovers and couples; others are for college kids with raging hormones, but Railay is for social, sophisticated travelers who appreciate delicious beachside meals and cool beers. (Planes connect from Bangkok to Phuket every hour. Flying time is about one hour. From Phuket Airport it is a two-hour taxi ride to Krabi or Ao Nang.) Anywhere you stay on Railay is great, and you are bound to find a room from $20 to $50 a night. My favorite place is a bungalow on the Railay Beach side.

10. Ride an icon. What could be more enchanting than traveling through Thailand on the world-famous *Orient Express*? For the ultimate in travel, jump on the *Thai Explorer*. Your trip departs from Bangkok with visits to Ayutthaya, Chiang Mai, Lampang, and the infamous River Kwai en route. Don't forget your Agatha Christie books. Check out www.orient-express.com.

VIETNAM

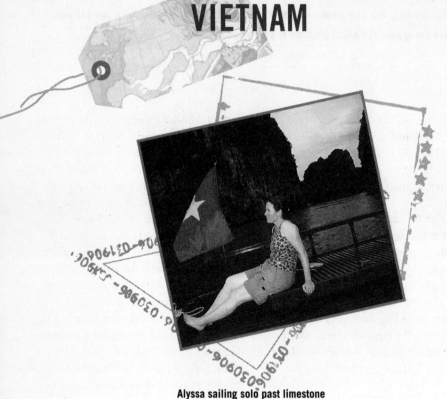

**Alyssa sailing solo past limestone
formations in Halong Bay.**

Why This Place Rocks
for Flying Solo

- - - - - - - - - - - - - - -

*V*ietnam is a slinky strip of land on
the Indochinese Peninsula, gently cupping Laos and Cambodia
with its western border. As you make
your way down from the northern cultural capital of Hanoi to the southern
heartbeat of Ho Chi Minh City (still
known as Saigon to locals), the life of
this amazing culture unfolds in brilliant
color. This is the Vietnam of conical hats
bobbing in flat rice fields and wandering
blue-gray water buffalo. This is the Vietnam of zipping motor scooters puffing
smoke and teetering bicycles ridden beyond their capacity holding full families
and their groceries. This is living history,

where pâté and truffles are served alongside spring rolls and steaming bowls of pho. And you might hear wisps of French and Russian in the mouths of elders. This is a culture still steeped in traditions, where it is believed that angry dragons forged each limestone grotto in Halong Bay and that chewing betel nuts will cure an ill temper.

So long a taboo subject or an object of tragedy, Vietnam is making a concerted effort to bring visitors to its handsome, serene nation the size of New Mexico. Women's silk ao dai gowns flutter to the sounds of gongs and moon-shaped lutes, recalling a time when Vietnam was not just a war. Luxury resorts are popping up along the pristine coastline, and grapefruits, persimmons, and mangos grow wild in the lush jungles and forests. The solo sister will feel welcomed by the locals with their gentle, kind nature. You will be moved to tears by the scenery and the history. The sheer joy that accompanies the simplicity and beauty of the Vietnamese lifestyle will have you questioning the details you sweat in your daily reality. Let Vietnam touch you and you'll never be the same again.

Culture: 4

French Quarters, Buddhist temples, Confucian libraries, and French villas are the architectural manifestations of the special cultural meld you'll see in Vietnam, each one representing a period in history that has made the country what it is today. You might even hear some Russian or Czech from those brought up in Communist Vietnam, or see youngsters gnawing on baguettes, a food staple left behind by the French occupation from the mid-nineteenth-century to World War II. Physical and emotional scars from the American-Vietnam conflict are still present in the country—be an aware and sensitive traveler.

Activity: 3

It's all about two-wheels in Vietnam, and you'll probably tire yourself out pedaling around town. And unless you sign up for one of the adventure tours I recommend, you won't be getting much exercise. When all else fails, you can usually find a group of people doing tai chi by the riverside.

Weather: 4

There are two seasons in Vietnam: the cold and the hot. The cold season is from November to April and the hot season is from May to October. It rains about 100 days a year, so it's wise to bring an umbrella to keep dry. The temperature in winter is colder than you might expect. The summers are not good for makeup or hair with muggy, hot days.

Social: 4

It will be largely up to you to set your scene in Vietnam. If you want a social scene that involves more people than the number that came over with you on the plane, the first choice you'll make is between the bustle of fast-moving Ho Chi Minh City or less frenetic Hanoi. In Ho Chi Minh City, hear live music at Vasco's or dance till the sun comes up at Allez Boo. In Hanoi, try Half Man Half Noodle or simply saunter down Bao Khanh/Hang Hanh Streets in the Old Quarter to find a selection of nightspots. Or try an organized tour—you will always be with other like-minded travelers from around the world.

Flying Foreplay

Darling, you are going somewhere very, very, very far where not many people speak your native language. You will need to be a bit more prepared than if you were heading to, say, Amsterdam.

Ho Chi who? Please, please don't go to this country without knowing your history. You'll encounter many opinions and conflicting facts about the tragic war that terrorized Vietnam not too long ago, and your trip will be so much more meaningful if you can look at everything with an informed eye.

Adjust your expectations. After you do all that learnin', you might be envisioning the Vietnam of *Platoon* or *Apocalypse Now*. The Vietnam of today is a vigorous and lively nation that's trying its darnedest to attract tourists. Picture dragon boats floating through serene green harbors, not Robin Williams yelling, "Goooood morning, Vietnam!"

Think tours. I'm all for sisters going solo (obviously), but a partner-in-*voyage* could come in handy here, where you might be walking long distances through open countrysides or wandering ancient abandoned pagodas at sunset. Though you are almost certain to bond with expats and fellow travelers you meet there, it could be especially nice to have a few guaranteed peregrination pals.

Read Before You Go

These are not uplifting stories about the beautiful landscape and wonderful people who call Vietnam home; they are tales of truth that took place before and after the Vietnam War.

A Good Scent from a Strange Mountain: Stories, by Robert Olen Butler (won the Pulitzer Prize)

The Quiet American, by Graham Greene
We Should Never Meet: Stories, by Aimee Phan

Vietnam Accessories

Bring your meds. This is the trip for your minipharmacy. Take a small supply of anything and everything you might need. No reason to take a whole box of Alka-Seltzer or Midol unless you plan on being there for a month. Even if you don't think you need it, take it. I don't want to scare you, but think diarrhea, cramps, sleeplessness, motion sickness, etc. At least you know you'll have medication if you need it, and if you don't need it, perhaps someone you meet on your adventure will. Oh, and pack Cipro!

Keep covered. Monsoons mean it's rainy but not cold. Don't let a jacket cramp your style or make you unnecessarily perspire.

Strap it on. A backpack is best for carrying around your belongings. Make sure it's got great zippers so you don't drop anything. If you plan on hitting some of the chic city spots, take a small handbag so you don't look like a clod while sipping champagne.

Check Out a Traditional Vietnamese Opera

Every Thursday at 7 p.m., there is a performance at the Ly Club in the theatre/restaurant located on the ground floor. Tickets are around $6. Ly Club, 51 Ly Thai To Street, Hanoi; tel: 84-4-936-3069.

Girly products. Bring your favorite feminine products because you won't find a plethora of feminine sanitary accoutrements. If you take tampons, bring the ones with paper applicators—or no applicators. Plastic is not good for their bad plumbing.

Bad hair daze. Hate leaving your shampoo collection behind? Don't like the dishwashing soap–like toiletries that are offered in travel sizes? Bring your own dearest shower goodies! You can find small, empty travel-sized plastic bottles at your local drugstore. Fill them with the conditioner that you can't live without. Tip: run the shampoo/conditioner containers under warm water first to make the product easier to pour.

Antibacterial wash. Never a bad idea, especially in a country where not all toilets are of the porcelain persuasion.

Cover up. Bring a bathing suit. Going nude is not a good option here; the locals won't take too kindly to it.

Don't get bugged. It's the tropics and bugs love it here. Make sure you have plenty of protection from the biting kind.

The Top 10 Extraordinary Experiences

1.   Bike the Ho Chi Minh Trail—Hanoi to Phong Nha. Imagine riding through the pine-scented forests of Dalat Plateau to the lush tropical waterways of the Mekong Delta with a crew of biking enthusiasts. Exotissimo offers a rare opportunity to mountain bike through off-road trails where you get to jump over bumps and cycle around buffaloes. Your tour starts in Hanoi and ends in Phong Nha National Park—that's a whopping 300 miles over seven days. This is a really remote trip—don't plan on bunking at any 5-star locales here. It's more like a tent and a warm meal. But what a way to see this incredible place! They do offer shorter rides for you wimps. You can take a shower when you get home, or better yet book a few nights at one of the many spas on your way home. Exotissimo; www. exotissimo.com.

2.   Sail back in time on Halong Bay. One of the great natural wonders of the world and a UNESCO World Heritage Site, Halong Bay covers an area of 950 miles where thousands of mysterious limestone islands and grottoes rise from the clear, emerald waters of the Gulf of Bac Bo. The majestic beauty of the bay and its islands is fully appreciated only while meandering among the islands, fjords, and inlets. And the best way to experience this wonder is on board the *Emeraude*, a classic single-wheeled paddle steamer straight out of the 1920s. Eat breakfast out on the deck and enjoy a late-morning massage or tai chi session. Midafternoon, relax while getting a foot massage, sipping a gin and tonic, and admiring the incredible view of the islands. Halong Bay is a four-hour bus journey from Hanoi. Tel: 84-4-934-0888; www.emeraude-cruises.com.

3.   Kayak with dragons on Halong Bay.
The Vietnamese believe that the jagged limestone islands of Halong Bay are the work of dragons that dropped them from the sky to protect the bay from invaders. And to get an up-close and intimate view of these amazing rock formations, try kayaking the "Descending Dragon." You can go out for a day with a group, or you can join a multiadventure tour group that will take you from kayaking to biking to hiking. A few different websites you might want to check out include www.greentrail-indochina.com, www. travelsvietnam .com, www.snowlion.com, and www.vietnamstay.com.

4.   Spend 24 hours on Hanoi's 36 Streets. In the heart of Hanoi, you will find one of the most curious places to go shopping. The locals call it 36 Streets. It is where dozens of narrow streets weave in and out of the ancient area of Hanoi. You really can find anything you possibly want—from handmade silk shirts to wooden coffins—it's all here. Businesses here were once taxed according to the width of their storefront, so you will find itty-bitty stores with an incredible selection of wares. Old-world and modernity come together here with weathered faces selling goods and Internet cafés brimming with young travelers checking their e-mail. Just follow the Silk Road to these golden quarters.

5.   Watch water puppets in Hanoi. There is no business like show business and here in Hanoi they really know how to put on a puppet show with a watery stage. Yup, puppets on water. The puppeteers stand waist-deep in the water and manipulate the puppets, making them do incredible water stunts. Think *Cirque de Soleil* with puppets. The water hides the puppeteers and their strings, creating an amazing stage that reflects the wooden actors, fireworks, and props.

Silk

You must get something made at Kenly Silk when you are in Hanoi or Ho Chi Minh City. It takes around three days to make whatever you want. Just bring in a picture, and wham-bam, you got yourself a new outfit! They will even deliver your couture treasures to your hotel. 108 Hang Gai, Hanoi; tel: 84-4-826-7236, fax: 84-4-828-9785; kenlysilk-hn@hn.vnn.vn.

Also 132 Le Thanh Ton—Dist, Ho Chi Minh City; tel: 84-8-829-3847, fax: 84-8-829-3847; www.kenlysilk.com.

The puppeteers sing while the band bangs out percussion music. Make sure to get seats up front, so you can really experience the action. Mua Roi Nuoc Theatre near Hoan Kiem Lake, 57 Dihn Tien Hoang Str, Hanoi.

6. Visit a museum in Hanoi dedicated to women. There is something pretty special about a city that has a museum dedicated to women. And in Hanoi, you will find the Women's Museum, the first national museum of this type in Vietnam. The museum was created to capture the simplicity of local women's everyday lives. Designed by female architect Tran Xuan Diem, its domed ceiling centerpiece, rising over the marble floor, is modeled after a woman's breast, complete with globe lights representing drops of breast milk. From rice pots to rifles, the museum displays clothes, photos, and other memorabilia belonging to local and national heroines. Hanoi Women's Museum, 36 Ly Thong Kiet Street, Hanoi; tel: 825-9129.

7. Be a part of Ultimate Hanoi. Ultimate Frisbee, that is. The Hanoi Ultimate Club hosts a Frisbee game twice a week, and you can watch a game or even join a pickup game—you can participate the first time for free, but if you get addicted, you'll have to pay a members' fee. Expats and locals alike come to flick the disc around, so even if you don't have a mean toss, this is a great way to meet friendly, active people. Try to catch a game when you first get into town— you are bound to meet a ton of English speakers who can tell you all about what's going on in Hanoi while you are there.

Get full information/locations

(and order a bad-ass T-shirt or a really cool commie Frisbee) at www.hanoi-ultimate.com.

8. Get Luxe in Saigon. Saigon is now called Ho Chi Minh City. Although that fabulous name that takes you back to the French Indochina era of martinis and colonial decadence has vanished, luxury still abounds. For the ultimate in fabulous, check out these haute spots:

The Rex Bar. A rooftop bar adorned with jet-setters and style mavens. 141 Nguyen Hue Boul; tel: 84-8-829-2185; www.rexhotelvietnam.com.

Park Hyatt Saigon. The brand-new addition filled with global glitterati. 2 Lam Son Square; tel: 84-8-824-1234.

Hotel Majestic. With seven different bars and restaurants, and a full spa, you are sure to stay happy and pampered. 1 Dong Khoi Street; tel: 84-8-829-5517; www.majesticsaigon.com.vn.

Q Bar. Look out for rock stars and prima donnas sipping expensive drinks. 7 Cong Truong Lam Son; tel: 84-8-823-3479.

And if you must have your luxe with your Hanoi, then definitely stop in for a drink at the hundred-year-old Metropole Hotel. 15 Ngo Quyen Street; tel: 84-4-826-6919, fax: 84-4-826-6920.

9. Go down with history in Ho Chi Minh City. Sometimes it's good to take a day for a little reality check. It's fabulous living like a first-class frequent flyer, but travel is the perfect opportunity to learn more about history. If you are visiting Ho Chi Minh City (old Saigon), then spend a day going out to the Cu Chi area. Here, you can explore the 75-miles of intricate tunnels the Viet Cong used in the Vietnam War. You'll crawl through very narrow tunnels, crouch in former conference rooms and closet-sized hospitals, lie down in sleeping chambers, and get a one-of-a-kind view of the Viet Cong's secret life. Listen to propaganda about "evil Americans" and learn about what really happened during the Vietnam War. Expect to be a changed person and have a new perspective on war after this tour.

10. Buy some art in Ho Chi Minh City and Hanoi. Vietnamese contemporary art is taking off in places like San Francisco and New York. Why should you spend a fortune buying art from a snooty gallery when you can buy it straight from the source in Hanoi and Ho Chi Minh City? Hanoi has been the center of arts in Vietnam, producing some of the most talented artists in the country. You will find an endless selection of galleries to visit in both cities. Hanoi Studio, located on Trang Tien Street, is worth a visit. You will find another Hanoi Studio in Ho Chi Minh City as well, located on Dong Du Street.

MIDDLE EAST

DUBAI, UNITED ARAB EMIRATES

Jennifer trades in her Beemer
for some bedouin wheels.

Why This Place Rocks for Flying Solo

Just twenty-five years ago, Dubai was a one-camel town, with a few nomadic Arabs called Bedouins crossing over its impressive sand dunes. Today, it's an amazing mingling of Arabic and Western cultures in a sprawling, cosmopolitan city. Dubai's list of attractions include world-class shopping, dramatic futuristic architecture, the first 7-star hotel on earth, and grown-up adventures that leave you feeling like a kid again. While Istanbul may wear the crown as the historical crossroads of civilization, Dubai certainly tops the charts as the crossroads for the new millennium. With 80 percent of its population having immigrated from the far reaches of the planet, expect to eavesdrop on conversations in almost every language in the world. With such a diverse crowd, you are sure to find the exact cuisine you long for—be it Mexican, Moroccan, or Mediterranean.

Innovation and *creation* are the buzzwords in Dubai: if you can dream it, someone can make it happen. Need more land? Build a huge island shaped as a palm tree that can be seen from space. Love the water? Rocket up and down waterslides at the oasis-themed Wild Wadi Waterpark, or plan a future visit to the soon-to-be-constructed underwater hotel. Miss the snow? Don't worry, there's an indoor ski resort, or snap up one of the apartments at the ice-themed residential community known as the Snowdome (complete with indoor mountain range).

Seated on the Persian Gulf, Dubai is one of seven emirates or states that make up the United Arab Emirates. The Al-Maktoum family, producing the sheikhs who rule Dubai, have demonstrated incredible foresight in developing Dubai as a multifaceted city with much more than oil to boast (oil now represents only a small percentage of the country's overall revenue). Thanks to its international population, Dubai is an inspiring example of Middle-Eastern cultural tolerance and harmony. While strolling down the marble-lined halls of the opulent and prolific shopping malls, you can find white-robed Emirati men with red-checkered headdresses, as well as Western fashionistas in Pradas and Manolos, all shopping and strolling in harmony. Solo women can feel equally comfortable in anything from chic capri-and-stiletto ensembles to head-to-toe traditional black coverings, or an elegant sari. Anything goes in Dubai!

Culture: 2

While Dubai is currently developing its cultural appeal, it is certainly not the city's raison d'être. The Dubai Museum, Sheikh Saeed al-Maktoum House (housing a historical photograph exhibit), and Heritage Village will quickly tell you everything you need to know about Dubai's recent history as an oasis for the dwindling Bedouin nomads. For music and cinema, coordinate your visit to coincide with the Dubai International Film Festival (mid-December) or the International Jazz Festival, which includes ever so much more than jazz (January).

Activity: 5

In Dubai, you will find everything from world-class golfing, prestigious equestrian centers, exhilarating sandboarding expeditions, to exciting Formula One racing. But for an activity that exercises both your legs *and* your pocketbook, get out there and do as the locals do: *Shop!*

Weather: 4

Someone once told me that Dubai has two seasons: summer and hell. Unless you like hanging out in a blast furnace, avoid traveling here in July and August. For the rest of the year, the temperatures range from pleasantly warm to a little hot.

Social: 4

You will be pleasantly surprised to discover that nearly everyone you encounter in Dubai speaks English. And as a solo gal in a Muslim-but-Western-friendly country, you can expect to be treated cordially and with respect nearly everywhere you go. As for clubbing, Dubai's nightlife is a mind-blurring world unto its own—with each new

Hotels

With each Jumeirah Beach hotel trying to outdo the other, hotel prices continue to creep toward the stratosphere. Many Jumeirah hotels have more pocket-friendly partner properties in the city, with free shuttle transport to the beach and use of the hotel facilities.

club trying to top the charts in terms of decadence, style, and funky gimmicks. You will not lack for opportunities to party like a rock star 'til the sun comes up. Many clubs offer ladies nights with super drink discounts, but choose your destination carefully so as not to end up being confused for the Eastern European prostitutes that frequent some of the seedier joints.

Flying Foreplay

You can pretty much buy whatever you desire, so do not worry if you forget to pack that oh-so-important "it" thing. You're likely to find it in Dubai anyway.

Cultural clothing. Dress to impress with your chic-est warm weather threads, but leave plenty of room to come home with new fashion finds! But remember, this *is* a Muslim country, so less skin is best for a solo diva. If you plan on visiting the more Arabic areas, such as the souks and the Jumeirah mosque (which allows non-Muslim visitors on designated days), be sure to bring something that covers your arms and legs.

Check the calendar. July and August? Don't even think about it (remember,

this is a desert). December? Book early as the film festival fills up hotel rooms, as does the shopping festival in January and February.

Setting Your Scene

Taxis are cheap, but the thrice-daily, rush-hour traffic jams are world class, so plan carefully where you want to call home during your stay. Be aware that the *entire* city is under construction, so be flexible and bring earplugs if you like to sleep late.

Jumeirah Beach. If Gulf views, stylish hotels, and all that is luxury ring your bell, then you and your Louis Vuitton bag should feel right at home on Jumeirah Beach. A long strip of sand down the Persian Gulf, Jumeirah Beach is home to the 7-star Burj-Al-Arab (the landmark of Dubai), the Jumeirah Beach Hotel, the Mina A'Salam, and many more. Jumeirah Beach Road is perpetually under construction, so bring your patience when you step into the taxi.

Deira. Deira's got souks, and souks mean shopping! As Arabia's historic predecessor to the shopping mall, a souk is where local bargains abound. A good place to stay if you want to spend the day haggling for gold, silver, spices, perfume, water pipes, henna, carpets, and even tacky Arabic souvenirs. A bad place to stay if you want to lie by the hotel pool, as many of the hotels in Deira sit right under the flight path to the Dubai International Airport.

Bur Dubai. *Bur* means "old" in Arabic, and so Bur Dubai is home to many of the historical sights in Dubai, including the Dubai Museum and the Heritage House. Walk or boat along Dubai Creek, have a traditional meal, but don't plan on doing much more in Bur Dubai.

Sheikh Zayed Road. The skyscrapers of Sheikh Zayed Road are noticeable from anywhere in Dubai. Enjoy a fine look over the city from a rooftop bar in one of the spanking new high-rise hotels. While there's not much else to do on Sheikh Zayed Road, it is a fairly central location to all the other sites.

Dubai Accessories

English magazines. *Time Out Dubai* and *What's On* are the must-have local magazines for current happenings. *Emirates Woman* gives you a peek inside the world of an expat Dubai diva. *Dubai Explore* provides all the info on local recreation.

Best books. You won't find a large array of English-language guidebooks on Dubai, but *Lonely Planet Dubai* and *Dubai Explorer* just about cover it all. For a photographic tour of Dubai, pick up the eye-boggling *Dubai Life & Times: Through the Lens of Noor Ali Rashid*, the royal photographer. British author Patricia Holton provides a glimpse inside the world of Arab women in her book *Mother Without a Mask: A Westerner's Story of Her Arab Family*.

The Top 10 Extraordinary Experiences

1. Bash the dunes, smoke the shisha. Whatever you do, do not miss a half-day desert safari! For a reasonable sum (about 85 euros at press time), you can be picked up at your hotel in a large four-by-four and whisked outside the city to the rolling sand dunes. After a good hour of dune bashing, mixed with stops to visit a camel farm and a sunset view from the top of your own personal dune, you arrive at a beautiful Bedouin camp filled with colorful carpets and low pillows. An Arabic dinner under the stars will fill your belly, while girls draped in black will paint henna designs on your arm and a dazzling belly dancer will entertain your eyes. Not impressed yet? Try a camel ride under the stars, à la T. E. Lawrence, and wrap up the day like a native by smoking apple shisha in the water pipes that are readily available at the camp. Arabian Adventures provides an excellent all-inclusive experience (dinner includes beer and wine) for about $100, and will pick you up and return you to your hotel. Tel: +971 4 303 4888.

2. Shop like an Arabian princess. With its vast variety of ways to spend your money combined with the celebratory no-sales-tax law, Dubai is quickly overtaking the likes of Paris, Milan, and Rome as the shopping capital of the world. Call in sick for a week, pretend your great-aunt died, but do whatever you have to do to get here for the four-week citywide

Royal Mirage

To properly understand the meaning of Arabian opulence, visit the One & Only Royal Mirage Resort on Jumeirah Beach. This three-in-one megaresort pays tribute to Arabian architecture in a way that would impress even the most spoiled sheikh.

Shopping Festival from January to February. Best of all, if you fly Emirates Airlines, they will graciously bump up the luggage allowance on your way out of the country. Looking for a pharaoh? Even King Tut himself would feel right at home at the Egyptian-style Wafi City shopping mall in Bur Dubai. Feeling *Italiano*? Head to the Venetian-themed Mercato mall on Jumeirah Beach Road.

3. See those camels and ponies go! For a taste of authentic bohemian life of the nomadic Bedouins, go to the races. The early bird gets much more than the worm at the 7 a.m. camel races outside of town at the Dubai Camel Racecourse (Thursday/Friday only). Tel: +971-4-338-2324.

If you like ponies, princes, and cold, hard cash, then plan on spending a day in March at the Dubai World Cup, the most expensive horse race in the world. The purse is a lovely $6 million going to the fair steed who laps the lanes the fastest. This world-famous race and all its celebrations are at Nad Al Sheba Racecourse. www.dubaiworldcup.com.

4. Cruise the creek. Take a *dhow* (traditional boat) cruise along the Dubai Creek, soaking up the sights on both the Deira and Bur Dubai sides, and perhaps a jaunt out into the Gulf as well. Follow it up with some al fresco dining on the creek near Heritage Village. Coastline

Leisure (tel: +971-4-398-4867) provides one-hour tours throughout the day leaving from the Sheraton Dubai Creek.

5. Drink in the view. Enjoy a drink and a variety of tapas on the Bahri Bar terrace at the super-luxe, Arabic-themed Mina A'Salam hotel. It's free to gape at the 7-star Burj-Al-Arab, Dubai's world-famous catamaran-shaped landmark, which lights up with multicolors at night. Afterward, if so inclined, you can walk to the "Burj" (as the locals call it) and drop 50 euros simply for the pleasure of walking in the door. Jumeirah Road; Bahri Bar, tel: +971-4-366-8888; Burj-Al-Arab, tel: +971-4-301-7000.

6. Ride the wave. For the ultimate attitude adjustment, scream and holler your way through 12 acres of waterslides, caves, tunnels, pools, and grottoes. Test the strength of your heart with a thrilling freefall drop down Jumeirah Sceirah. Jumeirah Road, at the entrance to the Burj-Al-Arab; tel: +971-4-348-4444; www.wildwadi.com.

7. Hit the slopes. At Mall of the Emirates, you can buy everything from 10-karat diamond broaches to sexy lingerie. When that gets boring, spend a few hours on the slopes at the indoor "Ski Dubai" facility. You don't have to worry about ski clothing or equipment either. Ski Dubai has thought of it all and offers guests the use of winter clothing and ski and snowboard equipment.

8.   Hone your haggling skills. Give your eyes, nose, and ears a special treat with a stroll through the glistening gold souks, the fragrant spice and perfume souks, the covered souk, and everything in between. The gold souk is reputed to be one of the largest in the Middle East. You will need to ready yourself for some vigorous bargaining, but it's worth every golden minute. Located in Deira.

9.   Find your inner Cleopatra. Treat yourself like the diva you are at the glorious Cleopatra Spa. With a variety of massage treatments and henna body art to pamper your every inch, you may never want to leave. Wafi City Pyramids, Al-Qataiyat Road; tel: +971-4-324-7700.

10.   See a movie. Yes, there is something free in Dubai! After all that shopping and skiing, or haggling and water sliding, head over to Movie Under the Stars. You can catch a free movie on Saturday and Sunday nights at 8 p.m. You never really know what you'll end up seeing, but it is a fun and free adventure. Wafi City Rooftop.

OCEANIA

PORT DOUGLAS, AUSTRALIA

Marina lounging at the
Mirage Hotel.

Why This Place Rocks for Flying Solo

*T*ucked away above the Tropic of Cancer and below Cape Tribulation is the tiny coastal town of Port Douglas. Port Douglas isn't your run-of-the-mill beach destination—this place is teeming with all kinds of life—wildlife, nightlife, highlife, the list goes on. Here you can check out some of the most amazing species of animals around, and I'm talking about Australian men. As for all those other things that swim, crawl, bite, and run, you can see plenty of those, too. It does take some time to get to Port Douglas from the Northern Hemisphere, but it's well worth the trip because everyone who finally gets to

Port Douglas really wants to be there. It's like a pilgrimage for the religiously active. It helps that Australian people are over-the-top friendly, everyone speaks English, and they love to party like, well, Australians.

So for all you women who want to know what happens down under, Port Douglas is the place. The quintessential Australian destination, it's far enough away from urban sprawl—not that there's much in Australia anyway—and close enough to civilization that you can find (almost) anything you want. You get to have your extreme tropical outback experience while staying in hotels that supply hot water and telephones.

From jumping out of perfectly good airplanes 14,000 feet above sea level to riding not-so-wild Brumbies through the rain forest, Port Douglas is super-duper for a girl with guts. And for you not-so-wild ones, you'll find miles of white, sandy beaches to explore, along with some pretty interesting places to meet locals. Between snorkeling, scuba diving, hiking, exploring, horseback riding, swimming, and Jet Skiing, you'll be sure to meet a cast of characters straight out of a Crocodile Dundee movie. In general, the guys are hot and tanned, the beer is cold and frosty, and the climate is just right.

Culture: 1

What! No culture? You'll get over it after your first scuba lesson with one of the many certified and deliciously handsome instructors who'll teach you to dive in the Great Barrier Reef. You'll spot some of the world's most outrageous sea creatures in the sea, and on land, you'll explore the incredibly lush Daintree Rain Forest. No other place in the world puts on a land and sea nature show like Port Douglas.

Activity: 5

Port Douglas is a natural amusement park for sports lovers. Spend a day swinging on the golf course, ride a horse, try scuba diving, or get lost in the rain forest on a nature hike with Aboriginals. The climate is perfect for spending your days outdoors and it's easy to keep your heart pumping.

Weather: 4

If you come at the right time of year, the weather is marvelous. The air is moist and filled with sweet, tropical scents. The days are toasty, and at night, the temperature dips oh so slowly. But like anything that's too good to be true, they've got only two seasons here: wet and dry. Come when it's dry, otherwise your hair will hate you, but more importantly, the water will be too stirred up to really enjoy the Great Barrier Reef.

Social: 5

By the time you leave, you'll know how to say "G'Day" like a local—along with a few other good Aussie sayings! You'll have a "heap" of new friends from "whoop whoop." Every night is a great night to go meet new "mates," over a "pot" of beer or a "Bundy and coke."

Flying Foreplay

H ere are a few tips to keep your trip a happy one. Queensland (the state that Port Douglas is in) is lined with some of the most jaw-dropping remote beaches and rain forests in the world, but they also are known for a few less-happy things.

A hole in Oz. Yup, there is a hole in the ozone right above Australia. So, that

Good Eats

For good food with both local and lodge guests, visit Port O' Call Bistro in Port O' Call Lodge, Port St. at Craven Close.

means you need to keep your skin protected big time. I'm talking 50 plus SPF. None of that wimpy 4 or 8 will work here; you'll fry.

Wear protection. The Australian men are known to bite, but you don't need to worry about them. Protect yourself from the mosquitoes with spray-on repellant. And keep the repellant off your acrylic nails; it's been known to ruin them.

Stay dry. As I mentioned, there are only two seasons in Port Douglas, wet and dry. Wet season is from December to April (hot and wet). Dry season is from May to November (warm and dry). You only want to go during the dry season.

Clothing optional. Port Douglas is very casual, so you don't need to pack your business suit. Bring lots of bathing suits because, with the humidity, it can take a day for your swimming togs to dry.

Port Douglas Accessories

Bite me! And those bugs will, if you give them a chance. From the moment you rise and shine to the time you hit the sheets, stay covered in bug repellent.

Skin sense. The sun is hotter and more ornery in Oz than in the rest of the world. Stay slathered in high SPF sunscreen that is waterproof.

All-terrain shoes. Plan on jumping from sand to sailboats, and going rock climbing and horse riding. You'll need shoes that protect your cute pedi-ed toes, as well as keep you sure-footed.

The Top 10 Extraordinary Experiences

1. Snorkel in the Great Barrier Reef. Diving down into the warm waters of the Great Barrier Reef, you enter an unbelievable world of timeless creatures and colorful coral. You don't need any training to snorkel. At first it can be a bit frightening—so much water, so little you—but once you get past your apprehension, the sea world opens up to you. The boats will take you to the reef at the very edge of Australia's Continental Shelf, to an underwater world of dazzling kaleidoscope brilliance. www.quicksilver-cruises.com.

2. Sail with the locals. The yacht club on a Wednesday night is the place to be. Get there about 4:30 p.m. and ask for the captain who's taking people sailing that night. Like most Aussies, you'll usually find him at the bar. Put your name down and buy your lovely sailor a drink. You can also buy a few for the road, or should I say sea. Once you get back to dry land, feast on a great, cheap pub meal with the other sailors, locals, and visitors who know about this little secret. Walk over to Port Douglas Yacht Club, or ask any local how to get there.

3. Giddy up! If you ever dreamt about riding with the man from Snowy River, then this is your chance. Spend a glorious day riding a horse through the thick, lush rain forest or gallop along the sandy coast of Wonga Beach, or perhaps you'll want to get lost in sweet sugar cane fields. Mowbray Valley Trail Rides, tel: (61)(7) 4099 3268; or Wonga Beach Equestrian Centre, tel: (61)(7) 4098 7583.

4. Ride Thunder. Rafting the Mighty Tully River is an awesome adventure for the girl who appreciates insane rafting through the rain forest. You'll get picked up at your hotel before the sun rises (but you can sleep on the way down) and spend the whole day out on the raft with a dozen of your new friends. www.ragingthunder.com.

5. Jump! There are things you only do once in your life, and skydiving is one of them. Because Australians aren't too concerned about details, they tend to take you up higher than most skydiving places allow. For the biggest adrenaline rush in your life, call Paul at Paul's Parachuting. Drop the extra cash for a video of your jump; it's worth the money! Tel: (61)(7) 4051 8855; www.paulsparachuting.com.au.

6. Meet some swingers. After all that swimming, try some swinging at the Mirage Country Club. This place is truly a golfer's paradise. Rated as one of the world's best resort courses, complete with crocodiles and tropical birds. Those kind gents at Mirage offer one-on-one professional golf instructors. So, if you ever thought about taking up golf, this is the place to do it. Davidson Street, Port Douglas; tel: (61)(7) 4099 5888.

7. Bike 'n' Hike. If you can't decide on what to do all day, why not do a little bit of each? How about a day of biking, hiking, and swimming in natural lagoons in the Mowbray Valley, near Port Douglas, with a small group of other travelers? You don't need to be in iron man shape to enjoy this trilogy of treats. Bike 'n' Hike; tel: (61)(7) 4099 4000.

8. Soar above the rain forest. The Sky Rail glides you on an amazing experience over Australia's World Heritage, an amazing tropical rain forest canopy. Rides go for about five miles over pristine rain forest, where you explore the wonders of an ancient tropical forest. Here, you can learn about one of the most botanically fascinating and diverse areas on earth. www.skyrail.com.au.

9. Get jiggy with Aboriginals. Take a guided walk deep in the rain forest with the KuKu-Yalanji Aboriginal tribe. These gentle natives will teach you about bush medicines and food, Dreamtime legends, and together you'll view cave paintings and visit sacred sites their families have called home for tens of thousands of years. The tour is followed by a Dreamtime story over billy tea and damper in a bark warun (shelter). KuKu-Yalanji Dreamtime Tours; tel: (61)(7) 4098 2595. For an even more intimate Aboriginal experience, ride with full-blooded Aboriginal Hazel Douglas of Native Guide Safari Tours, tel: (61)(7) 4098 2206; www.native guidesafaritours.com.au. She takes visitors on 4-wheel-drive tours of the Aboriginal way of life in the rain forest. She shares her traditional knowledge of plants, animals, Dreamtime myths, and Aboriginal history on a full-day tour.

10. Dine with the stars. Yes, this place is frequented by lots of famous people, but the stars I'm talking about are the ones you see when you look up.

Nestled in the fragrant rain forest, under palm trees and open sky, you'll find Nautilus restaurant. The food is marvelous and the setting is magical. This is one of my favorite dining experiences in the world. Nautilus, tel: (61)(7) 4099 5330; www.nautilus-restaurant.com.au.

QUEENSTOWN, NEW ZEALAND

Pamela chilling on Fox Glacier.

Why This Place Rocks for Flying Solo

Sometimes what you're looking for can only be found after a long journey to the metaphoric ends of the earth. Other times, you really have to go to the ends of the earth. If you're looking for a place with spectacular land-scapes, thrilling sports, jolts of endorphins, and welcoming locals—you'll find it in Queenstown, New Zealand. This handsome, buzzing town was given, and heartily embraces, the title of Adventure Capital of the World. These crazy kiwis (what they are endearingly called, not because of the fruit but the birds that live on the New Zealand islands) were the ones to set up

The Bus

Have a Remarkable Experience and jump aboard a 1937 Chevrolet Bus for a tour through Queenstown and Arrowtown, taking in the culture, scenery, art, and history of the region. Tel: 03 409 8578; www.remarkableexperience.com.

the first commercial bungee-jumping site in the world, so expect them to be a bit extreme when it comes to experimenting with sports.

Queenstown is the kind of place that makes you think about how far you're willing to go. Are you up for pushing your mental and physical stamina to the edge? Does the thought of free-falling and speed boating excite you to the point of goose bumps? And if you're not sure where your personal boundaries lie, take a chance and find out. This will be the trip to expand your spectrum of experiences and find out who you actually are. How many times in your life will you be able to encounter the overwhelming magnificence of the outdoors, jet boat, heli-ski, bungee jump, and white-water raft all in 48 hours? And for you less ambitious girls, try a funyak or funcanoe, take a four-wheel-drive trip to Macetown or Skippers Canyon, or treat yourself to a massage or treatment in one of the many spas in town. Or you can just hang out in one of the many pubs, sip a glass of the region's famous Pinot Noir, and socialize with other adventure-lovers who traverse the planet to chill under the Southern Skies. Paris has the Eiffel Tower, London has Big Ben, and New Zealand has unbridled natural beauty, endearing people, and more sheep per capita than any place on the planet.

Culture: 3

Like a cultural cocktail of ingredients pulled from all corners of the globe, New Zealand is an exotic mix of British, Maori, and Polynesian with a dash of Scots to round out the flavor. The rich native heritage of the island courses through everyday life, making New Zealand the not-so-monochromatic destination you might think.

Activity: 5

Pick your element: earth, water, or air. Whether you're a biking beauty, a fishing fan, a hot-air ballooning honey, or a wild rafting woman, Queenstown's got you covered. Bring your courageous spirit and an open mind. The activities in this part of the world are a bit over-the-top.

Weather: 3

Shift your seasonal paradigm; New Zealand's weather is opposite of the Northern Hemisphere. A great way to get a tan in the winter or snow burn in the summer, check the weather before you pack your bags. Most travelers visit New Zealand during the sunny summer months (November–February), when temperatures are warmer and the tourism industry is humming. Queenstown enjoys four distinct seasons, from summer sun, autumn leaves, winter après-ski style, and spring blossoms.

Minus Five

Check out an ice bar called Minus Five, where everything, including the glasses, is made from ice. Everyone dresses in heavy coats, so it doesn't matter if you forgot your slinky cocktail dress. They serve vodka (it's the only liquor that doesn't freeze at that temperature) and set your drink limit to three. Apparently alcohol has a different effect on you at colder temperatures. Feel free to lick the walls: tongues only stick at 20 to 30 degrees below zero. Steamer Wharf; tel: +64 3 442 6050; www.minus5.co.nz.

Activities from town (with the exception of skiing and snowboarding) run year-round.

Social: 5

Overlook the fact that New Zealand has more sheep than people. Because when it comes to a good night on the town, these folks are anything but sheepish with strangers. A good pub meal and a few beers after a heavy day of fervent activities set the social scene here. In Queenstown, every night is a Saturday, and you can easily move from pub to cocktail bar to club.

Flying Foreplay

Planning on risking life or limb? New Zealand has fantastic medical facilities, but there's no such thing as a free crutch. Doctors usually like to be paid immediately for their services. Be sure to purchase travelers' insurance if your policy doesn't cover you abroad.

Read Before You Go

The Bone People: A Novel, by Keri Hulme

Straying from the Flock: Travels in New Zealand, by Alexander Elder
The Whale Rider, by Witi Ihimaera

Queenstown Accessories

Sweet shoes. Hiking shoes are necessary if you plan to climb the hills around town; you didn't see the Hobbits trekking around in heels, did you?
Picture it! The stunning natural landscape provides the perfect backdrop for your "Look at me! I'm in New Zealand!" blog entries to show your jealous friends.

The Top 10 Extraordinary Experiences

1. **Try a combination platter.** Not sure if you want to spend a whole day bungee jumping because you want to try some crazy jet boating? But then rafting sounds fun, too? Here are a few places that offer attractive package deals, so you can do it all in one day:
Info & Track. They offer the Shotover High Five, which combines the

Current Events

Get a current listing of events at www.queenstown-nz.co.nz/information/Events.

Shotover Jet with a helicopter ride to Skyline for luging and a gondola ride down the mountain. 37 Shotover Street.

Awesome Foursome. Combine the Nevis Highwire Bungee with the Shotover Jet, a gorgeous helicopter ride, and a Shotover raft trip. Insane!

Ultimate Trio. Combine the Kawarau Jet with a tandem skydive and rafting. Want the true test of your stamina? Go for the Adventure Marathon—it's an adrenaline combination for true die-hards.

Queenstown Combos. This outfit has a dozen different packages to choose from. If you want more adrenaline, it's not a problem for these folks. Tel: 0800-423-836 in NZ, or 03-442-7318; www.combos.co.nz.

Triple Challenge Combination Trip. This five-hour trip offered by Queenstown Rafting dares you to strap on your life jacket, soar into the clouds, then work your oars till you're dripping with sweat and river water . . . in a good way. Tel: 0800-RAFTING (0800-723-8464).

2. Follow in the footsteps of the Fellowship. Even if you're not a geeky goddess, you can appreciate the mythical beauty of the scenery in the *Lord of the Rings* trilogy. Lucky for all of you, you don't have to travel to Middle Earth to feel like you're in fairy forests and princes' realms. *Lord of the Rings* was filmed primarily in nearby Glenorchy, a tiny village surrounded by blue ice glaciers, rolling rock meadows, and primeval tree canopies, where you'll feel like your fantasy world has come to life.

3. Take the plunge! Give new meaning to your mom's favorite saying, "Well if your friends all jumped off a bridge, would you follow?" Even if none of your friends have had a big, thick rubber band tied to their legs and willingly jumped off a bridge face-first, you can!

Kawarau Suspension Bridge. This bridge is 141 feet high (but looks higher when you're about to jump) and was the world's first commercial bungee operation.

The Ledge. It's 154 feet feet high and has the Wild Side and the Mild Side. It's located near town, and if you are more of a night jumper, they do offer nocturnal dives.

Nevis Highwire Bungee. At 440 feet over the Kawarau River, it's the tallest bungee site in New Zealand.

Bungy Tours. You don't have to jump with this new tour out at Kawarau Bungy Centre, which explores the history behind bungee and how it all started. It might, however, change your mind and inspire you to take the leap!

4. Trot with Sam. Saddle up for a guided horse trek across the tussock-covered hills of Moonlight Country. Ride among the animals on a classic New Zealand deer farm and enjoy spectacular alpine views of the Remarkables and Coronet Peak ski areas. You'll see grazing elk and rare white fallow deer on the 800-acre Doonholme farm. Sturdy shoes and long pants are a must for this ride. Sam, the yellow Labrador, will insist on coming with you on your ride. Moonlight Stables; tel: 03-442-1229; www.moonlight country.com.

5. Sip in the spectacular. A gorgeous winery nestled between the rugged mountain of New Zealand and the Kawarau River Gorge, Chard Farm is the place to get drunk on a spectacular view while tasting a collection of Sauvignon Blanc, Chardonnay, Pinot Noir, and Riesling. The tasting room is open seven days a week. www.chardfarm.co.nz.

6. Snow ski in your summer. Why limit your ski bunny wardrobe to the winter? New Zealand's seasons are gloriously off kilter from the Northern Hemisphere, providing year-round opportunities to cut it up on the slopes. You'll find two gorgeous ski fields, Coronet Peak and the Remarkables, within a half-hour drive of the main town. Queenstown is internationally famous for ski slopes, so while you won't be sliding down the mountains alone, you'll certainly crash into fellow snow followers from around the globe. Check Snow New Zealand for all things ski/snow related. www.snow.co.nz.

7. Do some day tripping. Head to Fiordland and destinations such as Milford and Doubtful Sounds, where you'll find jagged fjords, crystal clear lakes, and if you're lucky, you'll spot bottlenose dolphins, fur seals, and rare penguins. Other destination spots such as Glenorchy, Wanaka, and Arrowtown are all within an easy drive. Oh, they drive on the other side of the road, so you might want to go with a tour group.

8. Dine in the sky. Take the gondola, reputed to be the steepest lift in the Southern Hemisphere, to the tip top of Bob's

Peak and gaze down on Queenstown while enjoying a cocktail or meal at the Skyline restaurant. And just when you thought you couldn't have any more fun, race down the hill in a luge. Make sure you don't eat too much before your harrowing ride down the mountain. www.skyline.co.nz.

9.   Release your inner farmgirl. New Zealand sure beats Green Acres, and set within the fantasy-like environment are a variety of organic farms that will house and feed you while you whistle the day away on their plots. Find out how green your thumbs really are. Those looking for something a little less rustic can check out Vacation Verde, a guide for travelers "who wish to have a wholesome holiday experience." www.wwoof.co.nz.

10.   Get wrapped in Frangipani!! After all that bungee jumping, river surfing, snow skiing, luging, and horseback riding, you deserve a tranquil afternoon of pampering. Limp over to Hush Spa for a Frangipani Body Nourish Wrap. Owned by a local mother-daughter team, Hush Spa is a soothing lull in the adrenaline storm that is Queenstown. Don't forget to breathe. Hush Spa, Level 2, Corner Robins and Gorge Roads, Queenstown; www.hushspa.co.nz.

SYDNEY, AUSTRALIA

Aimee at the top of the land
down under.

Why This Place Rocks for Flying Solo

*A*s a self-proclaimed world-class jet-setter, my goal is to visit as many places as I can before I kick the bucket. So, once I visit a destination, I tend to check that off my "to do" list. But there is something spellbinding about Sydney that draws me back like a lovestruck teenager. Perhaps it is breathtaking Darling Harbour, or possibly it's the dramatic opera house. Maybe it is the frisky folks on Bondi Beach, or could it be the spicy Kings Cross district, or maybe the lively Rocks area? I think it's a tasty cocktail of them all, topped with the outrageously spirited Aussies. Sydney is like that perfect friend you have. You know, no matter how long you hang out, or where you go, or what you do, it's always a blast. That's Sydney, the sparkling crown of Australia that reclines oh so comfortably between the Blue Mountains and the deep blue sea.

You'll never get sick of hearing "G'day" or enjoying the sunny weather that so kindly blesses the city 342 days a year. Although it is one of the most contemporary cities in the world, and one of the largest in the Southern Hemisphere, it has retained its small-town charm. So, unlike some destinations where you really shouldn't venture into particularly seedy parts of town, Sydney is pretty darn safe!

As the capital, Sydney puts the small continent's best face forward with progressive theater performances, cutting-edge adventure sports, and more events than they can fit in a calendar. Unlike Europe, Sydney is fairly young; you won't find a famous fifteenth-century artist who called Sydney home. But if Australian art only conjures images of boomerangs and didgeridoos, think again. Modern Aboriginal art is spellbinding with its symbolism and traditional forms. You'll find plenty of Aussies who will love to share a "pint" with you, and don't be surprised if your belly hurts from all the laughing you'll be doing. So, if you are ready to go beyond the international time zone, where the Southern Cross fills the midnight skies, and Dream-

time is a way of life, then get ready for a life-changing trip to one of the best cities in the world—Sydney, Australia.

Culture: 2

I have to admit that I tend to spend more time hanging out with the locals in chic bars and restaurants than visiting museums. But if you are interested in the history of Australia, you'll find a bounty of information at the Museum of Sydney. And for you art buffs, the Art Gallery of New South Wales has the largest collection of Aboriginal and Torres Strait Islander art.

Activity: 3

Sydney has plenty to leave you *bushwhacked* by the end of the day, if you are into water sports. Surfing classes on Bondi Beach, canoeing, fishing, swimming, and sailing are just a few things to *tucker* you out. You can find more to do if you leave the city center and venture out to the Blue Mountain ranges for hiking, mountain biking, and horseback riding.

Weather: 5

Once you get here, you'll see why I don't spend any time in the museums. It's just too darn pretty out! You can count on the weather being mild, with a pleasant breeze. Oh, remember that the seasons are the opposite from the Northern hemisphere. So winter in Sydney is in June, July, and August.

Waiters in Australia tend to be more laid-back than you would expect. They get paid a pretty decent salary, so tipping is not required, but certainly appreciated. If the service is with a smile, tip; if not, well . . .

Social: 5

Australians are great people. They work to live, not live to work. So, when the evening sets in, you are bound to find businesspeople meeting at a local pub for a refresher before heading home. And the weekends are alive with people filling the neighborhood restaurants and bars. Oh, and they all speak English (with a sometimes difficult-to-understand accent, but without a doubt, it is English).

Flying Foreplay

Sydney has all the luxuries any global goddess expects. You can drink the tap water, the food is delicious, the fruits and vegetables are amazing, and if you do get sick, you can find whatever you need. Plus they speak English here, so that's a huge plus! You might not understand their slang, though, so here are some important words:

Sheila: what they call chicks
Shout: to buy a round of drinks
Whoop whoop: someplace really far away
D&M: deep and meaningful conversation
Pint: a glass of beer

"G'day, *Sheila*, can I *shout* you a *pint*? Looks like you came from *whoop whoop*, or you just got done having a *D&M* with your girlfriend."

You will be crossing over the international date line and losing a day. So be prepared for a big case of jet lag. Just plan on resting when you land and try to set your system on Aussie time ASAP. Accept that you might lose another day catching up, so plan that into your schedule. Better safe than getting sick because you were pushing yourself too hard.

Read Before You Go

In a Sunburned Country, by Bill Bryson
The Monkey's Mask, by Dorothy Porter
Poor Man's Orange, by Ruth Park

Sydney Accessories

Okay . . . You knew a place as perfect as Sydney had to have something wrong with it, right? And yes, there is a big hole in the ozone just above the Sydney Opera House. Make sure you use a sunscreen with protection against both UVA (aging rays) and UVB (cancer/burning rays). It's a matter of health as well as fine line prevention.

Swimwear, darling. With 37 ocean and harbor beaches, you'll wonder why you brought clothes at all.

Beat Jet Lag

Try to expose yourself to as much sun as possible during the day, which will keep you more alert and slow your body's natural production of melatonin. Before you go to bed, take a supplementary dose of melatonin (it's an all-natural substance that won't give you the nasty side effects of some chemical remedies). You'll wake up refreshed and the only bags you'll have will be your luggage.

Little black dress. Sydney is casual, yet sophisticated. You can get away with wearing something simple if you dress it up with a scarf or nice shoes. A pashmina and some chandelier earrings can go a long way.

Freshen up. Unfortunately they still smoke in pubs, so you might want to bring some fabric freshener, like *Febreze*. Spritz your clothes before you go to bed and hang them up in the bathroom; you don't want to spend a fortune on dry-cleaning.

Cute tennis shoes. Think pink and blue Pumas, not your muggy running shoes from college. This town is more Sporty than Posh Spice, and you're going to want sturdy kicks to keep yourself grounded as you climb the Sydney Harbor Bridge or jog down the beach for your morning exercise.

The Top 10 Extraordinary Experiences

1. **Travel in the company of divas.** Just for one night, put away your dreams of meeting the man from Snowy River or Crocodile Dundee; it's more like Crocodile DIVA! If you own the *Pricilla Queen of the Desert* DVD or soundtrack, then Sydney by Diva is for you. They offer tours of the city, led by "professional" drag queens. Get ready to get caught up in the fake eyelashes and glitter of it all; they give free makeup advice, too. Tours

Neilson Bay

Take a State Transit Bus from the city and head toward Rosebay, where you can rent a kayak. As you head out from the beach, you will understand why Sydneysiders have a great love of the outdoors. In Neilson Bay you will paddle along some of the most expensive coastline in Australia, as you check out the local real estate and admire the yachts as they play in the harbor. Pull in at Neilson Bay Park for a swim in the harborside pool and enjoy a cool drink at the kiosk before heading back to Rose Bay.

Bondi Beach

A solo girl will love a day at Bondi Beach. This beachside playground simply sizzles in summer. Make sure you go here on a weekend when the surf clubs are in training and filled with bronzed Aussie lifesavers. The sight of our boys all buffed and in Speedos is certainly quite something!

are offered daily, as well as a special "Girlie Tour" once a year for women only. Well, people in women's clothing. www.sydneybydiva.com.

2.   Go Aussie extreme. For you adrenaline junkies, this is the sightseeing tour for you. Imagine flying through Sydney Harbour at 50 miles an hour, and if you are lucky, your boat will ride a wake and catch air. The boats used to get your heart racing are the same ones used for special forces and the police. You'll feel like you are breaking the laws of gravity on this once-in-a-lifetime frolic. Make sure you don't wear a skirt on this trip! Ocean Extreme, www.adrenalin.com.au.

3.   Visit the botanical gardens that Dracula built. You haven't lived until you've spent a gorgeous afternoon strolling through Sydney's Royal Botanic Gardens, just a short walk from the harbor. You'll delight in the cockatiels perched high in the treetops, and as you gaze at them, you'll notice that the large leaves around them are moving. Yes, children of the night, what sweet music they make—all those giant flying foxes squawking and jockeying for branch position with their brown-veined wings fluttering. Like the rest of us, these fruit-loving cousins to bats just can't get enough of this phenomenal park. Other exotic shocks include a collection of rare trees from around the world as well as Australia's own garden variety of flora

Bill's

You simply cannot leave Sydney without having breakfast at Bill's, a café located in the rather bohemian area of Darlinghurst. As you step through the sandstone entrance into the light-filled room, center stage is a large communal table with the latest magazines. The basic but "to-die-for menu" has locals lining up on a Saturday morning to eat the best scrambled eggs you can imagine, although I must say it's a tough choice with the ricotta hotcakes and honeycomb butter. Bill Granger is the owner and also author to a number of cookbooks that are essential for every girl's kitchen! 433 Liverpool Street.

The Paddington Market

This is the place to be on Saturdays, where you can explore stands filled with the creations of local designers, jewelry, and antiques.

and fauna. When it's finally time to step inside, visit no less than the world-class Art Gallery of New South Wales whose Aboriginal art collection is stunning. www.rbgsyd.nsw.gov.au/royal_botanic_gardens.

4. Paddle through the night. Night life has a totally new meaning after spending a few shadowy hours paddling in the Royal National Park after dark. Bundeena Sea Kayaks does a Night Owl paddling adventure where you explore the nocturnal wildlife and natural beauty of the pristine waterways that are just 45 minutes south of Sydney. Once the sun tucks under the horizon, your tour begins. You'll glide past dark beaches and bays on your way into the park. Don't worry, all the paddlers are armed with flashlights, safety gear, and an experienced guide who provides historical and nature information about the park. www.bundeenakayaks.com.au.

5. Reach for the stars. Climb the Sydney Harbour Bridge. Weave through catwalks like a kitten on the prowl, scale steep ladders like Spiderman, and finally, reach the summit of the bridge with an eagle's eye view of one of the most beautiful metropolises in the world. It is a 3.5-hour round trip. This is not for the faint-hearted or those who are not very fit. Remember to wear sturdy shoes and bring your camera for that perfect holiday card for your soon-to-be-jealous friends. www.bridgeclimb.com.

6. Be a koala's mommy. First off, a koala is not a bear—it is a marsupial and an endangered one at that. The zoo is a beautiful site with unreal views of Sydney behind it. But instead of one more stuffed toy souvenir to commemorate your visit, why not donate money to the zoo in honor of a particular animal? You can get a picture with a koala, and you'll get regular updates, becoming a real "Zoo Parent" to the critter, and a seriously cool gal to the appreciative staff of the zoo. If you have something against koalas, you can also "adopt" wombats, kangaroos, gibbons, Tasmanian devils, and more. Visit the "Get Involved" link at www.zoo.nsw.gov.au.

7. Don't want to break your nails on a guidebook? Sydney is the kind of city that you can easily go out and tackle by yourself. But if you want a truly unique insiders' peek into this awesome city, join the Secret Sights of Sydney offered by Night Cat Tours. Tours last around three hours.

Some of the fun:

- A magical history tour. You won't find this information in the guidebooks.
- Stunning photographic vantage points of the city, and people who can take your picture!

Ferry

By now you will understand that Sydneysiders crisscross this city by ferry for work and for play. So jump aboard the Watsons Bay ferry and head straight to this idyllic harborside suburb that was once a fishing village. Explore the quaint backstreets and stop off at the beach for a refreshing dip before walking along the cliff tops to the Gap Ravine. Just before you make your way back to the city, ensure you stop off at Watsons Bay Pub for a glittering view of the city, or you could try the famous Doyles fish and chips in the shady park.

- Walk down the back streets of the famous red light area—Kings Cross.
- Glamorous inner-city shopping precincts—Balmain, Kirribilli, and Darlinghurst.
- Champagne and photos under the Harbour Bridge.
- Complimentary dinner at a famous local café.
- Toast at the famous Opera Bar. Breathtaking harbor views and a glass of bubbly.

Night Cat Tours; www.nightcattours.com.

8. Take a walk from the Opera House to Woolloomooolloo. From the Sydney Opera House, head through the iron gates of the Royal Botanical Gardens and follow the pathway along the harbor side before making your way farther into the gardens, to the Art Gallery of New South Wales. Make sure you check out the Indigenous Artwork of native Aboriginals along with that of early Australia. A ten-minute stroll from here is the Finger Wharf Pier at Woolloomooloo, which has experienced a remarkable rebirth and has imaginatively

been converted into apartments and a row of fabulous "very Sydney" outdoor restaurants. Certainly a great spot to stop for a bite to eat before heading to the Tilbury Hotel for a late-afternoon drink with the locals. Should you be in need of a late-afternoon snack, you must stop by the famous Harry's Café de Wheels for a "mushy pea and mash meat pie." Don't forget the tomato sauce! That's ketchup to us "Yanks."

9. Enjoy happy hour on the Harbour. Spending time on the water while you are in Sydney is a requirement. Because the harbor is actually fairly inland, you don't get those nasty breezes you get on ocean cruises. The water is pretty calm and the views—wow—magnificent. For a perfect preamble to a night on the town, try Matilda's Sailing Cocktail Cruise. It is a wonderful hour-and-a-bit cruise that includes light canapés and a complimentary glass of wine, beer, or champagne. You are bound to meet other visitors, and don't be surprised if by the time you finish the cruise, you have a new group of friends. Matilda's Sailing Cocktail Cruise; www.matilda.com.au.

An Aussie Pub

If you are looking for some social interaction, head toward the historic Rocks area, which comes to life on the weekend with plenty of Aussie men . . . and women. The Australian Hotel has great local brews and an interesting selection of pizzas—don't forget to try the Crocodile Pizza. The Glenmore Hotel has great rooftop views. The Hero of Waterloo is Sydney's oldest pub and has some rather colorful locals telling interesting *yarns*.

10. Read poetry. One of the most beloved Australians is Banjo Patterson, a famous poet, farmer, horseman, and writer. Some of his most celebrated works you already know, because they are iconic Australian tunes and stories. They include "Waltzing Matilda" and "The Man from Snowy River." Go to a bookstore and pick up one of his poetry books, then spend an afternoon reading his poetry under the shade of a blooming wattle tree or huge gum tree. My favorite poem is "The Uplift."

Top Watering Holes

G o to www.seesydney.com.au for the latest list of solo-friendly joints:

Darlinghurst

Dugout Bar, The Burdekin: Underground ambience.
Mr Goodbar: Funky tunes.

Lime Bar, L'Otel: The polished and uber-chic.

Ruby Rabbit: That inner-city feel.

Q Bar: Late night drinks and dancing.

Woolloomooloo

W bar, Woolloomooloo Wharf, Zeta Bar at the Hilton Sydney: The classy party set.

Posh Lounge, Overseas Passenger Terminal: Top floor cocktails.

King's Cross

Hugo's Lounge, Bayswater Rd.: Models with the moves.

The Rocks

The Harbour View Hotel: Live acts with a view.

Paddington

Paddington Bowling Club: Sunday afternoon beer and bowls.

Paddington Inn: Elegant decor and beautiful people.

NORTH AMERICA

THE CARIBBEAN

Stacy playing around in the
Dominican Republic.

Why This Place Rocks
for Flying Solo

*I*f water the temperature of soft
kisses and glorious days playing in
the sun are tugging at your
wanderlust strings, then I have a place
for you. Just south of Florida floats a cultural archipelago of islands known as the
Caribbean. Yes, you've heard all about
the places where the hordes of obnoxious tourists go, but I have a few secret
enclaves and escapades for the solo flyer
who wants to have a boatload of fun. It
is hard to choose just one adventure to
share with you, so I'll be telling you
about ten different places that are just
waiting to sweep you out of your ho-
hum life for a bit of bedazzling fun.

These places will have you dancing your nights away under the warm, starry nights while you turn into a tropical social butterfly. It is not just Stella who can get her groove back—so can you.

From splashing around in the outrageously unreal waters of Turks and Caicos, to learning how to make jerk chicken in Jamaica, you can't get bored on these trips. Thinking about mastering your downward dog, or ready to try the flying trapeze? The opportunities are endless, darling. Unlike other chapters, where I take you to one supremely super solo place, in this chapter I introduce you to ten totally different tours, cruises, and retreats that are ideal for the girl on the go. As incredibly beautiful as the Caribbean is, it's not the kind of place where you should just pack your bags and head out to an island. Each island has a completely different feel—think Rastafarians to royalty. The last thing you want to be is stuck on the "honeymoon island" alone, or on an island packed with randy college students (right?). Choose to chill, sail with pirates in the Caribbean, or hike a volcano—whatever you want, the Caribbean's got it.

Culture: 4
Oh girl. This place is as spicy as conch fritters with tangy papaya sauce. Since Columbus, Europeans have been clamoring to own these incredible islands. At an unfortunate time in history, this was slave-trading central, so there is a rich African society here, too. The amalgamation of all these cultures has created a saucy slant on each of the islands once owned by countries like England, France, Spain, and The Netherlands. It's pretty awesome seeing traditional colonial homes painted yellow, filled with Caribbean steel drum music, and wrapped in fuchsia bougainvillea.

Activity: 5
If you want to sit on the beach all day nursing a piña colada, you can! But if want to dive, Jet Ski, parasail, swim, hike, jog, and play in the sand, then you are going to love it here, too.

Weather: 4
Walking out at night and getting tickled by the gentle Caribbean breeze is divine. And for most of the year, the weather is stellar, but from around June to November, Mother Nature doesn't play nice, and sends over hurricanes.

Social: 4
You are going to meet other fabulous travelers who want to get to know you. Of course, if you go somewhere that's not on my Top 10 list, I can't promise whom you'll meet. The Caribbean can be tricky when it comes to meeting like-minded people.

Snow Birds

High season in the Caribbean is December to April, where poor, freezing souls from Canada and Northern America fly down to thaw out.

Flying Foreplay

Did someone say hurricane? Many places have great deals during the hurricane season, but is it worth betting against Mother Nature to save a few bucks? It is your call, but I don't see global warming going away anytime soon.

Caribbean Accessories

You'll need the usual suspects on this trip: a bevy of swimsuits, a variety of sunscreens, rock star sunglasses, and a waterproof camera. You should also check with the different trips to see if there is anything else you need to bring. For example, if you decide to sail on a tall ship, you'll need to bring the right shoes.

Caribbean Books to Take on Your Trip

The Islandman Sings His Song, by Giftus R. John
A Salty Piece of Land, by Jimmy Buffet
Wide Sargasso Sea, by Jean Rhys

The Top 10 Extraordinary Experiences

1. Learn how to fly at Turks and Caicos. For you jet-setters who love to party with the European set, head to Club Med's Turkoise village. It is an adults-only resort that is brimming with gorgeous staff members from around the world. Club Med is a French company and they have a very strong European contingent at this village. You are more likely to hang out with a Frenchman than a frat boy from Fresno. Between the morning yoga classes, the water volleyball scrimmages, wind surfing, snorkeling, and dancing, you should fit in a few trapeze classes. A group of trained trapeze artists show you how to fly through the air with the greatest of ease. And if you are good, you can learn how to do a catch! If you are new to solo travel, this is a perfect first-time solo vacation. Beware, you princesses, Club Med is a casual, yet all-inclusive resort, and that means there is no poolside service—you'll have to get off your logo-clad booty and get your own glass of champagne. Club Med; www.clubmed.com.

2. Pretend to be a pirate on a tall ship. Ahoy, darling! How about sailing on a tall ship around the Caribbean islands? Imagine spending your days listening to the white sails snap with the fresh sea air while you learn how to crew a tall ship. The ship stops at secluded beaches, isolated coves, and sandy cays around the Windward Islands. During the trip, you'll have plenty of opportunities to go scuba diving and snorkeling. And if you want to learn how to dive, they offer a PADI course on board. You don't have to be a sailor to join the crew. Duties range from taking the helm and handling the ropes to keeping watch and setting the sails. The cruises go out for ten days and include your food and berth. The ship sets sail from Barbados. Tall Ship Adventures; www.tallship.org.

3. Detox in Paradise. After one of *those* killer weekends with your girlfriends— you know, an endless supply of food and cocktails, while dancing on bars—you will need to rest your liver and calm your soul. The Ashram on Paradise Island might be the place to do it—but only for you die-hard yogis. The property is beautiful and the staff is wonderful, but it is totally vegetarian and there are no private showers. You are coming here to meditate, improve your yogic practice, or become a certified yoga instructor. The prices are great for the remarkable location. They offer some impressive classes with world-renowned spiritual leaders and musicians. All the guests are on the same schedule: rise at 6 a.m. for meditation, then yoga, followed by breakfast and more yoga and meditation. The classes are in the evenings, and by 9 p.m. you are beat and ready for bed. The Ashram is located on tiny Paradise Island, which is across the canal from the bustling town of Nassau. So, if you are craving a platter of fried fish or conch balls, you can take a boat back to civilization. If you are yearning for a really fancy Caribbean dinner, head to Columbus Tavern. They serve a killer coffee cocktail that is set on fire. After all that downward dog, cabbage soup, and "ohming," you'll need a drink. Sivananda Ashram Yoga Retreat; P.O. Box N7550, Paradise Island; Nassau, Bahamas; tel: 800-441-2096 or 242-363-2902; www.my-yoga.net; Columbus Tavern; tel: 242-363-2534; www.columbustavern.com.

4.   Jamaican me hungry! Eat your way through Jamaica on the Taste of Jamaica tour. On this delicious escapade you go village hopping in central and south Jamaica. You learn how to cook Jamaican cuisine with the locals in their homes. The great thing is that you move from one family to another, so you really get to meet a bevy of beautiful Jamaicans who are excited to teach you about their cuisine and open up their homes to you. Country cuisine includes crazy dishes like ackee and saltfish with spicy calalloo, dumplings, bammy, and fried plantain. You will also get to try some of the tasty fruits of Jamaica like naseberry, ortaniques, starapples, and tangerines. For dessert try some sugar cane, plantain tarts, coconut gizzarders, and enjoy Appleton Rum specials at the Appleton Rum Factory. Just when you thought you were done, sample some hot peppered shrimp and fried fish and bammy in Middle Quarters with Billy Kerr and his family. Then you'll visit Little Ochi in Alligator Pond on a fishing beach and enjoy lobster, fish, and other seafood while looking at the sunset and chilling with the community. Taste of Jamaica tours; www.unique jamaica.com, click on "Unique

The Jungle

If you want a plush yoga retreat, check out Jungle Bay on the island of Dominica. This resort combines adventure and relaxation with tree-house rooms and laid-back Caribbean charm. Look it up at www.junglebaydominica.com.

Tours," then click on "Taste of Jamaica."

5.   Get jamming. For you wannabe yacht divas who are more interested in socializing than sailing, windjammers will fill your sails. They have a few different types of boats as well as different categories of cruises, so you can pick the one that is best for you. Party like a prom queen? Chill like a lizard? Explore like Jacques Cousteau? You bet! The ports include Grenada, St. Lucia, Trinidad, Freeport, Nassau, Aruba, St. Thomas, Antigua, St. Maarten, and Tortola. Phew. When you book, make sure to confirm that the boat you are on is a singles' cruise. Heaven forbid you end up on the love boat with a crew of newlyweds. Yikes! Don't bother knocking. Windjammer Cruises; www.windjammer.com.

6.   Stay at the world's best resort. Did I hear you say that you deserve the best? That's right, girl, and it's here in the Caribbean. Ladera Resort in St. Lucia has been voted the best hotel in the world by *Condé Nast Traveler*. It's time for you to cash out that pesky 401(k) plan and spend some quality time with the most important person in the world—you! The property has 25 open-air suites with

views from 1,100 feet above the sea and sunsets that will take your breath away. Yes, darling, you get your own private plunge pool and you don't even have to leave your room—ever. So bring all those trashy novels and glossy magazines you haven't read in months and treat yourself to a fabulous solo vacation. Of course, if you want to take a tour, go to the beach, fly a kite, or ride a horse, they will make it happen for you. That's why they are the best, after all. Ladera Resort; www.ladera.com.

7.   Discover the wilderness of Puerto Rico. Forget sleeping at 5-stars; how about sleeping under 5 million stars with the folks at Acampa Adventure Tours in Puerto Rico? Visit places straight out of a fairy tale like El Yunque, La Finca, Tanama River, and Caja de Muerto Island. For you lovers of nature, you can't get any closer than this prisitine, lush tropical environment. The team here really tries to focus on recreation, preservation, and education. So not only are you going to hike through some of the most amazing tropics in the Caribbean, but you will get to learn about how the ecosystem works and what you can do to save it. And to top it off, you will be with a fabulous group from Acampar. Some of their camping tours include:

- Toro Negro Water Trek
- Organic Tanama
- El Yunque Rainforest
- San Cristobol Canyon
- La Finca
- Mona Island Expedition
- Caja de Meurto Island
- Monagas Ropes and Trails

Acampar; tel: 787-706-0695; www.acampapr.com.

8. Take it easy. From the brilliant minds behind EasyJet comes EasyCruise. They offer your basic, no-nonsense cruise ship perfect for darlings who are watching their dollars. If you have never flown EasyJet, think of Southwest with a frisky attitude and way more fun. The islands they visit include starting in Barbados, then Martinique, St. Lucia, St. Vincent, the Grenadines, Grenada. These cruises are super-duper-popular with Europeans, so expect to meet a few boys from London and a team of chickas from Barcelona. Also, if you want to get off and spend a few days on one of the islands, they can help you arrange it. It's like a big hop-on-hop-off tour of the Caribbean! EasyCruise; www.easycruise.com.

9. Get going with Iguana Mama. For you active girls, the best way to explore the Dominican Republic's countryside and national parks is with Iguana Mama, a group of adventure and eco-tour guides. They specialize in seven-day mountain-biking trips, but the company also offers hiking, horseback riding, canyoning, whale watching, white water rafting, and a ton of other active day excursions. One of their most popular tours is the Cascading Day Hike. It includes trekking up the 27 waterfalls of Damajagua river where you ascend the rocky slopes of the river, then jump, slide, and swim back down the spectacular falls. Iguana Mama 1-800-849-4720; www.iguana mama.com.

10. Lounge with the ladies. At Oualie Beach Resort, on the island of Nevis, they offer a fabulous week called "Ladies Week Out." Yup, no men, no kids, no cell phones, just other lovely ladies from around the world unwinding by the pool. And if you want more fun than tanning, they've got you covered. They offer a bunch of great activities:

- Guided hiking tour in the rain forest
- Horseback-riding trips on mountain or beach trails
- Sailing and snorkeling trips on a catamaran

- Historic tours of the Alexander Hamilton and Nelson Museums, including a visit to the botanical gardens and the ruins of an old sugar plantation

- Guided off-road tours on mountain bikes

Oualie Beach Resort; tel: 869-469-9735; www.oualiebeach.com.

CRESTED BUTTE, COLORADO

Holly teaches in her "classroom" at Skywriter Ranch.

Why This Place Rocks for Flying Solo

A very insightful man once said, "You can please some of the people some of the time, but you can't please all of the people all of the time." He obviously didn't spend any time in the lovely town of Crested Butte, Colorado. Tucked away in the Rockies' High Country, this quaint town is the perfect enclave for the solo gal who wants some action.

The valley is heaven in the spring and summer, with colorful wildflowers carpeting the hillsides and meadows; in winter, the feathery white snow promises to bring plenty of fresh water for making that famous Rocky Mountain brew. If

Skywriter Series Fiction Workshops

Here's a life-enriching experience for people passionate about storytelling. Founded in 2004 by novelist and screenwriter Holly Payne, the Skywriter Series Fiction Workshops teach not only the craft of narrative fiction, but also the process of storytelling and the most important yet overlooked elements of story, structure, and design (necessary for both memoirs and creative nonfiction, too!). The workshops are playful yet vigorous and ensure a safe, supportive environment to explore your voice. Tel: 415-205-8331; http://skywriter.holly-payne.com.

you appreciate nature, the changing of seasons, and casual country living, then get ready to fly high in Colorado's jewel, Crested Butte.

This charming Main Street town has retained its rugged gold-mining history, these days glistening with high-end boutiques and spas. Elk Street is the Champs-Elysées of Crested Butte—and believe it or not, there's not a single chain restaurant or retailer in sight. *Fantastique!* Plenty of lovely shops, spas, restaurants, and cafés line Elk Street and its side streets.

Culture: 3

Crested Butte has a long history of welcoming newcomers. It was founded in the early 1870s by miners and ranchers who realized that this valley, with its plentiful land and rich ores, was the perfect place to call home. For a hundred years, miners looked for gold, silver, and coal, while ranchers tended their cattle. Following the closure of all area mines in the late 1960s and the downturn in the beef market, Crested Butte all but shut down. But a few brilliant residents decided to put up a ski lift and open a few day spas, turning the ghost town into the perfect destination for sports lovers and

spa junkies, with enough interesting places for history buffs.

Activity: 5

The thriving mountain village has fantastic skiing during the winter, and intense mountain biking, wild kayaking, and scenic hiking and horseback riding in the spring and summer. Intensity levels are all up to you. This place is not only for hardcore athletes who need to engage their adrenal glands daily; even channel surfers can find some low-intensity activities, like wildflower walks and creekside painting. Do be aware that at 9,000 feet, even a nature walk will feel like scaling Everest the first day or two.

Weather: 5

Crested Butte's weather is iconic: for a perfect representation of the seasons, this is your destination! In the winter, it turns into the perfect wonderland; in fall, the leaves turn red. Summer is hot, and spring is bursting with colorful wildflowers.

Social: 5

Whoo-hoo! This place is rocking all year round. The locals are friendly, helpful, and approachable. Thanks to its small size and the free shuttle that operates the two-mile drive from the Mount Crested Butte Resort to the town of Crested Butte, the town is easily manageable without a car. The bus stops at many of the hot spots, of which there are plenty!

Flying Foreplay

Gun it! Make sure you book yourself all the way to Gunnison Airport. From there, you'll need to take a shuttle. The drive up to Crested Butte from the airport is about 30 minutes. For a hassle-free lift to town, jump on the Alpine Express. The drivers are knowledgeable (one night Crested Butte's mayor himself was the driver of my shuttle!) and are happy to point out things along the way, like elk or moose in the distance. The shuttle costs $29 per person each way, and I recommend you make reservations before you depart. There is only one shuttle when a plane lands, and the bus frequently runs out of space.

Go cozy. Crested Butte is very casual, so good walking shoes, comfy clothes, and layers are the way to go. Leave your frilly stuff at home—this is not Aspen or St. Moritz.

Check the town's calendar. The locals love to party, and they keep their activities schedule pretty booked, from wild-flower festivals to the town's annual Alley Loop ski-course race. www.visit crestedbutte.com.

Crested Butte Accessories

Rocky Mountain high. Girl, this is the Rockies of Colorado, not the sandy beaches of Cancun. Dress warm in all seasons. Bring casual clothes that you can easily layer. Leave Gucci and YSL at home—this is Wrangler country.

Boots not Manolo Blahnik. *Style* is not a word often used here when describing clothes. So save your coveted labels for your trip to Ibiza.

Motion lotion. The altitude is high, the air is dry—you know what that means. Chapped lips and dehydrated skin. Bring all those potions you use to keep your skin baby smooth and don't be stingy when spreading.

The Top 10 Extraordinary Experiences

1. **Spank the slopes.** The skiing in Crested Butte is so darn good that the locals would prefer to keep the mountain to themselves. But the secret is out, so grab your sexy après-ski suit. For complete vacation packages, call Crested

Your appetite will be delightfully satisfied in this modest yet deliciously decadent town. For the perfect steak, indulge yourself at the Timberline (tel: 970-349-9831), where you'll find the best dry martini in town, along with specialties including buffalo, fresh trout, and chocolate soufflés. If playing pool and chilling with the colorful locals is more your style, join the fun at Kochevars Bar (tel: 970-349-6745) across the street. Or end your night with a sophisticated cocktail at the Princess Bar (tel: 970-349-0210)—they usually have live music on the weekends. How about riding a mechanical bull before enjoying a few margaritas and tacos? Head to the Powerhouse for a lope on their bull (tel: 970-349-5494) and a strawberry blended margarita—don't forget to buy a potent pot of their homemade salsa for your flight home. For a hearty prime rib dinner, try out the Wooden Nickel (tel: 970-349-6350). The Slogar is a Crested Butte institution, serving family-style chicken and steak dinners in a renovated brothel (tel: 970-349-5765).

Butte Vacations. They can set you up with everything from hotel rooms, spa treatments, and lift tickets. 800-544-8448; www.skicb.com.

2. Horse around. For you horse-loving adventurers, trot on over to Fantasy Ranch (970-349-5425; www.fantasyranch outfitters.com) for a 15-mile jaunt across the Rockies to Aspen. Eight hours later, you'll find yourself in Aspen, where your guide has already arranged a charming stay in a local bed-and-breakfast. There, you can soak off those eight hours in a hot tub overlooking the jagged peaks you just conquered on horseback. You'll feast in style with your fellow horsewomen at dinner, enjoy a breakfast made for cowgirls, and return on horseback to Crested Butte the next day. You might be saddle sore, but for that much quality time in the Himalayas of the West, it's well worth it. If that sounds like too much work, perhaps you should hike or bike over to Aspen, this time on a one-way jaunt. And for the princess experience, Gunnison Valley Aviation will be happy to pick you up in Aspen and fly you back to Crested Butte or Gunnison Airport. The ride back from Aspen is a forty-five-minute scenic tour in a 206 Cessna airplane.

3. Go fish. For you die-hard fly-fishers with lures on the brain, the lure of a Rockies fly-fishing adventure is undeniable. Give Troutfitters a call and they can take you out on a guided float and fly-fishing trip (tel: 970-349-1323; www.troutfitter.com). If you prefer a private fly-fishing trip, call Dragonfly Anglers (tel: 970-349-1228; www.dragonflyanglers.com).

4. Bike the Rockies. Mountain bikers will be blown away by the rugged terrain surrounding Crested Butte. There are plenty of breathtaking trails to explore. Rent a bike at Flatiron Sports (tel: 970-349-6656), or the Alpineer (tel: 800-223-4655). For hiking and backpacking trips, call Alpine Meadows (tel: 970-349-0800).

5. Take a ride to the top. If you want a bird's-eye view of the valley without worrying about working up a sweat, take a scenic chairlift tour at Crested Butte Mountain Resort (tel: 970-349-2262).

6. Frolic on the fairways. Many would say a place can't be perfect without an eighteen-hole golf course designed by Trent Jones, and in Crested Butte they have one! The Club at Crested Butte is an award-winning golf course that is open to the public (tel: 970-349-6127 or 800-628-5496).

7. Power shopping. If the sale rack is your idea of a hole in one, then the boutiques on Elk Street will keep your heart rate up. Explore the eclectic shops brimming with the cutest Western fashions this side of the Mississippi, as well as retailers offering fine handcrafted leather furniture. Perhaps it's that rhinestone and turquoise belt at Butte & Co. (tel: 970-349-6890) that melts your heart, or the red leather chair at the Princess that gives you joyful goose bumps—and yes, they'll ship anything.

8. Explore the city. From the top of Elk Street and back, you can spend at least a day browsing the shops between cups of fresh-brewed coffee and delightful eats, which include a tamale restaurant (Teocalli Tamale; tel: 970-349-2005) and handmade confectionary shop (Rocky Mountain Chocolate Factory; tel: 970-349-0933). The art galleries boast some of the finest pottery in the West. If you're lucky, you can find Mary Jursinvic at Creekside Pottery creating magic by turning earth into something heavenly, like vases crafted with horsehair and colorful tea sets (tel: 970-349-6459). Or perhaps Matthew Scalla will be at work sculpting an original piece of art on his potter's wheel just for you (tel: 970-349-6366).

9. Spend the day spa-ing. In this town you can spend a week just pampering yourself from spa to spa. During this very difficult process, you can also get your hair colored, nails polished, and teeth whitened!

Crested Butte Club. For the ultimate spa and bed-and-breakfast experience, check into this palace of pleasure. It is in the heart of town and within walking distance to absolutely everything. You can spend the day in their spa and health club, or spend the night on Egyptian cotton sheets with an open fireplace roaring as you sip your nightcap. After a hard day on the slopes, or out mountain biking, Crested Butte Club is heaven on earth. The service is fabulous, the rooms are divine, and the spa is heaven. This is my favorite place to spa and stay in Crested Butte. Tel: 800-815-CLUB.

A Day at the Spa. Located in the historic section of Crested Butte on Third and Elk, the spa offers body wraps, hot stones, a variety of facials, and Thai, Swedish, and sports massages. Tel: 970-275-1271.

About Face. 510 Elk Ave #3 All things to make your face beautiful, from dental hygiene and zoom power whitening to retail spa products for hair, skin, and body. They also have a makeup artist on staff. Tel: 970-349-0173.

An Essential Escape. In the Purple Mountain Bed and Breakfast at 7th and Gothic Avenue, licensed estheticians and massage therapists offer facials, body wraps, enzyme peels, waxing, eyelash and eyebrow tinting, and an array of massage therapies. Tel: 970-596-6857.

Natural Butte. 309 6th Street at Elk Ave A complete beauty experience, with skin care, massage, personalized haircuts, mani/pedis, and gel nails. Tel: 970-349-7775.

Oh Be Joyful. Traveling therapeutic massage service for those who don't want to leave their room. Tel: 970-209-0366.

10. Float away. Take an unforgettable balloon ride above the valley in spring. Glide above fields of Technicolor daydreams and watch hawks dance in the thermal jets. Enjoy the view at 1,000 feet above Crested Butte and don't forget to bring your camera. Alpine Outside; tel: 970-349-5011.

FAIRBANKS, ALASKA

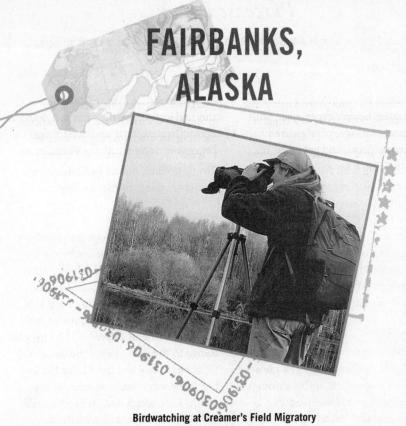

Birdwatching at Creamer's Field Migratory Refuge in Fairbanks.

Why This Place Rocks for Flying Solo

G irl, you can get *way* out of town without having to renew your passport! Fairbanks is Alaska's second-largest city and can be a winter wonderland for the solo flyer searching for outdoorsy entertainment. Nippy days, full of activities in Alaska's breath-taking expanses, fade slowly into cozy nights lounging around flickering fires accented by the Northern Lights dancing outside your window. Founded during the gold rush, Fairbanks maintains the same headstrong optimism of the would-be gold miners who first populated its streets. This snowy frontier has always attracted adventurers and explorers, and has grown into a city that pairs creature comforts with a rugged environment.

And if you needed more reasons to go: Fairbanks, along with Alaska as a whole, is one of the few places with about 21,000 more Alaskan dudes than divas according to the U.S. Census Bureau. We know that you're cute and charming in any demographic, but hey, can't beat those odds! With tongue-in-cheek, locals have a saying: "The odds are good but the goods are odd!"

Culture: 3

Fairbanks is part suburbia, part tundra, and part gold-mining town. The ghosts of prospectors past still amble through the streets, and you'll find plenty of gold rush memorabilia, including museums, converted gold dredge, and old-time saloons accommodating those old-time spirits. The Fairbanks Shakespeare Theatre hosts a 24-hour Bard-A-Thon, where all are invited to read and perform plays for a whole day straight. Between regular concerts, local symphony and ballet companies, and various dance clubs, inhabitants of Fairbanks have learned to keep themselves entertained for the long winters—certainly they can keep you entertained, too.

Activity: 5

If it can be done in the outdoors, it can be done in Fairbanks, Alaska. Skiing, dog sledding, snowshoeing, canoeing, and hiking are only a few ways to get your heart rate rising in this frosty playground. You can also try swing dancing, panning for gold, touring on a sternwheeler on the Chena and Tanana Rivers, golfing, hot air ballooning, or moose-tracking, to name a few.

Weather: 1

The extreme cold periods are greatly exaggerated by those who live below the 60-degree latitude. Schoolchildren play outside in −20 degrees F, not because Fairbanksians like to torture their kids, but rather the climate requires a whole different frame of reference. The Brooks Range to the north keeps the harsh Arctic winds at bay and the Alaska Range keeps the wet coastal weather to the south. Rare winds and an exceptionally dry climate, combined with the daily donning of hats, scarves, and gloves, make the cold not so cold.

Another myth is that it is dark all winter. The losing and gaining of light is a gradual process. In March, there is already nearly twelve hours of daylight. With almost 21 hours of "the Midnight Sun" daylight in June, summer temperatures routinely rise into the 70s and 80s. So be prepared with the layered look in winter and for variations in temperature during the summer. One day could be a tank top, shorts, and sandals, while the next might be a sweatshirt, jeans, and boots.

Social: 5

Alaska is known for its friendly, welcoming social scene, and Fairbanks—known as the "Golden Heart City"—has a healthy little social buzz going for itself. Perhaps since Mother Nature has provided them with such austere surroundings, Alaskans respond by developing bright, warm natures of their own. Fairbanks has retained much of its frontier village character while offering wine bars and first-class accommodations with Jacuzzi suites. After a long day of trekking, dog sledding, or skiing, the cushy stools of a cozy bar will seem like the only place you've ever wanted to go. Après-mush, anyone?

Flying Foreplay

*E*ven though it might not feel like it, Fairbanks is still in the good U.S. of A., so no need to get that dreaded typhoid shot. There are public buses and taxis as well as private and hotel shuttles. If you want more independence, make sure you've got your own set of wheels.

Read Before You Go

Call of the Wild, or *White Fang*, or *The Sea Wolf*, or *Klondike and Other Stories*, by Jack London
Into the Wild, by Jon Krakauer

Play with Fire and *A Cold-Blooded Business*, by Dana Stabenow
A Wolf in Death's Clothing and *Murder Most Grizzly*, by Elizabeth Quinn

Fairbanks Accessories

Warm clothes. Duh! Think snow bunny meets Boy Scout. Bring warm, cozy clothes and leave your full-body silk ski suit at home. The locals will look at you funny if you wear it in public.

A thermos. Good for porting drinks around with you, whether you want toasty hot cocoa on the river or warming red wine as you watch the Northern Lights shimmer and shimmy.

Hiking boots. These will be your main shoes while adventuring through the wilderness as well as exploring the city. Make sure they fit well, my dear.

The Top 10 Extraordinary Experiences

1. **Mush!** Fairbanks is a mecca for a spectrum of dogsledding enthusiasts, whether you're a hardcore musher or a first-time sledder. And if you've never been pulled around by a host of dogs (who aren't your ex's), then you've got

"Fairbanks Formal"

On a party invitation, this means anything is appropriate from a tux to a flannel shirt and jeans. Sometimes the richest guy at the party could be that man (possibly a miner) with the shabbiest clothes!

to try this crazy sport. Check out Sun Dog Express Dog Sled Tours (tel: 907-479-6983; www.mosquitonet.com/~sleddog), where you'll pay $25 for a snappy ride on the nippy slopes. A Taste of Alaska Lodge (tel: 907-488-7855; www.atasteofalaska.com) and Chena Hot Springs Resort (tel: 907-451-8104; www.chenahotspringsresort.com) also provide mushing opportunities along with their accommodations.

2. Watch a light show. For viewing the incredibly dramatic Aurora Borealis, you can take your chances and stay in the city and look up, or you can head out to these places:

Aurora Borealis Lodge was designed specifically for viewing the northern lights. Located on Cleary Summit, 20 miles north of Fairbanks, the lodge is situated away from the city lights that may hinder the sky view. North-facing large windows allow for optimal viewing conditions. Tel: 907-388-9954; www.AuroraCabin.com.

Northern Sky Lodge is located outside of town and is an ideal place to watch the northern lights from the end of August to mid-April. Tel: 907-388-9954; www.northernskylodge.com/aurora.htm.

3. Get a bird's-eye view of the forty-ninth state. For the true Alaskan experience,

take to the air and enjoy a unique look at Interior Alaska's awesome grandeur. To the south, Mt. McKinley is spectacular from the air. On your flight, be sure to watch for moose browsing in the willows or maybe even a bear with cubs. Perhaps you prefer heading north to the Arctic Circle and visiting a native village. On the way back you can view the newly built Fort Knox Gold Mine, the Alaska Pipeline, and check out the many historic gold dredges in the area. The view from your window is incredible . . . the vast beauty, breathtaking. Alaska Flying Tours; toll-free: 888-326-4424; tel: 907-457-4424; www.AlaskaFlyingTours.com; cranbrry@ptialaska.net.

4. Get wild! Experience true wilderness in the roadless Brooks Range alongside caribou, grizzly bears, wolves, and musk oxen. Eight- to twenty-two-day paddle and backpack trips are offered in Gates of the Arctic Park and Arctic Wildlife Refuge. They are all about small groups and love hosting solo gals. Arctic Wild—Alaska Adventures with Latitude; tel: 888-577-8203; www.arcticwild.com; info@arcticwild.com.

Discover Alaska's Arctic with one-day and multiday excursions that unfold the region's natural history and cultural heritage. Visit an Alaska Native village with no road access. More than nine destinations in Interior Alaska and the

Arctic north are offered by Northern Alaska Tour Company. Toll-Free: 800-474-1986; tel: 907-474-8600; www.northernalaska.com.

5. Soak away the shivers. After all that hiking, biking, mushing, and trekking, the healing water of Chena Hot Springs is the perfect place to rest your tired bones. The hot springs are over 100 years old and were frequented by Alaska natives before being settled by Westerners. The resort was "officially founded" after weary gold miners discovered that soaking in the oh-so-warm waters helped their aching bodies. www.chenahotsprings.com.

6. Eat and drink with the locals. For a night on the town with the local gentry, check out these popular digs:

Downtown, Café Alex Wine Bar is a trendy and popular place where you can sip wine and nosh on yummy plates from an all-appetizer menu of truly delicious food while listening to live music. 310 1st Ave.; tel: 907/452-2539.

Or three miles south of town on the Parks Highway, the Blue Loon has live music, lots of beer, good food, and a volleyball court outside. They even show movies! Tel: 907-457-5666; www.theblueloon.com.

A popular summer pastime is relishing the Midnight Sun with a local ale in hand from the decks of restaurants along the Chena River. Opt for the Pump House (tel: 907-479-8472; www.pumphouse.com), Pike's Landing (tel: 907-479-7113; www.pikeslodge.com), or Chena's (tel: 907-474-3644; www.riversedge.net).

7. Bike off your Baked Alaska. If mushing or skiing isn't your thing, then stick to some good ol' bike riding at 7 Bridges Boats and Bikes, at 7 Gables Inn. They'll even drop you off at the river and pick you up at your destination for $1.50 per mile out of town, with a $15 minimum. Guests at the inn get free rentals. 4312 Birch Lane; tel: 907-479-0751; www.7gablesinn.com/7bbb.

8. Shred the Moose. For you ski bunnies, Moose Mountain is the place to glide the days away. It's only 20 minutes from Fairbanks, so you can even go up for the day. And if you can't ski but want to learn, they do offer lessons in both skiing and snowboarding (www.shredthemoose.com). Mt. Aurora Skiland offers downhill skiing, dog

Arctic Learning

The University of Alaska–Fairbanks campus has lots of options for play and study. It's America's only Arctic university! The headquarters of the statewide university system, Fairbanks boasts the recently expanded University Museum of the North. Also outstanding are the Georgeson Botanical Garden (see what grows under the midnight sun . . . giant veggies and flowers!) and the Large Animal Research Center (musk oxen, caribou, reindeer, and babies!). See www.uaf.edu.

mushing, and aurora viewing (tel: 907-389-2314; www.skiland.org). The Nordic Ski Club of Fairbanks can glide you around the numerous cross-country trails throughout the winter (tel: 907-474-4244; www.nscfairbanks.org). Enjoy drinks in the heated viewing area overlooking the ice at the Fairbanks Curling Club (tel: 907-452-2875; www.curlfairbanks.org).

9.   Get artsy. The Fairbanks Summer Arts Festival encourages people of all ages to try something that they've always wanted to try! In two weeks' time, middle-aged mammas can be jammin' on steel drums. With group or private lessons, ice skaters of any level can gracefully advance to the next. The healing arts flourish with yoga and tai chi courses. Held on the University of Alaska–Fairbanks campus in June. Tel. 907-474-8869; www.fsaf.org.

10.   Be a dining diva. Get a table in downtown Fairbanks at LaVelle's Bistro, which has been called one of Alaska's best restaurants. Their extensive 3,000-bottle wine selection displayed behind glass in the main dining room is a lovely reminder of all your delicious sipping options. The menu combines varied international cuisines to scrumptious effect. Plus, many of the waiters are cute and single. LaVelle's Bistro; tel: 907-450-0555; www.lavellesbistro.com.

MOAB, UTAH

Sarah reclines in front of Delicate
Arch in Arches National Park.

Why This Place Rocks
for Flying Solo

You saw Thelma and Louise drive full-speed off the cliff in Moab's Canyonlands, but I recommend that you hit the brakes and stay awhile. Moab is a relatively small town, with only 5,000 permanent residents, but offers at least as many activities for the restless solo traveler. Most people who live in Moab were originally visitors who fell in love with the spot and planted roots here in the slickrock; the adoration of the town by its residents comes through in almost every interaction you'll have here. They are eager to share the love, especially with adventurous ladies traveling alone.

Yeee Haw!

Moab was a hangout for Butch Cassidy's Wild Bunch and other outlaw gangs of the 1800s.

This was formerly a uranium-mining town—no place for an honest woman—but has developed into a mecca for wild women of another sort. You're as likely to have a fierce female guide as a manly man on the trails. This is a significant boon for the adventurous sister who needs inspiration, or a little added security, to really let loose. Every female guide I met in Moab had a great story to tell, and immediately felt like a sister-in-arms in the battle to prove that women can rock out with the best of them.

And what a lovely spot to earn your adventure stripes. The Delicate Arch, made famous on Utah's brightly colored license plate, is only one standout in a collection of fascinating natural sculptures that include Balanced Rock and the Three Gossips. Moab's terrain is in a constant state of undress, with only a few shrubs and skimpy trees adorning the vast, flesh-colored shoulders and bare thighs of exposed rock. Bends and crevices seem more like soft skin than petrified sand, giving the area a feeling that is sensual and spiritual all at once. Each rock formation seems to have a face embedded within its outcroppings and indents. In Moab, nature looks back at you.

Culture: 3

This is an outdoorsy culture, if not a cult, where slickrock is hallowed and biking is sacred. Moab is rich with stories, legends, and cautionary tales. It seems that someone has intrepidly scaled each treacherous ridge, and someone else has fallen to his or her doom attempting the same feat. This is a town where it's not enough to look at the natural arches; a daredevil has to fly a plane cock-eyed through the narrow openings to really make an impression. Petroglyphs from Native American cultures still mark the orange rocks, reminders of adventurers past.

Activity: 5

Slather on the sunscreen and run wild! There are so many outdoor activities here that you could be spinning your bike wheels, hitting the slickrock with your hiking boots, or paddling your heart out down the Colorado River and never run out of new territory to cover. Check out Canyonlands National Park and Arches National Park, famous for unbelievable scenery (around 2,000 natural stone arches) and more than 20 miles of marked trails. Activity is not limited to the sunny months: you can snowshoe, cross-country ski, and snowmobile when Utah turns into a winter wonderland.

Weather: 4

Summer gets sizzling and winter's chill will have you wondering what happened to the desert air. Spring and fall are mild and enjoyable, and when most of Moab's events are held. Here's a tip: Winter is off-season for most tourists, but a time when Moab really shines. It gets a light

Moab Happenings

Moab Happenings is a comprehensive guide to everything that goes down in this Utah town. You can find printed copies in every store, restaurant, and bar, or check online at www.moabhappenings.com.

dusting of snow, giving the natural landscape and buildings alike a sugar-sprinkled quality. The cold eliminates the heat haze, as well as the carloads of sightseers, that can blur the view of the natural wonders during the hot summers.

Social: 3

Hmmm, I knew there had to be a catch somewhere! Utah has famously tight liquor laws that don't make it impossible to drink, but do require some extra effort on your part. For example, not every restaurant serves liquor, and even if they do, you have to ask for it—waiters are not allowed to suggest an alcoholic beverage to diners. There are a handful of fun nightspots on Main Street (see below in the Top 10) where you're likely to run into your cute river-rafting guide, and you all can share rounds of low-alcohol beers.

For a full description of Utah's liquor laws, visit www.alcbev.state.ut.us.

Flying Foreplay

Leave it. There are plenty of outfitters in Moab, so leave your trusty bike and favorite rafting oar at home. If it's to be had, it can be rented in Moab.

Get some wheels. Even if you plan to spend most of your time spinning on two wheels, you'll need to get to the parks and trailheads. It's the desert! Things are spread out. Call ahead and

the Moab Airport will be happy to arrange a car for you. Tel: 435-259-7419.

Book your bed. With the wide spectrum of accommodation options in Moab, ranging from a single tent to a luxury ranch, you'll always be able to find a place to stay, but book ahead to get what you want instead of what's available.

Carpe diem! No need to arrange your activities ahead of time. There's an abundance of quality tour companies who will accommodate you. See how you feel when you wake up that morning and go with the flow. Some days you just gotta ride the river; others are better suited for touring vineyards.

Read Before You Go

Above and Beyond Slickrock: Forty Mountain Bike Rides out of Moab, Utah, by Todd Campbell

Desert Solitaire, by Edward Abbey

Edward Abbey: A Life, by James M. Cahalan

Wind in the Rock, by Ann Zwinger

Moab Accessories

The basics. Bring your basic hiking accoutrements: a hat, sturdy boots, and a water bottle.

Slather it. Load up on gobs and gobs of sunscreen. This is a desert, and you'll need all the sun protection you can get. Yes, even in the winter, my dears.

Lights, camera! The scenery here is like nowhere else, and you'll need the snapshots to remind yourself it wasn't all just a surreal dream.

Keep kissable. The air is dry, so keep those lips moist with lip balm.

The Top 10 Extraordinary Experiences

1. Would you like some wine with your Wild, Wild West? In a valley that the Colorado River painstakingly carved out of auburn rocks, the Castle Creek Winery rests, unimposing and subtle. Part of the beautiful Red Cliffs Lodge, the winery produces a small but impressive lineup of wines including a buttery Chenin Blanc and a rich Pinot Noir. Highlights of the collection are a heady mix of Cabernet and Merlot called "Outlaw Red" and a kicky white named "Lily Rose." This lodge-cum-winery bustles in the spring-summer months, and the owners help arrange activities for their guests, including horseback riding, hiking, and rafting. In more laid-back moments, visitors soak in hot tubs or simply walk out on to their private decks to watch rafts glide by on the swift river. www.redcliffslodge.com.

Moab offers another local winery, Spanish Valley Vineyards, which is run by Cory and Stacy Dezelsky. The friendly husband and wife duo conducts tastings year-round (by appointment only in winter), and if you are lucky enough to come on a slow day, they'll gladly let you help bottle and cork their award-winning wines. www.moab-utah.com/spanishvalley winery.

Head straight to the Moab Information Center on Main Street. It's a veritable treasure trove of pamphlets, brochures, and information about anything and everything there is to do. You'll save yourself a lot of time, and open your eyes to all the possibilities, by making this your first stop.

2. Cruise during the starry, starry night. Not even Vincent van Gogh could capture the rarefied beauty of the Canyonlands when the sun sets. The Canyonlands by Night boat trip offers a one-of-a-kind view of the tall red rock cliffs that line the Colorado River. After enjoying a Dutch-oven dinner at dusk, cruise downriver and hear stories about the canyonlands illuminated on either side of you. At one point, all lights and engines are shut off, allowing you to drift silently in the dark and watch for shooting stars. Tel: 800-394-9978 or 435-259-5261; www.canyonlandsbynight.com.

3. Climb Wall Street. A stretch of highway is flanked by the meandering Colorado River on one side, and towering, sheer cliffs on the other. Beloved by rockclimbers who attempt to scale the cliffs year-round, the area is aptly called "Wall Street." You can see the anchors permanently affixed to the red stone. The walls are also covered with Native American petroglyphs, graffiti etched into the rock face on the shiny black patches called desert varnish (really oxidized manganese). More accomplished climbers can take part in the activities, but everyone can enjoy the display of real-life Spiderman (and woman!) climbing tactics.

4. Pleasure your peds. The beautiful Sorrel River Ranch offers a range of treatments at its luxurious spa. The spa's windows frame the gorgeous mesas that surround it, and the lavish services and scents will have you feeling like the luckiest gal this side of the Colorado River. The "Happy Feet Massage" lasts 25 minutes and revitalizes tired puppies. Your feet do so much for you . . . isn't it time to return the favor? Other treatments include a heated Desert Stone Massage and a Sea Weed Mud Wrap. Sorrel River Ranch Resort & Spa; Highway 128 Mile 17, Moab, Utah; www.sorrelriver.com.

5. What do John Wayne and Bon Jovi have in common? Why, it's Moab! Hundreds of movies and commercials have been filmed in this area, including John Wayne's *Rio Grande*, and the spirit of the film industry thrives in a small but enthusiastic Movie History Museum at Red Cliffs Lodge. The museum holds a mix of Moab movie memorabilia, including the recovered mannequin that went over the cliff in Geena Davis's place during the filming of *Thelma and Louise* nearby. A framed display informs the visitor that the enormous mesa visible from the lodge's dining room was the well-selected site of Bon Jovi's music video "Knockin' on Heaven's Door." For true movie buffettes, the Moab Information Center has printed guides of the key spots to hit on a Moab Area Movie Locations Auto Tour.

6. Be a VIP. Girl, you are already a VIP, but consider being another kind of VIP when you come to Moab. Apply to be a part of the Volunteer in Parks program, and lend a hand in the Arches National Park. You'll have to submit an application with your availability and area of interest ahead of time, and the National Park Service will place you as best they can. Fulfill your dreams of being Park Ranger Betty and help maintain one of the nation's most beautiful areas. Plus, I bet you'll look hot in the uniform. For more info and an application, visit the National Park Service's Volunteer in Parks website (www.nps.gov/volunteer).

7. Cruise in a Tomcar . . . or is that Tom in a Cruisecar? Either way, you've got a need for speed, and these sturdy little vehicles can satisfy your adrenaline itch. Tomcars, designed by the Israeli Army, are creating a buzz as the latest in all-terrain vehicles. Moab Adventure Center is currently the only local outfitter with these little yellow buggers, and they'll gladly take you on a tour through Moab's backcountry and sand dunes. Moab Adventure Center; tel: 888-622-4097; www.moabadventurecenter.com.

8. Write your way down the river. Tap into your inner intrepid author on a six-day river-writing journey through Canyonlands National Park. Let down your hair on this all-women adventure as you participate in writing workshops, drum circles, hiking, and rafting. Who cares if your body is not bikini ready—swim naked in the river, cover yourself

in red mud, and allow yourself to fully unwind in the company of fellow solo-traveling sisters. Howling at the moon is not required, but highly encouraged. Sheri Griffiths Expeditions; tel: reservations: 800-332-2439; office: 435-259-8229; www.griffithexp.com.

9. Mosey down Main Street. You don't have to hike long distances to find some of Moab's best spots. Check out these highlights of Main Street.

Mondo Café. Coffee is still legal in Utah. Come here for open mike night every Saturday and share your geology haiku with the laidback crowd. 59 South Main.

Arches Book Company. This is where the locals hang out. Browse books or sit with a coffee in a plush couch to people watch. 78 North Main.

The Peace Tree Juice Café. Enjoy a healthy wrap or some fresh wheat grass juice. 20 South Main.

Jailhouse Café. The former town jail has been painted pink and serves delicious ginger pancakes with apple butter. 101 North Main.

EklectiCafe. The decor looks like your favorite crazy aunt's living room, and the food is a refreshing change from some of the heartier food found in town. 352 North Main Street.

Marianne's Bakery. Any woman who thinks up fried cheesecake is a genius in my book. Marianne also sells her good-as-new day-old pastries at a great price for baked goods lovers on a budget. 92 East Center Street.

10. Which rock have you been hiding under? The Hole in the Rock is an earnest, if hokey, tribute to the Moab man who blasted his way to local infamy. Albert Christensen spent 12 years dynamiting and excavating 50,000 cubic feet of sandstone out of the face of a bulbous red cliff, creating a network of caves where he and his wife, Gladys, lived out the rest of their lives. Doubling as a diner for the uranium miners that flooded Moab in the 1950s, the caves served as home and final resting place to the quirky couple and is decorated in a style that can only be described as unique. Cave walls are painted a key lime green, stuffed favorite pets stand watch in dark corners, and each ridge in the chipped-away wall functions as a shelf to display Gladys's assorted kitsch. Today, the visitor can tour the home as well as the eclectic collection of Moab memorabilia that sits in a type of

kooky sculpture garden out front. Don't neglect the great photo op to be had in the petting zoo: an ostrich preening in front of the teepee in his pen, and the great red rock cliffs that make up the sweeping background. You can't miss this stop on Highway 191—giant white letters are painted on the red cliffs with an enormous arrow pointing to this particular Hole in the Rock. It's the stuff of legend. Hole in the Rock; 12 miles south of Moab, Utah, on US Highway 191; www.moab-utah.com/holeintherock.

Get dazzled at Delicate Arch

Whatever you do, be sure to make your way to Arches National Park (Highway

191, $10 vehicle admission fee). Touring through Moab's national parks is like walking through a watercolor painting of a different planet. Auburn rocks stretch and bend so unbelievably, you have to place your palm on the warm arches to believe they are real. Smooth and polished by the desert wind, rock pillars jut upward and bend like Mother Nature doing yoga, fiercely orange against a burning blue sky. Find your way up to Delicate Arch, an otherworldly spot to watch the sunset.

MONTREAL, CANADA

Anna at the Montreal Museum
of Fine Arts.

Why This Place Rocks
for Flying Solo

- - - - - - - - - - - - - - -

*I*t's easy to fall in love with Montreal instantly and completely. You just can't imagine how charming and European this North American outpost is. Montreal satisfies the continental cravings in us all with its magnificent boutique hotels and cobbled corners.

Complete with the romantic purr of the French tongue and a cuisine to satisfy it, Montreal seems otherworldly—part Canadian, part Gallic, and part miscellaneous with diverse communities all making their home here. World-class delights like the Formula One series are not generally found in the backyards of Yanks, yet here in Montreal, almost anything seems possible.

This sense of posh potential is especially felt in the summertime when the F1 cars fly on the Circuit Gilles—Villeneuve and when Montreal kicks off its annual Jazz Fest, a serious gathering of the heppest of the world's most talented cats. Above all, your mission, should you choose to accept it, is to embrace café society and stroll through *les rues et boulevards* of Montreal.

Culture: 4

Vieux-Montreal pleases even the most fastidious culture vultures with its old world sights and the sounds of a living French courtly language. Amazing English-language used bookshops like S.W. Welch (3878 St. Laurent Blvd.) are the perfect place to pick up a double cappuccino-long novella, and Montreal above all is renowned for its stylish interiors, beckoning boutique hotels and fantastic shopping both above ground and below in the malls of the Underground City.

Activity: 3

With a huge park in the center of the city, a long list of self-guided tours, and a popular annual marathon, the antsy diva will never have to idly twiddle her

The Language

Bien sûr, you took those three years of French in college. They won't help you now! Montreal French has evolved differently than its sister across the pond. Most scholars agree that Quebecois French is derived from the King's French or courtly French in France, because the colonial *mamans* had to drop their regional patois and find a common language to teach their *enfants*. Thus, this French has been undaunted by years of the linguistic adaptations found in the home of the Gauls. So put aside those dreams of bilingualism—your French will pretty much be Greek to them. *Quelle domage!*

French manicured thumbs. But I say let your imagination be the only thing that runs wild as you sip steamed chai and catch up on your journaling amid the charming daily life of metropolitan Montrealers. Would you like a pastry with that?

Weather: 3

Wonderful summers alone would give Montreal weather a 5, but the freezing winters that drive the population underground to do their shopping keeps this rating hovering in the middle. What Montreal lacks in the winter months it more than makes up for during glorious summers. The city more than thaws out with tons of international festivals on offer.

Social: 5

J'adore les Montrealers! What a wonderful city of people! Even the uber swankiest patrons of the sexiest boutique hotels are quick to start up conversations over breakfast. By the time your teapot is empty, you will have a napkin full of the names of beloved restaurants and city sights. I say "napkin," because you will be scribbling on the nearest paper once you realize that your newfound friends intend to give you an entire history of the local cuisine.

Flying Foreplay

Book a boutique hotel, darling! To get the quintessential Montreal experience, you have to stay somewhere superchic. Gorgeous boutique hotels beckon at every turn, and staying in Vieux-Montreal triples your style points. The best of the best include Le Place d'Armes Hotel & Suites, Hotel Gault, Nelligan, the Hotel St. Paul, and Hotels le Germain and Godin, located downtown.

Famous Sons and Daughters of Montreal

Geneviève Bujold
Leonard Cohen (see the film *Leonard Cohen I'm Your Man*)
The creators of Trivial Pursuit

Caroline Dhavernas
Céline Dion
Oscar Peterson
Caroline Rhea
Mordecai Richler
William Shatner
Norma Shearer

Montreal Accessories

Bring your arsenal of fabulous clothes and leave room to buy more. Fabulousness is encouraged in Montreal! This is definitely not the time to go dowager on us, darling. Think Paris! Think New York nightlife. Think Canadian dollar exchange rates! And think cute Canadian boys, *n'est-ce pas,* eh?

The Top 10 Extraordinary Experiences

1. **Spend a day wandering through Vieux-Montreal.** Here's where that old world charm really charms. It hardly seems possible that all you had to do to get here was drive or take a short flight. Doesn't

anyone want to check your visa? Don't worry, you'll be checking your Visa bill soon enough. Four-hundred-year-old streets are filled with art galleries, museums, well-worn churches, boutiques, and sidewalk cafés. At night romance oozes from every carefully lit edifice—a city-planning must since night falls early here in winter. You can walk clear to the St. Lawrence River and see the Old Port. Vieux this, old that—it's a wonder these places aren't more sensitive to their nomenclatures! www.vieux.montreal.qc.ca/eng/accueila.htm.

2.   Visit Mount Royal Park. The park that Central Park designer Frederick Law Olmsted built, Mount Royal has a lot to offer outdoorsy denizens. In a distant hilltop corner stands Saint Joseph's Oratory, which rewards with glorious city views. Whether you're exploring the park on cross-country skis and snowshoes or on foot or bicycle, you may not see all the park's treasures in one trip. If the weather's right, a picnic might be just the thing. Or a coffee at Smith House or a pedal boat around Beaver Lake. Sometimes the best thing about being in a city is the opportunity to take a break from it once in a while . . .

3.   It's art, darling, art. There are many museums here as befits so cosmopolitan a city. The purchase of a museum pass might make the most sense for the aesthetically driven diva. Passes of one to three days give you access to the many for the price of a few, a great deal if you plan to see at least three. These passes are good at such famed museums as the Montreal Museum of Fine Arts and the Musée d'art contemporain. The Bronfman (of Seagrams Canadian whiskey fame) Holocaust Museum is here, as well

as the fascinating Montreal Biodome. This is a wild place where you can walk from the Antarctic to the tropics in half a day—good for you! In addition to galleries galore, Montreal makes sure art comes to the masses in the form of various *maisons de la culture* scattered around the city that offer all manner of performances.

4.   Tour McGill University. Would you go to Cambridge, Mass, and not spend time at Harvard? Then definitely don't leave Montreal without spending some time at McGill. You'll feel smarter the minute you set foot on this campus where the elite of international intelligentsia go. Tours are free, and taking a Socratic stroll through these great halls of learning is a brilliant way to break up your sightseeing day. Conveniently located downtown, McGill's main campus will teach you a thing or two more about our neighbors to the North.

5.   Mont-Tremblant spas might make you tremble. Mont-Tremblant is the highest peak in these here parts, both in height and stature. Great for skiing in winter and hiking and rafting in the summer, this is the peak to patronize for spas galore. This gorgeous mountain is just an hour-and-a-quarter drive (60 miles) from Montreal. There are golf courses, too, and if window shopping is more your style, then spend a lovely weekend in the picturesque village at the base of the mountain with several ski-in/ski-out hotels including a very grand Fairmont.

6.   Enjoy summer in Montreal! Montreal is world famous for its International Jazz Fest and F1 series events. We've already discussed that burning rubber polo match, that car race for the croquet and coquette set. It's a decidedly Euro sport that fits perfectly with Montreal's cosmo vibe. And the annual Jazz Fest is nothing to sneeze your saxophone at. Top entertainers and their fans descend upon the city to the tune of tens of thousands of tourists. The best of the best as well as the rest take over the city, and concerts pop sciddly bop bop at venues all over town. www.montrealjazzfest.com; www.formula1.com.

7. Take your shopping underground. When it gets too frosty to shop (heaven forefend!), those savvy and fashionable Montrealers don't get cold feet. They head underground to their famous shopping mall. An entire city of commerce beneath winter's mean streets, this surprising answer to the chill factor wows with its sheer scale. Aptly called the Underground City, there are movie theaters down here as well as metro stops and shops, shops, shops! Great even on a rainy summer's day, it's fun to sink to the level of the Underground City. All those outfits and shoes for sale in that gorgeous Canadian currency? I must have died and gone to . . . oops, heaven is up!

8. Cloister yourself in café culture. Attention! Put that great big tourist map down. It's time to go into emergency Paris mode because Montreal's glamorous veins pulse with café au lait. Bring something to read or start writing something worth reading. Then settle in for a long afternoon at a small café table on some fabulous sidewalk, and let the rhythms of Montreal unfold before you like the buttery sweet layers of a croissant. The best café street is St. Laurent but you can easily discover your own favorite.

9. Find some spectator sports. Do I mean meeting cute boys or eavesdropping in a café? No I'm talking real sports. Like with equipment. Oh never mind . . . There is nothing sexier than the toothless grin of a real hockey player. The boys of baseball up and left a while ago, but the real men of the Montreal Canadiens are still around—those puck pushers who really know how to use their sticks. The Canadians have their own football league, and I don't mean soccer, though Montreal has a team for that, too, named the Alouettes. Buy an Alouette logo shirt and wear it at home. Kiss the first boy who recognizes it. A girl's got to have her standards.

10. I love the nightlife. We've saved the best tip for last for you disco divas! Montreal has a gorgeous, thrivingly fabulous nighttime scene. The very best of the very coolest is a little strip of places just near the Hotel Godin (a great place to crash afterward—www.hotelgodin.com). What might trip you up is the fact that Globe (3455 Blvd. St. Laurent) and Buona Notte (3518 Blvd. St. Laurent; www.buonanotte.com) are restaurants. Yes! But they morph into swank clubs once the last crème brûlée is served. So much the better for a new-to-town diva! It's easy to get into these popular places if you're already there eating dinner. You can watch the transformation from your table, and by the time you or someone else has paid the bill, you'll find yourself in the middle of a hot nightspot. The way Clark Kent rips off his clothes to reveal the superman beneath, so, too, do these hot little restaurants strip down for dessert to reveal the ultimate in Montreal partying. For a big club experience, jet over to Jet. The Grey Goose Sub Zero ice bar, literally made of ice, is the perfect place to chill this winter.

PLAYA DEL CARMEN, MEXICO

Teresa getting dolphin kisses
at Xcaret.

Why This Place Rocks for Flying Solo

*F*or the beauty on a budget who wants a fantastic cultural adventure while baking in the sun on a crystal blue beach, I've got the perfect destination for you! Forget the Mediterranean, and say "Hola" to the "Mexiterranean" and the charming village of Playa del Carmen. This small seaside town is a short 45-minute ride from Cancun Airport and a world away from the cheesy tourist trap of Cancun. The great thing about Playa (as the locals call it) is that the Europeans found it first, so you're more likely to meet sophisticated Germans and Italians than obnoxious tourists like you would in Cancun.

Club Med

If you are not ready to go all the way to Playa alone, spend a week at Club Med, Cancun, which is only 30 minutes from the airport. They will have a gorgeous Club Med staff member pick you up at the airport. This is a fabulous first-time adventure.

Playa's quaintness, along with its 5-star dining and unending list of water sports, is a great destination for any girl who's not too sure what she wants from her vacation. Sun, rest, parties, dancing, fitness, feasting, sailing, or sleeping? Basically, you can have it all. If you're a wannabe archeologist, there are a host of Mayan ruins to explore on day trips. For you athletic chicks, spend a week at the Bikini Boot Camp tightening up your buns. And for those of you who love the sun and want to chill with a margarita, you can do that just about anywhere in Playa. Oh, and for social butterflies, you'll be so busy dancing the nights away and partying with other beach-lovers that you might forget what day of the week it is.

Culture: 5

If you think Mexico is all about donkey shows, spring break silliness, and tequila slammers, then you need to learn more about this amazing country! Playa is the perfect place to explore Mexico's rich Indian ancestry, mystical ruins, and fascinating traditions. Just south of Playa is the city of Tulum—an unbelievable temple-turned-town built for the gods—equipped with pyramids, ruins, and ornate statues.

Activity: 5

If you don't want to see ruins or charge up pyramids, glide across the azure seas by Jet Ski, go sailing, and try cave diving.

For such a tiny town, there are plenty of activities to keep guests busy. If all that sounds boring, you can always try yoga, horse riding, or kite boarding. Tired just reading the list of things to do? How about a margarita and a day at the spa?

Weather: 5

Unless a hurricane is ripping through the Mayan Riviera, the weather is pretty darn nice. Hurricane season starts on June 1 and ends November 30. But other than that, it's smooth sailing under an *azul* sky.

Social: 5

First, you might want to learn a few Mexican phrases, then a couple German ones, and then try out a handful of Italian ones, too. It's not only the Mexicans who vacation in Playa, but Europeans as well. The list of nightspots is pretty long for such a short town and the drinks are always being poured somewhere. Everything is within walking or stumbling distance, depending.

Flying Foreplay

You might want to scope out a few details before you say "Sí" to Playa. And make sure you have some basic medical supplies before heading into rural territory.

Montezuma's revenge. He's real, and he loves messing up a solo girl's vacations. It must have something to do with that "sacrificing of virgins" stuff. So, make sure you take diarrhea medication with you.

Earplugs. This is a small town with a big party scene. Many of the parties are happening in venues near accommodations, so make sure you have hearing protection. That's unless you plan on being one of the noisemakers.

Spanish translation book. This locale is not a hotbed for English-speaking tourists (yet) so bring a Spanish translator. I like to use an electronic one where I can put in whole sentences.

Bug repellant. Ay yay yay. Some of the hotels don't have screened windows and bugs like to bite at night.

Playa del Carmen Accessories

Take one, or two? If you plan on lounging on the sandy beaches all day while sipping margaritas, then sporting your itty-bitty bikini is superb. But if Jet Skiing, playing with the dolphins, and cave diving is more your speed, you might want to bring a one-piece bathing suit.

Sombrero *por favor*. For those moments when you are chilling on a flotation device or swinging in a hammock—protect yourself from the sun. You know to bring sunscreen, right?

When night falls. In true Mexican tradition, the late afternoons are siesta time. Then, the sun drops and the parties begin. Dress changes dramatically from beach causal to sophisticated sexy.

Forget it? Buy it there! Playa is a well-stocked town, so you will find fun little boutiques lining the streets. They sell everything from colorful sarongs to darling handmade shoes.

The Top 10 Extraordinary Experiences

1. **Spend the day at Xcaret EcoPark.** This place is magical! If you can only do one thing between margaritas and lying on the beach, then this is it. The park is loaded with crazy things you'd never do or see in your real life. You can snorkel the underground river, walk through an unbelievably beautiful butterfly sanctuary, play with dolphins, watch sea turtles frolic—or whatever they do—and walk around real Mayan ruins. And at night you can watch a spectacular firelit Mayan ceremonial dance. You'll leave feeling like a Mayan princess. From Playa del Carmen, take a taxi or the Xcaret tour bus; it's less than 20 minutes away. www.xcaret.com/indexxc.php.

Frida Bar

For you Frida Kahlo lovers, have a drink at Frida Bar at Avenida 5 and Calle 12. Make sure to have your picture taken in front of the huge Frida portrait.

2. Ride the Fat Cat. Chill on a speedy 41-foot Catamaran with a crew of characters including Kimba, the snorkeling boxer. You can snorkel in a remote cove, check out Mayan ruins, explore Ritchie's island, or stay on the boat and indulge in Fat Cat's famous Rum Punch. www.playa.info/playa-del-carmen-info-fat-cat-catamaran.html.

3. Trek to Tulum and do the Bikini Boot Camp. Tulum is one of the most incredible ancient fortresses in the world. This picture-perfect place sits majestically on the edge of the Caribbean and was the seat of the Mayan empire. Take a day trip and walk the ruins, or better yet, after a few days of fun in Playa, check into Amansala's Bikini Boot Camp in Tulum. Days at Amansala include excursions to freshwater swimming holes, walks to nearby Mayan ruins, beachside massages and Mayan Clay Treatments, or just relax in a hammock on the beach. Tel: 011-52-984-100-0717; www.amansala.com.

4. Party on Fifth Avenue and beyond. Put on your sexy sarong and halter top and saunter from venue to venue enjoying a movable feast of cocktails and appetizers. Here's a list of some of my favorites:

Alux Cave. Eat dinner in a real cave festooned with dramatic lighting and spooky nooks and crannies. Enjoy dinner here, then head back to Fifth Avenue (Calle 5). Located about 5 blocks across the highway on your left on Juarez.

Blue Parrot. This place is always hopping and is a favorite with the locals and tourists. Between Calles 12 and 14; tel: 984-873-0083.

Capitan Tutix. If you're into seeing people dressed as jaguars juggling fire, then this is the place.

Kuba. You'll find this club next door to Tutix, and if Tutix is packed, chill here for a while.

Playa 69. The only gay bar on 5th is casual with friendly bartenders who can fill you in on the local scene. Located on the west side of 5th. Look for the sign.

Mambo Café. If you're into Cuban beats, then you will love this place. Balloons, foam dancing, and great music rule here.

Calypso. For you salsa lovers, dance the night away at Calypso and if you just want to listen, come when they have live salsa bands. Located on the second floor on the south side of Calle 6.

Rhumba Club. This is a salsa club located on the second floor of a shopping complex, behind the Domino's Pizza on Juarez Avenue. If you want to meet lots of tourists, head here.

5. Are you hot to trot? Just south of Playa you'll find some of the best horseback riding on the Mayan Riviera. Near the Calica Pier is Rancho Punta Venado, where you can enjoy an afternoon of horsing around on some of the finer ponies in town. Beware—some of these places have horses that look more like dead donkeys than healthy stallions. Rancho Punta Venado; tel: 984-877-9701.

6.   Do downward-facing dog. If your perfect vacation is more about morning yoga than margaritas past midnight, then you might want to check out Yoga By The Sea. Salute the sun in a studio facing the sea, followed by a quick dip in the ocean and a tropical fruit breakfast with coffee or tea. They offer daily classes or week-long programs. They even have Spanish classes! www.morethanyoga.com.

7.   Be a diving diva. Spend the day snorkeling in the gossamer blue waters of the Caribbean, or better yet, become a certified PADI diver. You can dive off the waters of Playa, or sail out to Cozumel Island. For a truly magical experience, leave the tourist waters near Playa and cruise out to the back, eastern side of Cozumel. For you really courageous girls, try underwater cavern diving. Tank-Ha Dive Center; tel: 984-873-0302; fax: 984-873-1355; www.tankha.com. Sealife Divers; www.sealifedivers.com.

8.   Spa it. After days of sun, sand, beach, and dancing . . . your body might cry out for some rest. If so, visit Spa Itza, a great day spa specializing in healing through water, massage, and authentic Mayan therapies. Treatments include Original Mayan Healing Bath, Sensory Floating Room, Massage Therapies, Hydro Remedies, Body Antidotes, Manicure, Facials, Pedicure, Body Waxing, Open Air Showers, Roof Top Dry Sauna, Roof Top Sun Bathing, Roof Top Vapor Lodge, and "Oxygen, Tea and Elixir Bar." Just what the witch doctor ordered! Reservations: (011-52) 984-803-2588;

from Playa: 803-2588; info@spaitza.com; www.spaitza.com.

9.   Ride a kite. Kite boarding is one of those sports that takes lots of time to figure out and you look like a clumsy idiot when you're learning to balance on a board while catching the wind and waves. So, Playa is the perfect place to master your skills. Nobody knows you! Plus you get to meet a ton of guys from around the world who are also learning to kite surf. The odds are in your favor; this ain't a chick sport! IKARUS Kite Boarding Shop; Calle 16 North and 5th Avenue; www.kiteboardmexico.com/web/english/home.htm; e-mail: contacto@ikaruskiteboarding.com.

10.   Cruise to Cozumel. Cozumel is a charming island about 30 minutes by ferry from Playa, and it's a great place to chill if you've kissed too many boys on the mainland. The Presidente InterContinental Cozumel Resort & Spa has an amazing spa that offers crazy treatments like the Mayan Journey, Mayan Moon Massage and Mayan Ceremony of Love. The hotel also offers a PADI Five Palm watersports operation, ideal for first-time divers. If you want to experience the Discover Scuba program or become a certified diver, the resort has first-class scuba facilities. Not into diving? Then spend your days lounging on the white sands beach, which is just minutes from the magnificent Palancar Reef, part of the second largest barrier reef in the world. For you golfing goddesses, the resort also has a putting green where you can hone your short game before heading out to the Cozumel Country Club. Presidente InterContinental Cozumel Resort & Spa; Carretera a Chankanaab km 6.5; Cozumel, Q. Roo, 77600, Mexico; tel: 800-327-0200; www.intercontinentalcozumel.com.

SAN FRANCISCO, CALIFORNIA

Judi dangles from a cable car at Powell and California.

Why This Place Rocks for Flying Solo

San Franciscans revel in entertaining and showing off their spectacular city. You'll feel their welcoming warmth, even if the temperature is a bit cool. This is a fem-powered town, where women don't think twice about dining alone or attending a show sans escort, unless that escort is their laptop. So, if you're ready for a liberating adventure where you're sure to encounter plenty of amazing people, pack your bags—because you're heading to San Francisco.

If San Francisco were a man, he would have the sophistication of James Bond and the adventurous spirit of Lawrence of Arabia. With designer shops lining the streets and bohemian cafés dotting the neighborhoods, this city is both elegant and eclectic. Scattered throughout this seven-by-seven-mile gem you'll find world-class restaurants, theaters, symphonics, operas, boutiques, museums, parks, and vibrant bars. You can't get bored in this city—it won't let you! Beyond the city's borders, further adventure awaits. There's great hiking and mountain biking in Marin, skiing in Tahoe, surfing, kayaking, and windsurfing up and down the coast, and golf courses everywhere you turn. All these activities are avidly supported by groups that love hosting solo women travelers.

Culture: 4.5

When it comes to culture, San Francisco is a world leader. Not because it's tied to one cultural path, but because it's not. You can find Asian fused with Mexican, Vietnamese blended with French—and I'm just talking about the people! With art galleries galore, miles of museums, clutters of cafés, and gorgeous historical landmarks around every corner, you'll be giving the city a standing ovation the entire time you're here.

Activity: 4

From Rollerblading on the Embarcadero to kayaking in Sausalito Bay, you can spend a week here just burning calories. San Francisco and its surroundings are packed with activities guaranteed to get your heart racing. (Even a nice stroll around the city can easily involve scaling several steep hills!) But if you simply want to relax with a mocha and a slice of cake at a cozy café, this city offers plenty of opportunities to rest as well.

Weather: 2

Mark Twain said it the best: "The coldest winter I ever spent was a summer in San Francisco." When in San Francisco, layer like the natives! Bring a jacket and a few sweaters because with the city's many microclimates, you can go from sunshine to fog in a few short blocks. What does stay warm (if not *hot*) all year round are the people. For look-but-don't-touch eye candy, think Castro boys. And to keep things hot while the fog rolls in, think Financial District suits, and scruffy Mission artists; for a summer of love, pluck a hippie from the Haight.

Social: 4

Better bring an empty little black book, because after a week in San Francisco you'll have it filled with names, numbers, e-mail addresses, and IM screen names. San Franciscans are friendly, social, and tech savvy to boot! They'll want to synch up with you in myriad ways. No wonder there's a song about leaving your heart here—you'll be feeling so comfortable around the locals that you'll soon be wearing your heart on your new designer sleeve.

Flying Foreplay

Take a moment to check a few things out before you press the "confirm your ticket" button. If you're hoping to meet cute, hetero dotcommers, make sure your itinerary doesn't overlap with Gay Pride Week. That might not slow you down, but other things can, like booking your golf trip during the rainy season or wanting to whale watch when the big blues are already in the Arctic.

Check the weather. San Francisco is by the beach, but not in a tropical way. It tends to rain in the fall and winter, and you'll find that it's surprisingly chilly during the summer, when the spectacular fog rolls in with white cotton-candy tendrils, lacing the Golden Gate Bridge in a downy drape. While not ideal for sunbathing, it's a poet's paradise!

Read Before You Go

Fogtown: A Novel, by Peter Plate
A Heartbreaking Work of Staggering Genius, by Dave Eggers

The Joy Luck Club, by Amy Tan
Oh the Glory of It All, by Sean Wilsey
Tales of the City, by Armistead Maupin

Setting Your Scene

There are a few wonderful neighborhoods in San Francisco that you can call home while you're in town. Here's a list of the top five areas that are safe, friendly, great for women, and close to attractions, restaurants, and shopping:

Embarcadero. This area is the new "it" spot. It sits on the edge of the bay, overlooking the iconic Ferry Plaza building and Bay Bridge. The Embarcadero is surrounded by great restaurants, new hotels, a waterfront promenade, and is a tram ride away from the ballpark—home of the San Francisco Giants. And during the winter, there's an ice-skating rink nearby.

- **Hotel Vitale.** A chic, cool place where the locals hang. Tel: 415-248-5924; www.hotelvitale.com
- **Hyatt Regency.** A San Francisco institution. They have a restaurant called the Equinox that rotates 360 degrees every hour. Tel: 800-233-1234; www.sanfrancisco.regency.hyatt.com
- **Harbor Court Inn.** One of the city's premier boutique hotels. Tel: 415-882-1300; www.harborcourthotel.com
- **Hotel Griffon.** Upscale boutique hotel on the waterfront. Tel: 415-495-2100; www.hotelgriffon.com

Fisherman's Wharf. For easy access to all the true San Francisco tourist spots, this is the place to stay. It is less expensive than the other locations because it has the largest selection of low-price hotel chains. It's my least favorite personally—but hey—you might like sweaty fishermen and the yapping of sea lions to sing you to sleep!

- **Argonaut Hotel.** Fabulous maritime-themed hotel right in the heart of Fisherman's Wharf. My number one choice in this area. Tel: 415-563-0800; www.argonauthotel.com
- **Sheraton at Fisherman's Wharf.** Your basic hotel with lobby, concierge, and all the services you need. Tel: 415-362-5500; www.sheratonatthewharf.com
- **Hyatt at Fisherman's Wharf.** Solid choice, but not my first. Tel: 415-563-1234; www.fishermanswharf.hyatt.com

Nob Hill. When San Franciscans want to get away, they go to Nob Hill. This ultra-luxe area in the heart of San Francisco is home to some world-famous hotels and private residences. There's not much nightlife up here, but it's great if you want to relax on the top of the world. Many rooms in these hotels have outstanding views—for a price. Forget buying that extra pair of Jimmy Choos.

- **Mark Hopkins.** Sleep at the top of the world. Tel: 415-392-3434; www.intercontinental.com
- **The Huntington.** A fabulous traditional boutique hotel. Tel: 415-474-5400; www.huntingtonhotel.com
- **Fairmont Hotel.** Stay at the hotel where *Hotel* was filmed. Tel: 800-469-6130.
- **Ritz Carlton.** For uber-luxe two blocks from the top of Nob Hill,

stay here. Tel: 415-773-6198; www.ritzcarlton.com

SOMA (South of Market Street). This is the favorite area for the local crowd, especially at night. Only in SOMA does the trendy mix so well with the seedy. Among warehouses and designer furniture stores, you'll find supertrendy hotels with busy bars, patronized by the offbeat beautiful people. If you want to be close to the Museum of Modern Art, downtown, and the ballpark, this is the place to stay.

- **Palomar.** A wonderful place for solo women. I highly recommend this friendly, centrally located hotel. Tel: 415-348-1111; www.kimptongroup.com
- **W.** Sexy hotel next to the Museum of Modern Art. Tel: 415-777-5300
- **St. Regis.** Pink champagne on ice and private butlers. Yum. Tel: 415-284-4000
- **Palace Hotel.** For any girl who wanted to be a princess, this is your chance. Tel: 415-512-1111
- **Four Seasons.** Complete with one of the best, swankiest gyms in the city, Sports Club LA. Tel: 415-633-3000

Union Square. Can you say shop till you drop? Well, if shopping is what you want to do, then this is the hood that you should crash. Stay out of the Tenderloin, which is between Geary and Market and Larkin and Taylor. This is not a safe area for women, and many hotel chains will say that they are "in the heart of the Theatre District," which means Tenderloin. These listed here are great and safe:

- **Clift Hotel.** This place is cool! Filled with rock stars and fash-

ionistas. Tel: 415-775-4700; www.IanSchrager.com

- **Sir Francis Drake.** A beautiful old hotel in the heart of Union Square. Tel: 415-395-8559
- **Prescot Hotel.** A lovely boutique hotel above the world-famous Postrio restaurant owned by Wolfgang Puck. Tel: 415-563-0303; www.prescotthotel.com
- **Hotel Diva.** For the diva in all of us. Just down the street from megashopping. Tel: 800-553-1900; www.hoteldiva.com

San Francisco Accessories

*J*ust as I never leave the house without makeup and a smile, I never visit a new town without knowing what to expect and what to bring. Here are the top five items you're sure to need in San Francisco:

Warm clothes. When it's summer in the rest of the world, San Francisco chooses to be the rebel child with windy nights, dramatic foggy mornings, and peekaboo sunshine. Bring those layers! Sweaters, scarves, and a nice coat will serve you well.

A good pair of walking shoes. You don't need to be a superathlete to enjoy walking this city, and you can easily manage San Francisco on foot as long as you're sporting a comfy pair of streetwalkers. I'd recommend a nice pair of boots or wedged-heeled shoes, so you don't get your heels stuck in the cable car lines or between the cobblestones in Jackson Square. And don't let the hills scare you—let *buns of steel* be your mantra.

Sexy-fine number. Every sport has its

uniform, and flirting is no exception. Don't leave home without that little black number. But if you forget, don't fret, because there are plenty of fabulous boutiques that can satisfy your need to sassify. And yes, you can wear skirts with boots in this town. Even Ugg boots.

Streetwise San Francisco Mini Metro Map. This handy, itty-bitty map (2.8 by 4 inches folded) gives you a clear overview of the city of San Francisco (how lost can a girl get in a city that's planned on a grid?), along with the public transportation routes. Find yours at www.streetwisemaps.com.

The Top 10 Extraordinary Experiences

1. Stroll across the Golden Gate Bridge. Spend the day in the Marina watching the local boys play Frisbee, check out the Palace of Fine Arts, explore Fort Point under the Golden Gate Bridge, then walk across the most spectacular span in the world. Leave early in the morning and plan on spending the whole day walking. No stilettos, sister.

2. Get crabs at Fisherman's Wharf. Start with a breakfast of champions at Ghi-

rardelli Square, where you can get more chocolate than you can handle. Visit the Maritime Museum to burn off a few calories before your lunch of fresh crab and clam chowder in a sourdough bowl. Walk through Pier 39 and end the day with an Irish coffee at the Buena Vista Café.

3. Ride a cable car to the top of the world. Start at Market Street at the Embarcadero and catch the California Street cable car. Get off at Mason and California. Have tea at the Fairmont or enjoy the legendary Top of the Mark sky bar. Get inspired at Grace Cathedral, the largest cathedral west of the Mississippi, where you can say a prayer or walk the Labyrinth. After all that religion, treat yourself to a dirty martini at the Huntington Hotel.

4. Go wine tasting in Napa Valley. No need to rent a car to go to the Valley of the Wines because there's plenty of tours that will drive you there. (Check out some recommendations in the excursion section of the local papers.) I also recommend that you try to spend the night in one of the smaller towns and enjoy a day of pampering. My favorite spas are the Sonoma Mission Inn in Sonoma and Calistoga Ranch in

Day Tripping

Book a walking tour with San Francisco City Guides when you first get into town. It's the perfect way to meet new friends, and the tours are free! Go to www.sfcityguides.org.

Calistoga. There are lots of couples there, so don't plan on meeting Mr. Perfect (you might, but he's probably married, so expect this part of your trip to be truly solo and restful).

5.   Take a ferry ride to Sausalito, Alcatraz, or Angel Island. Head to Fisherman's Wharf and check out the different bay tours. My favorite takes you by ferry to Sausalito, where you can spend the day shopping in the pristine, easy-to-walk town. Treat yourself to lunch overlooking the bay and San Francisco at Horizons; 558 Bridgeway, Sausalito; tel: 415-331-3232.

6.   Explore Chinatown. Go for a dim sum brunch and then stroll the small, crowded streets while searching for touristy trinkets. This is a great place to buy fun, inexpensive gifts like silk slippers, jade jewelry, and bamboo crafts. Start at Grant Street and Broadway and wind your way through the frenetic side streets.

7.   Feast at the Ferry Building. Eat your way through this historic building, home to famous San Francisco gourmet institutions like Cow Girl Creamery, Hog Island Oyster Company, Tsar Nicoulai Caviar, The Slanted Door, and Scharffen Berger Chocolate. Show up at happy hour, when the singles who work in the financial district (two blocks away) crash Hog Island Oyster Bar to celebrate.

8.   Hide away in Half Moon Bay. Rent a car and drive south down the breathtaking Highway One (or Devil's Slide, as the locals call it). Stop at Half Moon Bay and treat yourself to an overnight excursion of spa-ing and shopping. Stay in one of the historic bed and breakfasts on Main Street, or get the royal treatment at the Ritz Carlton overlooking the Pacific Ocean.

   Old Thyme Inn. Gorgeous B&B with decadent beds and hot tubs in the rooms. 779 Main Street; tel: 800-720-4277; www.oldthymeinn.com.

   Half Moon Bay Inn. Darling corner Inn in the heart of Half Moon Bay, great bar and restaurant. 401 Main Street; tel: 650-560-9758; www.halfmoonbayinn.com.

   Ritz Carlton. Play golf, practice tennis, or relax at one of the best spas on the West Coast. 1 Miramontes Point Road; tel: 650-712-7000; www.ritzcarlton.com.

9.   Revel in the Castro. Boy meets girl is great, but in this special part of the world it's all about boy meeting boy. The shops are insanely colorful and the cafés are delightful. Shops like Hot Cookie and Does Your Mother Know? and bars like Moby Dick and Daddy's set the outrageous tone. A solo gal can have tons of fun hitting the bars and dance clubs here—sometimes it's nice to be in a roomful of men who won't make you suffer through cheesy pickup lines. The Castro also boasts some amazing restaurants, the only places around here guaranteed to quench your oral fixations.

10. Head out to Haight-Ashbury. Oh man, if you wondered what it was like in the sixties, then head over to "The Haight," as the locals call it. You might think that this love-filled neighborhood forgot to wind up its clocks because, by the look of things, it's still 7 p.m., 1969.

Top 10 Solo Dining Places

A table for one is all it takes for a delicious dinner in the city. Here are my favorite solo-savvy places. You'll find that the wait staff is friendly (aka gorgeous and attentive) and the food is fabulous.

La Mediterranee—lunch or dinner (my all-time favorite!), Pacific Heights, 1761 Fillmore Street; tel: 415-921-2956.

Betelnut—lunch or dinner, Cow Hollow—Marina, 2030 Union Street; tel: 415-929-8855.

Bistro Aix—dinner, Marina, 3340 Steiner; tel: 415-202-0100.

Hog Island Oyster Company—lunch or dinner, Embarcadero, 1 Ferry Building; tel: 415-391-7117.

The Curbside Café—lunch or dinner, Pacific Heights, 2455 California; tel: 415-929-9030.

Rose Pistola—lunch or dinner, North Beach, 532 Columbus Avenue; tel: 415-399-0499.

Fillmore Grill—lunch, Pacific Heights, 2298 Fillmore Street; tel: 415-776-7600.

Cafe Claude—Lunch, Union Square—Downtown, 7 Claude Lane; tel: 415-392-3505.

Café De La Press—breakfast, lunch, dinner, and aprés shopping. Union Square; 352 Grant Avenue; tel: 415-398-2680.

Cha Cha Cha—lunch or dinner, SOMA and Haight-Ashbury; tel: 415-648-0504.

SOUTH BEACH, FLORIDA

Jordan checking out the view
in South Beach.

Why This Place Rocks for Flying Solo

Every time my plane screeches to a halt at Miami Airport, an ear-to-ear grin illuminates my face. Thoughts of dancing all night long with gorgeous Cuban men, power shopping in over-the-top boutiques, and chilling poolside with a mojito in hand swirl in my head. I rent my convertible and motor straight to Miami's South Beach, the exotic gem of American's eastern coastline—making sure that I've got the right beats pumping out of the car while I cruise. South Beach is a tiny piece of urban oceanfront heaven that is a dawn-to-dawn playground for open-shirted men and stiletto-tottering ladies alike. It is *the* hot spot where unique Art Deco architecture meets the front cover of *Vogue* magazine. Forget Los Angeles—this is where the celebs flock to go wild, and if you want to be counted among their numbers, you gotta hop a plane, train, or boat to South Beach, *amiga*.

As sizzling and body-hugging as a leopard-print miniskirt on a summer day, South Beach is a racy and heart-pounding tribute to all that is *fiesta*. Beaded Brazilian flip-flops by day, rhinestone stilettos by night, and fun, fun, fun 24-7. The solo sister needs only the proper tools and wardrobe to blend in, or stand out, depending on what she wants. There's no shortage of tipsy travelers wanting to share their merriment, and it's easy to make friends with men and women who also want to leave their hum-drum lives back home. *"Amo South Beach."* I love South Beach, and South Beach will love you, too. But be properly equipped—South Beach is the *haute* amusement park of the glitterati, fashionistas, and rock stars. Don't show up looking like a tourist, you will get kicked to the curb. South Beach doesn't do ugly.

Culture: 4

This is the closest to Cuban cum Ibiza you can get without leaving the continental United States or getting arrested for visiting a trade embargo country. Mix a little bit of Latin flavor and a touch of hedonism with a lot of sun worship, and you have South Beach culture. It is a potent mixture of spicy atmosphere, delicious yet ephemeral people, and sweet, dirty dancing.

Activity: 2

Dancing burns lots of calories. The more men you dance with, the more calories you burn. And if you define accidentally stumbling into a fashion photo shoot as "activity," you're set.

Weather: 5

Ahhh, that sun. South Beach is a year-round destination, with gorgeous weather in different forms every month. Keep your eyes on the storm watch, though. Florida is susceptible to hurricanes known to sweep through the region. Thunderstorms can put on an amazing show; just make sure you are not in the water or holding an umbrella. You might get more electric action than expected.

Social: 5

Walking around here, you'll see all those venues you thought existed only in your favorite glossy magazine: Nobu, Prive, and Mansion are just a few of the famous club names that regularly pop up in gossip round-ups of what some fabulous person is doing where. Dress the part and you, too, can be fabulous in South Beach. Maybe you'll even get your picture in a gossip column. Wouldn't *that* make your friends jealous!

Flying Foreplay

*E*ven though you'll feel like you left the United States, you haven't, so you don't need to worry about packing the kitchen sink or all your over-the-counter hangover medicine. You'll find that stuff everywhere.

Remember, darling, you are not staying in the town of Miami, you are partying like a princess in South Beach. Do not book an online travel package to Miami because there is a chance you will end up nowhere near the beach. This is the trip where you pull out your credit card for ocean views at a prime address. Here are five hotels in the area you want to be:

Hotel Astor, 956 Washington Avenue, Miami Beach, Florida

Hotel Nash, 1120 Collins Avenue, Miami Beach, Florida

Catalina, 1732 Collins Avenue, Miami Beach, Florida

Las Brisas South Beach Dorset, 1720 Collins Avenue, Miami Beach, Florida

The Savoy, 425 Ocean Drive, Miami Beach, Florida

Fake bake! That way you won't look like you stumbled off the plane from Juno, Alaska.

Wax on, wax off. I know it's unpleasant, but you're going to want to be smooth as a baby's bottom in this bikini-oriented town. You're not in Europe, ladies, this is Florida! For touch-ups once you get there, go to Uni K Wax Center (771 17th St.; tel: 305-531-7777). These people are real pros, which are the only kind you should have when it comes to hot wax and your skin.

Mani/pedicures. You'll be in flip-flops all day, so your tootsies have nowhere to hide. Never neglect your toenails when you're getting ready for South Beach.

So be it. Feel like you'll never get your bod up to South Beach standards? Don't sweat it. There are all kinds of body types and shapes that you'll see relaxing on the white sands. The whole point of South Beach is to rock out with your bad self; don't limit your good times because the tube top's running a little tight. Get out there and enjoy it. But a month or two on the South Beach Diet is a good plan if you want to shed some pounds before you go!

Party in the Mansion

The Mansion (1235 Washington Avenue) is open Thursday through Sunday, 11 p.m. to 5 a.m. Arrive early, looking like the jet-setting goddess that you are, to avoid a prolonged wait. Cover charges range between $20 and $30. If the line's too long there (or the crowd that night isn't up to your standards), try BED (tel: 305-532-9070). Monday night is Ladies Night, and girls come early to eat for free before the club gets wild around 11 p.m.

Read Before You Go

*B*ooks? Too heavy to carry in your beach tote, sunshine. Grab a magazine and indulge in some reading as intellectual as a scantily clad supermodel frolicking in South Beach.

South Beach Accessories

Bag it. Bring your sexiest, biggest beach tote bag. You'll be walking around all day, going from chic breakfast restaurant to hot boutiques, to cool beach, and then bar hopping. Where else will you stash your coconut-flavored sunscreen, Jackie-O sunglasses, water bottle, towel, breath mints, waterproof mascara, *Vanity Fair*, etc.?

All things that glitter. Pull out the big guns. That means your sexiest swimsuits, tiniest tank tops, and strappiest sandals. Pack all your *big* jewelry. If you don't own any, then bring a credit card with a low interest and a high credit limit.

Good reads. Trashy magazines and romance novels, for when you just can't focus on *The Economist.*

Scarface. I mean scarf. They are great for taming your wild beach hair and perfect for splashing color on drab outfits. I wore one as a skirt once. Yeah, baby!

A terrific towel. Chairs aren't free, and you'll want to stake your territory from the encroaching, oily sunbathers.

A spectrum of SPFs. Bring goop that protects, some that smells delicious, and ones that make your skin glisten in the sun. Use a lip balm that has SPF as well. You want to keep those lips moisturized; you never know whom you might kiss.

The Top 10 Extraordinary Experiences

1. **Do the Mango tango.** Mango's Tropical Café is one of my favorite dancing venues in the world. It is kinda over-the-top, but the music is awesome! Located in the heart of South Beach, Mango's is the quintessential Caribbean hot spot. Gorgeous men ask you to dance every song, beautiful women dance on the bars, cocktails are the size of my femur bone, and there's endless Latin music—until the sun comes up. Go for dance

lessons during the day; stay to use what you've learned after the sun sets. This spot is known for having the best-looking staff in Florida, and all employees are required to know how to salsa, merengue, lambada, and tango. That's a lot of people whose job it is to make sure your booty gets shaking. Even the bartenders are dancers. They perform dances and don costumes from all over the world. Be sure to try their signature Mango Mambo, made from ice, rum, mango passion liqueur, banana liqueur, and mango juice. Liquid courage, my friends! Mango's Tropical Cafe, 900 Ocean Drive, Miami Beach; tel: 305-673-4422; www.mangostropicalcafe.com.

2.   Shop for vintage Chanel. C. Madeleine's boutique has the country's largest collection of dazzling clothing and accessories from the past century. History is seen here through the eyes of style icons like Coco Chanel, Emilio Pucci, and Diane von Furstenberg. There are two things you need for C. Madeleine's: credit and a car. Like its fashions, C. Madeleine's is off the beaten path, about thirty minutes from South Beach. There's not much to see in the area, so don't blink—if you're not looking, you'll miss it. What is wonderful—and breathtaking—about C. Madeleine's is its sheer selection of items and the passion they evoke. With 10,000 square feet of vintage heaven, one could easily get lost, if it weren't for the meticulous attention given to each era, color, trend, and current event. Depending on the theme or upcoming holiday, clothing and accessories are showcased in vignettes throughout the store. Highlights include Think Pink, a section dedicated to *Sex and the City*, and *Chinioserie*, which highlights Asian-influenced fashions. In my

favorite section—*Logorific*—you can find any logo you desire: from Louis Vuitton to Chanel, it's all for sale. And every piece is hand-selected by the owner, C. Madeleine herself. C. Madeleine's, 13702 Biscayne Boulevard, North Miami Beach, Florida 33181; tel: 305-945-7770; www.cmadeleines.com.

3.   Discover the Deco nation. Local historians and architects conduct Art Deco District guided walking tours. You'll get an introduction to Art Deco, Mediterranean Revival, and the Miami Beach Architectural Historic District. The 90-minute walking tours of Ocean Drive and beyond depart from the Art Deco Welcome Center.

For independent jet-setters, do a self-guided audio tour walk through Miami Beach's Art Deco District and its architectural history. Audio tours are available at the Welcome Center seven days a week, from 10 a.m. to 4 p.m. Art Deco Welcome Center, 1001 Ocean Drive, Miami Beach; tel: 305-531-3484; www.mdpl.org/tours.html.

4.   Be a DJ Diva. Now that you know how to dance, it's time to learn how to scratch. Scratch DJ academy is the first academy in the world to feature a curriculum and tutorials showcased by celebrity instructors. This is the only place where aspiring and amateur *DivaJ's* can come to learn or improve their mixing, blending, scratching, and beat-juggling skills from some of the best DJ's in the world. In addition to the fundamentals, you'll learn the philosophy and business know-how you need to either start or enhance your soon-to-be DJ-ing career. Oh, and think of the guys you'll meet. Tel: *305-535-2599*; www.scratch.com.

5. Swim with the dolphins. After all that dancing with the beautiful men of South Beach, head to the ocean and dance with the most gorgeous creatures in the sea—dolphins! A swim with the dolphins at the Miami Seaquarium is a once-in-a-lifetime experience. Make sure to wear a one-piece when you go—the dolphins take you on this ride, and if you're not careful, your bikini top can come off. Miami Seaquarium; tel: 305-361-5705; www.miamiseaquarium.com.

6. Join two feet and one guy. Kevin Doran of Two Foot Tours offers an insider's trek through South Beach. Kevin provides a look at local history, dazzling ecology, wondrous architecture, and of course, delicious, salacious, nonfattening gossip. From the causeways to the Deco District to Millionaire's Row and Fisher Island, hear about the personalities and forces that have helped shape this singular environment into one of the world's most compelling destinations. Connect with Kevin before exploring on your own two feet. You will see some very familiar places in an altogether different way and leave Miami Beach with more than just a suntan. www.twofoottours.com.

7. Sex it up. Just what you need to do after basking in the sun and drinking tall tropical drinks is go into a museum dedicated to erotic art. Imagine the fun you'll have that night! The World Erotic Art Museum is one of Florida's hottest attractions. It's smack dab in the heart of the South Beach Art Deco District. And it has the world's largest public collection of erotic art (I wonder who has the largest *private* collection!) with thousands of historical and contemporary pieces on view. This truly unique and stimulating museum is the dream and realization of

world-renowned erotic arts collector Naomi Wilzig, who has dedicated years of her life to searching and acquiring this mind-blowing collection. And she's been kind enough to share her toys with us! World Erotic Art Museum (WEAM), 1205 Washington Avenue, Miami Beach, Florida 33139; tel: 866-969-WEAM or 305-532-9336; www.weam.com.

8. Take a lazy chic tour. For you rock stars who drank too much and danced your feet off, but still want to see South Beach before you have to go back to reality, Florida Ever-Glides (www.floridaever-glides.com.) comes to your rescue. You don't have to lift a foot or a finger to enjoy these tours on Segway Human Transporters. You'll cruise along learning all about South Beach's sordid past and racy present. The tours will glide through a ton of scenic/historic Miami Beach locations, including:

- Art Deco District & South Beach
- Miami Beach Marina
- Southpointe Park/Cruise Ships
- And other fascinating points of interest

9. Pamper your body and mind. By the end of your week, you are going to be sore. And if you're not, then you did not do South Beach properly! So, after all that decadence, your body is going to need a bit of love (and not the kind you got from Juan). The Spa at the Setai is ready to take your body and do a bit of healing work on it before you have to head back to the office. This place is a haven of serenity and peace—far away from the addictive beats of the nightclubs and bars. The philosophy behind the spa is derived from an ancient Sanskrit legend of the gods, who embarked

Red Velvet Ropes

They are notoriously impassable obstacles to the club of your choice. Here's a tip: Try calling the club during the day and ask to be put on the guest list. This usually works as long as you agree to be there before midnight.

on a quest for a natural elixir of immortality and eternal youth. Just what South Beach is all about. My favorite massage is the Thai massage. If you stay at the hotel, you can enjoy Sunrise or Sunset Meditation overlooking the Atlantic Ocean. www.setai.com.

10. Camina the Espanola Way. Get lost in the gritty village of Espanola Way, where you'll find bohemian shops nestled in the salmon-colored buildings and European restaurants serving spicy cuisine to a crowd less pretentious than those promenading on "The Strip" in South Beach. On Saturdays and Sundays, Espanola Way is packed with stalls selling every-thing from fresh flowers to semiprecious jewelry. The activity doesn't go down with the sun: stick around for the nocturnal street fairs on weekends and grab some shopping fuel at Tapas y Tintos, the best tapas place in South Beach. Art Circuit offers a night walking tour of the galleries and unique shops of historic Espanola Way on the third Thursday of each month, 7 to 10 p.m. And you can find the Miami Beach Cinematheque and Gallery there, where you can catch up on the latest independent films. Between Washington and Pennsylvania Avenues and 14th and 15th Streets, Miami Beach, FL 33139; tel: 305-531-5322; www.gmcvb.com.

WAIKIKI, HAWAII

Anna sunbathing at Diamond Head.

Why This Place Rocks for Flying Solo

----

*W*hy Waikiki? With big surf kahunas rolling in and out with the tide and the amphibious skills of all those Marines stationed here, Waikiki can be way kiki, if you know what I mean. This hottest beach in Honolulu is nestled beneath the shadow of hikable Diamond Head. It's paradise without the paranoia—the sea, the sand, and good old Uncle Sam spare you from having to bring a passport or change money. With a local Dole Plantation piña colada in your hand, you'll feel far away from home, even though USPS stamps adorn all your postcards. It's the ultimate easy vacation.

Hula Lessons

Here's a fantastic way to learn about the Hawaiian culture. Tell a story with your hands and another with your hips! The Outrigger Reef offers a "Rhythms of the Ocean" hula/yoga class if you're interested in becoming one with the ocean. Inquire at your hotel's activity desk or ask your concierge to find you the nearest hula class.

A solo traveler can come away with a lot of new skills if she plays her cards right. Not those skills! I mean that you can learn to hula dance if you want. Or overcome any hang-ups and give hanging ten a try. Have you ever parasailed before? Then why not go for it? Make your Hawaiian trip a magical one by taking away a memorable and exciting new skill or two. Or party like a rock star until you have no memory at all. It's totally up to you!

Culture: 2

Hawaii does have its share of history: Before it was a U.S. territory, it had a reigning monarchy. And you can take a tour of powerful Pearl Harbor memorials, but you'll spend most of your time in Hawaii *making* history, wink wink. The native Hawaiian culture is rich and fascinating, don't get me wrong, but it is something that you will have to seek out beneath the veneer of contrived tourist luaus. You'll catch a hula show or two with your dinners, and even a Polynesian dance performance if you buy tickets, but as far as the culture of Waikiki itself, it's more about partying, flirting, tanning, and drunken karaoke. And that's okay!

Activity: 5

No, dear, a booze cruise doesn't count as a water sport! But sailing counts, and you can break out the Sex Wax and learn how to surf. You can jog on the beach, too, and learn how to windsurf, go Jet Skiing and get wet and wild about a million different ways. Hike Diamond Head, surf, and even cliff dive if you must—there are tons of water and land sports guaranteed to keep your bikini booty in shape!

Weather: 4

It's paradise, but not all year round like you might think. I was there one February and almost froze my little bikini off! It was like sixty degrees—frostbite! But with temperatures on average in the seventies and eighties, it will almost certainly beat your local weather most of the time. Pashmina plus a thong—that's my song.

Social: 5

Who isn't friendly in this island paradise? Maybe too friendly! There are always interesting military boys around to tell you their faraway tales, and you'll hear them all if you grab a share table at Duke's. It's guaranteed that you'll meet someone. Many someones. People are here to relax and have a good time. Aren't you?

Flying Foreplay

Hawaiian time for Haoles. They call it Hawaiian time and it's just what you need even if you think it's not. So don't get frustrated. It usually takes us haoles a few days to get into the island's gentle rhythm—we need to detox and unwind from our multitasking mainland life. Things move slowly here on this island paradise. Who needs to rush? What are you so stressed out about, *brah*? You need to take it easy. There's plenty of time for those *da' kine* waves.

Waikiki Accessories

Beach bag. Most reasonably priced hotels are a few blocks from the beach. So, to avoid running back to your hotel every hour, bring a big beach bag filled with all your beach essentials.

Prudent purse. Bring a purse that wraps over your shoulder, so you don't have to set it down when dancing with all the hot guys. Fill it with just the essentials: lipstick, digital camera, room key, cash, and condoms.

Wrap it. The temperature can drop sometimes, so pack a shawl, wrap, sweater, or lightweight jacket—just in case.

Read Before You Go

Hawaii, by James A. Michener
Kaiulani, Crown Princess of Hawaii, by Nancy and Jean Francis Webb

The Top 10 Extraordinary Experiences

1. **Take surfing lessons from a big kahuna!** Maybe you're a pro and just

want to brush up on your sick skills. But if you're a beginner, now is the perfect time to try it! The water is warm and the Waikiki waves are gentle—not like its gnarly cousin, the North Shore. That you can work up to. Check out the Hans Hedermann Surf School at the Sheraton Waikiki. You will be amazed at how fast you get up on your board. What a rush—more than just walking on water, you'll feel like you're standing on top of it as it rolls toward the beach. You are Aphrodite among the waves, queen of all you survey. For an added layer of safety (you never know when you might need mouth to mouth!), try the Hawaiian Fire Surf School, which offers surf lessons given by off-duty Honolulu City firefighters. You'll be in good—and manly—hands as you undertake your surfing endeavor. Help, help, I'm *drowning* . . .

2.   Enjoy a share table at Duke's Canoe Club. Oh girl, this is ground zero for socializing! Duke's is legendary—you can't go to Waikiki and not go to Duke's, especially if you are traveling alone. Sit down in the middle of a great big empty table and let it fill up around you! If you're there first, you've got dibs. Tell the ugly guys and honeymooners that you're saving the chairs, and tell that hot group of boys to sit down! There's a standing Sunday beach party at 4 p.m. that is tons of fun, as well as a great happy hour with Jonnah on the

guitar, Monday to Thursday at 4 p.m. Both of these are musts. www.dukeswaikiki.com.

3.   Have your fish and watch them, too, at the Oceanarium. Take tables with a view to the next level and come to the Pacific Beach Hotel's Oceanarium, where you can get a table right next to their three-story aquarium. While feeding yourself, stick around for the fishes' feeding time. Why not do something nice for your solo self by hiring one of the Oceanarium's divers to write a message on an underwater sign—like your cell phone number followed by, "Call me." Or "Happy Birthday to Me!" Otherwise you'll be stuck with divers announcing Iris and Scooter's fifty-year anniversary all day. Talk about ruining one's appetite . . . www.pacificbeachhotel.com /ocean.cfm.

4.   Take a booze cruise. Ahoy there, Captain Morgan! Tell Jack Daniels to hoist the mainsail! Avast, Johnny Walker—I'll make ye walk the plank! Yes this is booze cruise central, and all your best friends should already be aboard. Catch a beautiful Mai Tai Catamaran from Waikiki Beach. You'll see all the guys down there trying to fill their boats up. The cruises aren't long but they're cheap, and the booze ain't top shelf, but the punch'll get you pretty punchy. The best thing about having the merchandise on the beach beforehand is that you get to pick your captain, honey. Even the views of your hot crew will be dominated by the sight of the beach and Diamond Head from the crystal blue water.

5. Let your inner MTV Spring Break chick thrive. You'll be wild on Hawaii if you play your cards right. What happens in Waikiki stays here. It's true! Unless you want to brag to your friends back home. You can two-step with the Southern boys at Nashville Waikiki, get your inner spring break on at a foam party, and even go on a real live pub crawl. Look for the guys with the binders hanging out in front of the Waikiki International Market, where you'll be shopping anyway, and buy a pub crawl ticket from them. Then let the games begin! Think of it as an Oahu rite of passage. For about sixty bucks you'll get a drink at each of the five bars you visit and a commemorative photo of the group, which you should immediately hide from your mother.

6. Get leid on Maunakea Street. Honolulu's Chinatown is where all the floral action's at. This special street is home to many famous lei makers. Stop in any of the lei stands and see firsthand how the intricate lei is created by masterful hands. Many of the shops have been family owned for generations, and you'll soon find your favorite. A tangible and fragrant symbol of the Hawaiian aloha spirit, buy a beautiful lei for yourself or for someone else's special occasion. The lei makers will work with you to put together a beautiful and personal creation and will let you know which flowers are not allowed off the island. California especially is really picky about incoming flora, and you don't want to be singularly responsible for destroying all those wine grapes, right?

7. Visit `Iolani Palace. A National Historic Landmark and the only royal house in the entire country, the 'Iolani Palace is a truly unique experience. Why not give your skin a break for half a day and come tour this regal downtown Honolulu habitat? After a tour of the palace and grounds, you might want to stay forever, but if you were imprisoned here like her Highness Queen Lili'uokalani, you might change your tune. Or write one in your time of confinement. The last of the Hawaiian royals, the queen was relegated to an upstairs bedroom with a single lady in waiting. With nothing better to do, this accomplished musician and songwriter penned the famous "Aloha Oe." Hawaii eventually fell into our hands after that. But don't worry— our government apologized forty years later. www.iolanipalace.org.

8. All hail Ala Moana Mall!! The world's largest open-air mall and mecca for the

---

Don't Get Teed Off, Darling

Hawaii is a golf hole in one! Both the Koolau Golf Club and Arnold Palmer's Turtle Bay have high *Golf Digest* rankings.

---

serious designer logo junkie, this isn't your local Louis Vuitton or Versace. That's because legions of Japanese shoppers have upped the ante, causing retailers here to bend over backward to please their love for logos. Check Dior and Chanel for hard-to-find items and bring home the treasures that your girlfriends would kill for. Then hit the food court for kahlua pork instead of the usual corn dog fare. Fun! And remember, girls, time your visit right for the big seasonal sales! I got 60 percent off at the Versace store when I was there. And I have the magenta logo purse to prove it! Ala Moana Center, 1450 Ala Moana Boulevard, Honolulu, HI 96814; tel: 808-955-9517.

9. Visit the Bishop Museum. I love love love the Hawaiian Hall in this museum. Full of Hawaiian cultural *objets* and old photos of the Hawaiian royals, and bits and pieces from all the major world cultures who've impacted these islands, the Bishop Museum is an elegant tribute to Hawaii's history. The converted Victorian house is warm and inviting, and during the day you may catch an art or dance demonstration. It also has children's exhibitions, a Polynesian center, a planetarium, a huge natural science component, and even a Hawaiian sports hall of fame. www.bishopmuseum.org.

10. Hike up Diamond Head. What a magical place. I know people who've gotten married in some of its most sacred spots. The summit of this crater offers spectacular views but not shady trails, so plan your hike early in the day and bring lots of water. Can't you just come home early one night? I promise this hike is worth it. You've seen this beautiful natural monument from the sea on your booze cruise—now see people like you and other kaleidoscopic sails and windsurf fins below you as a reward for the fact that you kicked the private major out early enough to get some good sleep.

WHISTLER, CANADA

**Katie strikes a pose
in Whistler.**

Why This Place Rocks
for Flying Solo

Y ou'll be whistling all the way to
Whistler if you are an adventure
diva who thrives on mountain
fun. This pristine destination, snuggled
up in the Canadian Rockies, has the
most terrain and the biggest vertical
drop of any sky resort in North America.
That makes Whistler an obvious winter
destination for solo women skiers and
snowboarders. And if the ski runs don't
impress you, then the après-ski fun will.
This is a pedestrian-friendly village
where skiers simply walk from one chic
venue to the next trendy nightspot. Even
as the snow thaws in summer, towering
mountains draw hikers and adventurers

Fire and Ice

From December to March, come out to enjoy the dazzling Fire & Ice Welcome Night, celebrated every Sunday at 6:30 p.m. at the base of the Village Gondolas. Guests are welcomed by performers using an eclectic mix of music, dance, and spinning fire to entertain. World-class athletes flip and spin through a burning ring of fire during a fireworks display right on the mountain.

from around the world. Just like in the snow seasons, the après-hiking festivities in town make this destination a top choice for you social solo sisters year round.

You don't have to be a heavy-duty athlete to enjoy what this little slice of British Columbia has to offer. Whistler's numerous art, music, and wine festivals enchant all connoisseurs of the good life. Events abound in this Canadian gem, and so do a bevy of delightful travelers and locals who are sure to make your trip spectacular. Between the killer skiing, phenomenal mountain biking, and the socializing, Whistler is a prime destination for any darling looking to have a socially infused outdoor vacation. The Winter Olympic Games will be held here in 2010, but until then, let the flirting games begin! Nothing like a hot Canadian skier to go with your hot toddy.

Culture: 2

Whistler isn't exactly known for its cultural activities, considering that less than 100 years ago its population was composed of approximately five very lonely people. Since then, the magnificent slopes have drawn people from all over the globe, making the town international if not cultural. You are sure to find

something happening around town; it just won't be the unveiling of works by Picasso.

Activity: 5

Whistler is one of the most action-packed places in North America. A ski season that stretches from early November until late May makes this divine destination an obvious winner for ski bunnies. But even nonskiers can enjoy a magical snow-filled vacation in this easily managed resort town. Snowshoe through fairy-tale forests, take a sleigh ride through snow-covered trees, or scale a frozen waterfall. Less known are the variety of activities offered at Whistler in the spring and summer months. World-class golf, horseback riding, mountain biking, or alpine hiking are just a few of the adventures you can have at Whistler after the snow has melted.

Weather: 2

If you like snow, then Whistler gets a 5 in the weather department, with the average annual snowfall being over 30 feet. In the summer months however, Whistler is often as sunny and warm as a Californian cheerleader, with temperatures reaching well into the eighties.

Hot Spots

Some of the best clubs and pubs in the village include Moe Joe's, a fun spot to dance with live bands on certain days, and Dubh Linn Gate, which keeps guests buzzing with over 90 international brews to choose from and live Irish music. If you still have some energy left, head to Tommy Africa's for some of the best DJ's and dancing in Whistler (it even boasts go-go dancers)! Sip a sex on the beach while you lounge by the fireplace at Buffalo Bill's. And if, at the end of the night, you're feeling more than a little bit sloshed, Whistler is small enough that it's most likely a short walk back to your hotel (if you can remember where it is!).

Social: 3

Compared to most ski resorts, Whistler has a ton of fabulous opportunities for socializing, flirting, chatting, and meeting new friends. At night, choose from close to 100 restaurants ranging from cozy diners to some of the highest-ranked restaurants in Canada. After dinner, you'll find the crowds heading to hear live jazz or knock back a few cocktails at one of the many pubs and clubs.

Flying Foreplay

Whistler is 75 miles from Vancouver, B.C. Don't rent a car: you won't be driving once you get there as the town is small and everything is centrally located.

- A new train service can get you from Vancouver to Whistler. Check out www.tourismwhistler.com for more details.
- You can take the Greyhound bus to Whistler for around C$25.

Round-trip fare between Vancouver's Pacific Central Station and Whistler on Greyhound is C$50 total, including tax. If you start from the airport, you will first have to get from there to Pacific Central Station. Greyhound; tel: 800-661-8747.

- You can take a taxi from the Vancouver Airport to Whistler for about C$250. From downtown Vancouver to Whistler, the taxi is about C$200.
- You can take a limousine from the Vancouver Airport to Whistler for C$325.
- Perimeter Coach Lines travels directly from the airport to Whistler for about C$60 per person one way. The trip takes about 2.5 hours.

Bring all the outdoor equipment you might need. While Whistler has plenty of outdoor equipment rental shops, the cost of renting can add up, but the convenience of not toting your skis and mountain bike may be worth it. You could be spending that money you save on an après-ski (or hike) massage.

Pique your interest. Check out *Pique NewsMagazine*, which lists events and concerts. Find around town, or on-line at www.piquenewsmagazine.com.

Read Before You Go

The Daring Game, by Kit Pearson
The Return of the Canoe Societies, by Rosemary Patterson

Whistler Accessories

Warm but thin layers. Even in the summertime Whistler can be frigid at night so polypropylene and fleece are musts.

Sunscreen and moisturizer. The cold wind, blinding snow, and high altitude can leave you dry and burned—load it on! Bring lip balm, too, just in case you

want to kiss the boys with those moist lips of yours.

A bathing suit. Most places have hot tubs so you can defrost after a day on the slopes. You might meet a few friendly faces while hot tubbing, so bring a cute suit.

The Top 10 Extraordinary Experiences

1. **Mush it!** It's just you, a team of eager huskies, untouched winter wilderness, and endless terrain. Once in your life you need to go on a dog-sledding adventure. This amazing tour takes you farther into the Whistler backcountry and straight through a spectacular, snowy paradise. A professional musher will teach you how to harness and handle your own dog team, and everything you need to know to drive your own sled on this extended journey. At the end the dogs get treats

Walk-a-Dog

Make the day of a homeless canine friend and walk a dog from WAG (Whistler Animals Galore). Volunteers are welcome to pop in and walk a dog or visit with the kitties in the cattery at designated times. You know guys will totally stop and talk to you with your pooch.

and the guests enjoy hot chocolate and cookies. Go to www.whistlerblackcomb.com, click "Things to do."

2. Hell, Yeah! Looking for a wild adventure and amazing alpine terrain? Catch a ride in a helicopter and experience an uninterrupted 6,000-foot run through virgin powder. You'll feel like a superhero or 007 racing through the show after jumping out of a helicopter. I don't know what's more fun, the ride up, or the adrenaline rush going down. Heli skiing/snowboarding gives you access to an area more than 60 times the size of the Whistler/Blackcomb ski area, and you'll have it mostly to yourself! Whistler Heli-Skiing, The Crystal Lodge #3—4241 Village Stroll, Box 368,

Whistler; tel: 604-932-4105, toll-free: 1-888-HELISKI (435-4754); www.whistlerheliskiing.com.

3. Frolic at the market. From June through October enjoy the Whistler Farmers Market. If you are sore from mountain biking or backpacking (or whatever), spend a sunny Sunday strolling around this heavenly outdoor market. Organic produce, fresh-baked bread, and desserts provide tasty snacks, and homemade soaps, jewelry, and handmade knits make wonderful gifts for your less jet-worthy girls back home. After the market, spend the rest of the day sauntering around the pedestrian-only alpine village and shopping at some of the 200 shops.

Roxy's

A great snowboarding school for those of you who are already fairly good is Roxy Women's All-Star Snowboard Camps: All women all the time. To get into this program, you must be able to link turns. Take it from there. This is a warm, positive environment that will help you get to that next level fast. From freeriding to terrain parks, the options here are yours to explore. You'll get video to help you along and the après is a riot, complete with your new friends, a few prizes, and lots of the day's triumphs to share. You won't see me here. I can't snowboard, but I hear it's great!!

4. Fly on the zipline. For you daredevils who just can't get enough craziness, try a trip through the air on a zipline. Harness up and then experience the excitement of soaring along ziplines suspended above old-growth rain forest and a breathtaking river below. Pause before or after the exhilarating ride to learn about the forest ecology and enjoy the serenity of the tree canopy. You'll get exclusive access to areas of rare and untouched ancient coastal temperate rain forest, all only minutes from Whistler Village. Tours operate in all weather conditions, 365 days a year. Zip Trek Tours; www.ziptrek.com.

5. Scale Ice. If you ever wanted to scale a vertical sheet of ice while rock climbing like Spiderman, here's your chance. Ice climbing involves strapping into a harness and using crampons and picks to scale a frozen waterfall. The sport definitely takes some bicep action and a fondness for adrenaline, but it can be one of the most rewarding winter sports ever. While it's certainly challenging, ice climbing's not only for fit and experienced climbers. Give it a try! This is your chance to experience the incomparable feeling of climbing up ice with technical equipment in a safe and beginner's environment. Whistler Alpine Guides Bureau; www.whistlerguides .com/winter.

6. Take a tour to see bald eagles. Unlike the United States, where the bald eagle has dwindled to the point of endangerment, the Squamish River region hosts the highest number of bald eagles in the world. Though they don't enjoy national mascot status here, the fierce fliers flock to Canada, especially in the Whistler area, to feed on spawning salmon. From November to February, tours allow you to leisurely float down the Squamish River, where you'll see countless bald eagles in their natural habitat. Some tours include a narrated walking tour and binoculars. Dress warmly and don't forget your camera. The Whistler Activity Centre; tel: 604-938-2769 (locally), or toll-free: 877-991-9988.

7. Kayak down the River of Golden Dreams. Row, row, row your boat gently down the River of Golden Dreams. Rent a kayak or canoe or take a guided tour down one of Whistler's most popular rivers. You are likely to see incredible wildlife like deer, fish, birds, and possibly even a black bear strolling along the riverbank. Keep your voice down and your head up and you're guaranteed to catch a glimpse of a wild river denizen. Whistler's five lakes and numerous rivers are just waiting to be kayaked, canoed, white-water rafted, windsurfed, and sailed, making this an obvious summer destination for water sport enthusiasts.

8. Your skis, madame. Hate lugging skis, boots, and boards to the mountain? Don't want to break a nail? Care to swoosh down the slopes in only the latest gear? Want a heads-up on the hottest trails (and nightspots)? Four Seasons Resort Whistler has the answers to your alpine anxieties. They offer an amazing ski concierge service that will arrange lift tickets, lessons, top-of-the-line rental equipment, private tour guides, even boot warming for you! After a long day on the slopes, they're also at the ready to whisk away equipment so that you can swiftly enjoy whatever après-ski activities you're into. Who said you needed a man to take you skiing?

Four Seasons Resort Whistler; tel: 604-966-2659.

9. Skate on a lake. Forget spinning in circles around an indoor skating rink—complete your triple lutzes surrounded by snow-covered mountains for hours of exercise beneath an enormous sky, then enjoy hot cider by a crackling fire.

10. Enjoy a sleigh ride and a fondue dinner. Snuggle up under thick blankets while a pair of draft horses pull your sleigh past frozen lakes and through old-growth forests. Absorb the silence of Whistler at night, with the only sound being the jingle bells from the sleigh. End your evening at a chalet and enjoy a three-course fondue dinner!

CENTRAL AMERICA

BELIZE

Ellen enjoying a treetop oasis in the middle of the jungle.

Why This Place Rocks for Flying Solo

- - - - - - - - - - - - - -

O
h please, send me to Belize!"
When you have had enough of
rush-hour traffic, and your
boyfriend pisses you off again, and your
boss just doesn't understand, take a deep
breath and get your butt down to Belize.

It is the perfect place for a solo sister to
seize that much-needed chill pill and
spend some time nurturing the divine
soul within. Tucked between Mexico
and Guatemala, Belize is a forgotten
Garden of Eden—a vivid fairytale oasis
teeming with life. Its colorful history is
rich with pirates, Mayan kings, and pot-
smoking Rastafarians. Not bad for a
place slightly smaller than Massachusetts.

And unlike anywhere else south of the U.S. border, almost everyone in Belize speaks English (owing to the fact that Belize was an English colony for more than a hundred years), making it a brilliant destination for the linguistically challenged.

It is a place where smog, pollution, and toxins don't exist—nor does that frenetic pace of the life you've been living. The air is fresh, scented with ginger and jasmine. Peaceful rivers thriving with wildlife crisscross the fertile countryside. Along the coast are sandy beaches and pristine seas where mountains of coral rise to the surface. Belize is the essence of nature, above and below the waterline. This country has been so underdeveloped that Hummingbird Highway, the main road that connects this tiny country, was unpaved until 2000. Because it is just beginning to be recognized as a tourist destination, many of Belize's immaculate beaches, stunning reefs, and tropical rain forests are untouched. Belize is a stunning example of ecotourism at its best, a miniature wonderland which has unsurpassed adventure waiting around every turn.

Culture: 3

Belize is rich in culture in its own funky, laid-back way. Probably the most significant cultural experience in Belize is exploring the ancient Mayan ruins that are scattered throughout the country. Climb a Mayan pyramid in the lush tropical forest and journey into the ancient past. Once part of great ceremonial and trading centers, majestic pyramids and temples lie mysteriously broken and nearly silent except for the occasional screech of a parrot or the throaty roar of a howler monkey.

Activity: 5

Belize is the ultimate outdoor adventure destination. The perfect place to let your inner Indiana Jones run wild. Dive into a Technicolor aquarium at the longest barrier reef in the Western Hemisphere, hike deep into the Mayan mountains, slither into underground caves through a magical realm of subterranean wonders, drink in life under a 1,000-foot waterfall, go fishing in some of the richest waters in the world, and take a boat trip up a twisting river with overhanging vines, toucans darting between trees, and crocodiles lurking just below the surface. The shimmering Caribbean waters are perfect for swimming, sailing, windsurfing, and Jet-Skiing.

Weather: 5

The best word to describe the weather in Belize is *perfect*. Summer is the rainy season, but temperatures never fall below a comfortable level. But if you prefer to be dry for most of the day (there are still daily thunderstorms, but they are brief), the best time to visit is between November and April. It's best to bring long pants and long-sleeve shirts and heavy boots if you are going into the jungle for protection from bugs, but don't pack your parka. A light rain jacket and long pants will keep you warm for the occasional cool evenings.

Social: 3

Throughout Belize, reggae, soca, pulsating punta rock, calypso, and Latin beats resound. These tantalizing rhythms get you dancing in no time. The Cayes offer a bit more of a social scene than the mainland. Ambergris Caye is dominated by casual seaside pubs, and after the sun goes down, the volume goes up in the Jaguar Temple Club and also at Fido's, which has live entertainment. The Princess Hotel and Casino in Belize City and Cayo District feature slot machines and performances in a Vegas-style floorshow. Throughout the districts, a mix of music flourishes. In Dangriga, you can see punta (Belize's unofficial national dance), a rhythmic shuffling of the feet with plenty of movement below the waist, but little above it. Casa Picasso in Ambergris Caye offers a bit of European twist, with tapas, pastas, and a martini lounge. Visit: www.ambergriscaye.com for more details.

Flying Foreplay

Wheels. Rent a car before you land in Belize. It is usually cheaper from the United States and will guarantee you the flexibility of having your own transportation. Check the car thoroughly before getting too far. Make sure there is a spare tire and a working jack, all the doors lock, the windows roll down, and also ask to have *all* existing damage—even small dents—noted on your contract.

Read about Belize. You are visiting a third-world country, kinda. So know a bit about the society and the spicy melting pot of cultures that live there. *Belize Moon Handbook* provides a good brief history and description of the different groups.

Pay to leave. Belize Departure Tax is paid at the airport when leaving, so make sure you have an extra US$35 tucked away in your hiking bag. This must be paid in US dollars.

Read Before You Go

Beka Lamb, by Zee Edgell
High Adventure, by Donald Westlake
I Spent It All in Belize, by Emory King
Journey to the Sky: A Novel About the True Adventures of Two Men in Search of the Lost Maya Kingdom, by Jamake Highwater

Belize Accessories

*I*f you plan on heading to a caye to dive and lie in the sun, all you need is your bathing suit and light clothing, but if you are planning to delve into the depths of the darkest jungle, be sure to have thick clothing to keep out the bugs, the most toxic, potent bug spray you can find, and earplugs so that you can soften the screech of monkeys and buzzing of insects. Also, a headlamp makes exploring caves a lot easier. An underwater camera can be a blast (but you can also rent them in Belize at most hotels and tour companies).

Plan on hiking? Bring sturdy tennis shoes or hiking boots to tackle the lush, and sometimes squishy, rain forest.

Keep warm. Yes, this is the tropics, but sometimes cold blasts from Canada can reach Belize, especially in December and January. So, bring your layers if you plan on visiting in the winter.

Tour tips. Most of the tours you'll take in Belize will be awesome, and you'll be glad you went with a group of pros instead of wandering into the jungle or out to sea alone. Here are some tips to make sure you get the best tour operator:

1. Make sure that your tour guide (not just the tour operator) is licensed by the Belize Tourism Board.
2. Find out what's included in the cost of your tour. Often entry fees and lunch are not included in the quoted price.
3. Ask how many others will be on the tour. An overcrowded vehicle can be misery. Also, the larger the group, the more waiting around you do.
4. Ask to see the boat or vehicle you will be spending the day in. Make sure it meets your comfort and safety standards.

The Top 10 Extraordinary Experiences

1. **Meet a manatee.** Spend a glorious afternoon swimming with the angels of the sea, the gentlest, most darling animal that lives in the warm Caribbean waters. Manatees are an endangered species and the largest manatee population in the Caribbean and Central America is found in Belize. Many tours guarantee that you will see a manatee or they will refund your money. Peek in on these sleeping giants, the ocean's only herbivorous mammal, as they lazily munch sea grass. The wonder of watching these huge animals in their natural habitat is a sight you won't soon forget. Full-day trips include lunch, snorkeling, and of course, a chance to see the manatee. Manatee Excursion, tel: 501-226-3221; San Pedro Town, Belize; e-mail: seabelize@btl.net; www.greendragonbelize.com or www.gocayecaulker.com.

2. **Hike through the jungle.** As dawn breaks and the mist rises through the lush canopy, explore the jungle as it awakens. In the company of an expert naturalist guide, you'll learn about the intricacies of a habitat that is home to creatures as diverse as the puma, the impressive black howler monkey, the tenacious jaguarundi, and the vividly colored keel-billed toucan. Lamanai Outpost Lodge is located one hour by car and one hour by boat from the airport in the heart of the Belize jungle and offers all-inclusive packages that include two excursions per night's stay. They will pick you up at the airport and fly you back to Belize Airport via charter plane. www.lamanai.com.

Lamanai excursions:

Early Morning
6:00—Breakfast on the River
6:30—Jungle Dawn
6:00—Sunrise Canoeing

Morning
8:00—Lamanai Maya Ruins
9:00—Cultural Immersion—Mennonites
7:30—Howler Trek

Afternoon
4:00—Sunset Cocktail Cruise
4:00—Sunset Airboat Cruise
4:00—Maya Medicine Walk

After Dinner
7:30—Crocodile Encounter
8:00—Spotlight River Safari

3. Go diving. Belize offers all ranges of diving—from shore diving in shallow water to the Great Blue Hole at over 200 feet deep. The barrier reefs offer excellent diving for beginners such as at Hol Chan Marine Park (recently expanded to include Shark-Ray Alley) a few miles south of Ambergris Caye. Many dive sites offer a range of dives from beginning to experienced. To See Belize; tel: 877-222-3549; www.toseebelize.com.

4. Visit Mayan ruins. Grab your camera and hiking books and get ready for an adventure right out of an action movie. In Belize you have quite a few Mayan ruin options, so you can find one that fits your needs. Xunantunich Ruins is pretty easy to get to and the most restored ruin in Belize. It's about eight miles from the Guatemalan border and you can always find a tour group heading out that way. Suspended high on a hill with views of the Mopan River, this complex was a major ceremonial axis during the classic pe-

riod of the Maya. Altun Ha Ruins is close to Belize City and many companies offer half-day tours. Caracol Ruins is Belize's largest Mayan ruin. Located in the heart of the Chiquibul Forest and only seven miles from the Guatemalan border, Caracol is much larger than nearby Tikal, which has not yet been restored. Tours to Caracol are common from all lodges in the San Ignacio area, and usually include a stop at Rio On Pools and Rio Frio cave. E-mail: info@belize-trips.com.

5. Breathe. Bring your twisted body, frazzled nerves, and tense shoulders to Belize Yoga Vacation Retreat, where you can unwind with daily sessions of Hatha yoga in one of the most spectacular settings in the world. Here you can awaken your mind, body, and spirit in this sacred Mayan land through the gentle practice of yoga. Become one with nature and rediscover your connection to the intricate web of life. A week of this and you are sure to be at peace and the real world will be a lot easier to handle when you get home. Belize Jungle Dome, Banana Bank, Belmopan, Cayo District, Belize; tel: 501-822-2124; e-mail: info@greendragonbelize .com; www.greendragonbelize.com.

6. Explore an ancient Mayan-worshipped cave. First rappel down a 300-foot sinkhole, then paddle through miles of underground rivers and cathedral-size crystal chambers. You will feel like you entered a scene from Harry Potter. See Mayan ceremonial grounds, where pottery artifacts and skeletal remains of sacrificial victims still lie. Dramatic waterfalls cascade hundreds of feet from the mountains above ancient Mayan ruins that have been buried by the jungle for almost 1,500 years. www.cavesbranch.com.

7. Pet a butterfly. Maybe not pet, but you can visit one of the most impressive collections of butterflies in the world. Located in the Cayo district, between limestone hills covered with lush vegetation, you will find Green Hills, the Belize Butterfly Ranch and Botanical Collections. Flocks of butterflies, from brilliant blue to gorgeous orange, dazzling yellow to intriguing gray, fly freely in 2,700 square feet of beautifully landscaped flight areas. It's the largest live butterfly display in Belize. www.belizex.com/green_hills.htm.

8. Go to the birds. Even if you generally just lump all flying-egg-laying animals you see into one generic "bird" category, the birds in Belize may make you take a second glance. In fact, they may so completely captivate that you'll be arguing whether the red-winged wonder that just flew over was a keel-billed toucan or a blue-crowned motmot. Belize, with its diversity of habitats, makes it home to over 500 species of colorful birds. Almost all resorts and tour companies offer birding trips. But Birding in Belize is a company that specializes in it. www.birdinginbelize.com.

9. Get stranded on a deserted island. If you ever dreamed of being left alone on an island to explore your vices, here is your chance! Many of the cayes and beach resorts can speed you off in a jet boat to a tiny, white sand island and leave you for the day. Bronze your body, snorkel in sparkling turquoise water, and play out your fantasies of being stranded on a deserted island. Bring your sunscreen, trashy novels, and big beach towel, and melt away your worries under a palm tree.

10. Go sea kayaking. Enjoy the tranquility of the sea from your own boat. Explore mangroves and estuaries, discover your own islands, perhaps see manatees or giant manta rays, and peer into the darkness of the deep water of Blue Hole. Fish from your kayak, bird watch, or bring your snorkeling gear and take a dip. To See Belize; tel: 877-222-3549; www.toseebelize.com.

CARTAGENA DE INDIAS, COLOMBIA

Suzanne shops for bananas fresh off
the cart in Cartegena.

Why This Place Rocks
for Flying Solo

So named because of that man who went looking for India and refused to ask for directions, Cartagena de Indias, hereafter Cartagena, was from its inception the fantasy of Spanish fortune seekers and their galleon ships full of plunder and slaves. Its strategic location for transporting booty back to Spain was second to none in the New World, so much so that a mighty stone wall and fort were built to protect Cartagena from invasion. The wall, the fort, and so much Spanish colonial architecture survive today that UNESCO has declared this city a World Heritage Site.

The question is where to begin exploring this legendary city? Does morbid curiosity pull you toward the Palace of the Spanish Inquisition to see ancient devices of horror, or are you drawn to that brightly painted square where street vendors have laid out beautiful crosses on the pavement? Do you stop to browse under the protective eye of armed policemen trying to act casual around the perimeter? Whatever you decide to do, it will be wonderful. And safe.

Culture: 5

The Spanish have left their indelible mark of both inspired godliness and misguided wickedness on the streets of Cartagena. With monasteries and churches and even a house of torture, Cartagena remains witness to the entire span of the Spanish heart and soul. Not to be outdone, the passionate Colombian people inscribe their own history, struggles, dreams, and everyday life upon the beautiful city. A donkey cart on the street, a mime chatting with a man selling cutlery from a box on his head, and African dancers entertaining in the plazas—this is Cartagena today.

Activity: 3

If you are a diva impervious to heat, then Cartagena is for you. It's fun to walk around and try on Colombia souvenir T-shirts, but some of us might need coffee ice cream in hand at all times to beat the heat. Now why isn't window shopping a sport? It sure feels like one when the temperature rises. One thing I do know—your shutter finger will certainly get its workout snapping away at period architecture and fascinating people. Beyond the walls of the Old City lies the Caribbean Sea, beckoning to you to dive, snorkel, and swim in its bath-temperature waters. Are you a fisherwoman? Because deep-sea fishing here is world-class.

Weather: 4

Sun rules the Caribbean shores of Cartagena. You can and should wear your tiniest clothes packed tightly in your smallest suitcase. Micro-miniskirts in January! Don't brag too much in postcards sent to New England friends. It will start off hot and then get hotter as the sun warms up for its main show. Nights are blessedly cooler with a gentle breeze just perfect for dinner outdoors in one of the many plazas. Plan for nineties by day and seventies by night. You might not even need a *pashmina*! Of course, if you come during the rainy season, especially late summer and fall, you'll need an umbrella.

Safety First

Your first question will undoubtedly be about safety. Colombia, you'll say to yourself, I'm not so sure. . . . Cartagena is safe, but the minute you board a bus to Bogota, you are on your own. Pick up taxis only from hotels, be city smart at all times, and you should be fine. No public transportation for you! This is the same edict that our diplomatic staff receives. While major airline travel should be okay, other Colombian destinations are not quite the oasis of safety that Cartagena is.

Love and Other Demons

Love and Other Demons, by Gabriel Garcia Marquez, is a haunting tale about the legend of a young girl who once lived in the Santa Clara Hotel when it was a monastery. When crews began converting the building into a 5-star hotel, they were instructed to empty out all the ancient graves including this little girl's. Her crypt broke, and out tumbled sixty feet of bright copper hair. Rapunzelita?

Social: 4

What fun and wild people are here! They are outrageous; they dress like pop stars and carry themselves like royalty. Cartagenans are full of pride and love to talk about their city. Especially in Spanish. Do you speak Spanish? As in, *donde estan los emeralds*? Street vendors can be aggressive but will smile appreciatively when you begin your savvy bargaining game. Even if your encounter is all gestures and pointing, it's still fun to interact with the locals.

Flying Foreplay

Do not be afraid. Cartagena is not as threatening to tourists as other places in Colombia might be. One woman I asked said that the reason it's so safe here is that this is a small town and everyone talks. A stealthy guerrilla wouldn't stand a chance of going unnoticed. Cartagena is a place where you can breathe a sigh of relief and let all sixty feet of your hair down. Because this is the ultimate retreat for Colombians, especially wealthy Colombians, they are certainly not going to let the bad element spoil it! Think of it as Colombia's Hawaii.

Best of the Books

*L*ove and Other Demons, by Gabriel Garcia Marquez, Colombian Nobel Prize in Literature recipient. Having owned the salmon-colored house across the street from Hotel Santa Clara for many years, this famous author did not have far to commute when he was researching this novel. No doubt he was inspired by his neighbor's legends and the transformation of this old sanctuary of prayer into a suave 5-star hotel.

Cartagena Accessories

GPS and ATM. Cash money and a good sense of direction will serve you well during your time here! The Old City inside the wall is a winding conglomeration of rainbow plazas and streets that change aliases block to block, as the gorgeous tiled street signs on buildings will attest. It's easy to get lost. As far as money goes, you can use yours or change it for theirs. But don't stand there riffling through your wallet looking for small change among the big bills, baby. Have small bills readily available in a pocket or purse compartment.

The Dungeon

Did you ever think that the only way to curb your shopping habit was to lock yourself up and throw away the key? Well, now you can enjoy incarceration *while* you shop! Las Bóvedas is a darling row of tiny shops that used to be a military dungeon. That's what *bovedas* means. Here you will find great souvenirs and all manner of Colombian products, including those yummy coffee candies. You have to buy a bag or two and take them back to the office!

The ultimate tour guide. English-, French-, and Spanish-speaking Marelvy Pena is the ultimate local guide for hire. Tel: 666-3991 or 315-760-5034 (cell); marepenahall@hotmail.com.

The Top 10 Extraordinary Experiences

1. Have drinks and watch for invading Spaniards. Because no one's been around to invade lately, a hot nightspot called Café del Mar (yes, like Ibiza) has sprung up on top of the old colonial wall. Here the fashionable gather and recline across trendy beds languishing atop the wide stone wall. Come early for drinks and stay for a DJ and dancing later in the night. From this lofty vantage point you'll be able to grab a good local beer and watch people walking along the Caribbean Sea shore. Beyond the sea you'll see the skyscraper skyline of the business area. Baluarte de Santo Domingo, Centro Historico; tel: 66-46-513.

2. Shop for emeralds and gold and silver filigree. Hey, if it's what they're famous for, you can't argue with that. Isn't it important to come away with something special to the culture? Like tons of fabulous new jewelry? There are even gold and emerald museums. You'll feel like a Spanish galleon ship yourself as you transport your New World booty back home.

3. Visit Hotel Sofitel Santa Clara. A 5-star hotel and legendary converted monastery from the 1600s, this is the perfect place to let pampering and history

La India Catalina

She's the diva of the Old City, and you will see her in a traffic circle just outside town, and again at the entrance to the Film Festival building. Her story reads like Pocahontas, a major Native American female figure who is still revered today. Cartagena is a city primed for diva worship between La India Catalina and the city's own patroness saint, a beloved incarnation of the Virgin Mary who has her own feast day in February.

collide. Sign up for a spa appointment or enjoy lunch in one of the lovely restaurants. Then wander through the lush courtyard under cool balconies spying on the hotel's former life. You'll see confessionals with tiny fences for faces and remarkable artifacts preserved in cases. The rentable party room was once the chapel, and its missing gilded altar now lives at La Popa Monastery. If you make the wise decision to stay at this hotel, and if you grow tired of their glamorous pool scene, you can talk to the concierge about booking an excursion to their own private Caribbean island. *Dios mio!*

4.   Care to square dance? Enjoy yourself in one of Cartagena's many squares and plazas! Some are all about art, some brim with street vendors whom you must barter with, and at night they all turn into lively café table scenes where delicious dinners are the least thing on everyone's agenda. The Colombians didn't get all dressed up just for the salad course! Maybe dancers and musicians will come by and entertain you. You'll certainly be entertained watching teenagers try to wrangle away from their embarrassing parents or tourists overpaying cigar vendors for fake Cohibas. You'll invent seedy stories to go along with that older man and his young, lithe companion. How fun!

5.   Take a horse-drawn carriage around town. If you speak Spanish, great, and if not, just smile and nod as the driver explains the sights. The clomping sound of hooves in the sensual night air is just the thing after a delicious outdoor meal. Hopefully you've already checked a lot of these sites off your list, and if you do discover something new, now is a good time to plan your next day. Or perhaps you'd rather wait and see what the gorgeous Latin hunk you're snuggled up to wants to do in the morning . . .

6.   Drench yourself in Artagena. There's so much art here! The Modern Art Museum exhibit I caught was dedicated to Colombian native Fernando Botero, whose ample statue of Gertrudis always lies languidly in the plaza outside. It is considered good luck to fondle her nipples. Art Cartagena happens at the end of every year and showcases the best local craftspeople in the country. They'll be selling their wares at the Claustro de la Merced in the Old City. Cartagena even has its own International Film Festival. There is so much beauty here that it is totally overwhelming to the beholding eye.

7.   La Popa Monastery. It would be worth it to come to this most gorgeous of vista points just for the views. But as usual

Chiva

What on earth are those crazy buses all about? You will see them go by—rowdily painted old school buses and, yes, wait for it, there are live *bands* on these buses! These are Chiva Buses—roving pub-crawl party buses that stop at tons of bars and discos. If you're thinking of climbing aboard, run the idea by your hotel's staff and see if they think it's a good idea.

The Doors

What's behind Door Number 2? You've fallen in love with Cartagena's architecture, especially those tiny doors set in giant doors! You laugh every time a person emerges from a people-sized door. The big doors were once needed for horse carriages while the small ones were for people on foot. That's the secret—these tiny and big door setups mean that the house is a big one, a traditional mansion, and behind these funny doors lie the most exquisite courtyards you've ever seen. So the next time you see a person coming out of a people door, try to catch a glimpse of the magical world inside. You might even ask in your sweetest voice if you can take a peek.

with Cartagena, there is so much more. The flowered balconies and ancient well in the convent's courtyard speak of another era, as the honored list of monastic superiors on the wall, starting from the 1600s, will attest. Here you will find monastery-turned-hotel Santa Clara's original gilded altar and a case on the wall filled with tiny charms. These were symbolic gifts once made to the Virgin to request her healing powers. Outside, as you gaze at the glittering city below and watch large vultures playing on puffy air currents, you'll thank yourself, or a higher power, for this trip to Cartagena.

8. Stroll through San Felipe Fort. What's a stone wall without a fortified fort? You really need the whole set to be effective. And San Felipe was certainly effective in its day. Lord help any invading forces unlucky enough to storm this fortress. You'll see, as you wander around, just how many ways there are to surprise and kill invaders. Tunnels and passageways with deadly cubbyholes and even brilliant trompe l'oeil arrangements left invaders confused, vulnerable and dead. Above the colonial carnage flies a huge Colombian flag that makes a great photo.

9. Check out the Palace of the Spanish Inquisition. Inquire within if you want to hear the whole awful story about punishments meted out by the Spanish Inquisitors. This horror house is the real original deal, splendid architecture and all. Check out all the diabolical instruments of torture, maybe before you've had your lunch. Then take a moment to enjoy the beautiful courtyard before delving into more of Cartagena's history. The palace also boasts many pre-Colombian artifacts and other not-so-deadly museum-quality memorabilia.

10. Visit the Archipelago of Our Lady of the Rosario. But you can call her Rosario. Located an hour-ish away by speedboat, if you are feeling adventurous enough to leave your fortified Old City, these beautiful Caribbean coral islands and nature preserve are a wonderful day or overnight trip. It's easy to forget that you're on the sea when there's so much on land to do in Cartagena. On the Islas del Rosario, you can swim, snorkel, and scuba dive; you can relax and read a book, or you can check out the aquarium and other living exhibits.

PANAMA CITY, PANAMA

**Stephanie loving the moment
at Panama City.**

Why This Place Rocks
for Flying Solo

*I*t's exotic but close, rain-foresty but you can drink the tap water, remote yet home to one of the world's most amazing marvels of engineering. And it is a boomtown. The world is snapping up Panamanian prop-erty, and half the travelers here right now are prospectors sifting real estate gold. Why?

Because you don't have to fly far, you won't have to change any money, and you won't have to hunt for bottled water every time you want to brush your teeth. And yet Panama is a lush paradise rivaling Costa Rica for rain forests and surpassing it in migratory bird populations.

There are sloths in the trumpet trees, toucans in the air, and fantastic hotels and restaurants in the city. Being the supremely convenient destination it is, Panama City even has its own rain forest within city limits!

Outside the city you can surf and hike through more rain forests. Beaches from both oceans await your snorkel fins. Or you can spa yourself silly. You might think you need only a few days here, but you could easily stay a week and not see everything. And as I always say, if it's good enough for three seasons of *Survivor*, it's good enough for me.

Culture: 4

Panama has several thriving indigenous cultures—real, honest-to-goodness peoples living as they have for hundreds of years. You'll find the Kunas with their beaded wrists and ankles in the San Blas Islands, the Embera in Darien Province, and others around Bocas del Toro. You can visit their villages and support their populations by buying handicrafts. There are also fascinating museums about the Canal and its history. And the Smithsonian has gone Panama crazy! I saw at least three separate research stations. They all keep irregular hours but you can definitely visit and see what they're all about.

Activity: 5

Water, water everywhere! Surf, hike, sail, snorkel, go fishing, go diving, go camping, go bird watching. Play sun goddess on a beach and *National Geographic* explorer in the jungles. Make contact with indigenous tribes and kayak through thick virgin forests. Sometimes canoeing down narrow rivers is the only way to get through. And sometimes getting a massage at the end of the day is the only way to cope.

Weather: 4

The weather is hot in the winter and hotter in the summer. The two seasons, rain and no rain, alternate to keep the engines of the rain forest flora pumping out all that oxygen. If it's too hot in the sun or your daiquiri starts to melt, duck under a tree or a canopy of trees to adjust the mercury to your liking. Evenings are pleasant, and your stay will be, too, if you drink lots of water and remember that sunblock. Dawn and dusk are sublimely well temperature controlled, but the mosquitoes are less so at these times so wrap a *pashmina* around those sexy, tanned shoulders.

Eco-Friendly

What's in an eco-resort? Panama is above all a glorious treasure of natural abundance and ecological marvels. Our humble presence can either destroy the very wonders that brought us here, or we can increase sustainability over the long term by encouraging beneficial local practices. When talking to a place that calls itself an eco-resort, make sure that they are truly adhering to sustainable practices. Your travel dollars send powerful messages. Panama is on the brink of a North American travel boom. Let's make sure that the boom doesn't turn into a total eco-bust.

Social: 4

Habla Espanol? It's not totally *necesario* but it will definitely help. Your first conversations will be haggling with taxi drivers. Later, you'll work up to drinking with the locals in the bars on Calle Uruguay. The more you wander around town, the more you'll chat with the international set who are here looking at property. And the more you chat with everyone, the more you will weave together a communal guidebook, because Panama has not yet been discovered by zillions of tourists. That's why it's wonderful to compare notes with fellow travelers. In fact, it's fairly crucial!

Flying Foreplay

Make reservations. If the December holiday season is your game, then let Rule Number 1 be to plan ahead. Not only are you fighting for space with other Americans who are slowly hearing the call to Panama, but the rest of Central and South America are on the move, and they already know about Panamanian delights. You won't have a prayer in the world of getting flights and accommodations if you don't make reservations ahead of time. That means both to and from Panama as well as within it. Bocas del Toro in particular only has so much room for surfers.

Check with the CDC. Malaria does exist in some of the islands and forests outside Panama City, as well as the other usual tropical suspects. How much you prepare depends on how far you want to go. There is an excellent possibility that, even if you've planned to stick close to the city, you will meet travelers who've just gotten back from somewhere with enticing tales. Suddenly you want to go to the San Blas Islands but all you've got is suntan oil. Try to plan ahead!

Media Mentionables

*R*ent the movie *Noriega: God's Favorite*. Bob Hoskins plays a great general, and after 120 minutes, you will be an expert on Panama's history. It's sort of like *Scarface* meets *Patton*.

Panama Jack by Joachim Bamrud explores the question on everyone's mind—what happens if someone else takes over the Canal, like China? It's fun fiction until you consider the strides that China has been making in Central and South America of late. How many yuan did you say it was to cross?

Panama Accessories

Field guides for fauna! Panama gets loads of migratory flocks because it boasts winged travelers from two oceans. Look for chestnut mandible toucans, slaty-tailed trogons, scarlet-rumped caciques, and the resplendent quetzal. A general field guide is also good so you'll know your tapirs and coatis. Leaf cutter ants and blindingly blue morpho butterflies abound, and howler monkeys and sloths hang out in the trees.

A great travel agent. What time does the train to Portobello leave? Aren't there any hotels in Bocas that aren't full? What do you mean, there are beautiful islands off the coast of Nicaragua that are only an hour's plane ride away? These questions and more will plague you unless you are favored by the wise guidance of Alba N. Ducreux at the Servicios de Viajes at the Riande Continental Hotel. 8475 Zona 7; tel: 507-269-4569 or 263-9999, extension 772; turismo2@hotelesriande.com.

The Top 10 Extraordinary Experiences

1. Watch the Panama Canal in action. The Miraflores Visitors Center at the Miraflores Locks is spectacular. Check out the whole scene as long as you're there—the installations and exhibits and the brief, English language movie. Then here's what you do: There's a restaurant upstairs that is rumored to be "expensive," so tourists avoid it. But it's

101 Uses for a Trumpet Tree

Either I'm crazy, or those leaves are walking away from me! It's a mind-bogglingly long string of leaf-cutter ants with their plunder of leaves held high. All day they work to collect the leaves that make their nests, following the path set that morning by their queen. She's home watching *Oprah*. They also harvest the leaves in their dank nests because soon yummy mushrooms will sprout. Who else likes the trumpet tree? Sloths do, of course! The total antithesis to busy ants, these slowest of mammals hang out in high branches. You'd think with their bloodshot eyes and mellow demeanor, that they're stoned. They are! Stoney slothies! Trumpet tree leaves are intense, man. Even human locals will smoke the stuff if nothing else is around.

not, and it has this great balcony that overlooks the Canal where you can eat lunch right above all the action. Grab a seat right next to the edge! Now relax, unwind, have a coffee, and watch the chambers fill with water and empty as humongous cargo and cruise ships go through, maneuvered along by tiny tugboats and small land trains. It's like maritime cabaret, *sí!*

2.   Take a ferry to Isla Taboga. The little flower island is so charming! You will love it, if you can get there. There are two possible piers from which the once-a-day boat leaves. And it's first come, first served, so get there at least an hour early. The first day I was taken to the right pier at the wrong time. Then I was taken to the wrong pier at the right time. Inexplicably, an unscheduled boat just happened to appear and took us bewildered boaters to Taboga. However you manage to get there, you will love strolling through the beautiful town and then sunning and swimming on the main beach. You can either stay overnight or take the last-and-only boat back. The best part of this trip is being on the water among all the ships waiting their turn for the Panama Canal. Definitely check with your hotel's concierge about the ferry times and piers. Then double-check this opinion with a second opinion—perhaps a fellow traveler or another member of the hotel staff. www.taboga.panamanow.com.

3.   Be a shopping fanatic! Become fanatical about Fanatixx, the superstore that aims to please. It's full of shoes, clothes, and much more with prices ranging from about $1 to the splurge price of $12. You will go shopping crazy! There are other stores like this in many of the malls on Via Espana near the Riande Continental Hotel. Across the street from the entrance to the Hotel El Panama is the best *mola* shop! *Molas* are traditional textile art made by the Kunas. This store is second-generation woman-owned and the proprietor knows everything there is to know about *molas* and buys directly from Kuna villagers. *Molas* celebrate all facets of Panamanian life like plants and animals, birds like the harpy eagle, and more abstract geometric forms.

4.   Enjoy a night out on Calle Uruguay. This is the fun street. With its bars, clubs, and great restaurants, Calle Uruguay is perfect for a one-stop night. No need to go elsewhere! Walk from restaurant to restaurant, checking out menus, grab a table somewhere outside (remember pants or a *pashmina* to protect your legs from mosquitoes) or inside, and marvel at the cool décor. Smoke a tobacco hookah at a sports bar, order exotic frozen drinks, and watch the crowds go by. Then get your *groovita* on at the clubs and have fun!

5.   Visit the endangered harpy eagles at the Summit Zoo. This is the national bird of Panama, a creature so fierce that it can snatch up monkeys and sloths from trees in its deadly big-as-bear claws. Like many of her raptor relatives, she's endangered, and she's one of the biggest birds in her class with wingspans of six feet. The Summit Botanical Garden and Zoo is one of the only harpy breeding facilities in the world. See the harpies in their huge habitat and also check out the film about them. This is probably the only time you will see harpies in Panama

Taxi!

Taxis are very cheap here and you can and should rent them for the day. The trick is not to let them rent *you* for the day. Don't agree to a taxi that costs more than a few dollars from Calle Uruguay to Amador Causeway. Rent a taxi for a full day for as little as forty dollars. There is a rumor that they can be had for about ten bucks a day, but my bargaining Spanish is not that good. You never know what you'll get—a town car or a car you pray for as you ride along in it or a car decked out with a DVD player under the rearview mirror. You'll forget the scenery as you gaze at Sharkira's shaking hips, but hopefully the driver will keep his eyes on the road.

unless you brave the thick and possibly dangerous rain forests of Darien Province. As long as you're at the zoo, you might give the tapirs a quick nod and feed the howler monkeys.

6.   **Experience the Gamboa Resort.** You've earned this! Take a break from sightseeing and indulge in this gorgeous rain forest resort. You'll get the royal treatment in the spa and feel like a princess on perfectly landscaped grounds. The property has butterfly, orchid, and reptile exhibits for you to discover on an afternoon walk in between all the excursions you reserved. The tour desk offers experiences for every passion: a morning of bird watching on the famous Pipeline Road, a monkey island boat tour to see howlers in their natural habitats, and an aerial tram canopy tour and observation tower where you can get high up in the trumpet trees and eye to eye with the sloths. The pool and bar are gorgeous, and many of the rooms' patios have hammocks. Discover the old world library upstairs in the main lobby. www.gamboaresort.com.

7.   **Tour Panama City in its old and older incarnations.** Colonial Casco Viejo is old, but there is an even *older* old Panama, too (Panamá Viejo, or old Panama City), a place of sun-bleached ruins and fallen stones. Casco Viejo is a baby in comparison full of romantically run-down churches and a seaside promenade of Panamá Viejo, where Kuna women come to sell textile wares. The Museo del Canal is here and offers a sophisticated and engaging account of the Canal's history. Now go back deeper into history and see the skeletons of an attacked city. Creep around the ruins strewn like boulders around the grassy fields. One Panama ruined, one Panama getting on in years, and one Panama thriving with tourists and nightlife. Make sure to tackle all three!

8.   **Get out of Dodge.** If you're ready to check out the rest of Panama, let me break it down for you. If you love to surf, Santa Catalina is a great, albeit long, day trip from Panama City. You can stay overnight if you like, but the lodgings are quite primitive. The best surf spot

that has the best town is Bocas del Toro. Definitely plan to stay a few nights here in an eco-resort enjoying water sports and hanging out in the funky little town. Another overnight trip is to Boquete. Here you can visit the Ruiz Coffee Plantation to see how the world's favorite stimulant is grown (www.caferuiz.com). Near Boquete is Volcan Baru, which offers a challenging hike to its summit. You'll have to get up at the crack of dawn to beat the heat, but the uphill battle will reward you beyond measure with its views on a clear day. Your grandkids will never get tired of this story—about the time when you climbed to the top of the world and saw two oceans at the same time. Definitely make hotel reservations ahead of time, especially in Bocas, and use a great local travel agent or concierge to help you with flights and other details.

9. Amble around Amador Causeway. A great place to catch the elusive ferry to Taboga, the Amador Causeway is an old U.S. army base turned entertainment center with daytime and nighttime offerings. During the day you can visit the Smithsonian Tropical Research Station, where you can learn about sea life from both of Panama's oceans. You can watch ships pass under the Bridge of the Americas and wonder if any of them are your Taboga ferry. If you are a runner, this is a great place to start off your day—the long and palm-treed promenade was conceived in jogging heaven. Cycling is fun, too. At night, choose one of the many lively restaurants and savor your lobster as you gaze at the city skyline. Day or night, be sure you have your camera so you can capture the great Panama City skyline views.

10. Indulge in investment property fantasies. Take a free tour of one of the many spec properties going up in the area—no one has to know that the only Panama you plan to own are the shells you picked up at the beach. Cranes spike the skyline as far as the eye can see— Panama City is literally growing right in

---

Hotel Insider

You might be an intercontinental type of girl, but my friend Karla told me about the very interesting deal to be had at the Hotel Continental Riande. The hotel is across the street from the cheap shopping malls of Via Espana, walking distance from Calle Uruguay, and for an extra ten dollars on top of your already cheap room rate, you get unlimited free Internet access as well as free cocktails at happy hour. There is also a private breakfast room right on your floor. The open-air lobby is filled with kooky organs (of the church variety), and in addition to an adjoining casino with penny slot machines, the best travel agency in town is at the other end of the lobby. Check it out at www.hotelesriande.com/hoteles/menuconti.html.

front of you! Take advantage of air-conditioned show rooms and staged demo apartments that are nicer than yours back home. Don't you want to see what the buzz is about? And if you *are* a diva with a nest egg . . . it's time to become an international real estate tycoon!

SOUTH
AMERICA

BUENOS AIRES, ARGENTINA

Wanda climbing Pasaje de la Detensa.

Why This Place Rocks for Flying Solo

*B*uenos Aires is the Paris of South America, and who doesn't like Paris? But instead of wonderfully pompous Parisians, picture a wave of Italian émigrés well versed in South American flair. Add a dash of Evita the Diva to the mix and you've got the cobbled concoction that is Buenos Aires. With the city as your lead, your travel tango will leave you with more questions than answers as you follow the twists and turns of Argentine history.

Argentineans are as friendly as they are gorgeous, and while per capita the locals might spend more money on therapy and breast implants than most of the world, these quests for self-improvement have obviously worked out. Besides a stunning populace, your senses will also delight in gourmet cuisine and the sensual feel of a body in motion pressed up against yours. I was thinking salsa club; what were you thinking?

With an economic crash like our Great Depression and some governmental glitches along the way, Buenos Aires desperately wants to rise from its geopolitical ashes. While everything seems fine now, you need only scratch the surface to find devastation. Sadly fortuitously, this means rock-bottom prices for travelers once you fork over for that expensive airline ticket.

Culture: 5

Even though it's almost at the end of the world, many cultures have managed to come through Buenos Aires and leave their mark. There are old Jewish synagogues and authentic Italian bakeries. Evita's legacy lures divas from around the globe to inhale the aura of their ultimate teacher. In fact, Argentine history reads like a who's who of international infamy with a soap opera cast of generals, dictators, and shady war criminals. Oh, the things you will learn!

Activity: 4

Whether you're walking around town or dancing in the arms of deft leads, your heart rate will always be up in Buenos Aires. That flush on your cheeks matches the hue of the sunrise that beckons you to bed after another unforgettable night. You're alive! And beyond BA is a wild and untamed world of pampas and glaciers and waterfalls. There's Patagonia and gaucho love songs and the lure of Antarctica. I think you'll manage to stay busy.

Weather: 4

Winter, I mean, summer? Since the seasons are hemisphere switched, it feels like Rio in December and San Francisco in August. Double-check temperatures when you start planning your trip. Depending on what you want to do, now is always the right time to go to Buenos Aires.

Social: 5

The people are gorgeous, their restaurants and hotels are hip . . . it's all so glorious

So many tangos, so little time! This exotic dance has been spun off more times than *CSI* into lots of styles and technical subcategories, but certainly there remains a difference between Argentine and American tangos. What you're mesmerized by here in BA might not be offered at dance studios back home, so make sure you specify your tango preferences. Or be a tango tart and try them all!

that if you aren't getting private tango lessons every night, you must have taken a wrong turn! The only time you will grit your teeth in a social situation is when your jaws clutch a rose on the dance floor. That is the only thorny situation I can imagine you getting into. The people are passionate and fascinating, their backgrounds are incredibly diverse, and their stories can be heart wrenching. Please talk with the locals to learn more about the intense march of history here and how it has affected them.

Flying Foreplay

Protect thyself, part one. This is a friendly, flirtatious, passionate place with beautiful men waiting to dance with you. However far you want that dance to go is up to you. I'm just saying, like my mother said to me, be prepared. Whose products of protection do you want to rely on? The smashed ones from his wallet or the mint condition ones in your makeup bag?

Protect thyself, part two. If you choose to go home alone after a magical night out, do take precautions. Be careful not to mention the name of your

hotel. Always take a taxi home. Feel free to be paranoid and take a circuitous route. Do not give out your room number or last name. Make sure that the rose of your safety is guarded with many sharp thorns.

Media Mentionables

Books: Anything by Jorge Luis Borges
Movies: *Evita* and *Motorcycle Diaries*
Music: Listen to some tango music before you go—it's not what you expect. It sounds more like old-fashioned parlor music than meringue.

Buenos Aires Accessories

Leave room for leather! Do you like leather? Then be sure to head to Florida Street to the Maybe store and get some custom-made leather outfits. *Prêt-a-porter* is so last century. It'll only take a day or two at the most, and at these low prices, it's worth the wait. And after shopping for hides, why not dine on steak at La Cabrera? The food is so good that you'll tell your tailor to leave an extra millimeter or two in the waist. Plan to hit this or other custom leather shops at the beginning of your trip so you'll have time for fittings and fixings if they don't turn out right.

The Top 10 Extraordinary Experiences

1. Cry for her in Argentina. Start your trip off right by paying your respects to the ultimate diva. In life she was powerful and in death she retains that power as a symbol for Argentina and for women around the world. Recoleta Cemetery, in upscale Recoleta (wherein you must shop), is where Eva, "I am my own woman," Peron now rests. Celebrate her life at the Evita Museum in Palermo (2988 Lafinur Street). And finally, gaze up at that famous Casa Rosada balcony and picture La Devita inspiring the masses.

2. Spa yourself healthy at the Aqua Vita Medical Spa. Health and looking twenty do not come cheap, except when they do! The Aqua Vita Medical Spa (Aqua *E*-vita?) offers the best spa care at the most incredible prices. Rejuvenating hydrotherapy and bountiful beauty and body treatments are the perfect remedy for a body twisted by tango. Let the heated mineral baths lift and release those fishnet stocking indentations right off your thighs . . . www.aquavitamedicalspa.com.

Graffiti Grown Up?

You won't be sure what to make of it at first—you know it's spray paint, but it's so kind of within the lines. So *nice* looking. The counterculture is talking to you, and it's using the voice of graffiti stencil art. Scholars are studying it and artists are evolving it, and you are the spectator caught in the middle. It's up to you to provide a reaction. Keep an eye out for stencil graffiti all around town.

3. Tango in San Telmo. Tango is spontaneous in San Telmo! It runs like honey down Buenos Aires cobblestones, and a rousing performance will be nearly impossible to avoid. Sundays in Plaza Dorrego are best—who doesn't like flea markets and antiques with their sexy dance performances, a sort of shopping two-step as you hunt for treasures to the tango soundtrack? This area is lovingly preserved and maintains the feel of a bygone era. You'll want to come away with a vintage purchase to match this vintage experience!

4. See the Louvre of South America. The Museum of Modern Latin American Art is what the Louvre is to European grand masters and mistresses. You'll find the fantastic Frida Kahlo represented here alongside the works of her naughty hubbie, Diego Rivera. Colombia's Botero is here, too, and many great artists whom you might not know. How proud this institution will be to expand your art history knowledge! Avenida Figueroa Alcorta 3415; tel: +54-11-4808-6598; www.malba.org.ar.

5. Explore the insides and outsides of shopping. Florida Street should have been named after a state like New York or California for all the great boutique shopping and mall shopping on offer here! You'll find your trendy and upscale old friends along the avenue, and you'll make some new shop friends, too. Leather is always a must in Argentina, so pay close attention to purse and belt stores, not to mention Maybe's custom leather items. If it's raining or you just feel like worshipping in a temple of shopping, then head to the Galerias Pacifico mall, also on Florida Street. This mall has a romantic history—its nineteenth-century inception was inspired by the French Bon Marche movement. Notice the beautiful murals crafted by famous painters as you hop from shop to shop. Check their website (www.galeriaspacifico.com.ar/_ingles/inf_turistica.htm) for free coupons and offers for tourists.

6. Fly to Iguaçu Falls. Argentina is a big country and this is relatively far—a plane ride away. But most classic Argentina travel itineraries do include a stop here at one of the world's largest waterfalls.

Uruguay

Who are you calling a Punta del Este? With party beaches, casinos, and hip hotels spilling over with international glitterati, this may not be how you pictured Uruguay. It's close enough to BA to fly or take a ferry. So jet-set on over today because in a few years everybody else will.

These massive and spectacular silt brown river waterfalls are raw with power and volume. Water heaves over slick precipices and pushes out toward the ocean. The dense water sheds its bulk second after second yet never seems to miss a drop. You can walk out over a metal grate and get face to face with the top of the falls, or grab a plastic parka and hop on a boat near the bottom of the falls. Just don't wear your new custom-made suede skirt.

7. Stay at the Faena Hotel and Universe. Light-years away from its competitors, the Faena is a hip universe of its own. The very hottest hotel in town . . . wait, you mean you haven't stayed in a hotel with its own hammam before? With a gorgeous spa, restaurants, pool, nightspot, and library, to call this your home away from home will insult the hotel unless your home is a palace staffed to the hilt. Nothing oils the gears of the precision vacation like a 5-star concierge. Shoot for the moon and ask for the stars, girl! Check out www.faenahotelanduniverse.com.

8. Indulge in dulce de leche! A spread, a candy, an ice cream, a flavor, a pastry, a cookie, a calling . . . dulce de leche is a melty, carmely, milky treat and regional specialty. Alfajores are the Argentine answer to the Oreo with dulce de leche at the center of this cookie universe. You simply must indulge in dulce de leche while you are here. Be the sweetie you are and bring back jars for your friends (and for midnight snacks at your house).

9. See the Teatro Colon. *Que bella!* A palace of performance, this breathtaking preserved theater is a must see, perhaps even more so than any individual concert. This glorious edifice nearly upstages all its visiting artists. So even if you can't find the time for a performance, you must take audience with the theater itself. Oh, if these walls could talk, I mean sing . . . Offering the holy trinity of ballet, opera, and symphony programs, if you don't want to experience a concert here (the equivalent of attending mass at the Vatican or a Knicks game courtside), then take a behind-the-scenes tour to see everything that goes into making a performance happen.

10. Estancia thyself, cowgirl! You'll never find yourself a rough and tumble gaucho in the city. No, you'll have to go outside city limits to find traditional ranches. Argentina is like the Texas of South America, famous for its fine fillies and cattle. Ranchers abound and so do charming ranch houses fit for the curious rope 'em and ride 'em diva. Some estancias traffic in cattle and others raise polo ponies. Some are sumptuous and others put you to work. Decide what you're looking for and then say "Howdy!" to your perfect estancia outing or overnight.

MACHU PICCHU, PERU

Jen finds a bit of the dharma on top of
the Andean world.

Why This Place Rocks
for Flying Solo

_P_icture a magical vortex between
the gods and man, where the
heavens open up and spill out
blessings of rainbows, rays of sun, and
fog. And the earth reaches up with waves
of steam, heat, and mountains. On this
sacred land, god and man are one. Incans
called this place Machu Picchu. A fair
land where hummingbirds the size of
seagulls buzz through caves of flowering
vines and shimmering waterfalls dance
in the morning sun. If you're ready for
an adventure that includes your body,
mind, and spirit, then Machu Picchu will
satisfy the trilogy of self-exploration.
Plan on a workout that includes tiring

your muscles, expanding your mind, and empowering your soul.

If you're in a quandary between spending another week with your girl-friends shopping in Palm Beach or going solo to Machu Picchu, pick the latter. You won't be disappointed. As one with a slight cynical edge, it can be difficult to inspire me. But the second my eyes opened up on the terraced landscape of Machu Picchu, I began to cry. This land is sacred and I could feel it. It's power moved through my body like the breeze through the trees, it moved parts of me that others couldn't touch, and it warmed me up and took my breath away. It will do the same to you, so get ready to bring your backpack instead of your bikini, and pack your camera in-stead of your Chanel sunglasses. It's worth it, I promise.

Culture: 5

No pictures you've seen or descriptions you've heard can compare to the mo-ment when you look out over Machu Picchu's splendor. Take a guidebook and a few days to really engage in the facts and myths of Machu Picchu. The stone skeleton of a city that lay forgotten for so long in the misty mountains waits for you to decide what it's all about.

Activity: 5

Machu Picchu was hidden from the world for centuries because it was so well tucked away in mountainous ter-rain; hiking and exploring those same mountains will be your main source of activity. Remember: Machu Picchu is high-altitude so drink lots of water and nap if you feel peaked. (Come to think of it, that's good advice for any location!) Keep the altitude in mind when drinking alcohol as well . . . as every good ski

bunny knows, you'll feel more effects with less air up in the mountains. Use moderation, or you'll be explaining to the UNESCO rangers why you're pole dancing on the Incan sundial.

Weather: 1

You don't come to Machu Picchu for the climate. From June to October the mornings are warm with brilliant sun-shine and can get quite cool in the shade. At night, temperatures can plummet into freezing. From December to April, showers and downpours are common, followed by bright, intense sunshine.

Social: 4

Hikers, trekkers, pilgrims, and everyday-leisure travelers explore Machu Picchu and are all pretty friendly. It's easy to strike up a conversation with others who are also on the way to the city in the sky. If you take the train, the last stop before Machu Picchu is an itty-bitty town called Aguas Calientes, and it's always packed with backpackers who love to chat over a "pisco sour" (Peruvian alcoholic drink) and corn chips.

Flying Foreplay

*B*asically, you're going to be out in the middle of nowhere for a week or more, so make sure you have your itinerary locked and loaded.

Book your accommodations ahead of time. Accommodations near the ruins can be hard to find, especially during the peak seasons. Camping is prohib-ited; so don't bother bringing your tent. If you want to stay in a hotel near the ruins, then Aguas Calientes is the best place to stay. For you girls who are all about "location, location, location," then the only place to stay is the 32-room Machu Picchu Sanctuary Lodge. It's a 5-star resort that kisses the entrance to the ruins. Spend a few days there checking out the ruins, then trek back to your room for a massage and dinner. www.monasterio .orient-express.com.

Check trail regulations. If you plan on trail blazing, you'll have to do it with a registered guide. In the hopes of protecting the forest and the ruins, foot traffic is limited.

Read Before You Go

Cut Stones and Crossroads: A Journey into the Two Worlds of Peru, Ronald Wright
Into the Fire, by Linda Davies
The Sunflower, by Richard Paul Evans

Machu Picchu Accessories

A Camelbak. This is the best way to keep water near and dear to your mouth: a backpack with a water pouch and straw built right in. Camelbak's motto is "Hydrate or die." You should keep your whistle wet when exploring this ancient Incan paradise.

A great camera. And film! Unless it's digital (and if digital, bring a backup SD card for all the incredible pictures you're going to take).

Toilet paper. No matter how luxe or unluxe you plan on going, you might want to pack some TP, just in case. Wet wipes are great, too, but if you plan on hiking, remember you need to take all nonorganic stuff off the mountain with you.

Solid hiking shoes. Make sure you try them out before you get up there; nothing is worse than blisters.

A leather-bound journal. Or whatever kind of journal that will represent this trip. Some of the most eloquent poets have been rendered wordless by the beauty of Machu Picchu; tap into the inspiration yourself and get your impressions down on paper. If all else fails, write bawdy limericks about that Italian tour group that just walked by.

Bug repellant. Civilization might have forgotten Machu Picchu, but this location has always been buzzing for insects. Mosquitoes and gnats still wage war against the foreigners traipsing around the ruins, and you're well advised to defend yourself with some heavy-duty repellant.

The Top 10 Extraordinary Experiences

1. **Explore the Sacred Valley.** To get to Machu Picchu, you need to fly into Cuzco, which towers at around 12,000 feet above sea level and is known for getting the strongest of people ill with altitude sickness. Unless you want to spend a day feeling lousy (think really bad college hangover), head to lower ground as quickly as possible. Ideally, you will arrange for a guide to drive you through the Sacred Valley, where you can acclimate a bit easier. The Valley is filled with mysterious ruins, amazing terraced gardens, and whistling Incan graves. Your guide will then drop you off at the train station; there you take the train to Aguas Calientes, which is the town below Machu Picchu. Having a guide through the Sacred Valley is really worth the time and money.

2. **Drink or chew coco.** Yes, it's made from the same leaves as that ego drug of the eighties. But hey, it's organic! You can find matte coco tea everywhere, but my personal favorite is chewing the leaves from the coco plant for that extra pick-me-up. It's legal, so don't worry, you're not breaking any laws. Heaven forbid I'd make you do something illegal. Just don't try to bring it home. Your best bet is to hire a guide and ask him to show you how to squish up the leaves and chew them. They taste nasty, but while in Peru . . .

Back at the base of Machu Picchu, look for a shrine called Intihuatana. It's a sundial perched on a granite tower also known as "the hitching post of the sun." See if you can synchronize your watch with the sundial. If you can, two gold stars for you.

3.   Trek the trail. For you die-hard hikers, why not try a 4-to-7-day hike on the Incan trail? Walk through cloud forests, sleep in green pastures, explore overgrown Inca ruins hidden from the world, witness the stunning vistas of the Urubamba River valley, and be one with nature and her incredible fauna and flora. And if that wasn't enough to excite you, the climax of waking up to the silent wonders of Machu Picchu at the end of your hike is mesmerizing.

4.   Soar above the clouds. Well, not really. You can hike Wayna Picchu, the big, spiky mountain you see in all the iconic pictures of Machu Picchu. The hike is approximately a half-mile up and is super duper steep. You'll find ropes and chains at points for you to pull yourself up. It can be a bit frightening at times, but with a bit of courage and a few coco leaves, you'll do fine! Plan on spending at least two hours round trip. I like meditating on the other side of the peak, with my back facing Machu Picchu. It's easy to find a quiet place to watch the incredible clouds roll across the Andes, journal, or silently pray.

5.   Order a rock-water combo. If you have 11 days to spare and you love adventure, then this is the trip for you. It is a fantastic combination of hiking and rafting with one of my favorite outfit-

ters in the world—Bio Bio Expeditions. You'll hike the Inca Trail to Machu Picchu and then raft the Apurimac River. It is an unbeatable combination of sheer excitement and adrenaline fun. The stunning simplicity and grandeur of Machu Picchu is a fitting reward after hiking the Inca Trail. Your hike is followed by a few days on the Apurimac River where you get to play in the deep granite gorge, inviting white sand beaches, and ride world-class white water. This Peru adventure trip is one of the best in the world and your Bio Bio guides are awesome. Tel: 800-246-7238; www.bbxrafting.com.

6.   Lunch with the gods. Machu Picchu Sanctuary Lodge, at 8,200 feet above sea level, is the only hotel located within Machu Picchu Inca citadel. If you don't want to drop the dough to spend the night, then how about lunch? While you eat, gaze out the windows at the city that time almost forgot. www.monasterio.orient-express.com.

7.   Leave a light footprint. No, I don't mean cut back on the Peruvian pastries—instead focus on leaving no trace in this gorgeous site. An estimated half a million people visit Machu Picchu yearly, and UNESCO is concerned about the possible damage that tourists are causing to one of their Heritage Sites. Be aware of your impact (stilettos can leave wicked track marks) and pack out all your trash, darling.

8.   Sip some heaven. For you girls who get drug tested and don't want to risk chewing coco, I have the perfect treat for you. Passed down from the Mayan culture, the Incans who inhabited Machu Picchu loved to drink hot chocolate. Find a steaming, creamy cup at the Inca Planet Café in Aguas Calientes. It's out of this earthly world.

9.   Get hot and steamy. Snugly located at the base of Machu Picchu and resting deep in the lush rain forest is the tiny town of Aguas Calientes. Underground hot sulfur springs burst from the rocky earth in steaming pools where you can soak your aching muscles, just like in the good old days of the Sun God.

10. Get candles in Cuzco. Once you get used to the altitude, you can head back to Cuzco and enjoy the magnificent city. The Incan translation of the name is "the belly button of the earth." The Incans believed that Cuzco was the center of the earth and universe, and you can see why when you're there. It's a charming town with lots of great restaurants and shops. Make sure to find the candle-making street, where you can buy huge, ornate, hand-made candles. They come in all the colors of the rainbow and are embedded with gold foiling and pictures of saints and Jesus. They're supposed to be used at the cathedral, but they look great on secular mantlepieces and candelabras as well. The candles are cheap and make great gifts!

RIO DE JANEIRO, BRAZIL

Maureen relaxing in Rio.

Why This Place Rocks for Flying Solo

*I*f you are ready to live—I mean really live—where you go beyond your comfort zone and dive into a culture that is as passionate as it is mysterious, then Rio de Janeiro is your destination. Rio is a fantasy, a place down the Amazon River from Wonderland. It is a steamy city where the gentry meets the jungle. In Rio, you have to leave your inhibitions at home and pack your best samba moves, tiniest bikini, and Portuguese dictionary. This is a city that knows how to party and has the unabashed attitude to prove it as one of the great global jet-setters' hangouts.

The Girl

"The Girl from Ipanema," written by Antonio Carlos Jobim and Tom Jobim, was inspired by Helô Pinheiro, an eighteen-year-old girl who lived in Ipanema. Every day, she would stroll past the popular Veloso café on the way to the beach. Rua Vinicius de Moraes 49 A, Ipanema.

Rio is protected by Corcovado, the huge, iconic Christ with his outstretched arms and adorned with a massive granite crown called Sugar Loaf. You might find that just walking down the fragrant streets of Ipanema evokes deep secret desires you can't explain. Let go and enjoy the inner heat of this urban, tropical paradise. With high-end neighborhoods lining the translucent ocean and less-friendly areas bumping up to the city's limits, Rio is a place where you can have an exhilarating time exploring alone, but know your boundaries. Just like anything worth having, there is a risk. Though it has a dangerous side, Rio de Janeiro is one of my favorite cities in the world. The giddy excitement I feel when I walk along the wide promenades of Copacabana beach is better than Christmas morning. Like the trill of Carmen Miranda's tongue set to the beat of Bossa Nova, Rio enchants and seduces, promises and delivers. Brazilians consider themselves to be quite distinct from other Latin American cultures, and by the time you're on your flight back home, exhausted and probably still sprinkled in glitter from the night before, you'll agree. If there was a destination that could transform you into a jet-setting diva with more passion, sensuality, and joy for life, Rio is the place.

Culture: 4

You don't have to walk into a museum to experience Rio's unique culture. Just sunbathing on Copacabana Beach as the local boys serve you freshly made *caipirinhas* with crushed ice and limes gives you a taste of the rich culture here. One part Portuguese, one part African, and one part Amazonian make up the distinct global fusion of this fascinating destination.

Activity: 4

Expect an impromptu volleyball match with a group of scantily clad athletes, or an all-night dance session in one of the many nightclubs. Don't expect 9 a.m. kickboxing class—you probably just got to bed. Beachside you can rent bikes, kayaks, and rollerblades. Inland you can hike the jungle, go white-water rafting, and try hang gliding.

Weather: 4

Brazil is in the tropics, so during the summertime (October–March) the weather is hot, hot, hot, and wonderfully humid. Your hair and skin will love you after spending time here. The rest of the year it's just mildly warm. Rio is in the Southern Hemisphere, so the seasons are the opposite of the Northern Hemisphere.

Churrascarias

Brazilians love their BBQ restaurants (called *churrascarias*) and your trip to Rio would not be complete without a visit to one of these. Churrascarias are delicious restaurants where you pay fixed prices to eat as much meat as you want. The meat selections include beef, lamb, pork, and sometimes chicken served off big metal skewers. You will be given a sign that is green on one side and red on the other. This lets your waiter know if you want more meat or if you are filled to the gills with BBQ. Visit Porcão, a favorite churrascaria, for a real gut-busting experience (Rua Barão da Torre, 218, Ipanema).

Social: 5

Though Carnival is the burning hot sun of the social solar system, there are a wide range of events that orbit year-round. With world-famous clubs like Baronetti and Bombar in Ipanema, you will never be short of a dance partner. All I ask is that you stay especially alert; this is not the place to lose yourself in the moment (i.e., drink *caipirinhas* until you can't see straight). Play it smart and you'll play it safe.

Flying Foreplay

Brazil + the Internet = love. There is an abundance of great Internet resources for traveling to Rio:

www.ipanema.com: The "Insider's Guide," this quirky site features "Rio for Beginners."

www.brazilmax.com: BrazilMax is the self-proclaimed "Hip Gringos' Guide to Brazil."

www.maria-brazil.org: Maria-Brazil has helpful cultural tips and travel pointers.

www.thebraziliansound.com/video.htm : Check out this interesting and regularly updated site listing movies about Brazil.

Book it! The jet-set glitterati descend on Rio during Carnival, filling hotels and restaurant reservation lists. The two areas you want to stay in are Copacabana or Ipanema.

Speak to me. Brazil's mother tongue is Portuguese, unlike the Spanish used by its South American neighbors. It would be wise to bring a translation guide that has all the basics you will need. Though it probably won't help you understand what Brazilians are saying, you can bring out your rusty high school Spanish, which might be more effective than just gesturing. Most everyone speaks some English, but don't expect to have a deep and meaningful conversation with that drop-dead Brazilian you meet. It's not like you'll be saying much anyway.

Read Before You Go

Donna Flor and Her Two Husbands, by Jorge Amado

Locals

Use the locals as a resource. The concierge/front desk at your hotel will have good tips on where to go and what areas to avoid.

Hour of the Star, by Clarice Lispector
Soccer Madness, by Janet Lever

Brazilian Accessories

Protect your biggest organ. I know that *you* know that *everyone* knows that sunscreen is important, but it bears repeating. Don't burn your delicate skin to a crisp, even if you are after that basted-turkey bronze the locals seem to sport. Wear suntan lotion even on cloudy days; the "hidden sun" factor can be fierce in Rio.

Wax poetic. Plan on wearing itsy-bitsy teeny-weeny bikinis. So make sure you are smooth and hair-free every place your bikini won't cover. It's called a Brazilian wax for a reason!

Sweat the small stuff. Hot and sweaty is a good thing, but not when you're in your favorite turquoise silk tank top. Bring clothes that will mask sweat marks, not accentuate and preserve them for all time. *Light, colorful,* and *slinky* are the magic words.

Is that you, Tammie Faye? When I say Rio is hot, I'm not just referring to the beach populace. The weather is sure to do a number on your cosmetics, so think about downsizing. The last thing you want is raccoon eyes from melting mascara and a streaky face from dripping concealer. Find a lightly tinted face sunscreen and a lip gloss with SPF.

Bling-free zone. It's hard to restrain yourself in this capital of shiny objects, but you're well advised to leave the heavy-duty jewelry at home. Opt for sequins: they're just as glitzy but don't yell "Hey, I'm American and I'm loaded" to all passersby.

Hide it, or tie it down. Invest in a shoulder strap for your camera or keep it well tucked away. Consider bringing a disposable camera when touring more crowded, urban areas. You might lose some precious memories, but not a month's worth of rent in camera gadgets if you are on the wrong end of a pickpocket. Don't walk around Rio with a flimsy handbag or zipperless tote.

The Top 10 Extraordinary Experiences

1.   **Welcome to the Sambadrome!** One of the most memorable nights of my life was when I danced in the Carnival parade adorned in a huge feathered headdress. I danced with 25,000 others dressed in similarly outrageous costumes. The Brazilians love their samba so much that they have a huge stadium (seats 95,000 spectators and is a half-mile wide) called The Sambadrome. Just once in your life, you, too, need to don peacock feathers and a skimpy G-string and

dance like there is no tomorrow. At www.ipanema.com, you can sign up to dance in one of the samba school parades (there are four different schools, and much like college, each is known for a specialty). Bring a camera and take pictures of the action while spinning around pretending you know how to do the samba. www.ipanema.com.

2.   Is your name Lola? It can be . . . On Avenue Atlântica in Copacabana, you will find more than bronzed beauties with perfect bodies and handsome men playing volleyball. You will find one of the most gorgeous hotels in the world—the Copacabana Palace. If you are in for an inch, go the extra mile and stay here. If the beach gets a bit too sandy for you, just change your itty-bitty bikini and lounge by the decadent pool at the Copacabana Palace. Plan on coming here during Carnival, so you can attend the Copacabana Masquerade Ball. The hotel transforms into a fairytale with guests dressed in ball gowns and ornate masks dripping in rhinestones, feathers, and velvet. Copacabana Palace, Avenida Atlântica 1702, Rio de Janeiro; Tel: +55-21-2548-7070; www.copacabanapalace.com.br.

3.   You've heard the song . . . Now you, too, can be the "Girl from Ipanema." Ipanema is a sophisticated neighborhood that kisses Copacabana. Where Copacabana is the home to superstars and the mega-rich, Ipanema is a bit more subtle. Cute boutiques, darling cafés, and chic hotels fill this neighborhood. The night scene here is vibrant with streams of outdoor cafés and restaurants filling the sidewalks. During the day, Ipanema's beach is packed with some of the most attractive people you

will ever see. Spend the days shopping for that perfect bikini and adorable strappy sandals. Celebrate you success with a meal at a *churrascarias* and wash it down with a *caipirinha*.

4.   Hang on! Everybody takes the trolley to visit Corcovado (the Christ Redeemer statue) with his hands stretched out—and mind you, it is a fantastic sight. But not as fantastic as hang gliding past it. Imagine soaring by the Christ Redeemer or down through Sugar Loaf, with a professional guide who does all the work for you? Remember, you only live once and if you always wanted to know the thrill of flying like a bird, here's your chance. http://rioadventuretours.com; www.riohanggliding.com.

5.   Ride, sugar, ride. Okay, so soaring on top of or through the steep, tropical mountains of Rio is not your idea of fun. How about riding the Sugar Loaf cable car up the iconic mountain that jets out from Rio's skyline? The first cable car takes you up 550 feet to the Morro da Urca, where you can get a bite to eat and look around. The second cable car takes you the rest of the way to the summit for an impressive panoramic view of the city and Copacabana Beach. Av. Pasteur 520; tel: 21-2546-8400; open: daily 8 a.m. to 10 p.m.

6.   Spinning goes mobile. TheBus Bike is a high-tech bus equipped with stationary bikes inside. You are spinning, but you're on an air-conditioned bus, complete with a bathroom and lockers. You may be asking yourself, why not just bike instead of taking my spin class on the road? This can be a much more comfortable way to bike, without the worries of wacky Brazilian drivers, getting lost, or inhaling too much smog. The bus travels along the southern coast of Rio, Lagoa, and Barra da Tijuca. www.busbike.com.

7. See it step by step. If you happen to get a good night's sleep on Friday, then head over to the Rio Tourism office for a *gratis* "Rio on Foot" tour. The walks are free of charge and take place on Saturday afternoon in groups of up to 50 partici-pants. Tours offered include TIJUCA FOR-EST (Meeting: Afonso Viseu Square—Alto da Boa Vista), DOWNTOWN (Meeting: Asembléia St, 10), and BOTAFOGO (Meeting: Botafogo Subway Station—exit to the São Clemente St.). Riotur—City of Rio de Janeiro Tourism; www.rio dejaneiro-turismo.com.bp/en.

Or if you prefer a more intimate tour, then the guided tours by Professor Car-los Roquette will be perfect for you. Just tell him what you want to see and he can plan your tour accordingly: Colonial Rio, Baroque Rio, Imperial Rio, Old Rio, A Night at the Opera, Museums Circuit, Styles in Rio, and Modern Rio are some of the favorites he offers. Besides the tours, he can take you on excursions to Búzios, Petropolis, and Paraty. Roteiros Culturais; tel: 21-9911-3829; e-mail: culturalrio@ig.com.br; www.culturalrio.com.br.

8. So good, it sounds like Mmmmm . . . For you sailing sisters, this trip should be on your top-five list. Triple M tours sails across Guanabara Bay, where you get impressive views of Botafogo and Flamengo beaches, Sugar Loaf, and the coast of Icaraí. You sail over to a few de-serted islands as well. The trip is only four hours, so you will still have lots of time for more activities on the same day. Go to www.rio.rj.gov.br, search for sailing.

9. Go wild. After tackling the crazy nightlife in Rio, it's time to explore the wild jungle. Indiana Jungle Tours offers jeep expeditions and ecological walks. They can take you diving, teach you to climb trees with cables, and take you sailing or horseback riding. Tel: 21-2484-2279; napoles@indianajungle .com.br; www.indianajungle.com.br (in Portuguese). Tuareg Rafting & Expedições e Adventura is a whitewater rafting company that goes rafting just outside of Rio. You'll spend 2–3 hours on the river and the rest of the day you get to chill with your new friends over a Brazilian BBQ. Tel: 2238-0230 or 2570-4413; tuareg@tuaregraftin.com.br; www.tuaregrafting.com.br.

Carmen

The famous Brazilian bombshell Carmen Miranda has her own private museum. See some of her outrageous costumes and learn more about her life. Av. Rui Barbosa 560; www.carmenmiranda.net.

10. Operation vacation.
Rio is the plastic surgery capital of the world. Yup, the chance of meeting someone in Rio who has had a tummy tuck, butt implants, or face-lift is pretty high. So, while in Rome . . . Companies offer cosmetic vacations. Bring your sad, sagging, and bloated body and leave with a tanned, thin, and tight one! No one needs to know that your week in paradise included a nip and tuck. www.cosmeticvacations.com.

Conclusion

Step aside, Homer; this incredible odyssey has been way more exciting than yours! In this book, we've visited 50 amazing destinations, packed with over 500 magical things to do.

I trust that whizzing through the world solo is something you'll try at least once or do more often now that you have this handy-dandy guidebook. And if you've just returned from a solo sojourn, brava! You have now joined our ranks of jet-setters. The best part is that the memories you made will definitely last longer than your itty-bitty bikini tan lines or those blisters you got from hiking Machu Picchu.

And for those who are not ready to dive into solo travel, feel free to take your friends along on the adventures that fill these pages. Yes, this book has been written especially for the solo girl on the go. But you can have a ton of fun globetrotting with your girlfriends, too.

It's time to go out and create your own whirlwind story! Feel free to share your traveling tales with all of us at www.tangodiva.com.

Fly, girl, fly!
Teresa

Photo Credits

ABOUT THE AUTHOR

TERESA RODRIGUEZ WILLIAMSON is the founder of *Tango Diva*, the premier online women's travel magazine and marketing firm that is focused on empowering women through travel. A writer who inspires women to take the plunge and travel the world solo, both on trips and in their daily lives, Teresa's advice has been featured in *Marie Claire* magazine and the *New York Times*, *Wall Street Journal*, and *San Jose Mercury News*. She has spoken at universities and associations across the country, including Stanford University, the Fashion Institute of Design and Merchandising, San Francisco State University, and the American Marketing Association. She was named the 2006 Woman of the Year by the Leukemia & Lymphoma Society, San Francisco Chapter, for her dedication to raising money and awareness for blood cancers.

Teresa lived in Australia for five years, where she modeled and worked on a game show that would send her to exotic destinations around Australia. It was during this time that she fell in love with traveling and exploring the world. Now back in San Francisco, she is married and lives on the Coast. When she is not jet-setting, you can find her cantering through the hills of Half Moon Bay on her faithful steed, Fortune's Luck.